A SELECTION FROM
THE 10TH ANNUAL

J.P. Morgan
Summer Reading List

WITH BEST WISHES

Edward Grussen

J.P.Morgan

BORN DIGITAL

BORN DIGITAL

UNDERSTANDING THE
FIRST GENERATION
OF
DIGITAL NATIVES

John Palfrey *AND* Urs Gasser

BASIC
BOOKS

A MEMBER OF THE PERSEUS BOOKS GROUP
NEW YORK

Books published by Basic Books are available at special discounts for
bulk purchases in the United States by corporations, institutions,
and other organizations. For more information, please contact the
Special Markets Department at the Perseus Books Group, 2300
Chestnut Street, Suite 200, Philadelphia, PA 19103, or call (800)
810-4145, ext. 5000, or e-mail special.markets@perseusbooks.com.

Designed by Timm Bryson
Set in 11 point Berkeley

Library of Congress Cataloging-in-Publication Data
Palfrey, John.
  Born digital : understanding the first generation of digital natives /
John Palfrey and Urs Gasser.
      p. cm.
  Includes bibliographical references and index.
  ISBN 978-0-465-00515-4
  1. Information society—Social aspects. 2. Information
technology—Social aspects. 3. Technological innovations—Social
aspects. 4. Internet and children. 5. Internet and teenagers. 6.
Internet—Social aspects. 7. Technology—Social aspects. 8. Digital
media—Social aspects. I. Gasser, Urs. II. Title.

  HM851.P34 2008
  302.23'10835—dc22
                                    2008021538
10 9 8 7 6 5

FOR OUR DIGITAL NATIVES

Ananda AND Dave

Jack AND Emeline

CONTENTS

INTRODUCTION

YOU SEE THEM EVERYWHERE. THE TEENAGE GIRL WITH THE IPOD, SITTING across from you on the subway, frenetically typing messages into her cell phone. The whiz kid summer intern in your office who knows what to do when your e-mail client crashes. The eight-year-old who can beat you at any video game on the market—and types faster than you do, too. Even your niece's newborn baby in London, whom you've never met, but with whom you have bonded nonetheless, owing to the new batch of baby photos that arrive each week.

All of them are "Digital Natives." They were all born after 1980, when social digital technologies, such as Usenet and bulletin board systems, came online. They all have access to networked digital technologies. And they all have the skills to use those technologies. (Except for the baby—but she'll learn soon enough.)

Chances are, you've been impressed with some of the skills these Digital Natives possess. Maybe your young assistant has shown you a hilarious political satire online that you never would have found on your own, or made presentation materials for you that make your own PowerPoint slides seem medieval by comparison. Maybe your son has Photoshopped a cloud

1

out of a family vacation photo and turned it into the perfect Christmas card. Maybe that eight-year-old made a funny video on her own that tens of thousands of people watched on YouTube.

But there's also a good chance that a Digital Native has annoyed you. That same assistant, perhaps, writes inappropriately casual e-mails to your clients—and somehow still doesn't know how to put together an actual *printed* letter. Or maybe your daughter never comes down for dinner on time because she's always busy online, chatting with her friends. And when she does come down to dinner, she won't stop texting those same friends under the table.

Maybe you're even a bit frightened by these Digital Natives. Your son has told you, perhaps, that a boy in his ninth-grade class is putting up scary, violent messages on his Web page. Or you heard about that ring of college kids who hacked into a company website and stole 487 credit-card numbers before getting caught by police.

There is one thing you know for sure: These kids are different. They study, work, write, and interact with each other in ways that are very different from the ways that you did growing up. They read blogs rather than newspapers. They often meet each other online before they meet in person. They probably don't even know what a library card looks like, much less have one; and if they do, they've probably never used it. They get their music online—often for free, illegally—rather than buying it in record stores. They're more likely to send an instant message (IM) than to pick up the telephone to arrange a date later in the afternoon. They adopt and pal around with virtual Neopets online instead of pound puppies. And they're connected to one another by a common culture. Major aspects of their lives—social interactions, friendships, civic activities—are mediated by digital technologies. And they've never known any other way of life.

B eginning in the late 1970s, the world began to change—and fast. The first online bulletin board system (or "BBS," for short) let people with clunky computer equipment and access to telephone lines swap documents, read news online, and send one another messages. Usenet groups, organized around topics of interest to communities of users, became popular in the early 1980s. E-mail began to enter popular usage later in the 1980s. The World Wide Web made its debut in 1991, with easy-to-use browsers widely accessible a few years later. Search engines, portals, and e-commerce sites hit the scene in the late 1990s. By the turn of the millennium, the first social networks and blogs cropped up online. In 2001, Polaroid declared bankruptcy, just as sales of digital cameras started to take off. In 2006, Tower Records liquidated its stores; by 2008, iTunes had become the largest music retailer in the United States. Today, most young people in many societies around the world carry mobile devices—cell phones, Sidekicks, iPhones—at all times, and these devices don't just make phone calls; they also send text messages, surf the Internet, and download music.

This is the most rapid period of technological transformation ever, at least when it comes to information. The Chinese invented the printing press several *centuries* before Johannes Gutenberg developed the European printing press in the mid-1400s and churned out his first Bibles. Few people could afford the printed books made possible by presses for another several centuries. By contrast, the invention and adoption of digital technologies by more than a billion people worldwide has occurred over the span of a few decades. Despite the saturation of digital technologies in many cultures, no generation has yet lived from cradle to grave in the digital era.

No major aspect of modern life is untouched by the way many of us now use information technologies. Business, for instance, can be done more quickly and over greater distances, often with much less capital required to get up and running. Politicians e-mail their constituents, offer video introductions to their campaigns on their websites, and provide volunteers with sophisticated digital tools to organize events on their own. Even religion is being transformed: Priests and pastors, imams, rabbis, gurus, and even Buddhist monks have begun to reach their faithful through their weblogs.

Most notable, however, is the way the digital era has transformed how people live their lives and relate to one another and to the world around them. Some older people were there at the start, and these "Digital

Settlers"—though not native to the digital environment, because they grew up in an analog-only world—have helped to shape its contours. These older people are online, too, and often quite sophisticated in their use of these technologies, but they also continue to rely heavily on traditional, analog forms of interaction. Others less familiar with this environment, "Digital Immigrants," learned how to e-mail and use social networks late in life. You know them by the lame jokes and warnings about urban myths that they still forward to large cc: lists. Those who were born digital don't remember a world in which letters were printed and sent, much less hand-written, or where people met up at formal dances rather than on Facebook. The changing nature of human relationships is second nature to some, and learned behavior to others.

This narrative is about those who wear the earbuds of an iPod on the subway to their first job, not those of us who still remember how to operate a Sony Walkman or remember buying LPs or eight-track tapes. Much is changing beyond just how much young people pay (or don't pay) for their music. The young people becoming university students and new entrants in the workforce, while living much of their lives online, are different from us along many dimensions. Unlike those of us just a shade older, this new generation didn't have to relearn anything to live lives of digital immersion. They learned in digital the first time around; they only know a world that is digital.

Unlike most Digital Immigrants, Digital Natives live much of their lives online, without distinguishing between the online and the offline. Instead of thinking of their digital identity and their real-space identity as separate things, they just have an identity (with representations in two, or three, or more different spaces). They are joined by a set of common practices, including the amount of time they spend using digital technologies, their tendency to multitask, their tendency to express themselves and relate to one another in ways mediated by digital technologies, and their pattern of using the technologies to access and use information and create new knowledge and art forms. For these young people, new digital technologies—computers, cell phones, Sidekicks—are primary mediators of human-to-human connections. They have created a 24/7 network that blends the human with the technical to a degree we haven't experienced before, and it is transforming human relationships in fundamental ways. They feel as comfortable in online spaces as they do in offline ones. They don't think of their hybrid lives as anything remarkable. Digital Natives haven't known anything but a life connected to one another, and to the world of bits, in this manner.

Digital Natives are constantly connected. They have plenty of friends, in real space and in the virtual worlds—indeed, a growing collection of friends they keep a count of, often for the rest of the world to see, in their online social network sites.[1] Even as they sleep, connections are made online, in the background; they wake up to find them each day. Sometimes, these connections are to people the Digital Native would never have had a chance to meet in the offline world. Through social network sites, Digital Natives connect with and IM and share photos with friends all over the world. They may also collaborate creatively or politically in ways that would have been impossible thirty years ago. But in the course of this relentless connectivity, the very nature of relationships—even what it means to "befriend" someone—is changing. Online friendships are based on many of the same things as traditional friendships—shared interests, frequent interaction—but they nonetheless have a very different tenor: They are often fleeting; they are easy to enter into and easy to leave, without so much as a goodbye; and they are also perhaps enduring in ways we have yet to understand.

Digital Natives don't just experience friendship differently from their parents; they also relate to information differently. Consider the way Digital Natives experience music. Not so long ago, teenagers would go to a friend's house to listen to a new record. Or music could signal a shared intimacy: A teenage girl would give her new boyfriend a mixed tape, with song names carefully written onto the cassette lining, to signal her growing affection. Not everything has changed: Digital Natives still listen to copious amounts of music. And they still share lots of music. But the experience is far less likely than before to take place in physical space, with friends hanging out together to listen to a stereo system. The network lets them share music that they each, then, can hear through headphones, walking down the street or in their dorm rooms, mediated by an iPod or the iTunes Music System on their hard drive. The mixed tape has given way to the playlist, shared with friends and strangers alike through social networks online. A generation has come to expect music to be digitally formatted, often free for the taking, and endlessly shareable and portable.

Digital Natives are tremendously creative. It is impossible to say whether they are more or less creative than prior generations, but one thing is certain: They express themselves creatively in ways that are very different from the ways their parents did at their age. Many Digital Natives perceive information to be malleable; it is something they can control and reshape in new and interesting ways. That might mean editing a profile on MySpace or encyclopedia entries on Wikipedia, making a movie or online video, or downloading a hot music track—whether lawfully or not. Whether or not they realize it, they have come to have a degree of control over their cultural environment that is unprecedented. Digital Natives can learn how to use a new software program in a snap. They seemingly can take, upload, and edit pictures to share with friends online in their sleep. Digital Natives, at their most creative, are creating parallel worlds on sites like Second Life. And after they do, they record parts of that world and post a video of it on YouTube (if they live in California) or Daily Motion (if they live in Cannes) in a new art form called "machinima." Digital Natives can rework media, using off-the-shelf computer programs, in ways that would have seemed impossible a few short decades ago.

Digital Natives are coming to rely upon this connected space for virtually all of the information they need to live their lives. Research once meant a trip to a library to paw through a musty card catalog and puzzle over the Dewey Decimal System to find a book to pull off the shelves. Now, research means a Google search—and, for most, a visit to Wikipedia before diving deeper into a topic. They simply open a browser, punch in a search term, and dive away until they find what they want—or what they thought they wanted. Most Digital Natives don't buy the newspaper—ever. It's not that they don't read the news, it's just that they get it in new ways and in a wide variety of formats. And they have little use for those big maps you have to fold on the creases, or for TV listings, travel guides, or pamphlets of any sort; the print versions are not obsolete, but they do strike Digital

Natives as rather quaint. These changes, to be sure, are not all good, but they will be enduring.

Indeed, many aspects of the way in which Digital Natives lead their lives are cause for concern. Digital Natives' ideas about privacy, for instance, are different from those of their parents and grandparents. In the process of spending so much time in this digitally connected environment, Digital Natives are leaving more traces of themselves in public places online. At their best, they show off who they aspire to be and put their most creative selves before the world. At their worst, they put information online that may put them in danger, or that could humiliate them in years to come. With every hour they log online, they are leaving more tracks for marketers—and pedophiles, for that matter—to follow. There's more about them for admissions officers and potential employers—and potential dates—to find. The repercussions of these changes, in the decades to come, will be profound for all of us. But those who are growing up as Digital Natives are on track to pay the highest price.

Digital Natives will move markets and transform industries, education, and global politics. The changes they bring about as they move into the workforce could have an immensely positive effect on the world we live in. By and large, the digital revolution has already made this world a better place. And Digital Natives have every chance of propelling society further forward in myriad ways—if we let them.

But make no mistake: We are at a crossroads. There are two possible paths before us—one in which we destroy what is great about the Internet and about how young people use it, and one in which we make smart choices and head toward a bright future in a digital age. The stakes of our actions today are very high. The choices that we are making now will govern how our children and grandchildren live their lives in many important ways: how they shape their identities, protect their privacy, and keep themselves safe; how they create, understand, and shape the information that underlies the decision-making of their generation; and how they learn, innovate, and take responsibility as citizens. On one of these paths, we seek to constrain their creativity, self-expression, and innovation in public and private spheres; on the other, we embrace these things while minimizing the dangers that come with the new era.

Fear is the single biggest obstacle to getting started on that second path, the one where we realize the potential of digital technology and the way that Digital Natives are using it. Parents, educators, and psychologists all have legitimate reasons to worry about the digital environment in which young people are spending so much of their time. So do corporations, who see their revenues at risk in industry after industry—recorded entertainment, telephony, newspapers, and on and on. Lawmakers, responding to this sense of crisis, fear that they will pay a high price if they fail to act in the traditional manner to right these wrongs.

The media feeds this fear. News coverage is saturated with frightening stories of cyberbullying, online predators, Internet addiction, and online pornography. Of course parents worry. Parents worry most that their digitally connected kids are at risk of abduction when they spend hours a day in an uncontrolled digital environment where few things are precisely as they seem at first glance. They worry, too, about bullying that their children may encounter online, addiction to violent video games, and access to pornographic and hateful images.

Parents aren't the only ones who fear the impact of the Internet on young people. Teachers worry that they are out of step with the Digital Natives they are teaching, that the skills they have imparted over time are becoming either lost or obsolete, and that the pedagogy of our educational system cannot keep up with the changes in the digital landscape. Librarians, too, are reimagining their role: Instead of primarily organizing book titles in musty card catalogs and shelving the books in the stacks, they serve as guides to an increasingly variegated information environment. Companies in the entertainment industry worry that they'll lose their profits to piracy, and newspaper execs fear their readers are turning to Drudge, Google, blogs, or worse for their news.

As parents of Digital Natives, we take both the challenges and the opportunities of digital culture seriously. We share the concerns of many parents about the threats to the privacy of our children, to their safety, and to their education. We worry about the crush of too much information and the impact of violent games and images online. But as a culture of fear emerges around the online environment, we must put these real threats into per-spective; our children and future generations have tremendous opportuni-ties in store for them, not in spite of the digital age, but because of it.

We see promise in the way that Digital Natives are interacting with dig-ital information, expressing themselves in social environments, creating new art forms, dreaming up new business models, and starting new activist ventures. The purpose of this book is to separate what we need to worry about from what's not so scary, what we ought to resist from what we ought to embrace.

There is a huge risk that we, as a society, will fail to harness the good that can come from these opportunities as we seek to head off the worst of the problems. Fear, in many cases, is leading to overreaction, which in turn could give rise to greater problems as young people take detours around the roadblocks we think we are erecting. Instead of emphasizing education and giving young people the tools and skills they need to keep themselves safe, our lawmakers talk about banning certain websites or keeping kids under eighteen out of social networks. Instead of trying to figure out what's going on with kids and digital media, the entertainment industry has gone to war against them, suing its young customers by the tens of thousands. Instead of preparing kids to manage a complex and exploding informa-tion environment, governments around the world are passing laws against certain kinds of publications, making the banning of books look like a quaint, harmless activity. At the same time, we do next to nothing in terms of taking the kinds of steps that need to be taken if we are to address the real concerns facing kids.

Our goal in this book is to present the good and the bad in context and to suggest things that all of us—parents, teachers, leaders of companies, and lawmakers—can do to manage this extraordinary transition to a glob-ally connected society without shutting the whole thing down.

The hard problem at the core of this book is how to balance caution with en-couragement: How do we take effective steps to protect our children, as well as the interests of others, while allowing those same kids enough room to fig-ure things out on their own? If we can find this balance, in the process we will allow thousands of flowers to bloom online and empower our children to handle problems that will no doubt arise in their future. The solutions that will work are complicated ones. They will involve lots of different groups, including parents and educators as well as technology firms and lawmakers—and, critically, Digital Natives themselves.

In shaping solutions to the problems that arise, we need not think in radically new paradigms. Often, the old-fashioned solutions that have solved similar problems in the past will work in the digital age, too. Those solutions are engaged parenting, a good education, and common sense. A lot of the things we're worried about—bullying, stalking, copyright violations, and so forth—are things we've handled for decades, if not centuries. We can, as a society, handle them in the digital age, too, without the hysteria that has surrounded them. We too often overestimate the ways in which the online environment is different from real space, to our detriment.

Parents and teachers are on the front lines. They have the biggest responsibility and the most important role to play. But too often, parents and teachers aren't even involved in the decisions that young people are making. They cut themselves off from their Digital Native children because the language and cultural barriers are too great. What we hope parents and teachers will begin to understand as they read this book is that the traditional values and common sense that have served them well in the past will be relevant in this new world, too. Rather than banning the technologies or leaving kids to use them on their own in their bedrooms—two of the most common approaches—parents and teachers need to let Digital Natives be their guides into this new, connected way of living. Then the conversation can begin. To many of the questions that arise, common sense is a surprisingly good answer. For the others, we'll need to work together on creative solutions.

That said, parents and teachers need not, and should not, go it alone. As mentioned earlier, Digital Natives, their peers, technology companies, and lawmakers each have a role to play in solving these problems. Imagine a series of concentric circles, with the Digital Native at the center (see Figure 1). In many cases, the Digital Natives themselves are the ones who are best positioned to solve the problems that arise from their digital lives. Of course, it's not always realistic to put Digital Natives in charge, but it's important to start there all the same. One circle out, the family and close

friends of a Digital Native can have an impact, whether through guidance (in the case of Internet safety, for instance) or through collaborative development of social norms (in the case of intellectual property). The third circle includes teachers and mentors, who often can have a big impact on how Digital Natives navigate these environments. Fourth, we look to the technology companies that build software and offer services, which can also make a big difference in how these issues play out—and which must act accountably if that difference is going to be for the good. Fifth, we turn to the law and to law enforcement, often powerful instruments but usually blunt ones—and properly seen as a last resort.

We are not indifferent to the outcome of the many legal, political, and moral debates that this material engages. For one thing, we are both parents of Digital Natives. We care deeply about the world in which they are growing up, about the friendships they will make, about their safety, and about how they learn and engage with society at large. We are eager for them to become active, caring, global citizens.

For another thing, we are lawyers. We love the law. We believe strongly that the law is an essential part of organizing our democratic societies in a constructive way. The law is a crucial means to solving many social problems. But we are also lawyers who believe that the limits of law are sharply apparent in the context of many of the problems we are studying here. Despite the uncertainty inherent in predicting the future, now is the time to look ahead, whether as parents, as teachers, or as policy-makers, technologists, or Digital Natives, and to shape—without doing harm—the regulatory framework for the emerging digital space in ways that advance the public interest. In some cases, like the surge in online creativity, these trends point to opportunities we should harness. In others, such as the privacy problem or the cyberbullying problem, substantial dangers lurk in the digital future that we ought to head off at the pass. The law is rarely the right answer, but we should not hesitate to use it when it could do more good than harm. Technology companies can be encouraged to do the right thing on their own, especially when they know that future regulation is a possibility if they do not. And it's always important to have law enforcement as a backstop for the worst cases.

I n writing this book, we've been trying to capture a picture of something that is already kaleidoscopic in its complexity, and that changes substantially every few months. By the time this book is printed, it will already be starting to go out of date. It will still provide an introduction to the most serious issues of the digital explosion and how they affect our children, as well as a context in which to think about solutions, and these matters will be pertinent for a long time to come. But we did not want to stop there. Therefore, much of our work is online, so that we can update it over time. It's in the form of a wiki—at http://www.digitalnative.org/—and uses the same technology that powers Wikipedia, the extraordinary online encyclopedia and one of the subjects of this book. It is a technology that allows anyone who wants to participate in updating our work to do so.

Our methodology involved a combination of approaches. We learned a great deal from the best research done by others in the field: social scientists, psychologists, neuroscientists, developmental pediatricians, and librarians. We also conducted original research of our own. In order to understand more clearly the issues facing Digital Natives, we conducted a series of focus groups and interviews of young people. Our goal was not to undertake a comprehensive study, but rather to take an in-depth look at the way young people relate to information and one another.

We spoke in detail to young people from around the world about the technologies they use, how they express their identities online, and what they think about privacy and safety. We asked them what they create in digital formats, what they know about intellectual property, how they research new topics and keep tabs on news about the world, and how they interact with one another. In all, we held about 100 conversations with young people in these formal settings. You will hear their voices, though without their names attached, throughout this book. Our research is also grounded in conversations that we held with about 150 additional informants, including other young people, their teachers, librarians, psychologists, and those who study them.

This culture is global in scope and nature. Whether physically based in Rio de Janeiro, Shanghai, Boston, Oslo, or Cape Town, Digital Natives—often young elites—form part of a global culture of their peers. They are connected to each other in terms of how they relate to information, how they relate to new technologies, and how they relate to one another. When they chat with each other, broadcast their latest videos, post messages on their blogs and social network profiles, or share the latest tunes over P2P networks, they do so across states, national boundaries, and continents. Parallel to their digital universe, Digital Natives are embedded in regional and local customs, habits, and values. These factors, among others—together with the social and economic context and the local laws—are likely to shape the ways in which Digital Natives use digital technology, how they can realize its opportunities, and how they will address the challenges it poses.

While researching and writing this book, we sought to identify both the common threads of the emerging global culture and to take into account regional and local differences. We have each logged hundreds of thousands of miles over the past few years, visiting dozens of countries and hundreds of places to speak with Digital Natives, their parents and teachers, representatives of software companies, and in several cases government officials. We interviewed them about the topics we're addressing in this book. We learned a lot from these conversations, and we hope that the insights that we brought back—from Eastern Europe, the Middle East, Asia, and Africa, among other destinations—are faithfully reflected in this book in one way or another.

As expensively educated academics in highly connected, wealthy societies, we come from places of great privilege. Both the opportunities and the problems outlined in this book take on different contours from perspectives other than our own. And there are many such other perspectives. Rather than calling Digital Natives a *generation*—an overstatement, especially in light of the fact that only 1 billion of the 6 billion people in the world even have access to digital technologies—we prefer to think of them as a *population*.

One of the most worrying things of all about digital culture is the huge divide it's opening up between the haves and have nots. This divide is regional: Wealthy countries like the United States and Switzerland have high levels of broadband access, high rates of literacy, and educational systems that (often) emphasize critical thinking. As a result, many kids in wealthy countries are Digital Natives. In the developing world, the technology is less prevalent, electricity often scarce, and literacy rates low, and the number of teachers who know how to instruct kids in the use of technologies is in short supply. There's a divide even within rich countries. In the United States, most kids can access the technology itself, but there are huge divides between those children who have the skills to use it effectively and those who do not.

The vast majority of young people born in the world today are not growing up as Digital Natives. There is a yawning participation gap between those who are Digital Natives and those who are the same age, but who are not learning about digital technologies and living their lives in the same way.[2] For billions of people around the world, the problems facing Digital Natives are mere abstractions.

The biggest concern that we highlight in this book is the impact of the participation gap. The digital world offers new opportunities to those who know how to avail themselves of them. These opportunities make possible new forms of creativity, learning, entrepreneurship, and innovation. In the past, many have worried about the "digital divide," the separation between those with access to the network and those without access. This is a persistent problem, but it's not the whole problem. The harder issue arises when you realize that access to the technologies is not enough. Young people need to learn digital literacy—the skills to navigate this complicated, hybrid world that their peers are growing up in. This type of inequality must be overcome. The costs of leaving the participation gap unaddressed over time will be higher than we should be willing to bear.

This story is breaking all around us, around the world, at unprecedented speed. The bad news is that there are no easy answers to the puzzles that Digital Natives encounter as they navigate their digitally mediated lives or to the problem of the participation gap. The good news is that there is a lot that we can do as our children grow up, with them and for them. We each have a role to play in solving these problems. Most important of all, we need to prepare our Digital Natives and other young people to lead the way themselves toward a bright future in the digital age.

1

IDENTITIES

IDENTITY WAS ONCE A FAIRLY STRAIGHTFORWARD MATTER. IMAGINE A SIXTEEN-year-old living several hundred years ago, in the agrarian age. She had a home in a remote village. She had two forms of identity: a personal identity and a social identity. Her *personal* identity derived from the attributes that made her unique: her personal characteristics, her special interests, her favorite activities. By contrast, her family members, friends, and neighbors contributed to her *social* identity. These members of the community were responding, in part, to the way she portrayed herself to them in person. They could set eyes on her, and they based their judgments of who she was on what they saw. She expressed her identity through her dress, her manner of speaking, and her treatment of those with whom she came into contact.

These identities were not completely static. The girl could change many aspects of her personal identity as she wished. She could choose different clothes, express herself in a new way, develop new habits and interests. She could change parts of her social identity by associating with different people, adjusting her social relationships, and so forth. No matter how hard she tried, she wouldn't have been able to control her social identity completely, though; her family's status, gossip among neighbors, and other

factors outside her immediate influence could all affect it, too. And her social identity might shift with the passage of time. Important life events—
marriage and childbirth, struggles and successes—would have made a
difference. Despite these changes, her fellow villagers might still recall earlier versions.

If the girl wanted to change—or altogether abandon—aspects of her
social identity quickly, she would have to go beyond the small community where she grew up. If she moved to a nearby village, there would
likely still be some people who knew her, or knew of her through others.
Some would recall how she used to express herself, and could tell stories
about her. They would only be able to tell these stories orally; there were
few permanent, reliable records kept about any individual. Still, word
would spread.

If the girl wanted to change radically, she could move a sufficient distance away—say, to another town whose inhabitants had little communication with the residents of the town in which she had previously lived.
She could completely abandon her old social identity if she were willing
to travel far enough. It was possible, in the agrarian age, to disappear, to
cut off friends and family for good.

This kind of dramatic transformation became much more difficult with
the advent of the industrial age. New forms of transportation, rising standards of living, consumerism, and urbanization were among the forces
that would make it much easier for people to change aspects of their personal and social identities. More options would be available to a sixteen-
year-old girl in a nineteenth-century city than to one in a medieval village.
The city girl might change neighborhoods or her style of dress, like the
village girl, or she might join a different church or social club. She might
relocate briefly in one place and return to her old haunts, and so forth,
each time adjusting her personal identity in the process.

But in the industrial age, social identity was harder to control than it had
been before. A young woman of this era could hide in the crowd of a big
city, but she also might interact and build relationships with far more people in the course of everyday life than the girl in the rural village. More people could come to know of her and both shape and track her identity as

she went about her daily life. The advent of modern publishing enterprises (such as the daily newspaper), of various recording mechanisms (such as the camera), and of modern bureaucracies (such as administrative agencies that kept records on citizens) added new degrees of permanence to identity. She would be far less able to recreate her identity in a complete fashion than she would have been in the agrarian period. A photo of her in the uniform of a waitress at a hotel restaurant, for instance, could mark her identity in a persistent way. If she were to leave one place for another, a record of her move would be more likely to exist (though it still might not exist), and, thanks to greater mobility and postal systems, evidence of her new identity could be carried or mailed back to her previous homes.

The Internet age, in which Digital Natives are growing up, is prompting another large shift in what it means to build and manage one's identity.[1]

A sixteen-year-old girl's personal identity today is in some ways not all that different from what it would have been in the past. People still express themselves through their personal characteristics, interests, and activities in real space—at least in part. For a typical girl living in a wired society, the digital environment is simply an extension of the physical world. The fact that she lives part of her life in digitally mediated ways does not itself have a large impact on her personal identity. She might be more or less interested in digital activities inherently, but the effect of this interest is modest. She might express these personal characteristics online, but at its core, her personal identity is unlikely to be much different from what it would have been in a previous era.

A sixteen-year-old girl's social identity, however, may be quite different from what it would have been in the agrarian or industrial ages. In the digital age, her social identity may be shaped by associations that are visible to onlookers at any moment through connections in social networks like MySpace, Facebook, Bebo, or studiVZ, or through links in her blog to the blogs of others. In turn, the actions of her friends, and their shifting reputations, can affect her identity and her reputation in ways that third parties can observe. Although she can change many aspects of her personal identity quickly and easily, she may not be able to change certain aspects of her social identity. The net effect of the digital age—paradoxically—is to decrease her ability to control her social identity and how others perceive her. And while she can experiment with multiple identities online, she may well be more bound to a unitary identity than she would have been in a previous era.

To be sure, the Internet doesn't change the notion of identity altogether. Nor are all of its effects new or unfamiliar to us. In some ways the nature of identity in the Internet age resembles what it was in the agrarian past. Personal identity is much the same now as it was then. And despite the changes in the dynamics of social identity that are now taking place, in some ways even these dynamics remain the same.

From the perspective of a Digital Native, identity is not broken up into online and offline identities, or personal and social identities. Because these forms of identity exist simultaneously and are so closely linked to one another, Digital Natives almost never distinguish between the online and offline versions of themselves. They establish and communicate their identities simultaneously in the physical and digital worlds. The sixteen-year-old might be bound to being a tall Irish American girl in the physical world, while in digital space she can experiment with self-representation, sometimes in modest ways and sometimes dramatically. Her multiple representations inform her overall identity.

A sixteen-year-old girl can now create a new identity and go into an online environment where people do not know who she is, at least for a while. She might create a profile of herself in a new social network. She could present herself in a way that is strikingly different from the way she presents herself in real space. She could even create an avatar in a virtual world, such as Gaia or Club Penguin, or in a gaming environment, such as World of Warcraft, as a way to try out an identity that is not tethered to any other identity she's had in the past. Someone would have to do some serious digging on her to tie these multiple identities together. In this sense, our Digital Native could reinvent herself many times over without leaving her bedroom, much less her village. And she need not explore these identities successively over time; instead, she can create them all in one day and explore them simultaneously.

A sixteen-year-old Digital Native changes aspects of her personal and social identities almost constantly. She frequently updates expressions of her identity, whether in real space or online. Just as she changes her clothes or her hairstyle, she changes the photo on her Facebook, Orkut, or studiVZ page. She adds (and occasionally deletes) friends or entire profiles of herself. She might post late-night musings to her blog or upload a new video on YouTube (at the most creative end of the spectrum). Some of the digital ingredients of her identity change at the hands of others, too, as friends post items to social networks that have her name associated with them.

So identity formation among Digital Natives is different from identity formation among predigital generations in the sense that there is more experimentation and reinvention of identities, and there are different modes of expression, such as YouTube and blogging. These ways of expressing identity often seem more foreign to parents and teachers than they really are. Studies of online identity formation consistently suggest that despite the differences noted above, young people tend to express their personal and social identities online much as people always have in real space, and in ways that are consistent with their identities in real space.[2] Parents and teachers are right, however, that some aspects of online engagement are cause for concern. It is true that there is some good to be found in all of this: The possibility of greater exploration in identity formation offers terrific possibilities in terms of personal development.[3] But the risks associated with the way the identities of young people are being formed and accessed by others in this converged environment should be taken seriously—perhaps even more seriously than most parents and teachers now realize.

It would be too simple to say that the Internet age represents only an amplification of the trends that began to emerge in the industrial age. In fact, something quite new is happening: The use of new technologies by Digital Natives—the most sophisticated of wired young people—is leading to changes in our understanding of identity. The changes are far greater for social than for personal identity.

A sixteen-year-old has many more choices available to her when it comes to making minor modifications of her identity, compared with teenagers of previous generations. She can adjust aspects of an online identity on the fly, over the course of a day. In a common scenario, she might change the pictures that show up as part of her profile on a social network site or on her blog. In a rarer but more dramatic scenario, she might change her avatar—a picture of her face, or a full-length image of her whole body—on a social shopping site. On MyVirtualModel, for example, a sixteen-year-old can use an avatar to describe to the world how she dresses, using images of clothing and accessories to dress up her avatar in the clothes she favors—or those she would wear if she could afford it. She can bring this avatar with her as she experiences the Web. She can post it to her blog or to a social network profile for others to see.

Just as young people always have done, Digital Natives try out different aspects of identity in experimental ways, both online and offline. One of the long-standing debates in the literature of identity turns on the question of multiplicity. Some sociological theories suggest that young people have multiple selves; others argue that these multiple forms of representation come together into a more or less unitary self-construct.[4] The common thread among the many competing theories of identity is that people tend to have multiple self-representations—different levels of both personal and social identities—that together form a whole. In focus groups and interviews, most Digital Natives revealed that they had multiple self-representations. Where they disagreed was on what these multiple self-representations meant for identity: Some saw themselves as having one or more "identities" in the converged online and offline worlds, whereas others perceived themselves as having only one identity that was expressed in both contexts.

One of the paradoxes of the Internet age is that while a Digital Native's use of various technologies allows her a nearly infinite array of possibilities for recreating herself in a wide range of virtual platforms, it has bound her ever more tightly to a unitary identity in the real world. The capacities of all sorts of organizations to track and record an individual's movements have exploded since the industrial age. The extent to which the information that people reveal about themselves can be tracked from place to place continues to grow: It's much less likely that a sixteen-year-old girl of our time could simply move to another city and begin again, without people in the new place being able to learn about her past identity or identities if they were committed to doing so, as compared with her counterparts in the agrarian or industrial societies.

Young people—among many others—are using the Internet to share more personal information about themselves than ever before. This trend is a source of consternation to many parents and teachers, especially if the adults in the equation spend much less time online than their children or students. (Just to be perfectly clear: Young people are by no means breaking this new ground alone. Often, adults are exposing more about themselves, particularly if they participate in online dating, than their children.)

Much of what makes up a Digital Native girl's identity is information that she consciously puts forward to the world. This means what she's posted to her MySpace page or Facebook profile, her blog entries in Xanga or LiveJournal, or the stream of photographs in her Photobucket feed. For the most adventurous of Digital Natives, identity might be expressed through video clips in a YouTube feed, or through a model on MyVirtualModel, which might be included as a widget on a blog. Those in the younger set might have multiple avatars in Club Penguin, and their older, more sophisticated peers might express identity through World of Warcraft, Second Life, or other virtual worlds and gaming environments. Identity also includes the connections she makes to other people, the friends she claims in her social networks. These connections can be initiated through searches for other users with similar interests, or can be strengthened with friends made in the real world. The array of services that offer ways of expressing and honing a Digital Native's identity is dazzling.[5]

These intentional digital contributions to identity—in the form of inputs of shared personal information—are central to a Digital Native's emerging identity. A sixteen-year-old girl, within limits, has the ability to shape her identity with care and to change it over time to incorporate new ideas about how she wishes to be perceived. Through these many means, Digital Natives are much more willing than their grandparents were in their day to share personal information with others—both friends and people they haven't met face to face—in a public forum, which for a Digital Native is the Internet.

For Digital Immigrants, this is one of the greatest puzzles:[6] What drives Digital Natives to post so much information about themselves in digital publics? Why do Digital Natives share all this information about themselves online?[7]

There is no simple answer to this (misleadingly straightforward) question. There are hints, though, that one can derive from various scholarly disciplines: from psychology and sociology, from evolutionary biology and economics. A great many researchers, from a great many fields, are trying to make sense of Digital Natives' practice of disclosing vast amounts of personal data—everything from cell-phone numbers to vacation photos.

Psychologists have developed what they call the "disclosure decision model" to explain why a sixteen-year-old might reveal so much information to others. The underlying assumption is that people decide what personal information they will disclose, how they will disclose it, and to whom they will disclose it based on their evaluation of the possible rewards and risks. According to this model, the disclosure of personal information—say, a sixteen-year-old's posting of her hobbies online, or information about where she lives or about her tastes in music—is intended to achieve certain goals. Those goals might include social approval, intimacy, or relief of distress, among other things. Or they might include more mundane objectives, like saving money or time (for instance, disclosing a credit-card number to order a book online), or pleasure or altruism.[8]

According to the disclosure decision model, individuals examine—as rational actors—whether the disclosure of information in a given situation is indeed a good strategy for achieving desired goals in particular situations, and whether the expected benefits outweigh the risks.[9] But people, alas, are not purely rational, particularly not young people: There is reason to believe that young people systematically underestimate the risks of disclosure. There are no data to suggest that young people, whether Digital Natives or not, disclose more information than other people who spend large amounts of time online, but the risks they run are nonetheless substantial.

The risks that a sixteen-year-old girl runs include the likelihood that this information will be accessible to others for a long period of time and from contexts that she does not expect. The more information related to her financial life that she discloses online, for instance, the more she may be at risk of identity theft, one of the world's most common crimes.[10] At the time of disclosure, she faces a nearly impossible task in evaluating the costs and benefits of sharing information about her identity.

Rational utility models can only go so far in explaining why Digital Natives—and older people, for that matter—decide to disclose information. Such models help to explain why people risk revealing information like credit-card numbers to purchase a book. But they don't explain why Digital Natives reveal so much of themselves in chat rooms and on bulletin boards—the sites that absorb so much of their time and provide the most obvious platform for identity creation. Here, there is no obvious "gain" to be made from disclosing information. Meanwhile, there is tremendous risk in the form of the future uses to which the information may be put by third parties.

The answer, in these social situations, may be the idea of reciprocity. Social life for many people has a crucial online component; the virtual world complements and extends the offline social sphere. A series of norms about sharing information, and in turn gaining access to information about a peer, governs these interactions, and participants engage in intricate on-line rituals.[11] The expectation that one ought to reciprocate when someone else shares information about themselves, for example, may lead a sixteen-year-old to share information about herself with little regard for risks. These dynamics are easily observed in social network sites, where the act of "friending" someone often corresponds to granting that person greater access to information about oneself.[12]

Young people disclose information about themselves online to build trust with others and as an extension of their lives offline. When some-one sends an invitation by e-mail to connect on Facebook or studiVZ, a sixteen-year-old might look to see how many friends they have in com-mon. If they have several friends in common, she may be more likely to accept the friend request. In becoming a friend with someone online, a young person is vouching for that friend by linking to her profile. This dance tends to lead to cooperative behavior online. The friends become linked to one another, their social identities coupled through a public dis-play on a social network, and a Digital Native knows that her reputation, and the reputation of her friends, is at risk if she doesn't play nicely.[13] The disclosure of one particular type of information—public communication about friendships—represents a technique of impression management and self-presentation.[14] The structural design of online platforms both constrains and builds upon these means of building networks of identity and trust.[15]

As she shares information about her identity on Facebook or on her Xanga blog, a sixteen-year-old is providing clues to the psychological and sociological processes that underlie the social interactions of her peer group more broadly. On the one hand, the disclosure of personal information on her blog, social network site, or home page is a new form of peer communication that replaces old ones (such as diaries or letters). The disclosure can be understood as a means of developing her notion of personal identity and a means by which that personal identity evolves.[16] On the other hand, the revelation of personal data on the Internet helps her to establish group membership, which is central to her social identity. Think about Facebook's social structure: Users form a very large group of tens of millions, then subdivide themselves into many smaller networks and groups to which users can "subscribe." From these many network and group memberships, in turn, Digital Natives derive and express multiple social identities.[17]

There are reasons to be excited about the changes in identity in a digital age. Digital Natives are using networked public spaces as crucial environments to learn socialization as well as identity development.[18] In many cases, young people have moved to these networked public spaces because they feel they have been chased out of other public environments. Young people turn to online social networks as havens from other places that have become, in their view, constrained. In turn, in these online social networks, many good things are happening: Participants learn what it means to be friends, to develop identities, to experiment with status, and to interpret social cues.[19] These environments allow for identity play, an important part of the developmental or therapeutic stage in overall identity development.

The habit among young people of sharing many of the details of their everyday life, on Facebook or on their blogs, is neither random nor uncontrolled. They are learning as they go, and more conscious of what they are doing than they are perceived to be. The regular, often daily, exercise of going online allows a Digital Native to experiment with, develop, and learn to represent identity in a space that often feels more private, or at least more controlled, than it probably is. A Digital Native's identity is context-specific; its expression depends on who's asking, what environment they're in, and what day it is. These multiple identities complicate matters in terms of how Digital Natives think of themselves and present themselves to the rest of the world.[20] That level of complication is likely to grow over the course of a lifetime as Digital Natives live more and more of their lives online and as the number of environments in which they express themselves in various ways grows.

The Internet is a virtual laboratory for experiments in identity development. As Digital Natives enter their teenage years, an increasing number of them are creating online profiles as a cornerstone of their identities. For some, their primary Web presence is their blog, a very simple Web page with a mix of text and photos. Many young people include pictures of themselves, perhaps taken with a camera phone; and if a user clicks on the photo on the blog's front page, he or she is brought to a profile. A standard profile lists the blogger's first name, age, interests, the LiveJournal groups he or she is part of, and links to the blogger's MySpace and Photobucket pages, where more personal information can be found.

For many teenagers in the United States, MySpace is the primary tool for flirtation, relationships, and day-to-day communication. As one group of high-school students told us, a MySpace page plays many roles, and the stakes of participation are high:

> FEMALE 1: Because [on MySpace] you can, you know, communicate with your friends, you know, be funny, things like that.
> FEMALE 2: Learn about different things, too. Like it's not just like playing all the time.
> FEMALE 1: Express yourself.
> FEMALE 3: You have to express yourself I think is like one of the biggest parts. But the problem is you could express yourself wrongly.[21]

Social networks such as MySpace play an outsized role today—perhaps just for today, though—in terms of their place in the expression of identities of Digital Natives. If a teenage girl were to put in her real age (say, fourteen or sixteen) when she signed up for a MySpace page, access to her profile would be limited by the service. She might put in her real age because she doesn't want "creeps" looking at her pictures and knowing all about her. Only people she expressly approves as friends can access her page, including her photos, music, videos, and friends' comments about those items.

In other countries, Digital Natives are beginning to flock to similar services, such as studiVZ in German-speaking cultures and Mixi in Japan. Research has shown that Facebook continues to hold the upper hand in older and wealthier demographics. As one high-school student told us: "Facebook is like a white, preppy MySpace."[22] In a few years, if the past fickleness of each Internet generation is any indication, these services may well be eclipsed by others.[23]

Virtual worlds may be among the cool destinations that Digital Natives head toward next in droves. The potential for experimentation with personal and social identity in virtual worlds is obvious. The numbers of users of virtual worlds among young people are far smaller than in the social networks or on blogs today, but the devotees of virtual worlds (such as Second Life) often wrap themselves deeply into their experiences there. Second Life, among others, functions as a kind of parallel universe or fantasy world. Similarly, young kids on Club Penguin, or slightly older children on Gaia, are creating versions of themselves that interact with others online.

In virtual worlds, the key act of identity formation is the creation of an "avatar"[24]—a virtual representation of the computer user. In most instances, the avatar is a figure whose actions can be controlled by the user's computer mouse and keyboard. It is through this figure that the user interacts with the virtual world—both objects and other avatars (that is, other users). In many online games, the avatar is largely determined by the kind of role one chooses to play in the game's more or less predetermined storyline.

Second Life is among the most promising of the virtual worlds. Once a sixteen-year-old is "in world," she has a great deal of freedom in the creation of her avatars, and avatar design and appearance can be a significant aspect of in-world participation. Second Life provides tools that permit users to tailor the appearance of their avatars, allowing them to design everything from clothing to skin color to the shape of the avatar's nose.[25] Users can create an avatar that looks very much like themselves in terms of both physical appearance and dress. But they can also experiment with very different identities—for example, a female may choose a male avatar, and people of one race may choose an avatar with another skin tone; a participant may even design an avatar of nonhuman form, whether a real-world animal or a creature of fantasy.

Massively Multiplayer Online Games (MMOGs), such as World of Warcraft, play a far greater role today in the lives of Digital Natives than virtual worlds do. Digital Natives are driving a market for digital games with revenues in the billions of dollars per year, and these revenues are growing at a rate of 20 percent annually.[26] At a young age, part of the formation of identity now takes place through the mediation of such games. To see how this works, imagine that our Digital Native picks up a mobile device to play Forgotten Warrior, an Animé-style mobile multiplayer game where the player is a prince fighting bad guys in quest of saving the kidnapped princess. The game connects through the mobile device to a network of other gamers. This means a teenage boy could play with his sister in the seat beside him in the family minivan—or with anyone else who happens to be playing at the same moment, regardless of where they are in the world. And as he plays, he's creating another part of his digital identity online, in the character of a prince.

The growth trend in the online gaming industry is one of the clearest indications that a global culture is emerging, joining Digital Natives in countries around the world to one another. High-school students in Shanghai or Riyadh talk about many of the same online games that kids are talking about in Chicago or London. And it's not just that these games are played in multiple cultures: The connections run deeper than that. Often, kids compete with one another online across vast geographic distances. Other times, they collaborate—with money changing hands in the process. For the past several years, rich people in the West, some of them Digital Natives, have hired Chinese gamers to play for them to help their characters get to higher levels in online games. It's easy to imagine that, as captains of industry in the future, they will continue to look to outsourcing as an option to get other tricky tasks done at low cost. As kids, they're already paying someone else, halfway around the world, to do the work they don't want to do—all in the name of enhancing their identity.[27]

Just as there are reasons to be excited about identity development in the digital age, there are reasons, too, for concern.

One of the big differences between what Digital Natives are doing in creating and experimenting with their identities and in interacting with their peers online, and what their parents did as teens talking on the telephone, or hanging out at the local mall, is that the information that today's youth are placing into digital formats is easily accessed by anyone, including people whom they do not know. Versions of these identities and interactions will likely be around for a long time. It's no secret that the digital medium is characterized by high degrees of accessibility and persistence. Negotiating various audiences and contexts is fairly straightforward in the physical world (the way a young woman represents herself at her part-time job, through clothes and patterns of speech, might be different from the way she represents herself with friends). But online, Digital Natives are managing their identity representations in a space where dynamics of visibility, context, and audience are much more complex.[28]

Awareness among Digital Natives about how accessible and persistent online information is falls on a spectrum. Some Digital Natives we interviewed perceived their friends as the main audience of what they post online, whether on YouTube or their blog. Others were plainly more aware of the implications of the fact that many other viewers can see the personal information they put online.[29] As one high-school student told us:

> For me I know with MySpace and Facebook because a lot of my friends are adults on there that I work with, or like older people I've worked with, I always feel like I have to maintain a very professional—like I don't have like really—I don't have any inappropriate pictures on either. And like I am very simple because I don't want to like—yeah, I

don't—you don't want strangers to look at my profile and—I don't know. I just want to give a very simple and accurate, like, presentation of who I am. . . . I personally am very like, you know, I'm very careful about what I put on MySpace and Facebook in like making sure that that's what—that's who I feel I am.[30]

The process of building and managing identities in the Internet age is complex and full of possibilities for most young people growing up in wealthy, wired societies. Those who seek to control and shape the various personally identifiable data elements that are disclosed to third parties over the Internet throughout their lives will face constant challenges.[31] Unless technologies, the law, or social norms change radically, it will be a Sisyphean task. One student told us: "Some kids keep every picture on [their profile], which I think is really dumb. But it's their choice. If there were pictures taken at a party and kids were drinking or something, I don't want people seeing me in that position. I know that colleges are looking at kids' profiles more nowadays. I don't want to put myself in that position."[32]

Those who do not seek to control or shape their digital identity, whether because they are too unskilled to do so or because they are merely daunted by the likelihood of the rock rolling back down the mountain, may well face other problems in the future. They could come across employers reluctant to hire them or college admissions officers reluctant to accept them, dates who fail to show up at the appointed time and place, people who find them when they don't want to be found, or embarrassing conversations with their kids about what they did in their youth—all because a Google search turned up unflattering photos or incriminating or revealing text.

Among the many changes in what it means to form an identity in a digital age, two stand out as likely to have the most impact over time: instability and insecurity.

Instability, in this context, means that one's identity in the digital age changes frequently, and not always through the volitional acts of the person whose identity is at stake. A young person in a digital age faces a decrease in his or her ability to control identity as others perceive it.

Digital Natives change the personal information they share over the Internet all the time as they change their sense of self and how they wish to portray themselves. What it means to be a young person hasn't changed; what has changed is the manner in which young people choose to express themselves. The various online expressions of identity not only reflect a Digital Native's state of identity as he or she currently perceives it, but also shape that identity by influencing the Digital Native's perception of how others think about him or her. In this sense, the creation and revision of identity is a sort of feedback loop.

Making changes in self-presentation might be as simple as modifying a few aspects of a public profile on a social network. It might mean swapping out a photo or a self-description on a site like MySpace or Facebook, the expressions that a Digital Native's friends are most likely to see. Sometimes a Digital Native adjusts a dominant part of his or her digital identity by creating a new profile or gaming character, or switching platforms when one social network or virtual world goes from hot to passé. These changes can happen as often as every couple of months. Sometimes a Digital Native might just create a new identity within a given social network. Avatars—as the software developers at Linden Lab, the makers of Second Life, have seen to it—can die and then be revived. Or, an avatar might be able to cross platforms, so that the Digital Native's identity is persistent wherever he or she goes online; a teenage girl's avatar, for instance, might come with her as she makes her way through cyberspace on blogs, wikis, and other kinds of online environments. When she makes a switch to a new platform, her former identities don't really die, but remain as part of her complex sense of self—at least as perceived from the outside.

Just as the digital identity of a Digital Native is at once rich and interesting and easy to create, it is also fragile and vulnerable to manipulation and falsification. In the process of spending so much time in this digitally connected environment, Digital Natives are leaving more of themselves— more of their emerging identities—in what are effectively public spaces— "digital publics," or the "networked public sphere." The relationships that Digital Natives form with one another online also have a different tenor from face-to-face relationships: They are often fleeting; they are easy to enter into with a few mouse clicks; and they are easy to leave, without so much as a goodbye. But they are also perhaps enduring in ways we have yet to understand.

Another dominant feature of digital identities is that they are insecure. The identity of a sixteen-year-old is characterized by instability: It can change frequently. But when it is expressed online, it is also characterized by insecurity: It is hard for a sixteen-year-old girl in a wired society to control who can access or make changes to her identity. It would be impossible for her to secure her digital identity at any given moment, even if she wanted to. It would be nearly impossible for her to know who was able to access information about her identity, to control who could see that information, and to prevent that information from being changed by others.

This kind of insecurity isn't inherent in the concept of identity, digital or otherwise; there's nothing about the technology, or about the way that humans think about identity, that preordains its insecurity. It just happens to be the case at the present—and for the foreseeable future—that digital identities are insecure. They are insecure because of the way the technologies that Digital Natives use are designed. The challenge for the future will be to design technologies that allow users—Digital Natives and otherwise—to control access to the information that contributes to their identities, and to shape social norms that support this objective.[33]

There are also serious problems of inequality that arise in the context of digital identities. The Internet is the ultimate marketplace. As with all meritocracies, in the virtual world there is little in the way of equality. The participation gap—which separates those who have both digitally savvy skills and access to technologies from those who do not—still exists. Those less fortunate, or living in a less connected society, for better or for worse, may well have a less rich, less complex digital identity. Many people around the world, even the technology have-nots, will be findable online at some point in their lives. Often, this digital footprint will be left by others, not by the person so identified but by others who interact with him or her—doctors, government officials, companies, friends. These unsolicited contributions

to a digital identity—without the conscious sort that Digital Natives contribute themselves to balance the contributions of others—exacerbate the
effects of the participation gap.[34]

Identity in a digital age gives rise to two paradoxes.

The first is that a sixteen-year-old girl living in the digital age can adjust
her social identity with ease, but has far less ability to control how her
identity is perceived by others than she would have had in previous eras.
She has less ability than even someone living in a remote medieval village
to rid herself of previous identities. Social identities are much richer, more
varied, and more persistent—and far less under our control—than ever
before. She appears to have more control over her identity, but in fact she
has much less.

The second paradox is that, though a sixteen-year-old girl can create
multiple identities online with ease, she is more bound to a single identity
than ever before. The conventional understanding of identity holds that,
over time, one can create multiple versions of oneself. Each of these versions of identity can be tailored to specific audiences. One can express
oneself as a sophisticated, hard-driving executive in a public context, and
a gentle, supportive, loving spouse and parent in a private context. In each
of these contexts, one appears to be whatever identity is expressed. The
public and the private, in this conception, can be kept (largely) apart from
one another; they are compartmentalized. The identities may collide peri-
odically, such as when an employee brings his or her spouse to the company holiday party, but that convergence is occasional and fleeting. We've
built a legal system to regulate activities based upon certain understand-
ings of this distinction. You have a "reasonable expectation of privacy" in
a public context (which is to say, not much of an expectation at all) and
quite a different expectation in a private context (you perceive your private
matters to be free from intrusion, at least from the state, if not from most
private actors, too).

For young people in the digital age, there's an extent to which this traditional bifurcation holds—but it is, in fact, a very limited extent. Digital
Natives are certainly experimenting with multiple identities. Sometimes,
they are recreating or amplifying aspects of their real-space identities when

they go online. In other instances, they are experimenting online with who they are, trying on roles and looks and relationships that they might never dare to try on in "real space."[35] A young person may have a single identity online that is different from his or her everyday, real-space identity.[36] Or he or she may have a range of different online identities: one in MySpace, another in Facebook, one or more in World of Warcraft. Sometimes, these multiple identities are sustained as separate and kept distinct from one another. But from the perspective of the observer, it's also likely that these identities might converge—and converge even more than identities ever converged before the digital era.

The paradox arises because, from the perspective of the onlooker, much more of the Digital Native's identity may be visible at any one moment than was possible for individuals in pre-Internet eras. If the Digital Native has created multiple identities, those identities might be connected to create a much fuller picture of the individual than was possible before, spanning a greater period of time. Because of the use of digital technologies over the years, the result is more than a snapshot; instead it is more of a record of the individual's life that continues to accumulate over time. The version of the identity of a Digital Native that a given onlooker sees may depend a lot on how the onlooker accesses this morphing, sprawling identity. It might be by performing a single, simple Google search on the person's name and clicking on a large number of the search results. It might involve following a trail of links. Often, a Digital Native's LiveJournal or social network profile includes links to places where they have posted artistic creations, such as photographs, videos, or podcasts. The search might involve tracking a Digital Native's public expressions through social networks or a series of syndicated feeds, using a technology such as Really Simple Syndication (RSS).

Digital Natives are living more of their lives in networked publics.[37] The effect is that versions of a Digital Native girl's identity meant to be shared in one context—perhaps thought to be a semi-private context, such as a closed group within a social network or an island in Second Life—are very possibly combined with other versions of her identity in other contexts. Sometimes, Digital Natives misperceive such spaces as more private than they are. Or they may know very well that the spaces are public and disclose information about themselves anyway, for a range of reasons. But rarely do they have in view the full impact of their decision to disclose this information. An onlooker can look across these networked publics and pull multiple versions of someone's identity together into a single view. Over time, the identity of a Digital Native may come to look extremely different from the identity that the Digital Native intends to convey to the world.

The nature of identity is changing in the twenty-first century. These changes affect not just Digital Natives and other young people, but everyone living in wired societies. Digital Natives are absolutely right not to distinguish between "online" and "offline" identities. Increasingly, the identity of just about anyone living in a digital era is a synthesis of real-space and online expressions of self. And increasingly, what matters most is one's social identity, which is shaped not just by what one says about oneself and what one does in real space but also by what one's friends say and do.

This changing conception of identity presents both risks and opportunities. Young people—especially those who are Digital Natives—often know the risks they run by living their lives online. In some cases, they are extremely capable of evaluating those risks; in others, they are not, and they often make poor choices. While some of her peers may think their audience online is a relatively limited group of possible readers and listeners, a savvy Digital Native knows that as soon as she uploads something to her MySpace page, anyone on the Web might see it. She knows, too, that people likely will still be able to see it years from now.[38] And she knows that to cut herself off from self-expression in the digital space altogether would itself be a risk, just of another sort. She would risk being less connected to her wired friends, give up the opportunity to develop social skills that come from interaction both online and off, and lose the chance to engage in often quite safe forms of identity play and experimentation.

The biggest cause for concern is not the changes in identity themselves or even the habits of Digital Natives. Digital Natives often have the skills to manage their identities reasonably well in this shifting, hybrid environment. Most Digital Natives have an instinct about the workings of these two paradoxes at the core of identity formation and expression in a digital age. Much of the time, the Digital Natives are shaping the changing nature of identity, and how others come to perceive them, through their own actions. So the Digital Natives—the savvy users—are not in great danger. The people we should worry about instead are those users who fall on the other side of the participation gap: young people growing up in the digital age who do not have the digital literacy skills to control their identities. These paradoxes can be managed—and perhaps resolved—but only through a broad, all-hands-on-deck community effort, starting with young people themselves.

2

DOSSIERS

IN THE DIGITAL AGE, PEOPLE TRADE CONVENIENCE FOR CONTROL ALL THE time. Digital systems offer highly efficient means of leading lives in networked societies around the world. These conveniences enable consumers to buy more things that they want (or that marketers think they ought to want), voters to participate in civic life more easily, bureaucracies to offer shorter lines for the provision of services or payment of bills, employers to squeeze greater productivity out of their employees, doctors to provide better health care to their patients, and so forth. Taken together, all the digital information held, in many different hands, about a given person makes up his or her digital dossier.[1]

The primary cost of progress toward greater convenience, efficiency, and productivity via networked digital technologies is that individuals are losing control over these digital dossiers. In the technology business, what's collected is called "personally identifiable information," or "PII." Individuals are losing control of this information because the data-collection practices of corporations, among others, are changing at a rate that is faster than the rate of change for society's methods of protecting that data. In other words, the market for information about individuals is developing more quickly than the social norms that govern how people protect data about themselves. Neither the development of technologies, nor the law, has been much help to individuals in this regard.

These changes in the amount and types of information held about individuals mark both an extension and an acceleration of historical trends, not a clean break from the past. In previous eras, third parties held information about individuals, but in nowhere near the amounts held in the digital era. With the rise of the bureaucratic state in the industrial era, for instance, government agencies began to keep files on citizens. Businesses, too, have long kept records about their customers and their purchases. These files were not in a digital format, but they were files and they contained personally identifiable information. What's different in the digital age is that the speed with which these data-collection practices are growing has reached an extraordinary clip. The scope of what is being collected and the range of parties who are collecting it are both increasing. So, too, is the ability to use new technologies to aggregate and to search across multiple datasets to pull together a more accurate picture of an individual. And the fact that young people, whether Digital Natives or not, are setting out with such little control over their digital dossiers, right from the start, means that the information explosion could have a greater impact on their lives in years to come than it will have for their parents and grandparents.

There's a big difference between a digital identity and digital dossier. Does every bit of personally identifiable data about an eighteen-year-old count as part of her *identity*? No, plainly not. Her digital identity is a subset of her digital dossier. Her digital identity is composed of all those data elements that are disclosed online to third parties, whether it is by her choice or not. In simple terms, if the information comes up when someone Googles her name, it's definitely a part of her digital identity. If the information is associated with her name in a social environment like Facebook, MySpace, studiVZ, CyWorld, or World of Warcraft—even if it's not available to everyone on the Web—it is also part of her digital identity.

The digital dossier is a "superset": It's all the personally identifying information associated with her name, whether that information is accessible or not, and whether it is disclosed to third parties or not. So, for example, an eighteen-year-old woman's MySpace profile, with access controls set to allow anyone to see it, is part of both her digital identity and her digital dossier. Her medical record, held once by her pediatrician and now by her internist, is a part of her dossier, but not part of her identity, since only she, her doctor, and a few others (perhaps her insurance company or pharmacist) can see what's inside. The government, too, has a series of digital files on each person, beginning with the birth certificate. Data elements are added over time and include Social Security records, tax returns, marriage certificates, recorded deeds, and the like—even traffic violations and, in unfortunate cases, arrest records, fit into this category. These presumably remain part of the individual's digital dossier, though not necessarily his or her identity, throughout life.

The digital identity of any citizen of a wired society is composed not only of the data elements that this person contributes voluntarily, but also of the elements that *other* people contribute and collect about him or her. For young people, it's even harder than for those less engaged in digital cultures to control digital identity, given the ubiquity of information technologies in their lives and the social norms of sharing information about one's friends online. The ramifications for the security and privacy of these individuals are substantial. Those ramifications will only grow over time if the current trajectories hold.[2]

Unlike people born into previous generations, those who are born digital will grow up to have a large number of digital files kept about them, whether they like it or not, and these files begin to accumulate right from the start. These digital files will become key parts of their digital dossiers as they grow. And Digital Natives aren't alone in this; as with many of the phenomena discussed in this book, the same goes for many of us who weren't born digital but who are living at least part of our lives in a digital age.[3]

The amount of information that goes into the digital files kept about a baby born today is extraordinary. To see just how extraordinary, let's look at the digital dossier of a hypothetical baby: We'll call him Andy.

Andy's digital life begins well before he is born—before he even has a name. The first entry in his digital file is a sonogram that his proud parents-to-be affix to the refrigerator, anticipating the happy event of his birth. That same image is recreated in the hospital's database, the first formal record of Andy's life. With the shift from analog to digital, it has become cheap and easy to make a copy of just about any file. Any image or video file or sound file can be copied and stored at almost no marginal cost. In this case, with good reason, the obstetrician's team will copy Andy's image into a file for the pediatrician who will care for him after he's born.[4] Start counting: That's one digital file, copied in at least four places.

These digital files mark the first contributions to Andy's digital dossier.[5] Even before he is born, Andy's digital dossier exists in four places: at home, at the obstetrician's office, at the hospital where he is destined to be born, and in his pediatrician's office files. In each instance, the file is surrounded by different contextual information that will govern how it is used and whether it makes a difference, somehow, in Andy's life. The development of Andy's digital dossier—and to some extent his identity, too—is already held in multiple hands, out of his control and out of his parents' control.

As soon as Andy is born, the number of digital files on Andy continues to grow. So, too, does the number of things each file contains. Andy's barcoded bracelet lists a few more facts: Andy's gender, the time of birth, his mother's last name. These facts are attached to the photograph of the unborn child in the hospital's digital file. The bits on the bar code connect the analog—that is, the "real-life" infant—to his emerging digital file. These facts (and files), again, are shared with the pediatrician's office.

Very likely, nothing terrible will happen with the files in Andy's digital dossier up to this point; at least, one hopes not. With rare exceptions, national standards exist to protect the privacy of personal health information, at least in the United States and Europe. We shouldn't spend too much time worrying that these particular datasets will fall into the wrong hands.

What we ought to care about instead is the pattern that is starting to emerge. The problem is that far more information than ever before is being collected and stored in a format that others can possibly search, whether in the near term or in the distant future. The information is held in many different hands, and every party that has access to it is subject to its own rules about what can be done with it. Young people are not asked to make informed decisions about the data collected and stored about them, and even if they were, they would be in no position to make those decisions. Nor can they do much about the collection of the information after the fact. Over time, the problem only grows. Andy's parents do not have much more control over some of the information in Andy's file than he does; indeed, they lack control over the information in their own digital dossiers.

It is not only big institutions—companies, hospitals, governments—that are contributing to the explosion of information gathering about individuals that is going on. A baby's family members, caught up in the euphoria of his birth and wishing to share the news with friends, make contributions. Many families get into the act of adding data to the baby's digital dossier as soon as they bring him home from the hospital, especially now that so many Web services allow even nontechnical parents to upload photos, videos, and text to the Internet.

The contributions that Andy's family—and later his friends and others—make to the dossier are quite different from the contributions of the medical community. The digital information that is in the hands of his doctors is likely to stay more or less private over time, whereas the online postings about a Digital Native created by friends and family are immediately in public view and social. The public and the social bits are far more likely to become important parts of Andy's identity than the bits held by a doctor's office (though both remain relevant as the story unfolds).

The family posts baby pictures of Andy to services like Photobucket, Ofoto, Shutterfly, Facebook, and Flickr. As soon as the photos are posted online in these public places, the family sends out a batch of e-mails to tell people to log in and check out the whole collection. Friends who come to visit bring flowers and plush toys, and each leaves with more photos, stored initially on digital cameras and cell phones. Photographs are no longer just tangible items to be mailed to friends and family—they are computer bytes easily spread across the Internet. These friends, too, upload the pictures to their own photo-sharing sites as part of the welcoming process.

The scale of online photo-sharing is vast and growing quickly. Online social networks now host billions of photographs. Photobucket, a favorite of Digital Natives, claims to host more than 4.7 billion digital photographs as of 2008. Facebook, one of the world's leading social networks, reports more than 3 billion photographs, less than four years into its existence.

Other, similar services, taken together, host billions more. New, convenient services that aggregate photos and allow for image searching, with increasing amounts of metadata to help associate the images with people, come online every year.[6]

Andy's parents also use their cell phones to spread the happy news. Text messages using SMS—short message service, favored by teenagers the world over—are a highly efficient way for Andy's family to get word of the vital stats ("healthy Andy born 6 1b 8 oz. at 7:12 p.m. mom well too") to the cell phones, Sidekicks, Blackberries, and Treos of their wired friends. In turn, their friends post congratulatory messages to the family's weblog to welcome the new arrival. The blog posts include links back to the Photobucket and Flickr feeds, where a mother-lode of pictures, tagged with Andy's name, awaits online visitors.

The important point here is that the proliferation of copying makes the digital files wildly difficult to manage—and right off the bat. The process starts even before Andy's birth. After he's born, the ability of Andy's parents to control the information that is associated with him is immediately lost, and by the time Andy comes of age and begins to try to manage it for himself, the tangle of information will be even more impossible to unravel. In the digital age, there are more files in total than ever before, and there are more items in each file. Under current law in the United States, there's little incentive *not* to keep a file, even if the collectors of the information are unsure whether they'll ever have reason to open it or do anything about what's in there. This proliferation of personally identifiable information, without a serious counterweight on the other side, is dangerous.

This wasn't the case in previous eras. Limitations on record-keeping—like the high cost of data collection or the scarcity of physical storage space in an office building, or even limitations on e-mail storage space—are no longer major factors. And more of these files—whether in the form of images, audio files, videos, or flat text—can easily be searched. As new technologies make the aggregation and sorting of large datasets more cost effective, the incentive to keep the data gets all the more alluring for more and more people who interact with Digital Natives.

The way that Andy's digital dossier emerges demonstrates the problem about an individual's control over one's identity in a digital age. Some of the places where data about Andy is stored are protected; others are quite open, to groups of "friends" (say, in Facebook) or to the whole world (via a search engine). It is crucial for users to understand the context for each place, as the most sophisticated of the Digital Natives realize. For some data, it is fine for it to exist in public; in fact, that may be the point. For other data, there's an expectation that no one will ever come to see it. The problem, at its core, is that Andy doesn't get to make those decisions. It's possible that he will get smart about it by the time he is a teenager, but by then he will already be fighting a losing battle.

Even the digital information that we perceive to be out of reach from third parties may in fact be more accessible than we realize, now or in the future. We can only hope that the Social Security Administration's computer system, which processes and stores the application for Andy's new Social Security number, is a digital Fort Knox. But the biggest search engines—like Google and Baidu, China's largest search engine—are constantly improving the ability of their Web crawlers to unearth more and more data from the dark recesses of the Internet. These crawlers copy information, without asking permission, and dump it into a massive, structured global index. At the same time, social networks and other services hosting personally identifiable information are eager to get the traffic from these search engines, so they are exposing more and more about people to the likes of Google and Baidu. This combination of factors—the incentive for search engines to index all the world's information and the incentive of online service providers to draw people to information on their sites— means that information about Andy that was once in a silo is now in a more open, public space. A photograph of Andy that was uploaded to a service that his parents thought was just for friends might someday become not just part of his dossier, but part of his identity. We love the convenience of search engines, but we may come to regret the lack of control over personal information that we trade for that convenience.

The pattern that repeats itself through the Digital Native's life starts here: In our rush to take advantage of the conveniences of digital technologies, we may be giving up more control of the information about ourselves than we can now comprehend. The bits of information about a child born digital may only be loosely joined today, but from the perspective of an outsider, it will be increasingly easy to put the pieces together and to associate them with Andy himself. Andy will have to work very hard to even begin to manage his digital identity, much less his complete digital dossier, as it continues to emerge over the course of his life. Neither his parents, nor Andy himself, nor the state, can control it.

As Andy grows, he begins to contribute to his digital dossier himself as he starts to lead parts of his life online. Many parents say that their kids start to go online regularly between the ages of five and ten. In most households, their online time is supervised—despite the children's protests. This is the time when issues arise about what the kids are doing online. It's also the time, usually in kindergarten, when kids start to go online regularly at school. As Andy and his peers interact with digital services at home and in school, they begin, unwittingly, to add to the growth of their digital dossiers and to cede further control over information about themselves.

Consider PBSKids.org. It's a perfectly innocuous, appropriate website geared toward young children. Kids like Andy, at age five, enjoy games like those they find on "Between the Lions." Between the Lions includes free, interactive games that involve kids in fun exercises related to reciting the alphabet, identifying synonyms, and other early steps toward literacy. It uses characters from the TV show of the same name. Parents like the games, too, because they come from a safe, credible source and help their kids learn to read.

But there's a catch: In order to play the games, Andy (or his mom, more likely) has to download a bit of software made by a big technology company, Adobe. Big technology companies, as we'll see, hold enormous amounts of data about individuals. In the process of downloading the software, Andy's mom is prompted to tell Adobe whether she is over eighteen or not and provide her name and her e-mail address. If she creates an account for Andy, another few entries in the Digital Native's distributed digital file, held in another set of corporate hands, is born. Call those files number two (at PBS) and three (at Adobe). (Andy is also getting exposed to the corporate logo for Chick-fil-A, the sponsor for the website, every time he logs on to the website. His penchant for eating chicken nuggets every day is easier to explain with this bit of context. This is not the last time he'll be carefully targeted at a tender age by online marketers.)

The development of Andy's digital dossier gathers steam as he gets older and starts to engage more in the world at large. Just as the playtime environment for a child is moving online, so, too, is his learning environment, with further ramifications for his developing digital dossier. In a typical grade-school science class, the teacher may ask Andy to look up photos and information about the solar system on Google. He types in "solar system," "Pluto," "Neptune." Once he clicks the search button, a stream of information is sent to, and stored in, the Google servers. This includes the address associated with his school's computer (called an Internet Protocol, or IP, address), the date and time of his query, the browser he is using, and the unique cookie ID assigned to the computer. If he is registered as a Google user and is logged in when he does his searches (Andy probably is not, unless he's already over the age of thirteen or is willing to lie about it), Google associates these data with his personally identifiable information. Add a few more digital files to the list as Andy and his friends go about doing their schoolwork.

PBSKids and Google are far from alone in this regard. Andy, like many other children his age, may come to love Neopets. This online service gives him a virtual pet that he can feed and interact with online every day, just as he would with a real pet. When Andy signs up for Neopets, the company asks for his first name, his birthday, his gender, and his country, city, state, and zip code. Neopets doesn't actually require all this information at registration—there is no little asterisk beside the name box or the gender box. But Andy probably doesn't know what "denotes required field" means next to the big star at the bottom, so he will probably go ahead and fill out all the information. He may also have to provide the e-mail address that his dad helped him set up. Neopets gobbles up this info and gives him a cookie in his Web browser so that the site can track his online activity when he returns. Digital file number six.

In their desire to keep their children safe, some parents are adding further to the growing dossiers on their children, using advanced information technologies to track their children's whereabouts. This creates yet another set of files on their Digital Natives. Imagine that Andy is a latch-key kid when he's in middle school. His parents set up a website to show a live feed from a webcam that hangs over their front door. Parents with hectic work schedules and children with equally hectic schedules filled with school and lessons find this Web page reassuring. Either parent can check that Andy is home when he should be. The site may include no information other than the video feed, and a bit of computer code can keep out the search engines. Even with these limitations, though, the data feed, if stored, might constitute another type of entry in the growing set of personally identifiable data about Andy as he grows up.

Andy's parents would probably not think the video feed was extreme in any way. After all, if they were paranoid they could have resorted to even more draconian methods of tracking him. They could have implanted his T-shirts or pajamas with computer chips, called radio frequency identification (RFID) tags. Or they could have tracked him through the chips in a cell phone, which would have enabled them, after signing up with a special service, to log onto a website and check the location of the phone, updated every five minutes. By clicking on the child's name on the site, they would have been able to scan the last five records of his location—the closest address, accompanied by a red dot on a small map, listed with the time.

Schools have experimented with this idea of tracking the whereabouts of children, too. A school district in California tracked children based on a badge they had to carry around with an embedded RFID chip, before abandoning the program in 2005. Other school districts are still experimenting with this technology.[7] Eager to know where their children are at any moment, some parents and teachers are amassing a huge record of their kids' childhoods. There are plainly benefits to this sort of tracking in terms of keeping kids safe, especially when the children are young. Parents and teachers can keep close tabs on who is caring for their children and where their children are at any moment. But the cost of doing so is high. These forms of tracking can undermine the trust between parents and children, restrict the independence of children, and create a massive set of data about a child's life by the time the child enters adulthood.[8]

When Andy gets to college, he continues to trade convenience for control of his digital dossier. If he's become a Digital Native—comfortable with new technologies and using them on a daily basis without distinguishing between online and off—he will have a profile on MySpace or Facebook, or whatever the hot site is by the time he gets to college. For many students, these social networks function as a connecting force in their increasingly recorded social lives. Financial records, too, might enter the picture here: a swiped college ID to buy a bagel at the campus café, a PayPal transaction to buy an overdue birthday present for a friend, a nearly maxed-out credit card used for nights out with friends. GPS devices in cars they drive to parties and video cameras in dormitory entryways track their movements. The convenience of Andy's life as a Digital Native is fantastic. So, too, are the possibilities in terms of what all of this means for his identity—and for what may happen to his privacy.

Andy is not the only one contributing to his digital dossier in college. His friends are major contributors, too. There's a vast amount of information being published and collected about young people by their friends. The Internet makes it easy for anyone to publish information online about anyone else. Digital Natives are champs at publishing information about themselves and their friends as they go about forming their identities online. In the course of a day in the life of a college student, many of the basic social interactions between young people are recorded, whether through photographs, blog posts, comments to public message-boards in social software, or funny videos of kids eating at restaurants that might be uploaded to Daily Motion or YouTube on the fly.[9]

The emergence of the ubiquitous Internet is a key driver of the proliferation of Andy's digital dossier. Digital Natives now add more to one another's dossiers than ever before through their use of mobile devices that can record digital information, and they post this information instantly to the Internet and track what others are saying online. The fact that Andy can access the Internet from all manner of devices and can interact with people and input or view information on the fly at any time leads to more contributions to his digital dossier. And while some of these are voluntary—meaning that he contributes them himself—many are involuntary—that is, contributed by others without his permission and often without his knowledge. Mobile devices are increasingly the interface for Digital Natives to shape their identities and those of their peers.

Take, for example, an ordinary party of college students in a large urban area, anywhere in the wired world. Most Digital Natives carry cell phones. In fact, it's hard to buy a phone without a built-in camera and the ability to e-mail a photograph or send it to another phone. Facebook, Flickr, and other services enable a young person to take a photo of a group of friends at the party, type an e-mail address into the phone, add tags in the body of the e-mail, and upload the photo automatically to the Internet. Instantly and automatically, anyone who accesses Facebook or Flickr can see the newly updated photo, no matter where it was taken or where the person accessing it is located in physical space.

As Andy grows older, he may have a better sense of the trade-offs he is making between convenience and control of his digital dossier, but he is no more able to control the information about him than when he was much younger. His dossier, by the time he has entered the workforce, will be colossal in size and scope. On any given day in his life, there will be dozens of records about him in digital form either created or added to, from commercial transactions to health records to traces of his social interactions. His digital dossier will be held in thousands of hands. He may make better choices about incremental contributions to this dossier as time goes on, but he will be unable to get his arms around its enormity, much less to control what others can come to know about him.

T he problem with the rapid growth of digital dossiers is that the decisions about what to do about personal information are made by those who hold the information. The person who contributes information to a digital dossier may have a modicum of control up front, but he or she rarely exercises it. The person to whom the information relates— sometimes the person who contributed it, sometimes not—often has no control whatsoever about what happens to the data. The existence of these dossiers may not itself be problematic. But these many, daily, individual acts result in a rich, deep dataset associated with an individual that can be aggregated and searched. This process, start to finish, is only lightly regulated.

Digital Natives aren't oblivious to the fact that their digital dossiers are growing as they lead their lives mediated by digital technologies. They do not, however, seem particularly worried about it. As one male college student said, "The fact that, like, search engines can figure out—can track what everyone searches for, that CVS can track everything you buy. But I guess I just have to rely on the fact that they collect so much data no one will bother to look at mine to any extent."[10] Many other students make similar comments: They know that data is being collected about them, but they doubt that much will happen to them as a result.

Digital Natives tend to be sanguine on this score, and probably too sanguine. One way in which this sanguinity exposes itself is that they themselves use this kind of information all the time. To most Digital Natives, research, of nearly any sort, means a Google search. They go online to learn more about one another before going on a date or heading out for a party. They go online to settle arguments or to illustrate a point. Google has become a way of life—at a party, it's not uncommon for a computer to be broken out to show something obscure on Wikipedia or to settle a heated debate.

Even though many young people shake off the concerns about all the information collected about them, they, too, start to get worried when they look at it from a different angle: The idea of someone aggregating, searching through, and acting on the basis of that information later can be unnerving. For instance, Digital Natives make much of the way employers or admissions officers might use these data to research them before an interview. The same is true of young people researching prospective employers and bosses (usually through a Google search), or schools and professors (through specialized sites like RateMyProfessors.com, or MeinProf.de in Germany).

The lives of Digital Natives will be even more fantastic in twenty years, in many ways, than we can imagine today. No amount of imagination can do justice to the scale and scope of digital dossiers a few decades in the future. Technologies, how they are used, and social norms will continue to change, probably even more rapidly than they have in the recent past. What's enduring about the narratives of the lives of Digital Natives, growing up in wired societies, is that some of them will come to regret the trade-offs in control that they've made in the name of convenience and fun. And, for that matter, the same is true of those who do not happen to be Digital Natives but who also live their lives in wired ways.

No one—not young people, not their parents, not the government, and not any single corporation—controls the emerging digital dossier of a Digital Native. The series of digital files that make up the digital dossiers of any given Digital Native are many, varied, distributed, and persistent. For now, anyway.

As a society and as parents, educators, and individuals we are neither looking ahead to the implications of our digital present nor working together toward a digital future in which the privacy and safety of our kids is assured. In the meantime, we are failing to prepare our children for what their current lifestyle already means for them, for their friends, and for the way they relate to one another and to their society. Too often, we are leaving our children alone to shape their identities in a fragile, fast-moving, hard-to-control environment online. And too often, the decisions that we make in favor of convenience mean giving up control that, at some point in the future, we may wish we had retained.[11]

3

PRIVACY

DIGITAL PRIVACY HAS BEEN A HOT TOPIC SINCE THE INTERNET BECAME A popular medium in the mid-1990s. Never before has so much information about average citizens been so easily accessible to so many. That's true whether we live our lives the way Digital Natives do or not. There are many regional differences in how online privacy is treated in cultures around the world. Data privacy continues to be a key battleground in policy circles, in Brussels and in Washington in particular. But there's no clear consensus on what to do about it.

The lifestyles of young people around the world increase the difficulty, and importance, of addressing concerns about privacy in a digital age. Young people who are living their lives mediated by digital technologies will pay a high price, sometime down the road, for the way privacy is handled in this converged, hybrid environment. Most young people are extremely likely to leave something behind in cyberspace that will become a lot like a tattoo—something connected to them that they cannot get rid of later in life, even if they want to, without a great deal of difficulty.

As they lead their social lives mediated by online services, very few young people are thinking ahead to gauge the consequences of the data they are leaving behind them. They are not in a position to make good choices about what they want their digital dossiers to contain—or what their identities will look like—years from now.[1] Understandably, they're focused on living their lives, and their lives have a significant online component. The metrics that matter to them are how many friends they have in a particular hot social network, how many postings they attract to their Wall on Facebook, and who's saying what to whom online.

Many young people believe their conversations online are far more private than they are. The digital age has brought about new incentive to reveal information about oneself (social norms suggest that the more information you post online, the more friends you will attract) while reducing checks on imprudent behavior (an innate sense of privacy, or someone telling you "don't you dare go out dressed like that").[2] At no time in human history has information about a young person—or anyone, for that matter—been more freely and publicly accessible to so many others.[3]

Many parents and grandparents can't believe what their children and grandchildren are sharing online about themselves. In this fast-changing digital environment, expectations of privacy among young people are shifting. Meanwhile, too many parents and grandparents have checked themselves out of the conversation. Or, worse, they are doing exactly what they are telling their children not to do: sharing "too much" information about themselves and meeting strangers they have met online in unsafe places.[4] Revised expectations of privacy may have an implication for the protections that the Digital Native may receive under the law now and in the future.[5]

B y the time a Digital Native enters the workforce, there are hundreds— if not thousands—of digital files about her, held in different hands, each including a series of data-points that relate to her and her activities. There is no way for a Digital Native to know that each of these files exists. Even if she made it her full-time obsession, it would be impossible for her to stay on top of managing the files or even sorting out their sources and contents. And she wouldn't be able to correct the information even when it turned out to be inaccurate.[6]

The answer, though, is not to avoid the networked publics in which so many people—especially Digital Natives—are leading their lives. Instead, we need to develop more nuanced ways to navigate these new publics. And we need to rethink what this new way of living means for our law as it relates to data privacy, and devise the changes we need to make our legal system responsive to the problems that have become so apparent.

Imagine a college-aged Digital Native who decides that she's going to get serious about managing the digital information that someone can come to know about her. She starts, sensibly enough, by Googling herself: She goes to www.google.com and types in her full name. About 0.06 seconds later, Google returns a page with "Results 1–10 of about 691,000" for her name. The top results include her blog, her Photobucket feed, and a few other things that she intentionally put out into the world about herself. So far so good. She's more or less in control of the first few links that Google turns up about her. On these pages, she might reveal more than she ought to, but at least it's her choice, and she can usually edit her own pages.[7]

Google doesn't turn up everything that's in her digital dossier, which is a good thing. Some online services, including certain social software sites, block Google's spiders from entering. In these cases, information about a Digital Native can be found only by those who subscribe to the service and are permitted, by one rule or another, to view the profile. Likewise, the large, deep pools of data that information aggregators collect about a Digital Native are nowhere to be found, unless there's been a security breach of some kind. Medical records, academic history, credit-card information, online banking transactions, all those security cameras that capture our comings and goings: Most are in the "deep Web," where search engines today cannot reach.[8] Nonetheless, these data about her are out there in the ether, in databases that are connected to the network. Without her knowledge, companies are sharing these data about her in the interest of "understanding her preferences better" when she comes into contact with their online services.

Asked what someone could come to know about her, a young person is likely to focus on the handful of places where she knows there's personally identifiable information about her—some of which Google can reach, and others not—not on these hidden datasets. After all, she put much of it there herself: on her blog, on MySpace, on Facebook, on YouTube, on studiVZ (if she's in Germany), on Bebo (if she's in the United Kingdom), on CyWorld (if she's in South Korea), and so forth. There's a clear analog to the pre-Internet world: She might consider the picture that she posts of herself to her MySpace profile as roughly akin to the dress she chooses to wear to the prom, or just to school one day. It is an expression of who she is, what she likes, and how she positions herself in the world, like a new outfit; it's important to have a page with the newest, hottest thing. In the Internet age, however, the information that the Digital Native reveals about herself is sometimes quite detailed. It includes things like her cell-phone number, her home address, her birthdate, and other details that she would never intentionally reveal to strangers in the analog world.

In some cases, Digital Natives can keep a specific item off of a Google search. Many sites offer the option of restricting access to personal information. In Facebook or MySpace, for instance, it's pretty easy to specify who can see your profile—for example, "only my friends" or "some of my networks and all my friends."[9] Even though the default privacy settings in Facebook and MySpace make a fair amount of information about a user public, their controls are better than most in this regard. (There's evidence, however, that this may be changing as the pressures of real-world economics come to bear on Facebook's team. Facebook originally disallowed profiles of its users from showing up in Google searches, but it changed its policy in September 2007 to draw in more viewers to basic profiles.[10] Facebook has also begun to work with outside parties, such as Blockbuster and online retailer Overstock.com, to track purchases elsewhere on the Web and to target advertising based on what users do online.)

No matter how sophisticated a Digital Native may be about controlling the digital information about her, there are certain things that are likely to wind up in her digital dossier despite her best efforts to keep those data out. For instance, if she created a page or a profile in a social network or other online service devoted to a particular interest of hers, which initially did not expose information to search engines, she still might find her profile included in a search on her name years later. The reason is that virtually every service reserves the right, "in its sole discretion," to change its privacy settings at any time. As pressures mount on firms to attract more traffic to their sites, they may be tempted to expose more and more information to search engines to draw people in. Likewise, if she were to post a blog entry or a photograph or video to a blogging site, her content might well be copied to another page on the Internet, which might in turn eventually be indexed on the Web even if her initial post was private. The same might be true of e-mails sent to a listserv that is later archived to a public place on the Internet, and so forth. Consider also all the information that she has nothing to do with, but that is nevertheless accumulating about her: There are networks of sensors, cropping up around major metropolitan areas, that allow young people to find their friends who are strolling through another part of the city. Such location information can be displayed, for instance, on cell phones or other mobile devices. The point is simply that information shared in digital form in one context, according to an initial set of rules, may be presented to the world according to quite another set of rules later on.

Young people face a major privacy challenge with respect to information they post about themselves, let alone what other people post about them or what third parties collect about them. For starters, many young people are not aware of the choices they can make as they begin to use online services. And even for those who are aware of the choices, keeping track of privacy settings can be difficult; from a practical standpoint, young people are unlikely to attempt it. Digital Natives who understand the choices they are presented with may simply decide not to spend their time in this way. There is plenty of evidence to suggest that no one—whether native to digital life or not—reads privacy policies or does much to adjust the default settings for online services. None of the young people we talked to in focus groups and interviews reported putting care into reviewing these policies regularly. Even the most sophisticated young people made clear that they almost never read these policies or compared the privacy policies among services. At the same time, they were attracted to Web 2.0 technologies, with their high degrees of interactivity and their implicit encouragement to contribute data about oneself and one's friends.[11] These new technologies are a wonderful thing in terms of creativity, but the implications of their popularity on privacy over the long run is almost certain to be negative.[12]

Much of what is accessible about a young person via search was put into digital format by someone else, and much of the information in a Digital Native's dossier is contributed by her peers, both in the offline and online world. Links further down in the Google results about a young person lead to blog posts that other people have written about her, sometimes linking back to her blog, often including a picture of her that another person took and uploaded to the Internet. Links lead also to the Photobucket feeds of her classmates, who have tagged pictures of her, which come up high in the search results page as well. Flip over to the "image" tab on Google, and pictures of her and her friends, both new and old, appear by the dozens.

Sometimes, these data elements are meant to be disclosed publicly; sometimes they are meant to be kept private. But in any event, it's clear that the meaning of both "public" and "private" is shifting, at least if you listen to Digital Natives talk about it. Both kinds of data elements—those intended for public view and those thought to be restricted to a private audience—are increasingly represented in digital format, and both become part of the identity of a Digital Native. Even more troubling, a much wider range of things can come to be included in someone's public, social identity in this highly social online environment than was possible in the social environments of earlier eras. Elements such as videos, photos, or blog posts tagged online with a girl's name by a friend, for example, become part of her identity, and she may not immediately know it. Or an element might be added by a third party that comes to be associated with her identity via an automated mechanism besides Google, such as the visual search engine Riya.

Societies need to start taking seriously the privacy concerns that young people face. These problems are unlikely to go away on their own. In fact, they are more likely to be compounded over time. Parents, teachers, and policymakers need to concern themselves with both the shifting notion of identity and the expanding digital dossiers of our children, and they need to understand that these dossiers include contributions from a wide range of sources and are easily accessible to an even wider range of people, some of whom may use them for purposes we would not desire. Unless something changes, the ability of our children to control the information that proliferates about them on the Web will decline with each passing year.

I n February 2005, a company called ChoicePoint decided to do something quite awkward: It wrote to more than 100,000 people to tell them that the company had inadvertently released records about them. The funny thing was, most people getting the letters didn't know what ChoicePoint was. They had never heard of the company, and they certainly hadn't given it permission to create dossiers on them—much less to sell what was in those dossiers to third parties. To make things messier, Choice-Point had sold data about these people to fraud artists.[13] The U.S. Federal Trade Commission (FTC) said that over 800 people had become victims of identity theft as a result of the breach. ChoicePoint paid a fine of $15 million as part of a settlement with the government.[14]

ChoicePoint is a publicly traded company, based near Atlanta, Georgia, that collects data about people. It is in the business of being a "commercial data broker." This means that it pulls together information about many people from lots of other private firms and from government records, and then sells it to various buyers, such as private industry. ChoicePoint itself has acquired more than fifty other companies. According to the Electronic Privacy Information Center, it keeps tens of billions of records.[15]

By itself, the aggregation of information about individuals, by Choice-Point or any other firm, may not be a problem. Most people think it's creepy; and in some parts of the world, like Europe, lawyers would argue that it violates individual rights. But in the United States, it is perfectly lawful—and it can be highly profitable.

The first problem arises when ChoicePoint and other data gluttons do something with this aggregation of information about a young person—or anyone else, for that matter. It would go beyond mere "creepiness," for example, if health-insurance premiums were calculated based on data from online food orders, or if an online merchant's pricing system discriminated among customers based on their income or spending patterns. But set aside those concerns for a moment, and imagine that the company that aggregates personal information is completely responsible in terms of how its staff uses this personal information—that it doesn't do anything that crosses the "creepy" line. A young person might be willing to accept this trade-off in light of the many conveniences of a digital life.

Even if a young person consents to this regime—he prefers targeted on-line ads to untargeted ads, for instance—there still may be a problem lurking here. When a data-aggregation firm's security is insufficient, the data may be released to users who are not so responsible. In the case of Choice-Point, that's just what happened.[16] And ChoicePoint's dataset hasn't gotten smaller since the data breach occurred; instead, it has expanded enormously. ChoicePoint now has access to the data of Lexis-Nexis, another giant aggregator of personal information, because of an acquisition early in 2008.[17]

The recent history of data breaches should sound a call to action, but curiously, little has been done to decrease the likelihood of further breaches in the future, other than steps taken by firms themselves to improve their security.[18] Privacy zealots may sound paranoid when they tell these stories, but the stories aren't crazy. And they seem less crazy with each passing year. A pattern has emerged. More data is being collected by firms about individuals. The incentive to do so is clear. The better they get to know a consumer and the more they know about that person's needs, interests, and preferences, the better they can target their offers—for instance, by sending tailored ads. But at the same time, the incentives for the bad guys to break into those databases are also becoming ever more powerful. And human error is the biggest concern of all. Some studies point to the risk of a "digital Pearl Harbor" unless we get much more serious than we are about computer security (which in turn brings with it another series of problems).[19]

ChoicePoint is certainly not alone in failing to maintain the privacy of all the digital information entrusted to it. The employees of companies that have long track records and trusted relationships with their users sometimes do stupid things. In 2006, an AOL employee released the search data of 658,000 of its customers. Days later, the information could still be

accessed over the Web.[20] AOL claimed that the mistake did not result in
the release of any "personally identifiable information," but names and e-
mail addresses, among other information, appeared in the publicly accessible search strings. As an AOL spokesperson said in an e-mail: "This was
a screw-up."[21] The parent of T.J. Maxx and Marshalls, the discount retail-
ers, settled charges with the FTC for exposing the credit information of as
many as 45 million people to hackers. The same went for Reed Elsevier,
the giant European firm, which was accused of letting hundreds of thousands of records fall into the wrong hands.[22]

It's not only companies that make terrible errors when it comes to disclosing huge amounts of personal information in a digital format to those
who are not meant to have it. The British government managed to lose
control over copies of sensitive information on about 40 percent of the
country's population, including the majority of the children who live there.
The government admitted that two computer disks, with information
about 7.25 million families, went missing in the mail. The disks contained
the names of all the children and parents who had claimed a child benefit, along with dates of birth, addresses, national insurance numbers, and
bank account numbers.[23]

Privacy could become a problem for anyone who leads a life mediated in
part by digital technologies. More information is collected about us, and
held in more hands, and accessible to more people, than ever before.
Many of us—Digital Immigrants as well as Digital Natives and other
young people—are putting huge amounts of information about ourselves
online. In the case of young people, however, the problem is more acute
for a number of reasons.

In cultures around the world, young people are using interactive online tools, including social network sites like MySpace, Facebook, studiVZ,
Mixi, Bebo, and CyWorld. Web 2.0 technologies are flourishing in wired
cultures around the world, including China.[24] Sophos PLC conducted a
study that showed that 41 percent of Facebook users were willing to give
up personal information to a complete stranger—even to a person who was
completely made up.[25] In the process, young people disclose information

in ways that will make it more persistent than they expect. Some of the more savvy users realize the information will be persistent, but they disclose the information anyway, choosing not to worry about it for now. Nevertheless, they may find themselves regretting that they shared some information when it seems not to go away over time.

The constant emergence of new technologies compounds the problem. Young people are turning to mobile devices in droves. They use them to post more information about themselves and their friends into the ether. When they upload a photo to a social network, they may "tag" it with the name of one of their friends. This practice of "social tagging" makes for more efficient searching—but this is not necessarily better when it comes to protecting privacy. Search and database tools continue to improve at an astonishing rate. And companies like Riya are using technologies to make links between images that have been manually tagged by human beings and other images online that have not been tagged.[26] Apparently unrelated pieces of information can all of a sudden be put together by someone who wants to compile a full profile of a person; this information can then be used for business purposes, such as targeted marketing. In the aggregate, this information may reveal much more about a person than the same details would in isolation.

The problem of privacy is exacerbated for young people by the fact that we are just at the beginning of the digital age. Time, in this sense, is not on the side of those who are born digital. No one has yet been born digital and lived into adulthood. No one has yet experienced the aggregate effect of living a digitally mediated life over the course of eighty or ninety years. Digital Natives will be the first to experience the compounding effect of the creation of identities and digital dossiers over a long period of time. Given that there may be hundreds of bits of information in many different online files kept by different private parties on each Digital Native by the time he or she is a teenager, hundreds more that accumulate during the college years and young adulthood, and thousands by middle age, the absence of protections may have a far greater effect than society has anticipated. A single, isolated breach or use of aggregated data that occurs today may not seem very troubling. But the true impact over the long run is yet to be seen.

Every year, as more of the world is getting wired and more people are gaining skills and access to digital technologies, both the sheer amount of information in digital format and the potential scope of the harm from wrongdoing online grow. As the network grows, more and more people have the ability to post information to the network and to access information about others. This trend is a wonderful and important thing: We have a chance to share more information with more people around the world than ever before. A great example of this power is MIT's OpenCourseWare project, which makes materials about every class at MIT accessible to anyone in the world for self-teaching or for inclusion in school curricula. But from the perspective of young people and their privacy, there's a downside to the global access to information made possible by information technologies like the Internet. False or misleading information can be far more damaging to the individual when it appears on the Internet than if the same information were released verbally or in writing in a grade school environment, for instance. The same holds true of accurate, but still harmful, information. The extent of the damage caused by harmful information—in terms of who can access it, when, how, and over what period of time—continues to increase as the use of the technology increases.[27]

Young people need guidance from their parents and teachers to learn to navigate the digital landscape and to protect their personal information, but they rarely get it. It is hard for any young person to make sound, rational decisions about how to manage information about them—and nearly impossible if those around them aren't helping. This is one aspect of the problem that doesn't have to persist. The gap in digital literacy and participation that exists between young people, on the one hand, and their parents and teachers, on the other, has the most bite in this area. There's a lot that parents and teachers can say to help young people think about their emerging identities and digital dossiers that is currently going unsaid. Young people—especially those who are Digital Natives—are themselves setting the norms for how they share information, and these norms may or may not turn out to be a positive influence or to protect them sufficiently from harm. Since parents and teachers have not yet figured out how to deal with these same issues, it could be a time for dialogue. There is an enormous opportunity for Digital Natives and their parents to listen to one another and to establish shared, positive norms regarding privacy issues as we move forward in the digital age.[28]

In one way parents are unwittingly creating problems for their children who were born digital. Parents make decisions for their children that will be difficult, if not impossible, to undo. When it comes to digital privacy, extreme cases are not hard to imagine. Consider the impact of widely used, existing technologies like sensors, webcams, and radio frequency identification (RFID) tags. A latch-key kid who carries a cell phone with an RFID chip in it (or who has one embedded under his skin) might have an identity that's far more extensive than the Digital Native who is further off the grid. Automatic garage-door openers with digital feeds, or webcams at home, will likewise make for enormous amounts of data about the lives of ordinary children. The parents of children who are tracked by such devices no doubt mean well, but they are contributing data points to their child's digital identity that will continue to exist in the future. Much of the time, the data points are just the tracks children leave as they go through lives with increasingly connected, digital dimensions—born of tools that anxious parents deploy to try to keep them safe in the near term. That trade-off may be the right decision for the families involved, but it also may come with costs over time.[29]

Parents, still meaning well, make decisions to protect their children's health that may in turn have adverse implications for the privacy of those same kids. Digital technologies have wrought big changes in the health-care system, many of them good. There are great benefits to be gained by the use of digital technologies in health care. Having quick and easy access to medical records can save lives in emergency situations. It can reduce the cost of treatment in numerous ways, making health care more accessible. And parents of children born digital have to make hard decisions about the health care of their kids. To take advantage of some of the technological advances in health care, for instance, they may be prompted to give up even more control of a child's personal data.

Imagine that a young person—call her Natalie—is diagnosed with epilepsy. Like any style-conscious teenager, she rarely wears her identifying bracelet. Her parents worry that if something should happen to her, the

ER doctors won't know of her condition because the bracelet is in her drawer at home instead of on her wrist. Their local hospital has installed VeriChip technologies, which include scanners that can read the first FDA-approved human-implanted RFID chip. The doctors propose that Natalie get an RFID chip implanted in her arm.

Natalie is against the idea. She already resents the endless doctor visits and constant testing. VeriChip claims that this chip, implanted under her skin, may help save her life someday. It's also promoted as being "highly secure." Natalie, seeking to fend off her parents and her doctor, reads up on what the computer security experts say about it: that the VeriChip implantable RFID chip can be easily copied. Anybody capable of purchasing off-the-shelf electronics equipment and making a few modifications can impersonate the bearer of a chip and gain access to his or her medical records, among other things.[30] Ultimately, her parents make the decision for her: Health concerns trump the possible risk to her privacy.

As part of the procedure to implant the chip, the doctors give her parents forms to fill out. Among the pile of papers is a privacy agreement, to be signed by Natalie and her parents. This "agreement" is the required disclosure form that informs them of how patient information may be shared. Like most people, they don't really read it, because the consequences are too remote to consider, and it's too hard to understand anyway. Whether Natalie and her parents sign this agreement or not, the medical institution may be permitted to share patient information with certain third parties. Natalie's medical history—including records of all tests, doctor's visits, and illnesses—may be used without further consent. For example, her doctor may discuss her case and send data about Natalie to a CAT scan administrator. Her doctor may share information with health-care business associates, including law firms, accounting firms, accreditation organizations, credentialing services, billing services, and third-party administrators. And depending on her doctor's privacy agreement, Natalie's file may be shared with fundraising organizations—hence the annual "Epilepsy Cure" fundraising solicitations they receive in the mail.[31]

Natalie has become exposed by virtue of a decision her parents made for her. The decision may well have been in her best interest in the near term. But this medical information might be used against her later on—for example, to charge her higher health insurance rates—by the third parties with whom the doctor is permitted to share it, despite the legal protections afforded to health-related information. In an acute sense, the trade-off might well be the right one in this case. But the overall issue is chronic: Every day, we make individual decisions about privacy. Often, these decisions are made by or for young people without much consideration of the long-term, aggregate impact of ceding so much control over personal information to other people.

Young people are also at risk of losing control of information about themselves because of the way intellectual property law functions. The question of who "owns" information about a Digital Native is closely related to the question of what someone can come to know about another person. The creation of digital health-care records is a case in point. In some instances, the data that belong to a Digital Native, from a privacy standpoint, can become of great interest to a third party that wants to provide value-added services based on that information. Such a company may start looking for ways to claim data ownership to secure its business model.

Another example comes from the field of personalized medicine. Personalized medicine promises to be a booming business, if the hype spread by venture capitalists and entrepreneurs is to be believed. Before long, doctors will make recommendations for how to treat Digital Natives based upon an analysis of their gene sequence. This information will be held in a record in digital form. U.S. law allows for the patenting of gene sequences and methods of research and treatment related to them. Digital Natives may be in good hands with their doctors, the health-care companies that employ them, and the pharmaceutical companies that develop their medicines. But there's an awful lot of trust required to put the most personal details of our medical histories, and even our gene sequence information, into their hands.[32]

The concept of trust is at the heart of the privacy issue on the Internet.[33] Young people use the Internet to connect with one another, but what they may not realize is that through the Internet they are also connected to a large number of corporations and other institutions. These companies, and the government, hold vast and growing amounts of information about young people—data that we presume to be public as well as data that we expect to be kept private. Although Europe has a strong data-protection regime, general privacy laws do little to protect young people in many places around the world, including the United States.[34]

Young people make decisions every day about whom to trust. These are daily interactions and decisions. A young boy sends another "friend" request to a girl on Facebook. The girl thinks she might know the boy from a party she attended recently, or did they meet up on Gaia or in Second Life? She can't quite remember. But the picture in his profile looks nice enough, and he's got a lot of friends. They even have a few friends in common, which Facebook points out to her. So she accepts his friend request. Now, even though she has set her privacy controls on "friends only," he can see everything she posts to Facebook. She has to trust him not to do something harmful with her information, or to post information about her that in turn is harmful to her.

Young people have reason to trust their friends at school: They see them in class every day and know them; they may have known most of them for years. They have much less reason to trust people and companies they know less well. With good reason, young people turn over information to their schools and to their doctors. The people who work at schools and doctors' offices presumably do not intend to harvest the information for personal gain. Another concentric ring out, though, and the reasons for trust get more remote. There is little reason to trust social networks and search engines, for example; young people increasingly realize that the information shared with such sites will be used to sell them things, through targeted advertisements. The surveys that pop up all over the Web, asking for personal information but rarely saying who's asking, offer even less reason for a young person to entrust their data to them, even if forgoing the survey does mean giving up a $50 gift card to one's favorite restaurant.

This privacy issue is the Achilles' heel of Google, Microsoft, Facebook, MySpace, and other big companies that hold an increasing amount of data about us. The good news is that some of these companies are beginning to "compete" based on the quality of their privacy policies. But as these companies enter the health-care arena, as both Google and Microsoft are, that issue will continue to grow more acute. When Google or Microsoft

asks Internet users to trust them about the health-care data they're helping to collect, store, and find, they're asking a lot. When we are talking
about maintaining health information, getting it right might literally be a
matter of life and death for a Digital Native.[35]

The trust that young people place in corporations is often misplaced.
The rules can change at nearly any time under most terms of service and
privacy policies. The data can be released in a breach. And increasingly,
there are good economic incentives for companies to collect as much information about their users as possible and to keep it for as long as possible. It's little wonder that the world's intelligence communities are widely
believed to be developing semantic search capabilities for the purpose of
mining social network sites. Getting access to the personal, shared data of
so many young people today would be a boon to marketers as well as to
law-enforcement personnel. The sheer volume of information users post to
social network sites makes them rich resources for marketers, who would
love to get their hands on detailed descriptions of the lives of the young,
wired class of people born digital. And most social networks claim ownership over any data posted on the site—and, though they claim not to
sell user data, they reserve the right to do whatever they want with it.

Some argue that the answer to this problem of trust is the market. The
Web, after all, makes it easy to switch services. Don't like the privacy policy of one social network service? Then don't use the service. Just leave, set
up a new profile elsewhere, and bring your friends along. To some extent,
the practices of Digital Natives support this argument. They are constantly
switching platforms, searching for the coolest new thing, and they often
drop something in a matter of weeks if others also leave or it becomes
passé.

While appealing as an idea—generally, the low transaction cost of
switching services means that a market in strong privacy protections could
emerge—the argument doesn't hold up under scrutiny. Some of these services are deeply ingrained in the culture of Digital Natives. If MySpace or
Facebook were to betray the trust of some of their users, it's true that something might come along to take their place (in fact, it's a near certainty that
something will come along to take their place in youth culture at some

point). But in the meantime, for a young person who logs onto Facebook first thing every morning to get her "news feeds" about what her friends are up to, it may not be such an easy choice to walk away from this particularly sticky social space where all of her friends remain. Finally, with many of these services, a Digital Native has put a lot of her*self* into it. The act of switching services isn't as simple as switching which movie store you are going to rent from.

The issue is simple: It's too much to expect any Digital Native to manage a hundred relationships with a hundred companies and other institutions that hold data about her. There is nothing standard about their privacy policies (not that she reads them anyway). And in any event, the companies invariably retain the right to change these policies at their sole discretion. Either the Digital Native needs to gain more control over the data that abounds about her, or she has to come to trust the companies that she deals with—more than she should have to.

S o what can we do about privacy in a digital era? This is a problem that has vexed policymakers since the rise of the Internet. As with other complex problems in the digital era, there is no single, simple answer. In fact, it's possible that "privacy"—defined as we have historically defined it—will never be the same again, no matter what we do at this stage. But there certainly are things that we can—and should—do to address the privacy issues facing young people, whether they are Digital Natives or not.

There are two problems, each of which merits attention: One relates primarily to a Digital Native's *identity,* the other primarily to her *digital dossier.* Each problem has its own contours, and each requires different solutions. Existing law does not provide the answer for either one if we mean to protect the privacy of Digital Natives in anything like the fashion in which we've protected the privacy of our citizens in the past.

Any solution to the problem of privacy is going to require the involvement of multiple actors. With respect to the first set of data—the data that make up the Digital Native's identity—the person most capable of doing something about it is the Digital Native herself. Her parents, peers, teachers, and mentors also have a role to play. And the companies that provide the services she uses, or stores the data she transmits, have a part in improving the situation. Finally, perhaps the state can do something to help through its regulatory authority or enforcement of law.

The person who can do the most to protect her privacy over the long run is the Digital Native herself. She is not in a position to solve the problem completely, but she can sharply mitigate any potential harm through her own behavior. Common sense is the most important aspect of any solution to the privacy problem. Anytime a Digital Native is about to post a picture, she should ask herself: Would I want this picture I am about to post to be on the front page of the *New York Times,* or embedded at the top of my resumé or graduate school application? If not, don't post it online. Some Digital Natives are beginning to use this type of logic, often after having a bad experience or hearing of a friend who had one. In some cases, young people are at risk because they make poor decisions on a daily basis; in others, they are more sophisticated in their thinking about privacy than their parents and teachers, not less. Common sense will serve everyone well in this context.

Digital Natives can also help solve the problem of privacy by helping and educating each other. There is evidence that Digital Natives often educate one another about online protocol already. High school senior Sabena Suri, as a summer intern for CNETNews.com, wrote an article in which she offered some seemingly obvious advice to her peers. She said, for example, "Don't post makeout pictures on MySpace. Honestly, it's sad that I even have to spell this one out, but it makes me cringe when I see makeout pictures of my friends who have become an item. . . . Please save your passionate embraces for any place other than my computer screen. I wasn't invited to the date, so don't make me feel like I was there."[36]

One of the most promising solutions to the privacy problem is to emphasize peer-based learning and activism. Digital Natives are a social, connected, and resourceful bunch when they choose to be. There's good reason to believe that Digital Natives have the capacity to work together to effect change with respect to their online environments. In September

2006, Facebook introduced a new feature, called "news feeds," that broadcast changes in profiles and other happenings to the home pages on Facebook of everyone's friends. The release of this feature was a debacle for Facebook. The users of the service reacted with alarm: The service looked completely different, and it was because the minute details of most Facebook users' lives were splashed across the home pages of their friends.

Then, an astonishing thing happened. Students on Facebook used the features of the site to mobilize one another. Within a few days, 750,000 Facebook members joined the "Students against Facebook" group. The group articulated their concerns about the privacy aspects of the news feed feature. The Facebook team did just the right thing: They didn't argue. They listened. And they changed the service, in a manner that enhanced user privacy controls. In this simple example, Digital Natives showed their facility with the environment by using the tools of social networking to organize—in fact, they used the very feature (the "news feed") that they were protesting—and to prompt change in an increasingly powerful company. Within a few months, the news feed, with improved privacy controls, became one of Facebook's most popular features. Those concerned about subsequent changes to Facebook's privacy controls, such as the introduction of targeted ads based on purchasing habits at other sites, are wondering if Digital Natives and the company itself will learn from this experience.[37]

Parents and teachers, the next concentric ring out, have a crucial role to play in educating young people about privacy and protecting their identities. This role needs to start with modeling smart behavior. Often, parents and teachers disclose information about themselves online that they come to regret, especially in the context of teaching their children how to behave in digital environments. On the other extreme, it is difficult for parents and teachers who have no online identity to be credible, particularly if their children or students are Digital Natives. The first step for these adults has to be to engage in life online in constructive ways. Though often awkward at first, conversations between parents and their sons or daughters, or between teachers and students, about identity and privacy online are essential. Common sense—grounded in the experience of going online—goes a long way.

Parents often wonder whether they should track their kids' activities online. It's easy for parents to keep tabs on where their kids surf, what they post online, and so forth—there is special software designed to assist in this very task. There's an instant appeal to this approach: Parents want to know what their kids are up to online, especially when they're younger, and want to have a sense of who is communicating with them. So long as the children know that the tracking is going on, there's probably no real reason to worry about the use of tracking software in the home.

But it is worth listening to the cautions expressed by privacy advocates. They say that tracking kids' online activities will undermine trust between parents and kids. They note also that kids will get around the controls anyway, whether on the home computer or elsewhere. It's also worth listening to the young people themselves. Many Digital Natives say that when they know their parents are watching what they do online, they don't chat much on instant messaging or go to their personal MySpace pages on the shared home computer. Increasingly, the most heavy-handed online surveillance and tracking techniques used by parents in the home are backfiring. Young people have gone to these online spaces like MySpace and Facebook for a reason—often, because they feel alienated in other public spaces.[38] The answer is not to keep chasing them away from safe spaces into more remote zones.

One important—and often sensible—variation on the idea of tracking where kids go online is to keep the computer in a common space in the home. Parents can go online with young children and make it an activity that they do together.[39] They might also show kids how ordinary browsers track online activities; by watching their parents track their online activity using built-in tools, Digital Natives can see how easy it is for people to track their online activities on virtually any computer. Certainly, there's a place for knowing what your young kids are up to online, but perhaps there's also a point at which the controls are turned off and trust kicks in. Parents might consider limiting access to the Internet when their children are young, then allowing for increasing independence as they grow older and prove themselves mature enough to venture online without constant supervision.

Parents and teachers have far more to offer young people than they may think when it comes to teaching them about how to protect their identities online. The first challenge is to know enough to be credible. But once the conversation starts, everyone will be better off.

The third concentric ring out is for the technology companies, which also have an important role to play. Companies can make a great deal of difference through good technological design, both of interfaces (that make it easy for Digital Natives to make good choices about personal data) and controls (to keep certain people from getting access to their information, or to information about their friends).[40] The companies that host services used by large numbers of Digital Natives need to step up to the plate and work to protect the privacy of their users. The environment of light regulation in which they operate is predicated on their commitment to earning and maintaining the trust of those users. These companies, including but definitely not limited to the social networks, need to be more explicit about what they will do with user data, how long they will keep that data, and how users can go about deleting it themselves. The temptation for these companies has been to maintain maximum flexibility so that they can mine the data they've collected to support future revenue streams. From a public policy standpoint, that's completely the wrong approach. These companies ought to take major steps toward clarifying their privacy policies and making it easy for young people to control the data about themselves.[41] The paradigm needs to switch from a firm-centric model, where companies choose what to do with user data, to a user-centric model in which ordinary people—not just the most tech-savvy—can manage themselves.

The place of the law is not obvious in the context of information that a Digital Native—or anyone else for that matter—discloses about herself. If someone decides to disclose information about herself online, the checks on that behavior should be imposed by friends, family, or teachers, not by the state. The state does need to provide a crucial backstop, and in the

United States it already does. If a company says that it will do one thing, and it does another, then the Federal Trade Commission can hold the company responsible for its actions. This enforcement mechanism is crucial and, if anything, should be stepped up. The FTC is constantly understaffed and underfunded for its broad-based enforcement efforts like protecting user privacy.

In the same vein, the law could also mandate clear, simple labeling of privacy policies. The state mandates that certain consumer food products have a standard label to list the nutritional facts about the food. In the same manner, the state could make it easier for Digital Natives and others to manage their online identities by mandating that Web services provide clear, standardized labeling for their privacy policies. An icon-based system, making clear the most important aspects of the site's privacy policy (such as how long data is stored before it is deleted), could go a long way toward ensuring that Digital Natives at least know what they are getting themselves into when they post large amounts of information about themselves into a certain environment online. It's important to note that this need not be through a "law"—in theory, an industry consortium could take up this same charge without a state mandate. But to date, this has not happened. In the meantime, the lack of clarity about how companies treat personal information is a growing problem for Digital Natives—not to mention for everyone living in a digital era.

There is much more to be done when it comes to the second challenge, protecting the privacy of young people with respect to their digital dossiers. This challenge is greater than the challenge of managing online identity because there is much less that the young person and his or her family can do to solve the problem directly. And the challenge is doubly great because many of the economic incentives at play work in precisely the wrong direction at the moment.

A young person and her friends and family can't do all that much on their own about all the information third parties are collecting about her, let alone influence what the third parties do with it. She can limit the amount of time she spends online or in places where data will be collected about her, but all roads seem to lead to a more—not less—digitally connected existence for Digital Natives. And she can only be so careful. When it comes to her credit, she can call up Experian, TransUnion, or Equifax, if she lives in the United States, to ask about the data they've collected on her. For other kinds of data, there is no simple, legally mandated mechanism for her to use. Medical records, school records, records of where she goes online and the purchases she makes: All of these are pretty much unavoidable in our digital world.

Young people generally have very little idea what is being collected about them by third parties. One high-school student explained how confusing this lack of control can be:

> So I don't know how I feel right now just because I feel like anyone can have access to your stuff. And, like, do you accept that because you participate in using the Internet and technology like that or is there a way to fight that and create ways in which you can keep stuff private and keep stuff yours? . . . So, I mean, like if you give people like a situation, in terms of, this is this and you have to accept this if you choose to do this. Fine, but . . . Google . . . they don't tell people, "Oh, we track everything you do." Especially with youth, like people Google everything because they just think to. They don't know, like, where this information goes. They don't know that, like, when you log on to certain sites, like they keep track of like when you log on and what you write. So, I mean, I don't know. It's the fact that people don't know. . . . There's not enough transparency for young people to know and they participate very, like, unknowledgeable. That's what scares me because you don't know what that will end up looking at later on.[42]

The problems that come from the existence of digital dossiers can be mild—the targeting of advertisements in ways that are arguably attractive to Internet users—or they can be terrifying—in the case of identity theft, stalking, or being denied a job because of what someone found in a digital file.

With respect to data breaches, there's little or nothing that a single person can do. Ditto for the likelihood that someone working at a firm holding lots of data will let it out. And parents and teachers are just as powerless to help as Digital Natives are to help themselves. There's nothing that anyone could have done about what happened to the data about Digital Natives that ChoicePoint, AOL, or the British government were holding.

Technology companies and law-enforcement authorities have critical roles in this arena, as do those who collect lots of data about Digital Natives. Technology companies that create the systems to collect and store data about individuals have an obligation to build secure systems, and they ought to be held accountable under law when they do not. Services like social network sites and Internet Service Providers (ISPs) ought to tell users what they collect about them—such as "click-stream data" (the information about where one has surfed online)—and they ought to report who will receive and utilize that data.

The law can and should make a difference on behalf of young people to safeguard their growing digital dossiers. That said, it's important to understand that the law cannot solve the privacy problem on its own. If designed well, laws can do a lot of good in terms of helping protect the privacy of Digital Natives, especially by limiting the collection of data about them in the first place and establishing principles on how data, if collected, needs to be treated. European ISPs, for instance, can rely on tough privacy laws to respect the privacy of Digital Natives who are accused of sharing music over P2P networks.

In designing a legal solution to the problems presented by digital dossiers, it would be a terrible mistake to lose sight of the fact that this world is more connected than ever before. A violation of a young person's privacy may have ramifications far beyond his or her immediate community. Data about Digital Natives freely crosses geographic and political borders, unfettered in virtually all instances. A young woman may well be doing business with companies based in other countries that provide online services to her; that's certainly true if she's a European or an Asian person using U.S.-based systems. The problem is that the protections she enjoys in one country may not protect her in another context online. Any set of solutions that we come up with needs to take these cross-border considerations to heart.[43]

It's also important to bear in mind the costs of privacy regulation. To date, privacy laws have come not only with high costs but also, sometimes, with flaws in design and implementation. Privacy protections sometimes run up against free-speech rights, as there are many instances online where one person's (or company's, for that matter) speech may violate another person's privacy.[44] Consider, for instance, a case in which a Digital Native creates a website where she posts pictures, names, and possible IM names or cell-phone numbers of her classmates online to create her own social network site. Under European data-protection laws, her activity, no matter how well intended, may be a violation of data-protection laws. But this is not the case in the United States, where free speech in many instances trumps privacy. American law has yet to catch up to the changes in the way that Digital Natives are leading their social lives in networked publics.

Badly designed and overarching privacy legislation can hamper innovation. Many new applications and services are premised on the notion that people want to aggregate personal data in a single place online. Social network sites are one way to do this. But it is easy to see how less regulation might allow entrepreneurs to experiment with new business models, in turn creating jobs and economic growth in markets around the world.

It is also possible that privacy protections—however well intended—could make it tougher for law-enforcement personnel to do their jobs in tracking down criminals, who may seek to hide behind the same shields. Again, much depends on how carefully a privacy law is designed and what types of exemptions and limitations are built into it.

Americans trust companies more than they trust governments. In Europe, it's the other way around. In keeping with this distinction, personal information held in the hands of corporations receives much stronger protection in Europe than in the United States. However, Europeans are also wrestling with privacy protection on the Internet. First, it's questionable to what extent the existing laws in Europe are aligned with the current practices of Internet providers and users alike. Often, it feels like there's a mismatch between the laws on the books and what users are actually doing online.[45] Second, even in Europe, where there are tough privacy laws, the laws are rarely enforced. Only a handful of privacy-related cases have been

brought before Europe's highest courts, indicating that citizens pursue their
privacy rights in only a limited manner.

Many privacy advocates have called for omnibus data-protection laws—
big overhauls of the law that would conceivably seek to protect every aspect of personally identifiable information. The European Union passed
such a law, the Data Protection Directive, to harmonize the national privacy
laws across member states. An omnibus data-protection law certainly enhances user privacy, both by raising awareness and by providing a minimum level of protection, especially where more specific legislation has not
been enacted. However, in countries like the United States, where more
specific privacy laws are already in place, it remains contested whether the
merits of such one-size-fits-all laws outweigh their demerits. Omnibus
data-protection laws tend to be cumbersome—bringing with them unintended consequences and very high transaction costs for businesses—and
with benefits that are not yet clear to end users.[46]

If the law in a given country already provides for specific protections for
consumers, the value that can be added by omnibus legislation should be
weighed against the potential harms before it is enacted. Even if we sympathize with the general idea that we should use the law to protect our
privacy, we have to acknowledge that well-intended but overly broad or
badly drafted laws can do more harm than good in a quicksilver technological environment.

The law should let users decide what happens to data about them, not the
corporations that collect the data. This is the key lesson that we can learn
from European-style privacy laws: They put the individual in control of his
or her personal data. This approach to privacy has been less popular among
lawyers in the United States than among European lawyers, but it has recently received much attention among scientists and U.S. technology firms
that work on better ways to protect online privacy. The most powerful
change that we could make in privacy protection would be to shift toward
user-centric privacy controls, while providing adequate support to users in
their efforts to maintain these controls. Instead of thinking of personally
identifiable data as the "property" of those who collect it, we should shift
the focus to those to whom the data relates. There is no incentive for companies to change the paradigm on their own, absent legal intervention.[47]

Privacy laws should also make it easier for people to protect themselves once they decide to disclose personal information. A first approach would be to require companies that collect data on a massive scale, like Choice-Point, to produce reports about consumers upon demand, much as the credit-reporting agencies do, in a standard, understandable format. The cost of producing the reports could be shared with customers, as they are in the case of credit reports. New business models for intermediaries, to help users manage their data, might emerge, as analogs to MyFICO and others in the context of U.S. credit reporting. It may be tricky to determine who is subject to the rules and what they are required to report; however, these questions could be addressed in well-designed legislation. The big downside would be the cost to the companies that collect the information, which might well drive some or all out of business. But the interests of these particular businesses are outweighed by the growing importance of enabling users, including Digital Natives, to control what others can come to know about them.

We should focus on the development of a tailored legal regime to protect consumers from data breaches. The law should make clear what it means for an actor who collects personally identifiable information to be negligent in terms of computer security. Lawyers call this area of the law torts. Companies that store information about users should be held to a reasonable standard, under the law, for maintaining the security of their data collection and storage systems. In the event of a data breach, an individual or class of persons should be able to hold companies accountable for the breach. If companies do not meet this reasonable standard for security, they should be held liable. Today, these companies often get a free pass when they allow a breach.

The counterargument to this approach is that we can't hold companies liable for flawed computing systems. Why not? First, because every system has bugs, and second, because we want to encourage continued innovation in the computing industry. Both of these things are true. Microsoft, for instance, has not been held liable for every security breach of systems using its code. Hackers can break virtually any system. It's been absolutely the right thing to do not to hold Microsoft liable for all the bugs in its systems, despite the cost of these hassles to consumers.

What we propose is slightly different from the standard proposal to hold software providers liable for bugs. When a company holds personally identifiable data in a database, it needs to use industry-standard protections, which we think ought to be higher than they are today, to protect those data. And if they do not, they should be held liable. If some of that code came from Microsoft, and if it was below a reasonable industry standard, Microsoft, too, should share in paying that cost. We realize that this may require judges to call upon the expertise of computer security experts to determine a reasonable standard, but that sort of expertise is required by courts all the time. There's no reason why this pressing social need should be treated any differently just because the Internet or software is involved.[48]

Regardless of the protections put in place in one country, like the United States, we need to be mindful of the vulnerabilities caused by the global nature of the Web. Even if Google behaves perfectly and respectfully when it comes to a young person's data, it is entirely possible that someone in another country will gain access to data about that same person and will disclose it in harmful ways. True solutions to the digital privacy problem will not only be complex, they'll have to be global.

Digital Natives are growing up in the midst of a massive transition when it comes to privacy. Some things can be changed to protect them, and other things probably cannot. There's not much we can do about the fact that there will be a great deal of information collected, in digital format, about Digital Natives—and the rest of us. This information will be held in multiple places around the globe and accessible from many places around the globe. These facts are trade-offs that we, as societies, are choosing to accept as a cost of the convenience afforded by digital technologies. Attempts to curtail the volume of this information related to Digital Natives will fall short at this point; that's trying to turn back the clock. Many of the most obvious solutions—such as passing a very broad law, or reconciling international approaches to privacy—are likely to come with high costs of other kinds.

It's also critical that we help Digital Natives get smarter about controlling what they can and recognizing the risks inherent in releasing information into networked publics. There is good reason to believe that Digital Natives are open to receiving guidance in terms of how they think about privacy, but it's far from a foregone conclusion that everyone will get smart in this regard. Neither Digital Natives nor anyone else actually reads privacy policies or discriminates effectively among services. Students describe a false sense of confidence: They put information into online services without thinking about what the company may do with it down the line. There's a growing understanding about the issue, but not growing sophistication about how to control private information.

As this story of online privacy and our kids is breaking in front of us, we as societies are relying heavily, even more than we realize, on trust— of third parties we don't know well at all. Trust of corporations and governments and others who hold data about us is the primary mechanism ensuring our data integrity and personal privacy. In many instances, trust works very well. It should be the cornerstone of online strategies to protect privacy. We should work hard to leverage community-based, user-oriented controls of personal information. But we should also take steps to ensure, through law and the markets, that companies compete with one another to earn the trust that they are asking all of us to place in them. We need to find better ways to gauge whether or not to place trust in those who hold data about us, through more sophisticated reputation systems. And we should have strong forms of enforcement at the ready in cases where that trust has been misplaced in a corporation or in a group or individual. The cost of trust without verification in the online privacy context, especially in light of the lives that Digital Natives are leading today, is too high for us to do otherwise. If the current trajectories hold, that cost will only rise over time.

Ordinarily, children learn about whom to trust from their parents. As parents get more involved in their children's lives and as they help to shape their emerging identities, they ought to think about identity and what it means for their child in today's world. And we all ought to think of it in bigger, broader terms, understanding that digital technologies have put our identities into public view in a way that was never before possible. The idea of identity is more intricate than it has been historically, because so much more information can become personally identifiable, and because it can follow a Digital Native around for a long, long time. Though most people are never going to find out most of the digital information stored somewhere about a Digital Native, bits of that information can find its way into public spaces and become part of a Digital Native's identity. Perhaps everyone's identity will become so extensive online that these errant bits will make no difference in how Digital Natives are judged when they grow older; perhaps young people will solve the problem on their own. Either way, the digital revolution is in the process of blowing up traditional meanings of identity. We all need to take part in making the meaning of identity take shape again, in a way that does not leave this population of Digital Natives caught in an awkward period of transition.

Digital Natives, who live so much of their lives in networked publics, are unlikely to come to see privacy in the same terms that previous generations have, by and large. In the context of U.S. law, we have relied upon a classical distinction between the "public" and the "private." When that line is blurred or when that line moves, as it has in the lives of Digital Natives, the traditional legal mechanisms will not work as well as they have previously. A similar shift has occurred in the copyright environment: It's become so easy to make a copy of a creative work, and social norms are so strong, that a chasm has grown between what the law says and what Digital Natives do. The traditional legal definitions and mechanisms—in the privacy context as well as in the intellectual property context—fit awkwardly when changes of this magnitude occur.

The implications of this misfit are only likely to grow as Digital Natives continue to live more and more of their lives online. In this period of transition, as we rethink how the law should work, those who can do something about it—online technology companies, as well as parents and teachers—need to take on greater responsibility for helping Digital Natives make good choices about their personal information in networked publics.[49]

4

SAFETY

ALTHOUGH THE ISSUE OF ONLINE PRIVACY POSES REAL DANGERS AND GEN-
uine challenges, evidence shows that it is not what parents of Digital Natives are losing the most sleep over. The first concern for most
people is safety. Parents and teachers of Digital Natives worry a lot about
digital safety—far more than Digital Natives themselves do. It's often the
first thing that people mention on their list of concerns about what their
kids are up to online. Predators who search online for vulnerable minors; ubiquitous pornography; Internet addiction; cyberbullying—the
list of dangers lurking within the family computer goes on and on, stoked
by breathless nightly news stories about Internet-related crimes. A steady
stream of government reports reinforces anxieties about the strangers
our children will meet online, and the stalking—or worse—that may
come of it. These reports are often long on hyperbole but short on data.

The concerns about online safety are not new. Each safety concern has
a counterpart in the offline context that predates the Internet. As parents
of Digital Natives ourselves, we take these concerns seriously. But we also
believe that fear is getting in the way of taking a reasoned approach to online safety.

First, we need to catch our breath and remind ourselves that every radical new communications technology has brought with it new fears. When first introduced, most new technologies—including everyday things such as the automobile, radios, television, and microwave ovens—give rise to new anxieties, and even panics. People are generally afraid of the unknown, and they project their fears and fantasies onto the new technologies. Many of these fears are totally ungrounded in reality—microwave ovens do not, after all, cause radiation harmful to most humans. Some fears are exaggerated, often by a mainstream media eager to sell papers and attract viewers. Some fears, of course, are real. Most of the safety concerns that young people face online are overstated in the public discourse. By and large, the Internet is just a new medium for old kinds of bad behavior. Most of these problems can, and should, be handled by using the old techniques we already know. At the same time, it is important to resist the temptation to reach for simplistic, politically expedient solutions that will do more harm than good.

It's also important to grasp an essential point: There may be ways in which the Internet is exceptional, but few of them are in the area of safety. To be sure, there are contours to these digital safety risks that are different from their "real-space" counterparts. Some people argue that the potential harm to children may, in some cases, be greater, especially in the case of the psychological harms—but the data to support such assertions are thin, at best. Most important, the root of these problems is the same online as it is off. Parents have worried about versions of each of these problems before.

These safety risks don't seem unfamiliar to those who are immersed in what's actually going on online. Many of the strategies that have worked to protect children before will work here, with some modifications for the digital age. The best way to address these problems is not much different from the ways we've addressed similar problems in the past. But before getting to solutions, let's first look more closely at the safety issues themselves and take these concerns seriously.[1]

P arents are worried about safety in part because their kids are spending so much time online. It's true: Young people around the world are spending an increasing amount of their free time connected to the Internet. Each year, in many cultures, screen time switches further away from TV toward the Web and mobile devices. In some cultures, like South Korea, experts believe the average teenager spends two hours online per day.[2] In China, there's public concern about "Internet addiction," and centers that treat alcohol and drug addictions are opening their doors to receive young patients in this new category. And it's reasonable to ask whether we should worry about kids when they are alone online; after all, we worry when they are alone in the park, and the online environment is similar in some ways because we don't know who may be lurking there.

Is growing up as a Digital Native really more dangerous than it was for those of us who are older to grow up in the world before the Web? How worried should we really be? And about what, exactly?

The data do not suggest that the world is a more dangerous place for young people now that they spend so much of their time connected to one another through digital technologies. It's true that the contextual information found in cyberspace is different from the contextual information found in real space: Safety is an area where it helps a great deal to be a Digital Native, aware of the cues that indicate what's going on. To a Digital Native, the signposts are obvious—perhaps even more so than in real space. And safety aside, there are good reasons to allow young people— as they grow into their teenage years—to explore these spaces on their own, without constant supervision.

The challenge is to ensure that young people have the skills and the tools they need to navigate these new, hybrid environments in ways that keep them safe, online and offline. Plainly, young people will sometimes go unsupervised when they go online, just as they do when they are in real space. One study of families in New Zealand and the United States revealed that the vast majority of young females use the Internet in a way that is unmonitored by adults in their lives.[3] We should give as much attention to protecting young people from safety risks online as we do to the similar, and interrelated, risks in the offline world.

Digital Natives face two main kinds of safety risks, whether in cyberspace or real space. First, there's the psychological harm that can come from exposure to harmful images or from having damaging experiences online. These are old fears given new names: cyberbullying, cyberstalking, and so forth. In truth, it's just bullying and stalking, where the medium that the criminals use is the Internet. And second, there's the physical harm that can be inflicted offline by someone who finds his victim online. These risks are not new, nor are they exclusive to the online world. The Internet is simply a new medium through which bad things can happen.

One risk to kids—especially young children—is psychological harm from exposure to something that they're not ready to see. This harm could occur in the offline world as well as online; the risk is very similar in the two contexts.

The online world is full of every sort of image, story, and encounter that the human mind can come up with. Some of this information can be very disturbing. A young child going online doesn't have to do much to find himself exposed to images with graphic violence or sex that could cause him psychological harm. In Britain and France, legislators have been worrying about children seeing fights recorded on camera phones and posted to Internet services such as YouTube. Others fear the raw footage of wars and human rights abuses that are posted regularly to the Internet. The ready access of young people to pornography has concerned parents, teachers, librarians, and lawmakers since the Internet came into widespread use in the 1990s.[4]

Of course, the offline world is also full of disturbing images and events with great potential to traumatize a child. A young child walking with a parent, hand in hand, down the street might come across an image or an act that causes the parent to cover the child's eyes. (Then the parent has to figure out a plausible answer to the inevitable, wide-eyed: "What was *that*, Daddy?".) Children have access to mind-bending violence and sexually explicit images as soon as they learn how to use the television remote control. It is unlikely that many children make it through grade school without being exposed to inappropriate or disturbing behavior in the schoolyard—or at a family gathering, for that matter. The online world is hardly unique in this regard.

This is not to say that the online and offline worlds are identical. There are meaningful differences: the extraordinary ubiquity of potentially harmful information online, the ease of access to any Internet user regardless of age, and the lack of barriers between the young person online and the inappropriate content. And since the majority of a Digital Native's time online is spent without adult supervision, he is far less likely to have an adult nearby to help him process the disturbing material he has just encountered.

Let's start with the most common example that worried parents raise: pornography. In the online context, parents often point first to the concern that a child might be more likely to be exposed to all forms of pornography than they would in an offline setting. It's true: Porn is far easier to come by online than it was before the Internet's existence.

A single Google search using a remotely naughty word turns up many varieties of pornography, just a click or two away and free for the viewing. There are literally hundreds of thousands of adult sites on the Internet, which doesn't take into account the large number of amateur videos posted to general-purpose video sites such as Bright Cove or the adult section of Metacafe.[5] One expert claims that nearly all young kids come across pornography online while doing their homework.[6] Another reports that of the 42 percent of young Internet users in the United States who had been exposed to online pornography in the past year, 66 percent reported only unwanted exposure.[7] Some parents consider this exposure a major problem; others are less concerned.[8]

Pause here, just to get one thing straight: It is at least sometimes the case that children who encounter pornography online *are looking for it.* Though parents may choose to believe otherwise, that's a well-established fact. According to one set of surveys, 42 percent of kids between the ages of ten and seventeen have seen porn online. Two-thirds of the time the exposure was unwanted, mostly the result of the use of file-sharing programs; but in at least one-third of the cases, the children sought out the material.[9] And studies such as these almost certainly underrepresent the number of cases in which children sought out the pornography, for the obvious reason that some number of respondents may be ashamed to admit they sought out online porn.

That said, we should take seriously the fact that many children do encounter pornography online unintentionally, and also take seriously the concerns of parents who worry that such encounters could cause psychological harm. Is there a reason for online porn to be placed into a different category from offline porn, or for us to think about it in a significantly different way? When it comes to pornography, has the Internet introduced a problem that is new and different at its core, or has it only provided a new source for an old problem? What, if anything, is different about the Web when it comes to pornography?

The root cause and effects of pornography are certainly no different online than offline. One thing that sets the digital era apart from previous eras, though, is the likelihood that a young person may be confronted with pornographic images. This difference stems from the ubiquity of the material. Before the Internet, if a home had no pornographic materials in it, parents could be secure in the knowledge that a child at least could only come across it out in the world at large (or by a friend smuggling something into their home). In the Internet context, images and stories of this sort are accessible from any Internet-ready device—a laptop sitting around the house or a cell phone with a decent Web browser (though, to be clear, most Digital Natives rarely access the Web through these devices today).

The second difference is that the material is easy to access, regardless of age. In the pre-Internet era, a young person might have to convince a store clerk that he was of a certain age before the clerk would turn over a pornographic magazine from the top shelf in exchange for cash. These intermediaries were hardly foolproof, from a parent's perspective, but at least they might function as speed bumps. The kid had to come up with cash and a gullible salesclerk, at a minimum—or perhaps a salesclerk willing to accept a small bribe. A greater barrier still, the child would also have to confront the high potential for shame: shame at being caught buying the magazine, shame that the clerk happened to be in his sister's class in high school, or any number of other scenarios that are less likely to attach in the context of accessing images on a laptop in a bedroom at home behind a closed door.

There are no active, live intermediaries on the Internet. It's not that a young person couldn't be shamed as a result of behavior online; it's just that there's a perception of anonymity that is not as acute as in real space. There's plenty of online pornography that a Digital Native can access without even needing to prove his age or produce a credit card. There is nothing in the law, in the United States or elsewhere, that effectively stops minors from accessing online pornography. There's not much hope that these laws, or associated technologies, will accomplish a whole lot more on their own in the near term.

There are, ultimately, very few effective barriers between a young person and potentially harmful content online. And we have the power of the current generation of search technologies to thank, or to blame, for this state of affairs. In the real world, a small metal shield in the corner store stands between the idle young teen and the magazines on the top shelf. The physical segmentation at the video store between the Disney section and the adult titles—which are often in a separate room or have had their graphic covers removed—might be plenty to keep videos separated. Online, no such separation necessarily exists, unless an Internet company has chosen to take great care to create such barriers—or if someone, a parent or a teacher, has installed special commercial software to filter out pornographic material.

Young people may find themselves confronted with pornographic images whether they are seeking it or not. The unpredictability of when a pornographic image might present itself, even without explicit prompting by the Web surfer, sets the digital experience further apart from its offline analog. There's a very real possibility—frankly, a growing possibility—that a computer in a home or a school has been hacked. A computer that's been compromised might have software installed on it, surreptitiously, that causes pornographic images to pop up on the screen. As many as 60 million computers in the United States alone are infected with some kind of badware.[10] A very common flavor of this badware can cause unwanted pop-ups—really, ads, intended to cause the viewer to click on them and subscribe to a service, often a pornographic one—to appear on the screen.[11] The same images may appear in e-mail spam sent to a young person's inbox; obviously, a child with an e-mail address is bound to receive all sorts of spam without asking for it, just like the rest of us. Bad computer code and spam affect people equally regardless of age.

Parents and teachers need to start by coming up to speed with what's happening online if they want to be in a position to protect their kids from harm. Very often, Digital Natives have better computer skills than their parents, and this means they can be more helpful in keeping computers safe from harmful images than parents and teachers can. The answer, in many cases, is basic computer literacy coupled with easily accessible commercial software and online services. By taking relatively simple steps, parents can prevent badware from creeping onto their home computers. When those measures fail, it is possible to remove the software offering the unwanted pop-ups. When parents and teachers feel stumped, asking their children to help might achieve two things: a cleaner computer, and the start to a positive conversation about what's going on online.[12]

Parents and educators should seek to engage with their children on the issue of pornography generally, not just with respect to online images. Young people are likely to see these images, whether online or offline. Computers can put these images in front of them, but so can a friend with a pornographic magazine. Parents and teachers can help their children and students to understand what they're seeing. The old guidance about talking to children about sex, so that they have a context for what they encounter, holds just as true in a digital age as it did for any other age. The conversation may just have to happen earlier.

In cyberspace, just as in the schoolyard, young people sometimes encounter bullying. Cyberbullying is the intentional use of any digital medium, including text-messaging, pagers, and phone calls, to harm others. And cyberbullies are, in most respects, like their classic schoolyard counterparts. The digital toolset they use just gives them additional ways to reach their targets—and at any time of day or night. The cyberbully can be anonymous to his victim, and he can disseminate harmful messages to an incredibly large audience with unprecedented speed. These digital messages persist in ways that schoolyard taunts never can.

Bullying, whether in the schoolyard or online, is a major concern for parents and educators because of the harm it can do to the victim. Young people are still in the process of developing their social competencies. Kids might not be capable of fully grasping the seriousness of their actions—especially in an online setting where they cannot see others' body language or facial reactions. Young people, in particular, rely on these visual and auditory cues to guide their behavior.[13] The anonymity of the online experience exacerbates the problem: If a young person cannot see the response of the person he is communicating with, chances are he will be even less empathetic than the schoolyard bully in his interactions and less likely to curb his actions.[14] It becomes easier to rationalize harmful behavior in a digital setting, where actions might not seem as "real" and the Digital Native doesn't see the reactions of the person he has just harmed, or even the reactions of bystanders. As a high-school student told us,

> I think people like say things that they would not normally say to your face because online when you're just writing something, like you don't have the person face-to-face. So, I know that . . . I've written an e-mail to one of my friends saying so many things that I wouldn't really say to her face because I'd feel bad saying it to her face. So, when it's like in an e-mail, you just feel less guilty.[15]

The damage that a Digital Native might do to another person in this context is only part of the problem: Years later, he may come to understand the impact of his behavior and feel regret, depending on the extent of the harm he has caused.

There are several possible reasons for this tendency to act more aggressively toward other people online than face to face. Psychologists call it the "disinhibition effect." Many people—young and old alike—are emboldened by the ability to be anonymous, feeling as if they will never get caught, even though we all leave digital traces behind. And many people (and not just Digital Natives) experience greater difficulty curbing their impulses online than they do in real-space social situations. Part of the issue is that there is a time delay between sending an e-mail and getting one back. The absence of an authority figure in an unmediated space empowers people to act on impulse. And some studies show that a heightened sense of the importance of self leads to disinhibition.[16] For young people who are still developing the ability to control their impulses, digital media become potentially dangerous tools.

How worried should we really be about cyberbullying? Studies suggest that bullying using online media is a rapidly growing phenomenon. But there's no reliable data to support the argument that cyberbullying is anything more or less than an extension of bullying into the converged environment of online and offline life. In one study, conducted in the United States in 2005, 25 percent of the respondents who were girls and 11 percent of the boy respondents said they had been bullied online.[17] Most kids—77 percent of those who reported having been cyberbullied—claimed that the cyberbully was someone they knew.[18] A majority of both boys and girls told researchers that the bullying had occurred mostly over instant messaging, a popular application among Digital Natives and the source of an endless stream of pop-ups and flashing icons on their personal computers.

The data, partial as they are, suggest that some young people are more likely than others to experience bullying online. Digital Natives who spend a lot of time online are more likely to be the targets of bullying online. Teens who are heavy Internet users, and content creators in particular, are especially vulnerable to cyberbullying. Girls are more likely to be victims than boys. According to a recent survey, about one-third of all teenagers who use the Internet say they have experienced online harassment.[19]

Harmful behavior moves seamlessly from the playground to the Internet, and often back again. Though there is no fundamental change in what is occurring when the online world is the stage rather than the playground, there are differences in the way the impact is felt by the person attacked and by those who can observe its occurrence. The fact that the bullying is occurring online means that it takes place in a public forum for all to see. The observers may include adults, who would not normally be privy to the transient, schoolyard variety of bullying. A local dispute, carried out in online public spaces, can become an international news story. It's hard to say whether public hazing that anyone, anywhere on the planet, can watch is worse than hazing that happens in real time in front of one's closest friends. Both are pretty lousy.[20]

When we asked Digital Natives what they thought the motives were behind cyberbullying, they agreed that adolescent behavior simply moves from the schoolyard or locker room to the Internet. Some teens argued that some kids might feel stronger, and more able to speak harshly to others, when they can hide behind a computer monitor. Others thought that intolerance and discrimination were key drivers.[21] Leading researchers have argued that the motives for the online form of bullying are much the same as for the offline variety, but that the medium mirrors and magnifies the bullying.[22] Much empirical and theoretical work needs to be done to gain a better understanding of this type of aggressive online behavior.

The dynamics of bullying are the same whether the bullying takes place online or offline, and bullying can move back and forth in either direction. "Cyberbullying" is not all that different from "bullying"; it's just put on the record in a more permanent way. Lauren Newby, a high-school sophomore from the Dallas, Texas suburbs, made national news when she encountered bullying in both realms: on a message board and on her front porch. Lauren suffers from multiple sclerosis. Online, the bullies posted nasty messages on a message board under a thread entitled, "Lauren is a fat cow MOO BITCH." Nothing was off limits on this board, apparently. The anonymous poster (or group of posters) harassed Lauren about her disease ("I guess I'll have to wait until you kill yourself which I hope is not long from now, or I'll have to wait until your disease kills you"). Her weight was also fair game ("people don't like you because you are a suicidal cow who can't stop eating"). Offline, someone—it is unclear if it was one of the people who was attacking her online—threw a bottle of acid at the front door of her home and vandalized her car. Lauren's case was a particularly bad one; most examples of bullying, online or offline, are less extreme.[23]

Lauren's case reveals that in some cases, cyberbullying may spill over into the offline world and lead to physical harm in real space. The fact that one form of torment took place online, and another at her home, makes plain that the underlying problem is the unchecked behavior of the bully, not the medium in which the harm occurs. Torment in a public place online, in front of a child's peers, by someone acting anonymously, and in a form that is irretrievable and could live on indefinitely in the virtual space can cause deep scars.[24] These taunts may become permanent artifacts of a young person's identity. But the harms that occur in real space can cause physical harm. And the embarrassment of being taunted in person, in front of one's friends, also may be acute.

The bullies found online are not always Digital Natives. Another national news story described the tragic fallout when Megan Meier, a girl from Dardenne Prairie, Missouri, found herself in an old-fashioned argument with two peers who had once been her friends. With the involvement of their parents, these two girls dreamt up a boy they thought might appeal to Megan. They created an online profile for this fictional boy. "He" became friends with Megan online by sending messages that suggested a romantic interest in her. Megan apparently became enamored of this fictional boy. When she learned that it was a hoax, she committed suicide. Dozens of news outlets reported the fact that both adults and children had participated in the hoax, and the story received international attention. Whether or not these adults actually wrote any of the hostile messages to Megan, it is plain that their judgment was terrible. Megan's story highlights the critical role, for good or ill, that adults play in the lives of their children, both online and off.[25]

Both Lauren's and Megan's stories are heartbreaking, but they do not reveal a dark truth about the Internet. Instead they speak to how human beings, young and old, treat one another, both online and offline. The technology may have enabled these particular stories to take the form that they did, but the underlying harm is nothing new: Bullying has always caused harm, both psychological and physical. The harm that is done by cyberbullying may be somewhat different from the harm done by bullying offline, but it is not necessarily better or worse. Most significant, though, is that the medium through which the acts occur seems foreign to many who don't spend a lot of time online. More cases of bullying are reaching public attention because they play out in networked public spaces.

Stories like Megan's and Lauren's get a lot of media attention. The harm caused is serious and real, and we need to work hard to prevent such incidents from happening in the future. But there is no data to suggest that there's more bullying now than in the past. Nor is there data to support the assertion that young people are tormenting one another more than in the past because the Internet makes it possible. The lesson is that we ought to redouble our efforts to stop harmful bullying, wherever it occurs, using strategies that get at bullying both offline and online.

If bullying that takes place online is hyped in the media, the danger posed by meeting strangers online is even more hyped. A small number of high-profile cases have led to a lot of fear. There is no evidence that young people are in more danger of abduction or sexual assault today than they were before the Internet existed. The data that we do have are inconclusive. Government reports in the United States point to anecdotal evidence of the risk to children—plainly, the "anecdotes" are all too real—but concurrently note the absence of a comprehensive set of data showing what is happening on this front nationwide.

The data we do have demonstrate that inasmuch as we should be worrying about the danger of violence on the Internet, we should be worrying about kids hurting each other psychologically—and not as focused, as we seem to be, on adults hurting kids physically. Recent academic studies reveal that there may be a slight decrease in the number of unwanted sexual solicitations online, but an increase in forms of online harassment of young people. The data about the psychological harm that young people are doing to one another are more troubling than the data about the likelihood that a young person will meet an adult online who will then do him harm.[26]

The majority of teens' online interactions are with people they already know. Girls, in particular, use social network sites like Facebook, studiVZ, or MySpace to reinforce preexisting relationships.[27] And teens in general use online tools primarily to communicate with their offline friends—gossiping, making plans for social outings, and the like.[28]

That said, stories about young people meeting new people online are not uncommon. Half or more of teens say they interact online with people they don't know.[29] Very often, the interface between the young person and the new friend is IM, chat, or a gaming environment.

This willingness to talk to strangers online can result, in the worst cases, in a young person being lured into a harmful real-space encounter. A young woman from Texas, called Julie Doe III in the court proceedings that arose from her case, created a MySpace profile at age fifteen. In 2006, a complete stranger to Julie found her online and reached out to her. He convinced Julie to meet him offline, then proceeded to drug her and sexually assault her when she showed up. He pleaded guilty to the charges brought by the police in the face of ample evidence and is now serving a ten-year sentence in Texas.[30] In civil court, four families have sued MySpace for not taking enough steps to protect their children.[31]

These cases remind us that, despite the absence of data to show that young people are at greater risk in an Internet era, there is reason enough for young people to be very cautious about how much information they share with others in networked public spaces about themselves and their whereabouts. Social network sites provide ample opportunity for a high-school or college student to post information about her whereabouts— dorm rooms, class schedules, where she'll be at a certain time—and often, plenty of photographs, which would allow strangers to identify her in real space. In some cases, a girl may be too generous (maybe the right word is "promiscuous") with her life's story. She may constantly update her information, giving a stalker more than enough data to go by when tracking her down in order to do her harm. As a young person travels through cyberspace, she leaves an extensive profile of herself online. This profile includes lots of digital tracks, most of which persist over time—enough for anyone to follow. Her life in real space runs parallel to the one in cyberspace, and a stranger who finds her online often will not have much trouble finding her offline.

Sometimes, those tracks are intended to be sexually provocative. Many young people, from the eighth grade up to the college years, describe a sense that their friends are revealing themselves too much, portraying themselves in sexually appealing ways online. As one junior-high girl told us, "Like a lot of people they put, like—some girls will be like in like bikinis or booty shorts and all that. And then you'll be like that's like—it's ridiculous, but then you'll see like how many comments they have. . . . And that's what you want to get is a lot of comments."[32]

A related problem is that cyber-mediated experiences lead some young people, especially when they first go online, to trust people they don't know. As one student told us, "I think that people trust people too quickly [online]."[33] A version of the disinhibition effect is at work here, too. When a young person perceives that he can leave the conversation at any time, the risk of connecting online seems low. There's an extent to which the online interactions can seem like games, or dreams. And a feeling of invisibility can embolden a young person to reveal more than she would in a face-to-face encounter.[34]

The good news is that the more sophisticated the young person is about online life in general, the less likely he or she seems to be to trust other people online. Digital Natives are often far more sophisticated than we give them credit for—and more sophisticated than their younger counterparts. The younger the user, in general, the less savvy he is about how to manage online interactions. Digital Natives are not guileless online any more than they are offline. Consider the comments of two young women who argued that, over time, they learned of the risks they might be running online. As a result, they changed their behaviors:

> FEMALE 1: I used to always be on the Internet. I used to like always be updating my websites and stuff like that. I used to go on Party Line. I used to go into like chat rooms and stuff. But now it's like now I'm older. It's like I don't want to talk to people that I don't know. Why I want to talk to you for? I don't know you.
>
> FEMALE 2: Yeah, you shouldn't be talking to, you know, some guy that you meet online and like thinking about going to meet him. When you're younger, it's like—it's easier to convince yourself that this is okay, even though my parents like keep shoving it into my head that, you know, don't talk to strangers.[35]

The facts about how young people interact with others online, and the risks they are running, point to the importance of better digital media literacy. Peer learning—where Digital Natives pick up skills by following the lead of their friends—is also plainly very important in the context of online safety. Social norms play a crucial role in how young people interact with their friends and with strangers online. And these facts also suggest that, rather than treating the online environment as an exotic space that presents wholly new dangers, we must reexamine the situation and redouble our efforts to follow tried-and-true approaches to keeping kids safe from psychological and physical harm, whether online or offline.

The Internet is not the root cause of cyberbullying. Nor is it the root cause of unwanted contact between minors and adults. The root causes for both of these dangers are the same as they were before the Internet came along: poor judgment, a lack of concern for the well-being of others, human depravity, mental illness, and so forth. These safety risks are perfectly real in the online context, however, just as they are in the offline context. And the technology of the Internet has complicated the situation. In an online environment, young people may be more likely to confront the age-old problem of bullying alone; and a young person may be caught off-guard and talk to a stranger with a false sense of security. But even though the environment in which the risks arise has changed, the harmful acts are still the same harmful acts. Bullies can shame their targets in front of a bigger audience online than they can in the schoolyard, but their taunts are no different. This point about digital safety—that the problems are the same problems, only carried out in a new medium and sometimes rendered more complex—is essential to understanding how to do something about it.

The best way to mitigate the Internet safety risks that our children face is to combine several strategies. The four primary tools at our disposal are education, technology development, social norms, and the law. The first, and most important, goal is to work together as a society, through education, to give young people the skills—often, not much more than common sense—to grow up safely, whether in the emerging digital social space or in traditional settings. The second is to put digital technologies themselves in the hands of kids, parents, teachers, police, and site operators to keep kids safe. The third thing we can do is to develop positive social norms around online life. Once these strategies are in place, the law—and classic law enforcement, in both online and offline settings—should serve as an essential backstop. We must take care to ensure that Digital Natives don't have to go it alone. That is why education—in the form of an open, ongoing, and honest conversation—must be the top priority.

The process needs to start with Digital Natives themselves. They are often in the best position to make the kinds of choices that will keep them safe. Our emphasis should be on giving them the skills and the tools they need to make the right choices. They need guidance from their peers, through peer learning, but they also need guidance from those, like parents and teachers, who are older and wiser. Many young people have reasonable instincts on this score. As one high-school student told us,

> The only time I ever accept a—like a friend request from either My-Space or Facebook is if they are like family of a friend and that friend, like, is like, "Yeah, they're alright people." Or if they are connected to the work I do and like I know they're—like legitly [sic] like interested in networking. I hate when people request you and they don't know you, or they come up very creepy, or they message you and say stuff like, "Oh, hey cutie" or "I think you're cool" or whatever.[36]

In our interviews and focus groups, we perceived a higher level of sophistication about safety issues in the oldest Digital Natives and among those who had spent the most time online.

The development and sharing of positive social norms for online behavior is an essential part of mitigating the risks that our children face in their lives. Digital Natives themselves are getting better at protecting themselves and their friends. Remember Lauren Newby? The poster of the offensive message remained anonymous, while Lauren's defenders not only signed their names, but also reprimanded the attacker for his or her anonymity. This proved an effective means of ending the harassment.

A new set of social cues is emerging, and Digital Natives are learning them. Emma Free, the only female computer science major in her class at the U.S. Military Academy, follows the commonsense rule her mom taught her: "If it's too good to be true, it is."[37] Emma and her mom are right. Common sense applies in cyberspace just as much as in real space. Along similar lines, the U.S. Postal Service and the National Center for Missing and Exploited Children have launched a clever campaign called 2 SMRT 4U, with teen actress Hayden Panettiere and other young people telling their stories in video postings and chatting about how to stay safe online.[38] The

campaign uses attractive, sensible-sounding young people to reach out to
their peers. Digital Natives may be best positioned to teach one another
how to be safer online.

Young people need strong allies to help them to understand these new
social cues and to counter the disinhibition effect that comes with lives
led, in part, online. Parents and teachers are on the front lines of preventing harm to our children in any context. That's as true in the digital
era as it has been in any other. The difference now is that parents and
teachers are often not in a strong position to help when it comes to matters of the Web, because they are not as engaged as their children in online life. It's this dynamic—the gap between a Digital Native and his
parents when it comes to Internet knowledge—that we must seek to
change first, before turning anywhere else for solutions to the problem of
safety on the Net.

Parents and teachers need to start by putting in the time it takes to understand how the digital environment works so that they can be credible
guides to young people. It's not that anyone has to use every new technology the minute it comes out. It would be unreasonable to expect all parents
to keep up with whether Xanga is cool now or if it's all about whatever New
New Thing (inevitably) has just arrived on the scene. And yet, anyone with
children living their lives partly online needs to understand the basic dynamics of digital culture. In general, parents are likely to find themselves reassured by what they find in the digital world; they will quickly discover
that the challenges of keeping children safe online are not much different
from the challenges of keeping them safe in other contexts.

The home is a good place for parents to begin. They must get smarter
about what their children are doing online, which need not be something
their kids do by themselves in an isolated part of the home. And they need
to be actively engaged with their children in a conversation about what's
going on online. To make the Internet a "safe space" for their children
when they are young, some parents choose to use controls such as filters
to block access to certain sites and to track where their kids are going online.[39] This is fine, but as the Digital Native grows, such close scrutiny
makes less sense and can backfire. The need for parents to be there for
their children is no less important, however. This is a perfect example of

how digital space is no different from real space: What's needed is good, involved parenting, not overbearing parenting.

Digital Natives should feel encouraged to discuss online matters with their parents—or their friends, for that matter. A simple conversation to discuss an online friendship—or a plan to meet someone he met online—might lead a young person to see what a risk he's taking if he meets his pen pal. Even if he does decide to meet this new friend, at least the parents could trail along and say hello too, and help to ensure that nothing goes awry. Such collaborations are most likely to happen if a young person feels he is in a position to ask for help, and it's essential for parents to do everything they can to foster open and honest conversations with their Digital Natives. We know, of course, that this is easier said than done.

Not talking about online activities is a mistake, and it could be a costly one. By letting their children remain isolated in digital space, and treating their activities there as different from activities in "real space," parents miss a chance to help their Digital Natives make good decisions about their own safety. A recent study showed what we all know: The more often "significant adults" talk to young people about their experiences online (and occasionally monitor what they are doing), the less likely the youth are to engage in risky behavior (defined as disclosing personal information, meeting up offline with someone they met online, or sharing photos with strangers). The young people who did not have the adult intervention were four times more likely to agree to meet up with someone they met online.[40]

The first conversation might well be awkward. Because many young people worry that telling their parents about negative online experiences could lead to these privileges being taken away, they are unlikely to be the ones to bring up the subject. It's important that parents initiate the conversation and keep coming back to it.[41] Asking about MySpace, studiVZ, and other social network sites can be a great way to start the conversation—not only to address privacy and safety concerns, but also to talk about what a child and his friends like about this or that site or game. By simply talking about what a child likes about the Web, parents can get to know their children better. In other instances, the Internet itself may make it easier for parents and kids to connect: Online technologies make conversations possible for parents and kids that they cannot have face to face—either because of the difficult nature of the topic or because of sheer distance. At Cornell, there's a webcam set up in the middle of campus. The "mom cam" lets parents remain connected to their children in a way that a simple phone call couldn't achieve. Students can coordinate with their moms to show up at the right spot when she's watching and wave to her—as in, "Yes, Mom, I'm off to class," or "No, Mom, I didn't wear a hat this morning."[42]

Many parents require their children to show them their profile on Facebook, MySpace, studiVZ, or whatever the popular social network of the day is. This practice can also lead to good conversations about the Web. Parents will hear about the subtle social cues their children pick up as they make their way through the space. Parents are likely to be surprised, and possibly reassured, at what they learn from their Digital Natives. No matter what, they will be better able to provide guidance as the conversation continues. Digital Natives may be annoyed at first, but they may well come to appreciate their parents' interest and concern. As one boy put it, "Well, I kind of feel like [my mom is] invading my privacy, but I know that she's really not because she just wants me to be safe."[43] Though kids may resist this parental interest in their online activities at first, many will end up getting into the spirit of the conversation, and some will tell their parents a great deal about the online environment.

Teachers and principals, too, need to step up their efforts to teach Digital Natives about the brave new world we all live in. Schools convey information about the Internet and impart skills related to digital safety to students in different ways, and there are lots of pedagogically sound ways to get the job done. Some educators have argued that an explicit curriculum on Internet safety should be mandatory. Others emphasize working Internet literacy more broadly into the curriculum at large. Another approach is to make space for students, parents, and teachers to educate one another about what's going on in cyberspace and to explore together ways to mitigate the risks that online life brings with it.

Though these safety concerns relate to a new space, they are not fundamentally new to parents and educators. There is no reason to separate cyberbullying from traditional bullying: A unit or dialogue on bullying can incorporate both. Nor is there any reason to treat the dangers posed by unknown persons online as something different from dangers posed by strangers offline. These bifurcations only reinforce an imaginary line between the "real" world and the "online" world that many young people already have a difficult time seeing. And studies show that a large percentage of cyberbullies were at some point in their lives victims of traditional bullying; the virtual world allows them to retaliate, regardless of their physical size.[44] Educators need to be addressing these core safety issues in both the offline and online contexts simultaneously.

Teachers should heed the same lesson facing parents: There's no way to share the knowledge and common sense that we have if we're not credible about the topics Digital Natives are struggling with. A lecture from a teacher who is obviously not up to speed about digital culture will only backfire. A clueless teacher is just as likely to find herself parodied on the Web by her clued-in students as not. If teachers—already overworked and underpaid—are not in a position to come up to speed on digital culture to be helpful guides to young people, schools may need at least a single teacher who can help build this capacity or teach an occasional session on Internet safety and literacy. Outside speakers, or even older Digital Natives who know the environment well, could help fill the void.

Technology companies have a strong incentive to keep young people safe online. The most popular online environments, such as social network sites, make money from advertising. These companies want to keep their young customers on their site for as long as possible, and they want them to visit as frequently as possible, so that they can present them with advertisements, which in turn pay for the operation of the site. The safer the young people perceive these sites to be, the more time they are likely to spend there. The same goes for the sites for young children, except that in this case it is the parents who appreciate safety online and allow the children to participate. In many cases, the people who work for technology companies want to keep young people safe because, as parents themselves, they simply want to do the right thing.

Although digital technologies, deployed in the home or by online service providers, do have a role to play in protecting kids, the technologies alone cannot ensure the safety of children. It's not the technologies, but how people interact with the technologies in their everyday lives, that we need to focus on. Facebook and MySpace, two of the fastest growing sites on the Web, are working on ways to use technologies to help young people learn how to pick up on the social cues that they need to understand in order to stay safe. Both sites have established ways for community members to report suspicious online behavior, and instituted rapid-response teams to act upon those reports, and this is an essential step in the right direction. Both companies have also sought to make privacy controls easier to use.

MySpace has provided a series of safety tools called "Zephyr" for parental use.[45] The software keeps a parent up to date about the key information that their children enter into the system, including name and age. These software changes are unlikely to please everyone, and they involve a delicate balance: The more parents can track their kids' movements, the less likely kids may be to use the service. So taking advantage of the safety measures could backfire, causing teens to transition faster than they otherwise would have to new frontiers of cyberspace. Systems like Zephyr hold promise, however, if their effect is to prompt parents and teens to talk about what's going on in social networks.[46] Some MySpace users who are fourteen or fifteen years old have told us that they have set their age to "100" to prevent the system from automatically setting their profiles to "private." This strange dynamic ought to prompt a conversation that could lead to kids being safer online and off.

New technologies can also help law-enforcement officers to keep kids safe online. State and federal child protection units spend a lot of time online tracking down people who would do harm to young people. The technology developers that build the services teens use most should incorporate ways of tracking unusual behavior on the site in an effort to pinpoint those who reach out to young kids inappropriately, and they should work with partners in law enforcement to keep these spaces safe.

New technologies are also still needed to help keep small children away from unwanted, graphic imagery online. Some technologies that do this are already available. Parents can set up a kid-friendly browser, for example, to identify the user of the computer as a child to all the websites he is visiting. One such browser now available is called kidrocket.org. To make this solution more effective, governments could require websites not to return any obscene material to anyone self-identifying as a child. There's a minimal obligation placed on the parent to set up the computer correctly for the child, and a minimal obligation placed on the website operator not to serve up content that a kid should not see. The net effect would be an efficient, relatively unobtrusive way to protect kids from content (and possibly contact) without forcing them to stay off the Internet altogether.

Some large technology firms have set a positive example for others by developing cross-disciplinary teams that focus exclusively on Internet safety. Microsoft has been a leader in this regard. The Internet safety team at Microsoft includes private investigators, former prosecutors, legal experts, and technologists. They have launched a multicity tour, called "Get Net Safe,"[47] and a website, at staysafe.org, that provides information for teenagers, parents, and others.[48]

The most noteworthy thing about Microsoft's staysafe.org is that it is not created by an adult, but by a Digital Native. The site highlights a short film called "Predator" that was made by a fourteen-year-old junior-high-school student from Utah. The film raises awareness about online safety risks.[49] Microsoft and its partners on Internet safety get it right: Tap into—and celebrate—the creativity of Digital Natives to help solve the problem. The film is a great conversation-starter, and it demonstrates the kind of connectivity that will help us as a society through this transition period, a time when many adults don't understand the first thing about their children's lives online.

Changes in the law and regulation are not the primary ways to protect our kids, but the role of the state is important all the same. The law, as a general matter, can offer a backstop in terms of keeping children safe. The law is better at some things than it is at others. In the United States, the law cannot help much in keeping young people away from pornographic images or bullying because of constitutional protections under the First Amendment for those who operate websites or post things on websites. But there's a fair amount that the law can do to keep young people safe from unwanted contact with others.

As a general rule, online service providers have gotten a free ride under the law in the United States. The Communications Decency Act (CDA) of

1996 grants broad immunity to service providers in the event that their users cause harm to others. This safe harbor, located in Section 230 of the act, covers most online intermediaries—including MySpace and other social networks—so long as they qualify as an "interactive computer service" that allows users to post material themselves. This part of the law was intended to enable companies to act as "good Samaritans" while enabling innovation to continue on the Internet. The CDA has generally served society well, on balance; it has been smart not to chill innovation and free speech by imposing too much liability on companies in the nascent online space. But that's not to say that all Internet intermediaries should be completely free of responsibility for anything that happens on their networks. Internet safety is one zone where greater liability might be reasonably imposed.

The scope of the immunity the CDA provides for online service providers is too broad. One of the costs of this immunity is that the parents of a child harmed online are barred from even reaching the question of whether a social network was negligent. In the Texas MySpace case, the judge said that the parents of Julie Doe III could not bring a negligence action against MySpace because of this law's safe harbor.[50] The U.S. District Judge Sam Sparks reasoned that the Communications Decency Act's Section 230 shielded MySpace from this type of liability for the acts of its users. The judge was probably right in his interpretation of the law as it is written. As a result, there was no ruling on the merits of whether MySpace had done enough to protect kids online. The lawyer for the families says they'll appeal.

In this particular case, it is entirely plausible that MySpace did nothing wrong under the law. And it's entirely plausible that the law should continue to protect MySpace from any liability for defamatory statements posted to its website by third parties. But the law—intended as a "good Samaritan" statute in part—should not preclude parents from bringing a claim of negligence against MySpace for failing to protect the safety of its users. Its new service, Zephyr, among many other efforts underway at MySpace, might end up serving this safety function effectively. The law shouldn't stand in the way of parents bringing a claim of negligence against an online service provider when a child has been harmed. There is no reason why a social network should be protected from liability related to the safety of young people simply because its business operates online.

In addition to strengthening private causes of action by clarifying that tort claims may be brought against online service providers when safety is at stake, the state should be given ample tools to punish those who harm young people, online or offline. It has long been illegal to hurt a child physically. The use of online technologies in the commission of a crime against a minor already allows federal prosecutors to go after the criminals using an expanded set of investigative tools and penalties. The law should be used to create further disincentives for people to commit these acts. Legislators should work hard to keep the relevant laws up to date and to ensure that law-enforcement officials have the tools and the resources they need, which too often is not the case. Those who hurt young people should be punished harshly. But it is unlikely that adjustments in the relevant criminal laws will make a lasting difference in terms of making Digital Natives safer than they could be.

There is not much the law can do to protect kids from bullying, whether online or off, but there are things that state actors can do to be part of the solution. Government authorities and child welfare nongovernmental organizations (NGOs) around the world are providing various types of support and assistance to victims of cyberbullying and their families. In the United States, the Department of Health and Human Services has established a helpful website with practical tips for parents, teachers, and students, including information on countermeasures and consequences for the victims and the perpetrators. In Europe, the Insafe website of the European Commission is a good starting point to learn about this phenomenon and possible remedies against it.

The law hasn't proved all that helpful when it comes to protecting kids from online pornography, either—but we should not expect it to be. In the United States, lawmakers have made several attempts to regulate material, like pornography, that may be harmful to minors. The Communications Decency Act, for instance, was designed to impose criminal penalties on anyone who used the Internet to make pornographic materials accessible to a person under eighteen years old. It required an age verification mechanism to prevent minors' access to pornography. The law didn't last long, though. A few years after Congress passed the CDA, the U.S. Supreme Court found that most aspects of the law were unconstitutional. The definitions used in the statute were too vague to survive First Amendment scrutiny and the proposed verification system for identifying those who accessed Web materials was not considered feasible. It wasn't a particularly close call. (Section 230 of the CDA, however, which provides the liability shield for online service providers, was not struck down and is still good law in the United States.)

In 1998, the U.S. Congress took another run at it, and again came up short of a workable solution. In response to the Supreme Court's prior decision and in order to pass constitutional scrutiny, the scope of the new law—called the Child Online Protection Act (COPA) of 1998—was limited in several ways. For example, the provisions covered only materials posted on the Internet by commercial publishers. Again, the law was challenged in the courts, and again, it was ultimately struck down on constitutional grounds following a complicated legal battle. Several state laws with the same purpose have shared a similar fate. To date, these proposed laws have been too sweeping and imprecise to meet the requirements of the First Amendment.

Even without a specific federal statute, government officials can still play an important role, in concert with private companies, to keep young people away from unwanted contact and content online. Law-enforcement authorities are working hard to ensure that social networks are doing their part to protect the safety of our children.[51] The attorneys general of forty-nine of the fifty states have reached an accord with MySpace to establish a task force, which we are chairing, to work toward a better understanding of the issues involved and to identify technological protections for users under age eighteen. This collaborative approach is the right way for law enforcement to address social network sites: We must work to encourage positive steps to protect kids without banning the social network sites altogether. An agreement reached between the New York State Attorney General and Facebook, which requires the involvement of a third-party monitor of safety practices at Facebook, is a similarly positive, collaborative step.

There's one legal strategy that does not make sense: The temptation to ban the use of certain technologies outright will prove counterproductive.

It's also probably not permissible under the U.S. Constitution. Banning the use of social networks would not protect young people from harm. The former attorney general of Massachusetts, Tom Reilly, for instance, in the midst of an unsuccessful campaign for governor, proposed a law that would ban people under the age of eighteen from using MySpace.[52] The Deleting Online Predators Act called for a ban on all social network sites and blogs in libraries and schools. It was proposed in the U.S. Congress in 2006 and reintroduced in 2007. The Protecting Children in the 21st Century Act, proposed in 2007, would ban social network sites from schools receiving federal funds and require those schools to educate children about appropriate online behavior. But this bill doesn't make much sense, either.[53] Banning a certain technology—especially a technology that Digital Natives plainly like and one that has such a significant educational potential—isn't going to help. Digital Natives are going to create digital publics.[54]

A ban on a single popular site, like MySpace, would not be enforceable. Clever Digital Natives who wanted to take part in online social networking could easily switch to another online service. It is in fact likely that a brand new service would have *fewer* protections for kids' safety than MySpace and Facebook, not more. Services like MySpace that have been around for a while are at least working with regulators and advocates for children to improve the safety of their space. And for those youth who rely on public libraries and schools to gain access to the Internet, a ban would only serve to end their already limited participation in their peers' social worlds. Most worrisome, a ban would mean giving up on the many wonderful things about digital life that lie ahead for societies able to harness its promise.

The key point of this chapter is one of the key points of this book. There's an unnecessary technology gap between young people and many of their parents and teachers. The net result of this gap is that our kids are too often at risk in an environment where some of them are prone to risky behavior, like conversing with strangers they'd never talk to in "real space." This gap also breeds and reinforces fear of new technologies, rather than encouraging positive steps to figure out how to live our lives together in a digital era.

There are many things we can do to address online safety. Instead of automatically seeking to ban the technologies, we need to focus on the root causes of the problems that are posing these real risks to our children. We ought to hone in on the source of the online disinhibition effect and combat the most extreme forms of it directly. We need to help kids understand the line between activities that are part of healthy experimentation and activities that constitute risky behavior, just as parents have done for their children since the dawn of time. Together, we need to figure out how to interpret the rich set of social cues online to keep one another safe. Companies that offer online services popular among young people need to commit to being part of the solution. And in working together, we need to be sure that we are helping those young people who are not Digital Natives. They are the young people who are most at risk, because they have less proficient digital literacy skills.

Parents and teachers need to become a much bigger part of the solution, and soon. Right now, things are headed in the wrong direction, with a huge gulf between parents and teachers, on one hand, and children, on the other, and too much fear-mongering in the public discourse about what Digital Natives are up to online. We can only become effective parts of the solution by immersing ourselves in these issues—at least enough to understand a bit about what's going on in digital culture. Our children, in many cases, will be our guides. In turn, we can help guide them through the bad neighborhoods of cyberspace, just as they guide one another. And we can help them to keep themselves safe, online and off, in the bargain.

5

CREATORS

I N OCTOBER 2006, *THE NEW YORKER* FEATURED A STORY ABOUT A MOVIE STAR who won an Oscar. It was not someone particularly famous—not Helen Mirren or Judi Dench or Meryl Streep, not Cate Blanchett. In fact, this Oscar winner is well-known only to those who spend a lot of time on YouTube. Her name is Stevie Ryan.

Stevie received her first "Oscar" when she was twenty-two. Like many people, she grew up dreaming of Hollywood stardom. Rather than succeeding in the way that her parents' generation might have, Stevie has become a star without the help of powerful, big-name movie producers. Stevie struck out on her own in Hollywood in the classic fashion, but it was in cyberspace that she found an audience. She created a character named Cynthia, an eighteen-year-old Latina woman from East L.A., who becomes better known as Little Loca. Stevie's "Oscar" arrives not on the Academy Awards but on YouTube, a few minutes into about the fortieth video she created. Her videos have been viewed well over a million times. New editions regularly attract an audience of tens of thousands of viewers. Stevie is in the top 100 video producers on YouTube of all time in terms of the number of regular viewers who subscribe to her channel.[1]

YouTube and the creation of online video has become a central part of Stevie's life. Shooting Little Loca videos and posting them to video-sharing sites became a full-time activity for her. Stevie Ryan has created a series of online personae for herself, as Cynthia (in the Little Loca videos) and as Stevie (on her own "tv" site). Little Loca is irreverent, self-assured, and appealing to her young audience, many of them Hispanic like Cynthia. The Oscar she received, it appeared, was real, stolen from a bar by a friend of Stevie's. The stolen Oscar, introduced to viewers on a couch in a YouTube video by a foul-mouthed young actress (who says in the video it was "heavy"), marked a shift underway in the manner that media is created and shared by young people.[2]

Stevie's not alone. The Internet has unleashed an explosion of creativity—and along with it thousands of new forms of creative expression—on a vast scale. These new forms of expression are unlike anything the world has ever seen before. Digital Natives are increasingly engaged in creating information, knowledge, and entertainment in online environments. Creating one's own TV shows, like the ones that Stevie specializes in, or making digital remixes of popular media are among the more spectacular examples of user-created content.

The creations of Digital Natives, however, are quite often limited to the thoroughly unspectacular: a new personal profile on Facebook, a posting on twitter.com ("Weather's nice here in Munich"), digital photos uploaded onto Photobucket or Shutterfly. Many Digital Natives are offering up contributions that fall somewhere on the spectrum between the mundane and the magnificent: editing an article on Wikipedia or programming a new Facebook application.

Approximately 64 percent of online teens in the United States have created some sort of content on the Internet.[3] (Older people aren't doing so badly in this dimension, either. Among adults, about a third of Internet users have created and shared user-generated content such as text, audio, video, categories or tags, and networks.[4]) The "power users" among young digital creators—age-wise, often clustering in their early to mid-twenties—engage extensively in blogging, creative forms of online game-playing, instant messaging, and the like.[5]

The phenomenon is truly global: In Hungary, Denmark, Iceland, Finland, Norway, Germany, Poland, and Luxembourg, for instance, a majority of young people have posted messages to chat rooms, online newsgroups, or forums.[6] Similarly, data for Asian countries show that home pages, blogs, and social network sites are extremely popular. Millions of Japanese write blogs and participate in social networking. About half of Korean Internet users have created websites or blogs. In China, blogs, bulletin boards, online communities, instant messaging, and the like are on the rise.[7] In our travels, we have found digital creators in every culture we have encountered. The phenomenon is one of the hallmarks of the emerging global culture of Digital Natives.

Of course, not all Digital Natives are participating in the creative renaissance that is happening online. The vast majority of kids are not rushing home after school to do anything so dramatic as to make political satires in the form of digital remixes. Only about one in four young people say they remix content of any kind into their own artistic creations such as artwork, photos, stories, videos, or the like.[8] Most digital creativity is of the unspectacular sort. What stands out to us is not the absolute (and relatively small) percentage of Digital Natives doing the most creative things online, but the extent to which this creativity represents an opportunity for learning, personal expression, individual autonomy, and political change. These examples of self-expression through digital media point toward greater engagement in remaking content, even in modest ways. This trajectory is particularly important for how we ought to be educating our kids in a digital era.[9]

A Facebook page is not, of course, an act of creation on par with the paintings of Leonardo da Vinci. Certainly, not all of the creations posted online— indeed, probably only a very small fraction of them—deserve the label "creative." It's therefore important to distinguish between "creation" and "creativity." "Creation" relates to any digital content made by a Digital Native, ranging from an apparently trivial update on Facebook ("Mike is . . . tired today") to an artistic video clip. "Creative," in contrast, is a differentiating term that has a qualitative connotation. The word suggests that the respective content created by the user is unique, useful (at least at the margins), and organized.[10] Consequently, a snapshot of the Notre Dame cathedral made by a French kid with her camera phone and uploaded directly from her mobile phone to the Internet is a creation, but not necessarily a creative one.

The Internet nevertheless has tremendous potential as a creative medium, particularly by comparison with other electronic media, and many Digital Natives have used this potential to create something more than snapshots from their camera phones. Television, for instance, is a noninteractive, one-to-many medium with a remarkable ability to transform everyone within sight into a couch potato. The only way we participate in it is by turning the television on or off, by switching the channel, or by changing the volume. At best, we might record something for viewing at a later time, perhaps omitting the commercials in the process. There is no easy way to interact with the content broadcast on a traditional television channel. Nonelectronic media are often designed with passive consumers in mind. Even in the case of a book—still among the most valued and revered media forms in the world—the activity level usually doesn't go beyond the sensorial, cognitive, and other neuropsychological processes that are necessary to perceive and process its content (what we call "reading").

In contrast, many of the most popular Internet applications require a much higher level of inter*activity* among users, applications, and with digital content. Today, there's little doubt that user activity that goes beyond mere consumption of content is a design feature of the Internet. In fact, the latest iteration of the Internet, the participatory Web (Web 2.0), is all about the millions of people who are becoming creators of digital content. Marketers call the output of these creators "user-generated content" (UGC) or "user-created content" (UCC). In combination with the social networks, this phenomenon of user-generated content is what the Web 2.0 buzz is all about. In its pure form, this shift moves us away from a world of largely passive consumers of content produced by a few powerful professionals toward communities of increasingly active users—often amateurs—who can produce and share their own TV shows on YouTube, publish their own news, or collaborate with others to rewrite online encyclopedias. In our view, that's a very good thing, and something that we ought to find ways to encourage.

Many Digital Natives are "creators" every day of their life. When they write new text for profiles of themselves in a social software environment, they are creating something that many of their friends will see later that day. If a college student updates his picture in Facebook or writes something on the profile page of a friend, a "news feed" is issued to all his friends to check out the changes on the relevant page. This combination—the ease of updating a personal page and the ability to send out a feed of those changes—has been wildly successful. It's what drives people from all around the world to visit billions of pages on Facebook per day.

Some Digital Natives also engage in more sophisticated acts than just updating their profiles. When they post video, when they make and share music, when they post and point to news, when they tag and bookmark stories on the Web, and when they make or ply new networks, they are creators. One of the most alluring, and often very creative, contributions of Digital Natives—and, to be sure, many Digital Immigrants as well—is their use of a new art form, a type of digital collage called the "remix" (sometimes also called a "mash-up"). Most people who use the Internet have encountered remixes, often forwarded by friends because they are funny or satirical. The remixes that mashed together Howard Dean's infamous scream in the primary election in January 2004 with music or other video clips are still on many people's iPods. Most popular television shows are remixed regularly as content creators use them to poke fun at characters or to make a point about a social issue.

Remixes allow Digital Natives and others to interact with cultural objects in a way that affects how cultures develop and are understood. Damien Randle, a financial adviser from Houston, Texas, formed a hip-hop group called "The Legendary K.O." along with his partner Micah Nickerson. The Legendary K.O. has successfully produced music at home and distributed it over the Web. After the rapper Kanye West spoke off script at the NBC Concert for Hurricane Relief and complained: "George Bush doesn't care about black people," they put together a song to express their view on the matter. Damien and Micah used samples from West's song "Gold Digger" and his speech on TV and added their own critical lyrics about the disastrous Katrina relief efforts. They say this whole process took them thirty minutes. Twenty-four hours later, the song had been downloaded 10,000 times. Later, it reached gold status with more than half a million downloads. Since then, the song has been turned into a series of videos that have been shared widely over the Internet.[11]

The point is that the new world of digital media gives users the opportunity to interact not only with peers, but also with content. Text, images, videos, and audio files are not only shared with peers, but also easily manipulated. Mixing and mashing have become common practices in cyberspace. Digital Natives have developed excellent research skills when it comes to digging up digital materials that can be remixed—young people variously call it ripping, chopping, blending, mashing, or just manipulating it—to create new forms of expression. The creative efforts of Digital Natives build upon the rich tapestry of digital content already spread across cyberspace.

Sampling, like the remix, also demonstrates this type of engagement with digital media. Sampling was popular with hip-hop and R&B artists long before the Internet came along. "Sampling" a song means to take a portion of one song and reuse it as an element in a new recording. "Mash-up"—a.k.a. "Bastard pop"—is a popular musical genre in which the vocal of one song is laid over the music of another. Among the most famous mash-ups to date has been D.J. Danger Mouse's *Grey Album*,[12] which uses the vocals of J-Z's *Black Album* and mashes it with a rearranged version of the Beatles' *White Album*. Although the legality of such mash-ups is often contested, some artists encourage their fans to remix songs from one album to combine them with tracks from another (for instance, David Bowie with his "David Bowie Mash-Up Contest"). Other forms of digital expression are "cut-ups" (humorous or satirical pieces of reconstructed spoken words and video materials, such as Johan Söderberg's "Endless Love," featuring G.W. Bush and Tony Blair),[13] spoofs (including political parodies, such as JibJab's "This Land"),[14] and "machinima," a technique of using video games or virtual worlds to develop narratives and short films.[15]

Along with remixes and sampling, fan fiction has become a promising new creative pursuit among Digital Natives. In "fan fic" stories, Digital Natives use characters from their favorite TV shows, movies, books, cartoons, and the like and develop new plots, settings, or situations for them. The fan-fic authors then post these stories online, often on fan sites. One of the most popular fan-fiction objects is Harry Potter. The Harry Potter fan-fiction site, www.harrypotterfanfiction.com, allows anyone to contribute by posting an individual story about life at Hogwarts. And many people do so—the website currently features more than 45,000 stories, according to its live ticker, and it gets some 40 million hits a month. Sharing these stories on fan-fiction sites with peers is an important part of the experience—and often, posters and other fans get together in person at informal "meet-ups" and even at full-blown conferences.

Mash-ups, fan fiction, and sampling: Each is a way of creating art based upon the works of others. The law labels these new art forms "derivative" works, meaning that they are new works derived from the copyrighted creativity of people who came before. What they have in common is that they build on existing creative works, like songs, videos, and text, to form a new creation. This "rip, mix, and burn" culture—with a hat-tip to Apple for the slogan—is at the core of the unfolding creative revolution in cyberspace.

These new creative forms are inherently in tension with existing copyright laws, and it is hardly surprising that they have garnered the attention of legal departments in big media companies. YouTube has been sued by Viacom for alleged copyright infringement by YouTube's users, many of whom have posted segments of television programs online without permission. Sometimes, these postings are straight rip-offs of the original files. Other times, they are creative rearrangements of songs, texts, pictures, and movies. These practices—creative and noncreative alike—are already generating litigation, and we can expect much more litigation before the legal issues surrounding these derivative works become clear. For the time being, this means that the way Digital Natives are interacting with digital media leaves them at risk for ongoing copyright liability.

Take the Harry Potter fan-fic site. Let's say a Digital Native posts a Harry Potter story on the Web that either Harry Potter author J.K. Rowling or the publisher of the Harry Potter books happens to disapprove of. Could the copyright owners do something against it?

The answer is most likely yes. Copyright law protects characters like Harry Potter and related forms of literary expression. The crucial point here is that copyright law grants the right holders of Harry Potter the *exclusive* right to make reproductions or so-called derivative works from it, so long as one of a few defenses, such as the fair use doctrine, does not apply. Derivative works are creations that are substantially copied from a preexisting work. Since fan fiction is all about the imitation of the original characters, their names and habits, and the like, the fan-fiction author is at risk of being sued for infringement of copyright law. In one case of Harry Potter pornography, a London-based law firm on behalf of Rowling and Warner Brothers sent out a so-called cease-and-desist letter and required a fan-fiction site to remove the pornographic story.[16]

The explosion of creativity online has given rise to new forms of expression and extended others, like sampling, to a broader population of creators. Creative reuse of the materials of others can lead to problems, though, in terms of copyright risks to the creators. When we combine this challenge to existing copyright law with the common practice of illegal file-sharing of music and movies, which we take up in detail in the next chapter, we see the makings of a legal trainwreck. And it is Digital Natives and traditional copyright holders who will be facing one another down.

Not all creative activity online involves the appropriation or reappropriation of other people's material without express permission. The movement toward digital creations and online creativity is about sharing. It is inherently social and collaborative. In many respects, it's about the power of *communities*.[17] The collective efforts of thousands of contributors—many of them Digital Natives—to build the world's largest encyclopedia, Wikipedia, is the most prominent example of collaborative content creation on the Internet.[18]

Jimmy Wales is a successful former commodities trader and digital entrepreneur. You'd be forgiven if you thought he was nuts when he created Wikipedia with the express goal of making it the world's greatest encyclopedia—free and online. The idea that an encyclopedia written by tens of thousands of people, none of whom were paid to contribute their work, could actually amount to anything remotely credible would have seemed absurd just a few years ago.

Wikipedia is not without its faults, many of them extremely relevant to the story of Digital Natives. But by nearly any measure, it has been wildly successful. It's the clearest example of the trend that online culture has made possible: We're shifting from a world of consumers to a world of creators of information. In contrast to the *Encyclopaedia Britannica* and other traditional encyclopedias, Wikipedia is not written by experts. (The experts, in the *Britannica* case, incidentally, are "professionals" who are paid to write their sections, and they claim copyright on those sections, unlike their Wikipedian counterparts.) Wikipedia is written collaboratively by an army of volunteers. These volunteers may well be experts in some areas, but they contribute to the project outside of their professional routines. And they include not only people born before the digital age but hordes of Digital Natives as well.

Wikipedia is built on an incredibly simple, powerful technology called a "wiki." A wiki is a website that functions more or less like an online Microsoft Word document that anyone can edit. On a wiki, any user can make an entry at any time. Users can also edit articles written by other people. If you're intrigued by the technology and want to play with a wiki, we encourage you to practice on the wiki we've created as we've written this book, found online at http://www.digitalnative.org/. Just be prepared to get hooked. Wikis are addictive, as the success of Wikipedia makes clear.[19]

The Wikipedia project started in 2001 with a single English-language edition. Today, Wikipedia contains over 6 million articles in 249 languages, including more than 1.6 million articles in English alone. These numbers are remarkable. More impressive, however, is the number of volunteers who have contributed to the project. As of September 2006, more than 280,000 users—a.k.a. "Wikipedians," or, as some would have it, "Wikimaniacs"—from around the world had made at least ten contributions each to Wikipedia.

An even more active group of 10,000 Wikipedians makes at least 100 contributions per person per month. Most of these active users have a subspecialty, a general area of interest and expertise where they focus their efforts. Some are interested in technology, so they edit the pages about software programs. The Windows Vista operating system has been a hot topic on Wikipedia since 2003, which was many years before its public release, and the full range of open-source technologies that are constantly evolving, such as the Linux operating system, likewise attract constant editing. Other digital creators, with online identities like "Scoobyirish"—a person who is clearly very into rock 'n' roll—focus on the extensive pages related to individual songs ("[I Can't Get No] Satisfaction" has a frequently updated page, for instance) and bands, both old and new (the band Wilco, for example, which hit it big online, has a substantial and well-edited page).

It's not just the number of authors and articles in Wikipedia that is astonishing. In our research, what struck us as most important is the extent to which so many young people have come to rely upon Wikipedia as a source of information. Wikipedia ranks among the top twelve most visited sites in the world. Its content is even cited by U.S. courts—and increasingly so. The creative, social, online habits of Digital Natives—and many older people as well—are fueling and being fueled by Wikipedia.

Wikipedia points both to the promise and to the peril of the Do-It-Yourself online culture in which Digital Natives are growing up. On the one hand, it's extraordinary that young people, among many others, are participating in the making and aggregating of human knowledge in digital form. It's crucial to note that this trend enables individuals to exercise greater autonomy through their ability to affect directly how narratives are told and retold. On the other hand, there are real concerns about cheating, plagiarism, lack of credibility, defamation—and much more—to which Wikipedia gives rise.

Music and encylopedias have been around for a long time, but virtual worlds and Massively Multiplayer Online Games (known online as MMOGs) are new to the Internet. In each of these cases, Digital Natives are creating much of the content.[20] Digital Natives have created entire virtual worlds online. World of Warcraft, EverQuest, Second Life, Active Worlds, Entropia Universe—these are all computing environments that support thousands of Digital Natives who might play simultaneously, each controlling one character in the game. (Many players frequently edit their virtual appearances—their "avatars"—to change their roles in the game, or play multiple roles within the virtual world.) These MMOGs range from Crazyracing Kartrider, a South Korean game in which players race cars against one another, to games in which players shoot people ("killing games"), or even serious, real-world simulation tools aimed at training professionals. They are "games," in a way, but to stop there would miss much of the point. These are entire worlds, where much of the content and the experience itself is created not by some game designer but by the users.

Several million accounts have been created in Second Life, an always-online, persistent, Earth-like fantasy world that is inhabited, all day and every day, by as many as 25,000 users simultaneously. Altogether there are hundreds of thousands of active residents, from many parts of the globe, who fly or walk around this world, sometimes for hours on end, exploring and developing this exotic environment. Sometimes they meet other residents and chat, much like they would in any other online chat room. Sometimes they participate in group activities, like musical events or the trading of virtual property. Most important for this story, residents of Second Life spend their time creating virtual items—buildings, furniture, machines, clothing, or artwork.

Second Life is, for the time being, not a scary environment. Its founders have established a world that is, by and large, conducive to self-expression and creativity, without excessive fear. There are some explicitly safe neighborhoods set up in Second Life to encourage younger Digital Natives to participate in this creative environment. A parallel world has emerged, set up especially for teens aged thirteen to seventeen. Teen Second Life (the "Teen Grid," or TSL) is screened for adult content. As in the Adult Grid, TSL users are creative, collaborative, and interested in self-expression. They become community leaders, entrepreneurs, game designers, DJs, and socialites.[21]

The key point about these worlds—and the link to creativity—is that they are built not by software developers, but by the people who "live" there, some of whom are Digital Natives. Second Life is a user-defined world. The residents themselves create most of the content. The developers at Linden

Lab, the makers of Second Life, provide three-dimensional modeling tools and a scripting language. These tools empower Second Life residents to create avatars, houses, landscapes, vehicles, machines, plants, and the like as parts of the virtual world. The creative part is left up to the inhabitants. Young people are erecting buildings based on original architectural designs; establishing islands, cities, and ports; and creating characters who themselves become famous "in-world." Though the percentage of young people in virtual worlds is modest, the creativity demonstrated by those who are in them is staggering—and inspiring.

W hat is it about the Internet that has made it such a fertile ground for creativity?

Certainly, one crucial factor is that users incur very low costs and can potentially reach enormous audiences. Unlike the cost of producing a traditional movie or record, the art forms that Digital Natives are pioneering cost very little. Theirs is a culture of creativity powered by ultra-simple, cheap technologies. Take the music industry, which has been transformed by the (intentional) sharing of music online. The availability of low-cost recording devices, cheap storage space, and affordable editing software, along with the availability of high-speed Internet connections to upload larger media files, has made it possible for individuals and bands to create and distribute their music without needing fancy equipment and expensive studio time.[22]

Another factor in this creative explosion is the technology infrastructure that allows people to access and then remix digital content. Half of the populations of rich regions like North America, northern Europe, and East Asia now access the Internet through a fast pipe—a broadband connection that can handle big files like video and audio content.[23] Affordable multimedia editing software suites such as Apple's popular iLife, for instance, are literally only a few mouse-clicks away. Apple's software includes, among other things, everything you need to edit and share photos, create and edit movies, record music and podcasts, and design and publish websites and blogs. Similarly, it's easy and relatively cheap to buy, say, a digital camera over an auction site like eBay in the United States, or Baazee.com in India, that allows you to shoot digital photos or video clips as raw materials for creative expression on platforms like Photobucket or YouTube.

New technologies also make it easier for Digital Natives to enjoy their friends' works. Young people who like to watch remixes, mash-ups, spoofs, cut-ups, and documentaries created by their peers depend on advanced infrastructure such as broadband connectivity, increased computing power, and greater storage capacity to interact with digital content. Applications and services that help users to search for peer-created content and then organize ("tag") it according to their own preferences have had a positive effect on this creative culture as well. "Tagging" functions as a demand-side, technology-enabled driver of user-created content. Here, "consumers" of user-created content are themselves increasingly turning into creators. More than a quarter of all online Americans (and especially younger users) have used the Internet to tag content, such as news stories or photographs they like, on social bookmarking sites such as Del.icio.us or Flickr. The tags are used to organize digital content such as photos or videos and make the images searchable by others.[24] Tagging is a creative act in itself, through which Digital Natives are adding context to online content. It makes works easier to find in the vast online environment, and because it is user-friendly, it encourages people to create and share content.

While computer processors, storage devices, and communications capacity help to enable large-scale production of information, knowledge, and culture on the Internet, social factors matter, too. Online interactive tools, combined with the willingness to share content and contribute to communities, change the media-consumption habits of Internet users significantly. Taken together, these factors will be among the most important drivers of user-created content in the years to come.[25]

Let's begin with the Digital Natives themselves. What motivates them to create and share digital content like videos, songs, and podcasts? Why are they writing fan fiction, creating mash-ups and spoofs? Why are hundreds of thousands of people working together for no pay to build up a virtual world or compose an online encyclopedia?

The motivations for digital creativity aren't any different from the motivations for other kinds of creativity. Young people have been creative since the dawn of time. The motivations for this creativity will sound very familiar.

In some cases, Digital Natives are motivated by the possibility of financial reward. Not all of the creative work happening online is happening for free. Consider, for instance, Anshe Chung, a virtual land baroness in Second Life who became the first real millionaire—in terms of real U.S. dollars. (Her name in real space is Ailin Graef.) She is the first, but by no means the only, person to make a small fortune by creating buildings and spaces within a virtual world for others to use. Anshe Chung Studios has grown into a business employing eighty people in the real world to create things for others in the virtual world.[26]

Other digital creators are looking for fame. Think of Stevie Ryan, who became famous by playing Little Loca on YouTube. Sites like YouTube, MySpace, and others that host user-generated content have helped a great many Digital Natives establish themselves as artists and propelled them to real fame. Some are karaoke champs; others are folk singers or lyricists, or contribute videos, photos, or other art forms. And not all of the people generating content are young people: One widower, at almost eighty years old, confessed via webcam that he was addicted to YouTube.[27] Platforms such as Sumo.tv, a TV channel that broadcasts user-generated content, or BBC's "Your News," featuring clips sent in by nonprofessional producers, are reasonably perceived as "talent auditions." While only the very lucky (or talented) few are able to translate their online creativity into real-world fame and fortune, these opportunities inevitably motivate many users to express their creativity.

The vast majority of Digital Natives are dreaming of neither fame nor fortune when they create online. Often, they simply want to express themselves, just as human beings have wanted to do since they first began painting in caves more than 30,000 years ago. The desire to express one's own beliefs and opinions—to share them with others—is central to human nature. Advancements in digital technologies have enabled practically any user with basic digital literacy skills and fast Internet access to engage in self-expression in creative ways and at low cost. The impulse is nothing new, but the forms of expression are. And the impact on cultures and on how they are understood will be vast.

The creative revolution in cyberspace is not only about who gets to say what to whom. It is also about the question of who gets to control the shaping of culture, the making of "meaning." This is one area in which the Internet is living up to its hype. The Internet, by giving people the ability to shape and reshape cultural understanding through digital creativity, has introduced something that is truly different. And it is Digital Natives who are best poised to engage in this process.

Consider again the story of Stevie Ryan. Stevie—regardless of her talent—would have faced extraordinarily long odds in striving to reach an audience of 25,000 viewers per week if she had to rely on Hollywood studios to get her there. Similarly, bloggers with audiences running in the tens of thousands today may never have gotten the chance to become star columnists with the *New York Times* or commentators on even local TV news stations. It is no longer the case that Rupert Murdoch and Katie Couric are the only ones who can tell the rest of the world how something happened. In the digital era, thousands of people describe the important moments and create the icons of our culture. And new gatekeepers, like Google and Baidu, Microsoft and DailyMotion, the companies that develop the technologies and offer the services, are emerging to fill the shoes of the old news conglomerates.

Digital technology gives everyone the means to express themselves, and it empowers them to speak—and to be heard by others, including those in power—in ways that previous generations could only have imagined. Creators no longer need to rely on the old gatekeepers like professional agencies, editorial boards, and producers. Digital technology allows creators "to route around" the traditional intermediaries by using the hardware and software in their dorms and homes.[28]

What's different about Digital Natives, compared to older Internet users who are participating in this creative revolution, is that they take the breakdown of the old hierarchy for granted. Nevertheless, they are proving their ability to exploit the new hierarchies that are emerging in place of the old ones. Digital Natives are growing up in a brave new world in which the decisions about what will or will not be produced no longer lie with a small number of content-industry professionals. Unlike older generations, which grew up relying on a small cluster of networks, newspapers, and film studios, Digital Natives presuppose their role as shapers of culture.

The fact that so many people can participate in the online cultural commons and make contributions to it has led to a culture that is far more diverse than it was even a few decades ago. And diversity matters. Diversity—wide distribution of information from a great variety of sources, each competing for the scarce commodity of attention—matters because it enhances democratic processes and democratic deliberation. Diversity provides people with the opportunity to access a wider range of perspectives. It draws people into public conversations by presenting ideas and forms of expression that may attract, challenge, or even repel them. In turn, diversity helps to drive participation, by young people and others, in public conversations.

Diversity matters also from a cultural perspective. A rich body of art and literature, varying lifestyles and ways of living together, and different languages, value systems, traditions, and beliefs doubtlessly make our lives more interesting. It's not all good—diversity can lead to too much information and information of dubious quality; there may be too few intermediaries to help us to choose, and we might face social fragmentation over time as multiple perspectives gain acceptance. But on balance, information diversity, with greater participation by young people, is a positive development that we believe will be good for the long-term health of our society.

The transition to "digitally loaded" art forms and types of discourse is not free of challenges. Many parents and teachers, for instance, fear that the Internet will replace other valuable forms of content creation—traditional forms, such as writing a short story on a blank piece of paper by using a simple pencil, or painting a picture with watercolors. This concern needs to be taken seriously. Our own observations suggest that the Internet does not *replace* traditional forms of content creation but rather *adds* to the long list of forms available. Of course, it is up to us to determine whether digital creativity will supplant other forms. Much depends on the choices that we as parents and teachers are making—whether, for instance, we encourage our children to use paper and crayons to make their first drawings or sit them in front of our PCs and let them draw with the mouse. Both from a developmental and cultural perspective, we should certainly be encouraging Digital Natives to use a broad range of media to express themselves—including low-tech media such as pens, crayons, watercolors, and paper, among others.

There are qualitative issues as well, of course. Many parents and teachers worry that the Internet, with its "rip, mix, and burn" culture, only fosters those forms of creation that are based on the practices of mixing and mashing, while neglecting other, more original modes of creativity. There can be little doubt that a large portion of the user-created content is based on previous work; in that sense, some of these derivative works aren't particularly "creative." But that critique ignores the extent to which creators of all sorts inevitably build on the shoulders of others.

Take Shakespeare as an example. No one would disagree that Shakespeare was a brilliant and creative mind, right? But it's common knowledge among Shakespeare experts that he adapted most of his plays from known, preexisting sources—and in the same way, dramatists, poets, novelists, filmmakers, and other artists later used his texts as the basis for their own adaptations. The point is that even the most creative works are often based on previous ones—creativity very often involves reference to, or even imitation of, one's predecessors.

There are few, if any, examples where Digital Natives have used digital technologies to generate something that is certainly of such creativity and beauty that it represents work for the ages, like a Shakespearean drama. But when photography was first introduced, it was dismissed by many as inartistic by comparison to painting, on the grounds that photography was merely documentary and couldn't improve upon nature. No credible source would say that today when looking at images by Weegee, Robert Mapplethorpe, Man Ray, or Richard Avedon. The video camera seemed like a hobbyist's toy until Thomas Vinterberg produced *The Celebration* in

1998. New information technologies do often give rise to creative new art forms. Though most of what is created today on YouTube or shared on Photobucket may seem worthless at first blush (and much of it may well be on second blush, too), there's ample evidence to suggest that extraordinary works of digital art lie in our future. Digital Natives are likely to be the artists who break us in and show us where this genre is heading.

The increasingly diverse digital universe places more of a burden on the so-called audience in several ways. This participatory digital environment requires all of us to become more media literate. It means that we will increasingly have the opportunity to evaluate news, music, and fiction, and all the other cultural forms that are emerging, for ourselves. It forces us to make choices, and in doing so, it stimulates us to develop the skills and routines we need to navigate the new media landscape.[29] The process of choosing itself is becoming a more and more important skill—and though it is intuitive to most Digital Natives, it is much more challenging to others.

In this future of digital creativity, certain canons are certain to collapse. In a world where an unviewably, unlistenably large number of videos and songs are available at any given moment, no single set of artists is going to dominate the way they used to. Viewers and listeners already face a tyranny of choice. They will have to decide for themselves whether to watch a Fellini film or YouTube videos of cats playing the piano (or, perhaps, a critique of the Fellini film that features piano-playing cats). But, as ever, it's the role of schools and parents to help shape the filters that young people apply to how they spend their time. Meanwhile, given the range of works of entertainment available now, our kids' tastes may well look very different from our own; perhaps we can learn from them as much as they can learn from us.

The most important point is that a participatory cyberspace presents great opportunities for Digital Natives to learn how to create and enjoy new expressive works. This process of creating happens with others and causes us to learn from others, often not in the home or the school but in networked publics online. Digital Natives are learning these lessons every day. And they are open to teaching the rest of us, at least any of us who are ready to listen. We need to pay attention, because the implications of this participatory culture are substantial for democracy, markets, and the law of intellectual property. If Digital Natives engage more critically with the cultures in which they are growing up, they stand a chance to remake those cultures in unprecedented ways.

The primary benefit of moving to a global online culture that is more participatory and that requires higher digital literacy skills is that it may lead to stronger democracies. This process of strengthening is not of the sort that we usually have in mind—like getting more people to vote on election day. This stronger democracy will stem from more people becoming engaged in the making, interpreting, and remaking of meaning in the culture. That's what Digital Natives are up to when they remix our culture. It could be what they are up to when they decide which news blogs and other sources of information they enjoy—but only if we manage to teach digital literacy effectively. The hardest question we'll have to answer is whether we will attempt to thwart this burgeoning online creativity in Digital Natives in the name of protecting crumbling institutions, or foster it, and the participatory culture it can lead us to.

6

PIRATES

WHEN IT COMES TO MEDIA, DIGITAL NATIVES SEEM LIKE A COMPLETELY different species from their parents and grandparents. Digital Natives don't remember photographs captured on a roll of film that had to be taken to the drugstore to be printed out; they think of digital images, instantly viewable and deletable and shareable with friends on the Internet. Digital Natives don't think of news and information as something that arrives in a mass of pulp on the doorstep in the morning; they think in terms of a massive, converged, often digital mash-up of headlines, blogs, videos, and podcasts. Most of all, Digital Natives don't think in terms of recorded music in the form of LPs, eight-tracks, cassette tapes, or even CDs, purchased at a record store; music, for them, exists in a digital format they can download from the Internet, move around, and share with their friends and relatives.

With so many forms of media available in digital formats, Digital Natives are breaking new creative ground. The most creative young people are interacting with news, works of entertainment, and other information in ways that were unimaginable a few years ago. These young people are not passive consumers of media that is broadcast to them, but rather active participants in the making of meaning in their culture. Their art form of the remix, where digital files are combined to create a new video or audio file, is already having an effect on cultural understanding around the world. And their creativity extends, too, to innovation in the form of new platforms and business models—including Napster, Facebook, and YouTube—for the distribution of digital media.

Creativity is the upside of this brave new world of digital media. The downside is law-breaking. The vast majority of Digital Natives are currently breaking copyright laws on a regular basis. By and large, many young people don't pay for music. Sometimes, they watch television shows or movies illegally. Often, they use the systems created by other Digital Natives in order to copy or watch the files. Many Digital Natives know that what they are doing is illegal; others are not so sure. Either way, the practice is pervasive. And an entire generation is thwarting the copyright law as they grow up, despite aggressive—at times even desperate—measures by industry groups and government enforcers to get them to stop.

Right or wrong, creative or destructive, civil disobedience or plain old stealing—the epidemic of file "sharing" among Digital Natives has forced us to rethink a system of copyright that is at odds with the dominant social norms of a generation. We need to think seriously about whether we are doing enough to get young people to focus on the costs of their law-breaking and whether they are accountable enough online. Most of the misguided "education" efforts to date, funded by industry groups representing copyright holders, have amounted to little more than finger-wagging campaigns. At the same time, we need to ensure that stopping piracy doesn't also mean stopping the new forms of creativity just taking hold among Digital Natives.

The story of how we got to this point begins with a Digital Native named Shawn Fanning.

Back in 1998, as a freshman at Northeastern University in Boston, Shawn wanted a convenient way to find music on the Web. More important, he wanted to share the latest tunes in MP3 format with his college friends. (MP3 is the groundbreaking coding and compression technology that allows the transmission of music over the Internet.) A few months later, at age nineteen, Shawn decided to leave college and become a digital entrepreneur. With the help of his uncle, he incorporated a company, and together with a friend, he developed and released, on June 1, 1999, the beta version of a cool piece of code that would later challenge an entire industry's business logic: Napster was born.

Napster turned out to be the first of a series of extremely popular peer-to-peer (P2P) file-sharing programs. It was also the beginning of a period in which a whole lot of young people (and old people, too) started to break the law. A lot.

Napster was easy to use. That was part of its genius. Sixteen months after the launch of Napster, more than 30 million people were using it to swap their music for free. Around 2.8 billion files per month were downloaded worldwide during Napster's peak.[1] Up to 40 percent of the registered users, though, were college kids in the United States—the first generation of kids born digital. Back in those days, Napster was consuming as much as a third of the bandwidth of many colleges.

Napster had an immediate impact on the music industry. Only a few months after the original Napster was released, the number of record albums sold—including CDs, tapes, and LPs—started to decline sharply after decades of growth.[2] Not surprisingly, the recording industry was not pleased about these developments. Almost overnight, it seemed, a handful of very powerful corporations—the record labels—had lost their previously very tight control over their products. Although piracy had existed long before Napster, the scale of the new challenge was shocking. Even more important, Napster mysteriously seemed to create a new type of "pirate." Young people across the world started to "steal" music from Madonna. (In a legal sense, anyone who uploads music on P2P networks is violating the intellectual property rights of the artists, whose interests are formally protected by the laws of virtually every nation in the world.)

From the perspective of the record labels, there was no reasonable doubt as to what was going on. P2P platforms like Napster were responsible for the massive decline in CD sales and the resulting collapse of profits. The decline has hit the billions of dollars for the music industry worldwide, according to its lobbying groups. The industry's argument seemed straightforward: Facing the possibility of getting music for free on Napster, consumers were no longer willing to pay for it in the brick-and-mortar music stores. (Later, several well-known economists painted a much more complex picture, challenging the notion of a direct causal relationship between P2P file-sharing and the drop in CD sales. Other studies, however, have supported the recording industry's argument, suggesting that file sharing reduced album sales by up to 30 percent.)

Leaders of the recording industry knew they had to do something if they were to gain back control of the music distribution process. And so they started suing people for copyright infringement. Instead of starting by suing the college students who were using the service, the music industry began by suing Shawn Fanning's Napster. In December 1999, only months after Napster's inception, A&M Records and seventeen other record companies filed a complaint against Napster for copyright infringement. Other lawsuits followed, filed by the band Metallica and major music publishers. The record labels argued that the millions of Napster users were violating their rights by trading music over the P2P network. From the perspective of the recording industry, Napster was ultimately responsible for this theft because it provided the core infrastructure of the service. Less than two years after Napster was created, the courts agreed with the recording industry: There was little doubt that the file sharing itself was illegal, and Napster shared some of the liability for what its millions of users were doing. After a few rounds of legal wrangling, Napster was effectively forced out of business in 2001.[3]

The rise and fall of Napster demonstrates the enormous appeal of digital media services to Digital Natives. Rarely in history has a service been created so quickly and inexpensively, aggregated tens of millions of users, and threatened to bring down a powerful, entrenched global industry. At the same time, the Napster story foreshadowed a fight that rages to this day. Oddly enough, the fight is between the recording industry and many of its customers. Rather than figuring out how to tap into the rush of Digital Natives to file-sharing services, the recording industry has dug in its heels and continues to fight back by suing nearly everyone it can. Since Napster, the entertainment industry has been tirelessly fighting the developers and distributors of file-sharing technology. A lot of time and money—some lawyers are getting rich from these disputes—have been spent to battle P2P providers, especially in the United States. But with little effect: Despite the risk of liability, and despite the fact that many are aware of the illegality of their actions, young people persist in sharing digital media files online.

The industry's victory over Napster did not put a stop to P2P file-sharing—not even close. Even as the Napster case was pending, technologists were developing new P2P services—despite, or perhaps because of, the music industry's fierce fight against them. The Napster ruling also offered some loopholes that were quickly identified by smart lawyers, activists, and geeks. And the popularity of online file-sharing, despite the Napster decision, continued to grow.

Before long, a new generation of P2P networks had attracted millions of users, just as Napster had before its demise. This second generation of networks, among them Grokster, eliminated one of the features that provided a handle for the plaintiffs. They got rid of centralized functions like indexing and cataloging that were part of the Napster technology, which gave rise to liability for the company offering the service. By altering their design in this way, the developers hoped to escape the liability that had ensnared Napster.

Not surprisingly, the recording industry wasn't going to let a few small technical adjustments get in the way of crushing Grokster. In 2001, MGM and other copyright holders brought suit against Grokster, Kazaa, and other similar services.[4] Grokster was effectively shut down after the Supreme Court ruled in 2005. In *Metro-Goldwin-Mayer v. Grokster*, three pieces of evidence were decisive. First, both internal documents and public advertisements showed that Grokster had been targeting users of the former Napster service that, by then, was well known for large-scale copyright infringement. Second, the company hadn't tried to develop filtering tools or the like to diminish copyright infringement on the part of its users. And third, Grokster's advertising-based model meant that revenues were linked to the use of the software. If popular works were traded, more people would be drawn to the service. Since the most popular songs were copyrighted, infringement brought Grokster more money. This didn't make Grokster look good. Despite the fact that Grokster was used for many lawful purposes—trading of perfectly legal files, alongside the illegal—the litigation pursued by the recording-industry process forced them out of business.

Net result: Yet another major P2P platform was gone. But the problems for intellectual property holders were not.

Why, despite the constant threat of legal action, do P2P services continue to thrive? Because these P2P services have something on their side that is bigger than the law: They're wildly popular. Pretty much everyone with access to a fast enough computing set-up, and definitely not just Digital Natives—have come to *love* file sharing. Shawn Fanning let the genie out of the bottle when he released Napster. Not even a federal court could put it back in.

Since Napster and Grokster have been shut down, millions of users have shared music over various P2P networks with different underlying technologies and fancy names, such as Kazaa, iMesh, LimeWire, Xolox, eDonkey, Overnet, or eMule, to name just a few. And P2P file-sharing is global. As one study points out, 66 percent of the P2P users originate from the United States, while Germany accounts for 5 percent, France for 3.5 percent, and Canada for 3.2 percent. In terms of per capita usage, Luxembourg has been the leader, with roughly 12 percent of the population on P2P networks, followed by Iceland, Finland, Norway, Ireland, and the United States.

Not surprisingly, P2P programs have been especially popular among students and other Digital Natives. P2P was born on the college campus and it sure hasn't left. A survey of 1,000 U.S. college and university students, for instance, revealed that 95 percent of the students were aware of popular P2P programs like Kazaa or Morpheus in 2003. In the same study, roughly two-thirds of the students responded that they had downloaded music from the Internet for free. Another report suggested that 56 percent of full-time students were downloading music from P2P platforms. Most studies have found that young people between the ages of eighteen and twenty-nine were most likely to use peer-to-peer file-sharing.[5]

Why are young people persistently engaging in large-scale copyright infringement? One answer is that many Digital Natives—not to mention quite a few adults—are confused about copyright law in the digital age. A great many people who use the Internet believe that virtually all forms of private, noncommercial copying of copyrighted works either *is* or *should be* allowed. One study found that over 50 percent of consumers believe it is legal to make copies of prerecorded CDs and share them among family members, while 29 percent believe that it's okay to make copies for a friend.[6] Especially in the early days of file sharing and absent widely publicized court rulings, it was far from clear whether sharing music online was legal or not. In fact, there are places in the world—like Switzerland—where the *downloading* of copyrighted files is not considered to be illegal. The *uploading* of files—posting them to Internet networks to make them available to others—is illegal virtually everywhere.

The entertainment industry has, however, pursued aggressive legal and educational campaigns to raise awareness about illegal file-sharing. To an extent, these efforts have been effective: Our research suggests that while most Digital Natives are still confused about the intricacies of copyright law, especially about what they *can* do creatively with copyrighted files, they know by now that downloading is illegal in the United States. As one junior-high-school student told us, "When I was like 11 . . . and I didn't know LimeWire was illegal, so I didn't think to ask anybody, I just downloaded it. But then I started reading everything, and I found out it was illegal."[7] But file sharing continues, despite the fact that many of the sharers now realize that their actions are illegal and punishable. What does it mean when so many otherwise law-abiding people break the law?

To understand the epidemic of file sharing, we have to understand social norms, which are extremely important regulators of human behavior. We teach our kids all day long to comply with social norms of all sorts, telling them to "share nicely," "don't push your sister," "please say hello to the nice police officer," and so on. Because young people in particular do not have a strong formal relationship with the law, social norms exert much more sway over their behavior, and can overwrite legal norms.[8]

Apply this logic to the problem of file sharing. Can strong social norms—norms of *sharing* (though not the sort that we ordinarily teach our kids, to be clear)—overwrite the norms set forth in copyright laws? This notion partly explains the P2P battle. One study revealed that of the 35 million Americans who downloaded music in 2003, 67 percent said that they did not care whether the downloaded music was copyrighted or not. Among the least concerned were younger people between the ages of eighteen and twenty-nine (72 percent).[9] A study by the Business Software Alliance from the same year indicated that 76 percent of the surveyed American college students believed that piracy of music or movies was acceptable in some or all instances.[10]

Our own focus groups revealed a similar lack of concern for legalities. Many of the Digital Natives we interviewed believed that sharing music and movies online was acceptable because it caused no harm. To share a song or a movie over the Internet is not the same as, for instance, taking away a CD from a friend. If a Digital Native takes away the CD from a friend, he has it but the friend no longer does. But if he copies his CD collection over P2P, he has it—but so does his friend. In the case of P2P, the Digital Natives generally saw no direct link between copying something and causing a loss to someone.

Of course, illegal file-sharing *can* harm someone—the copyright holder. The harm occurs if the artist or company that holds the rights is deprived of a sale of the recorded work that otherwise would have occurred. But Digital Natives tend not to grasp this concept. It's hard for Digital Natives to see how swapping a Lil Mam song could harm her, since it's on the Internet for free already. At a more general level, it is often difficult to picture the glamorous superstars of show business as "victims" in the first place— not to mention the big monopolists who produce these stars and starlets. With regard to the latter, some commentators have even characterized P2P file-sharing as a protest movement against an overcharging, stubborn music industry with an old-fashioned business model. File sharing, in this view, is a way of forcing the industry to listen to its clientele again. Some artists agree with the file-sharers, too, which clouds the message to young people. The popular hip-hop artist 50 Cent, for instance, argues that file-sharing doesn't hurt *artists,* but rather the *distributors* of the recorded entertainment.[11] Courtney Love said the same thing in an essay for Salon in 2000, concluding that "there are hundreds of artists ready to rewrite the rules."[12]

With 50 Cent, Courtney Love, and other artists providing rhetorical air-cover, many Digital Natives argue that music that is accessible online ought to be free. Free as in "free beer," rather than "free speech." There is a history to this idea. The Internet originated in an explicitly anticommercial culture—commercial sites had no place on the Internet until the mid-1990s. Combined with economic factors—what economists call high sunk costs and the low marginal cost of information—this anticorporate sensibility has led to an abundance of free online content of all types and quality. Content providers have had a hard time enforcing scarcity in the online environment. It's hard to charge for online information since there is always someone else producing—or making accessible—similar content for decent quality for free. Today's users may be willing to pay some amount of attention in return for content, as in the case of online advertisement, but they don't want to spend dollars or Swiss francs. For Digital Natives to pay for content, they often need to see clear benefits, such as ease of use or computer safety (for example, no virus-contaminated files) or other added value.

The study of the human brain provides further clues as to why so many honest people are "stealing" copyrighted songs from artists like Avril Lavigne. Researchers have started to formulate and test hypotheses about why our brains respond in significantly different ways to "property"—say, a bicycle—than to "intellectual property." A better understanding of the distinction that our brains draw between the two forms of property might lead to a better understanding of copyright infringement.[13] Recently, insights from behavioral studies and neuroscientific experiments about cooperative behavior have added reward processing and altruistic punishment to the mix of possible explanations for large-scale file-sharing among strangers.

Although there's still a long way to go, these research projects may one day help to explain the psychology and sociology of file sharing as well as attitudes about intellectual property rights (IPR) in general. These contributions might be of interest to legal scholars and policymakers when reexamining IPR doctrines. They might also be of interest to geeks who are working on platform design (resulting in what one scholar calls "charismatic code") or to businesspeople who are seeking to develop new business models in the digital media space that match the preferences of their consumers.[14]

The music industry's primary mistake was to underestimate the emergent culture of Digital Natives and to discount efforts to shift modes of distribution of digital media. In 2003, soon after the first victories against P2P in courts, the Recording Industry Association of America (RIAA) started to take direct legal action against the people who were sharing files. The cases initially focused on large-scale uploaders of music files. One problem with this strategy was that it meant suing the people that the record companies wanted to do business with in the first place: potential buyers of recorded entertainment. Never before had copyright law been used on such a massive scale to protect recorded works of entertainment: To date, the industry has sued more than 15,000 people in the United States alone. A significant percentage of the online population—many of them Digital Natives—found themselves transformed almost overnight from ordinary users of the Internet to the pirates of cyberspace, with an entire, powerful industry in hot pursuit.[15]

The international industry associations were not as quick to sue their consumers, but they caught on eventually. More patient than their U.S. counterpart, European copyright holders at first counted on technological forms of content protection, on the one hand, and promotion of public awareness through educational campaigns about the illegality of file sharing, on the other. In March 2004, however, the International Federation of the Phonographic Industry (IFPI) and its national branches launched a first wave of internationally orchestrated lawsuits against alleged file-sharers in Denmark, Germany, Italy, and Canada. Legal actions in the two largest European music markets, the United Kingdom and France, soon followed.

The number of both criminal and civil suits brought against users in more than fifteen countries is currently estimated to total somewhere around 15,000—about the same as the number of lawsuits filed by the RIAA in the United States.

This litigation campaign by the worldwide recording industries has been a disaster from the standpoint of public relations. An industry is unlikely to gain popularity by suing thousands of people for acts that a significant percentage of a society doesn't consider to be problematic. And the recording industry also hasn't shown much respect to its potential customers in its campaign. It has gone after Digital Natives, elderly people, and everyone in between.

Among the first cases to be filed in 2003 was a lawsuit against twelve-year-old Brianna LaHara of New York. Brianna, at the time a seventh grader, was reportedly storing more than 1,000 songs on her computer. According to news reports, Brianna believed that she was allowed to download the music from the Internet—partly because her mother paid a monthly subscription fee to be connected to the Web. Brianna's music library included everything from the latest songs from Christina Aguilera to the children's song "If You're Happy and You Know It." Facing a lawsuit with a maximum penalty of $150,000 per unauthorized song, the LaHara family didn't feel so happy anymore. They settled the lawsuit quickly by paying the plaintiffs $2,000, as have most other people who got sued. On average, defendants in these matters, most of whom are indeed liable for the infringement, are paying between $2,000 and $10,000 to the music labels to avoid expensive trials.[16]

The recording industry didn't help its case by making numerous high-profile errors in its campaign to put a stop to file sharing. For example, the RIAA sued a retired schoolteacher and sculptor, sixty-six-year-old Sarah Ward. Ward was accused of having swapped thousands of music files over Kazaa, resulting in millions of dollars' worth of damage. She explained in several interviews that she's neither computer-savvy nor interested in the hip-hop music she was allegedly downloading from Kazaa. Nor was someone else using her computer. In addition, it turned out that she owned a Macintosh—a computer that wasn't able to run Kazaa. Luckily for Ward, she had lawyers in her family who took up the case. The industry eventually dropped the case. Ward, for her part, says she is disappointed that the RIAA never apologized for its mistake.[17]

How did the RIAA respond to such stories? To quote a spokesperson: "When you fish with a net, you sometimes are going to catch a few dolphin."[18]

Let us be clear: We believe that copyright law is essential to the promotion of creative works and innovation more broadly. And we believe that it is important to uphold the rule of law, not to ignore rules that seem merely inconvenient. The Napster and Grokster cases, as well as the suits brought against file-sharers, have served at the very least a positive pedagogical function. Take note: Online file-sharing of copyrighted works is illegal in the United States and in most other jurisdictions in the world. But at the same time, the principle that the mechanical means of reproduction is not itself to blame for copyright infringement has also been upheld. The core theory that protects the Xerox machine and the VCR from being illegal— a theory established by the Supreme Court in the 1980s—still stands, which is a very good thing. And some businesses that were breaking the law in the United States have been disallowed from continuing their practices. The foundations for a movement toward greater accountability in the online music business are in place.

If our research is a good guide, file sharing is still extremely popular among Digital Natives around the world, despite the litigation campaigns. Nevertheless, it is possible, though far from certain, that a reduction in the use of P2P file-sharing is underway among young people. Kids, at least in the United States, may be losing some of their interest in downloading as they fear the consequences of legal action and dangerous files creeping onto their computers from polluted peer-to-peer networks. According to a recent study commissioned by the Business Software Alliance (BSA)—an industry organization devoted to strong intellectual property protections—kids between the ages of eight and eighteen are today much less likely to download copyrighted material from the Internet than they were two years ago. The study suggests that the percentage of young people who downloaded unauthorized copyrighted works dropped from 60 percent in 2004 to 36 percent in 2007.[19]

It seems unlikely that the reason behind the BSA's reported drop of downloading by teens, if true, has much to do with the litigation campaign. Surveys show that the pollution of the networks—spam, viruses, badware, and the like—ranks among the top reasons why Digital Natives (as well as other users) turn away from peer-to-peer networks.[20] All these statistics, of course, have to be taken with a grain of salt, particularly given their sources. The numbers are likely underreporting the prevalence of the activity itself, since there is greater understanding today that the act of downloading is illegal than before the litigation campaigns began. Survey respondents would be reluctant to admit to engaging in such activity. Our own focus groups and interviews gave us no reason to believe that a massive reduction in file sharing is in progress, though we certainly met a few earnest Digital Natives who said they accessed online music through lawful services such as iTunes—almost always because someone had given them a credit to spend down for a birthday gift or as a family policy.

The problem of Digital Natives and their penchant for illegal file-sharing may be intractable. The music industry has done little, through litigation and its education efforts, to solve the problem its members face. The real hope for solving it lies with the new possibilities for the monetization of digital distribution that have opened up since the launch of iTunes.

One of the effects of the litigation has been that some students don't download as much music, but they don't buy it, either. As one college student told us, without the slightest hint of irony: "I don't download music very much at all. I just get it from friends." A second student said: "I'm so used to it being free, I just can't imagine it being any other way. Like I would never pay for music now." And a third: "I'd say it's socially acceptable, obviously illegal, but, you know." For the recording industry to recover its relationship with the Digital Natives we met, its top executives will have to look beyond litigation: They will have to find a way other than through fear to reconnect with their customers.

Ultimately, those who wish to sell recorded music will have to find a way to make money from the sharing and downloading of files from the

Internet. It is easier said than done, but there are very good signs of progress in this regard. The runaway success of the iTunes business model is the first sign. The recent willingness of the recording companies to license their music more broadly to digital distributors is a second such sign. These innovations in business models hold out the greatest promise for resolving the digital media crisis, and bringing Digital Natives in from the cold.

The key breakthrough in the digital media crisis has been prompted neither by lawsuits nor by innovations in the recording industry. It took a visionary technologist. Steve Jobs and his colleagues at Apple have broken new ground—by giving Digital Natives the first attractive and viable option for going legit when it comes to digital media. The iTunes system is not the end-all-be-all to the problems of music and Digital Natives. It's not a panacea. But it represents the promise of listening carefully to Digital Natives and offering services that are more in step with emerging social norms—and which result in artists still getting paid. Today, iTunes is the largest music retailer in the United States, ahead of every record store—even ahead of Wal-Mart.[21]

On April 28, 2003, Apple, Inc., opened its iTunes Music Store in the United States. It allowed users to browse a catalog of initially over 200,000 tracks, to buy their favorite tunes for $0.99 per song or $9.99 per album, and to transfer the songs easily to their iPods. Today, the iTunes Store offers a music catalog with over 6 million songs for purchase. It has sold more than 3 billion songs to date, accounting for over 80 percent of online music sales in some countries.[22] Digital downloads represent the fastest area of growth for recorded entertainment.[23]

iTunes is no longer only about music. It's also the most popular outlet for movies online. It offers audiobooks, podcasts, and iPod games, among other things. No doubt about it: Apple—a device manufacturer, not a content owner—has changed the dynamic of the online media space in unexpected ways. The iTunes Store has become so successful and has such a strong market position in some countries that antitrust authorities have started investigating it.

Even though iTunes hasn't solved the problem of file sharing, it has moved the industry far more than the industry was willing to move on its own. iTunes is a good and crucial starting point. Though not a total solution for the digital media crisis—whether viewed from the perspective of artists, consumers, or the public at large—iTunes has released a flood of market-driven approaches to the thorny digital media challenge.[24] Besides filing lawsuits against Digital Natives and lobbying for tougher laws, the entertainment industry finally started teaming up with digital entrepreneurs, device manufacturers, cell-phone companies, and the like to offer legitimate sources for online content.[25]

The market developments in digital distribution since iTunes' launch in 2003 have been remarkable. The digital content industry is very dynamic and among the fastest-growing sectors of the industry. Today, Digital Natives and Immigrants alike can get digital content from literally hundreds of online stores across the world. A range of business models has emerged. Many Digital Natives are still getting music for free, but today they can choose from the still dominant pay-per-track model, like iTunes, or streaming subscription models, like Rhapsody or Napster 2.0 (the legal successor to Shawn Fanning's original business), where consumers can access for a monthly fee as many songs as they like. Usually, the online stores distribute songs and movies in a protected format—so-called digital rights management (DRM) systems—to control the number of times a song or video can be accessed, copied, or burned onto a CD. These DRM-protected services, though, have not become popular enough to resolve the file-sharing crisis.

The music industry has also begun to experiment with higher-priced songs that are DRM-free, which is an excellent development. It turns out that users—Digital Natives in particular—don't like to deal with DRM-imposed restrictions, and they've made their preferences on this score clear. The music industry is also experimenting with commercial P2P distribution. Services like Mercora, Musicmatch, or iMesh, for instance, offer users the ability to stream music that has been purchased by peers on the same network. The BBC uses the P2P software BitTorrent to distribute the episodes of various shows over the Internet. In many cases, P2P has become a promotional tool to spur purchase of digital content.

Several services have started to incorporate some of the key community features that are characteristic of P2P platforms, like shared playlists, recommendation systems, and P2P webradio services. The habits of Digital Natives in particular drive this trend toward more collaborative services and portals for music, movies, games, and other digital content. While offline sales revenue is still essential for the digital content industry, online business is the future. Although most of the new business models are at early stages and will take more time to develop, change is underway—and people are starting to make some money from digital media. In years to come, Digital Natives in affluent societies will have many more choices than ever before for how to search, acquire, use, and share their favorite music, movies, games, ring tones, and so forth in a global marketplace of entertainment.

W e've learned several lessons from the digital media crisis. First, the P2P technology story demonstrates what can happen when Internet applications with disruptive power mesh with the social norms of Digital Natives. Powerful institutions in traditional hierarchies, under threat, push back hard, then turn to more innovative solutions with time when the threats aren't enough. It's clear that the recording industry's primary response—the use of intellectual property laws in defense of threatened business models—is likely to be part of its strategy into the future, too, but there are early signs that leading companies, like Universal Music Group, are starting to distribute their music in more innovative ways. The Recording Industry Association of America contends that its members have licensed works to hundreds of partners in digital distribution.[26]

The second lesson we can learn from the P2P controversy is that the use of law in the context of digital technology can have an impact, but is not always successful. Although the RIAA and IFPI are trumpeting their legal campaigns against P2P platforms and file-sharers as a run-away success, file sharing is still popular and large-scale. To be sure, we aren't suggesting that the use of copyright law in courts is always meaningless. However, we *are* arguing that mass-scale litigation against potential customers is not a sustainable approach for any industry that wants to do business with them in the first place, particularly in a fast-changing technological environment where strong social norms are in play that are in tension with existing law.

There is a third lesson we should also heed: The use of copyright law to solve a problem of this scale can be associated with significant costs—costs not only for the parties involved, but also for the public at large. Copyright law, as interpreted through cases like *MGM v. Grokster* or as amended by legislation, might ultimately have unintended consequences, hampering technological innovation. Digital entrepreneurs—in particular, Digital Natives like Shawn Fanning—are particularly vulnerable to these side effects (one might argue that's as it should be). The danger of spillover effects and unwanted consequences even grows when we move from courtrooms to the halls of Congress. While it is still too early to report the negative impacts of the most recent incarnations of antipiracy legislation, experiences with other pieces of legislation suggest that we'll have to expect them sooner or later.

Decisions handed down by the courts in the wake of these battles can have a similar effect on innovation by Digital Natives. The *Grokster* opinion, as Solomonic as it may appear to have been, may well have its biggest negative impact on entrepreneurs who seek clarity in terms of the law as it relates to digital media. The problem is that the inducement standard set forth by the Supreme Court is not yet clearly understood by entrepreneurs who develop technologies that might be used for both lawful and unlawful ends. While the big companies—large consumer electronic manufacturers, for example—may have the money to pay expensive lawyers and the power to sit out years of litigation, digital entrepreneurs in their garages or living rooms may not. The digital entrepreneurs—those working on the cool technology that shapes the way Digital Natives will communicate tomorrow—might be driven away as they become reluctant to experiment with new technology or start a new business because the case law leaves it unclear what their legal responsibilities would be. In a way unintended by the courts involved, copyright law in today's quicksilver technological environment has a *negative* impact on innovation—innovation being the goal that intellectual property law is supposed to serve in the first place.

The same experiences also teach us how difficult it is to change copy-right law once it is in place. If we don't get it right the first time, we're in trouble.

Probably the most important lesson of all, however, is that all these is-sues are not things that can be delegated completely to lawyers and lob-byists. Copyright legislation, in particular, shapes the further evolution of technology. Bills that are championed by one industry, but locked in a pitched battle with another industry and its customers, can do much harm in this regard if they become law.

The people who will bear the costs of bad decisions made today are those who are born digital. If we care about the future of our kids, if we care about the ways in which they interact with information, communicate with each other, and find the music and movies they are looking for, and how they share their experiences online with their friends, we should take seriously the implications of the policies we are crafting today. We need to be extra careful when introducing new legal doctrines or thinking about the enactment of tougher copyright laws in response to technological change in the digital world.

There are dangers to an overemphasis on legal fixes to the digital media cri-sis. We ignore the social norms of Digital Natives at our peril. As we look ahead and seek to apply these lessons learned, we do so in the knowledge that things are getting more complicated, not less so, with the advent of the new technologies of Web 2.0. The most creative of Digital Natives spe-cialize in new forms of expression that are in inherent tension with the copyright law, which was framed hundreds of years ago; many remixes, for instance, use footage from CNN and clips from MTV. It shouldn't come as a surprise that these new forms of digital expression have garnered the at-tention of legal departments in big media companies. The fight over P2P distribution was just the beginning of the copyright war. The next wave of controversy in digital copyright is a series of lawsuits against companies like YouTube and its parent, Google, who have been sued by Viacom and the book-publishing industry, among many other litigants. A third wave of copyright litigation may well be about creative rearrangements of songs, texts, pictures, movies, and the like. Cases relating to fan fiction and music sampling are already emerging that point toward this new battleground.[27] These uses of technology are fun and attractive and laudable, but one can easily imagine variants that will give rise to copyright and trademark controversies ahead.

There's no denying that the digital media crisis is good for neither Digital Natives nor those who create and distribute recorded entertainment. And there's no denying that things are getting more complicated with copyright online, not less. The copyright war—a war of litigation involving content owners, Digital Natives, and technologists—has become a defining feature of the digital age. But it doesn't need to be.

Digital Natives do some creative things online, many of which we want to encourage. They also do some illegal things, closely related to these creative and lawful acts, which we want to discourage. The law and social norms are sharply at odds with one another. New technologies and services offer great promise, but they have not yet solved the crisis by any means. And policy interventions have muddied the waters, not made them clearer.

Despite the continued evolution of the relationship between digital media and Digital Natives, there is a series of interventions that would help. There's room for everyone to participate in resolving this mess. We propose five approaches.

First, do no harm. One of the key lessons of the recent digital past is that the use of restrictive copyright law—in fact, the law has become more and more restrictive over the past fifty years or so—is unlikely to be a sound response, on its own, to the manifold challenges posed by digital technology. The old rules about what it means to make a "copy" or a derivative work don't fit the digital environment and communities of practice very well. In some instances, these existing legal norms are disconnected from powerful social norms, as the example of file sharing illustrates. Even more dangerous than outdated rules, however, are inadequate new laws. Some of these new laws are inadequate because they are the product of unequal bargaining power and shift the balance away from the broader public interest and inexorably back toward right holders. In other cases, the laws are inadequate because they produce unforeseen and unintended consequences.

These inadequacies are harmful because they can easily hamper techno-logical innovation—the goal copyright is supposed to serve in the first place. In the digital age, lawmakers should therefore become more like physicians and follow one basic credo: First, do no harm.

Many of the recent proposals to reform copyright law around the world in response to the digital media crisis involve strengthening the protec-tions of copyright law, criminalizing more and more behavior, and in-creasing enforcement and penalties for copyright infringement. This instinct is wrong.

There may be a need for radical changes to the copyright law in re-sponse to changes in media forms, but simply piling on more protections to the age-old framework, which is ill-fitting to the digital era, is not the answer. Why? Frankly, we're less worried about the law's impact on P2P providers such as Grokster, or people who are sharing thousands of songs for free when they ought to be paying for them, than we are about the pos-sible side effects, such as adverse implications for privacy, creativity, and in-novation, of simply continuing to expand copyright protections. These expansions of the copyright laws will shape the future of cyberspace and the ways in which our kids can interact with each other in the future—and how they can innovate, whether as young entrepreneurs or as profes-sionals later in their careers. And there's ample evidence that innovation continues to abound in the online environment, with Digital Natives near the center of the action as leaders, employees, and customers. That's rea-son enough for us, as parents, to care about expanding copyright protec-tions, too—regardless of our viewpoints when it comes to P2P file-sharing.

Let 1,000 flowers bloom, but ensure that those who are in the garden are ac-countable for their actions. As a general matter, we trust in market forces on-line to make things better. It's not the first time that the entertainment industry has cried foul and argued that a new technology—here P2P—threatened the very foundations of the industry. Jack Valenti, head of the motion picture industry group, claimed in the early 1980s that the VCR was to the movie business what Jack the Ripper was to women.[28] A few decades later, the movie business has found itself making more money on VCR tapes and DVDs than it does at the theater.[29] The lessons of the past suggest that when judges and lawmakers restrain themselves from intervening too aggressively in the context of digital media, market competition usually solves the problem on its own.

In the current controversies about P2P distribution, we see similar market forces at play. Fierce competition among content providers, device manufacturers, technology providers, and others have led to promising experiments with new business models that provide users easy access to lawful digital content like music, movies, podcasts, audiobooks, and the like. Market dynamics are forcing the industry to adjust to the new technological environment and adapt to the new rules of cyberspace; iTunes and its progeny represent an extraordinary series of innovations. The transition period might be tough for some, but we have reason to be confident that these adaptations will ultimately benefit both users and creators. For this strategy to work, though, technology companies need to do their part by acting accountably—and not framing their businesses in such a way as to encourage unlawful acts by their users.

Use law as an enabler of the positive things Digital Natives are doing. While we trust in market forces and social norms to regulate, we don't dispute that the law can play a constructive role, too. Recent legal reform efforts to date have been generally focused on accomplishing the wrong things: increasing the punishment of lawbreakers, creating new causes of action to sue people, and so forth.[30] Law can be an effective constraint on behavior, which is what the entertainment industry hopes it will be in this context. That's not working in a way that will resolve this problem long-term.

The law should function as a "leveler"—creating a level playing field—and an "enabler" rather than just constraining behavior. Consider, for example, a successful project called Creative Commons. Creative Commons arose from the insight that it is difficult, under the copyright laws of most countries, to make clear to other people that they may use your copyrighted works in certain ways. Beginning in 2003, Creative Commons began to offer a range of licenses for the distribution of copyrighted works for anyone to use. More than 100 million of these licenses are in use today.[31] By building off a system grounded in existing copyright law—and translating licenses into both nonlawyerly and machine-readable form—Creative Commons makes it both possible and easy to give permission to others to reuse content in creative ways. If a young podcaster, for instance, licenses her latest podcast under an attribution, noncommercial, share-alike CC license, she allows the users of her work to copy, distribute, display, and perform it and to make derivative works as long as the resulting work is distributed under a license identical to the one she is using. No longer are all rights reserved, only some.[32]

Align incentives better. Economists are (most of the time) very smart people. One thing they know about is the incentive system. Right now, the incentive system is out of whack in the context of digital media. The series of lawsuits against Grokster, Napster, and individual file-sharers make clear that there is a misalignment among copyright holders, digital technology providers, and consumers. It doesn't have to be so. Technology companies like YouTube would be much better off striking deals with companies that hold copyrighted content, like the National Football League or Warner Brothers, and sharing the revenue that comes from people enjoying the content. And Digital Natives themselves, when they create things, can get in on the act, too, by sharing their works online in ways that benefit them—whether through popularity, social credits, future recording deals, or direct payment for their works. The goal should be for copyright holders, technologists, and their customers to exchange royalty checks with one another instead of legal complaints.

Educate, educate, educate. RIAA and IFPI have run massive educational campaigns in schools. Recently, the Curb Illegal Downloading on College Campuses Act of 2007 was introduced in U.S. Congress—with the express goal of using educational funds to reduce illegal downloading.

These campaigns get it wrong. They are strongly one-sided and geared toward protecting the central role of an industry struggling to pull itself out of a downward spiral. Digital Natives *do* need more education about copyright issues, about what they can do with digital content and what they cannot. But the message must be well balanced, which it will never be when it is created by the music industry's spin-doctors. It needs to be credible and creative. As part of a broader media literacy program, all aspects of copyright need to be taught—not only the part of the story about exclusive rights and control, but also the one about limitations and exceptions such as fair use, research and teaching exceptions, and the like.

In an environment where almost everything is possible, but not necessarily legal, it's crucial that we teach Digital Natives about their responsibilities, as well as about their rights. And it's important that we introduce this education at a relatively early age. Digital Natives will need these skills to navigate the network through which they are leading more and more of their lives. They will need this knowledge as they, too, increasingly become copyright holders as well as copyright users.

This also means that all of us Digital Immigrants, parents and teachers alike, will need to familiarize ourselves with copyright issues. We've heard from many, many parents and teachers that they do not understand the legal status of online file-sharing, and therefore cannot in turn help the Digital Natives who look to them for guidance. As in the case of privacy and safety, the process of avoiding more problems and taking advantage of what is great about the habits of Digital Natives must start with a new connection. Only then can we avoid repeating the wasteful conflicts of the P2P litigation wars and turn to the more important goal for society at large: to encourage the creativity of our Digital Natives.

7

QUALITY

O N MAY 26, 2005, SOMEONE ADDED THE FOLLOWING TEXT TO THE WIKIPEDIA biography of the well-known U.S. writer and journalist John Seigen-thaler, Sr.:

> John Seigenthaler Sr. was the assistant to Attorney General Robert Kennedy in the early 1960s. For a short time, he was thought to have been directly involved in the Kennedy assassinations of both John, and his brother, Bobby. Nothing was ever proven.
>
> John Seigenthaler moved to the Soviet Union in 1972, and re-turned to the United States in 1984. He started one of the country's largest public relations firms shortly thereafter.

Roughly four months after these paragraphs were added to Seigenthaler's biography on Wikipedia, one of his friends discovered the entry. Seigen-thaler was outraged to read that someone had accused him of possibly being involved in the Kennedy assassinations—by all accounts a falsehood.

Seigenthaler decided to fight back, using the mainstream media that he understood so well as the means of repairing his damaged reputation. In so doing, he set off an avalanche. While the false accusations were quickly removed from Wikipedia after he complained, a long public controversy followed. It soon came to light that an operations manager of a delivery service company in Nashville had posted the false information as some sort of joke, and he later apologized. So the controversy turned not on Seigenthaler's past, but rather on Wikipedia's accuracy. The online encyclopedia could inform or misinform; it empowered anyone who wanted to contribute to tell the story the way it was, but it also empowered those who decided to spread falsehoods. Regardless of whether any given Wikipedia entry is true or false, that entry is often the top link that comes up on Google for any given search term. And for young people, among many others, it's the first place to go for information.

On September 8, 2004, *60 Minutes Wednesday* aired a report about President George W. Bush's Texas Air National Guard Service. In the first half of the report, a *60 Minutes* reporter interviewed Ben Barnes, a former lieutenant governor of Texas and speaker of the Texas House of Representatives.[1] The topic was whether President Bush had received preferential treatment in being assigned to the Texas National Guard. In the second half of the broadcast, CBS presented documents to prove that Bush had applied pressure to be treated better than others in August 1973. Allegedly, the documents were taken from the files of then-Lt. Bush's commander; *60 Minutes* also reported that it had consulted with a document and handwriting expert who believed that the documents were authentic. Later on, CBS issued a statement that the experts had vouched for the document's authenticity.

Nineteen minutes after the broadcast began, a group of four bloggers began an interconnected, real-time investigation into the authenticity of the documents. They argued that the documents shown on CBS contained spacing and typographical constructions that would have been impossible using the electric typewriters available in 1973. Later, an investigation showed that there was a significant likelihood that the documents were forgeries. An independent review panel finally produced a 234-page report on the controversial CBS news segment, reviewing the journalistic routines that led up to it.[2]

I nformation quality issues are neither Internet-specific nor new to the digital age. The Seigenthaler and Bush stories were about factual inaccuracies; both became major international news stories. In one case, the biography of a well-known journalist was mischaracterized. In the other, the quality of documents and the conclusions drawn based on these materials were questionable. One inaccuracy emerged in a relatively novel niche of the digital online environment, the other in the context of a traditional and prestigious journalistic format.

The problem of sorting out inaccurate information from the truth is as old as civilization itself. At no time in world history has there been any lie-detection system to help sort fact from fiction.[3] That said, the advent of the Internet has spawned significant concerns about the challenges facing young people, who are growing up surrounded by so many information sources and so many services that let anyone become an author or an editor that it has become even more difficult than before to distinguish good information from bad. One of the big changes wrought by our use of the Internet is the way in which many of us create and consume information, knowledge, and entertainment. This is one of the complications to which the participatory Web gives rise. Wikipedia, the medium in which the Seigenthaler controversy took place, illustrates this shift most concretely. Its articles can be edited by anyone—at any time, for any reason—who has access to the Internet and basic digital literacy skills.

The way information is produced for the Web is often quite different from the way it is produced for traditional media. Wikipedia is the most obvious case in point. It's an open platform with very low costs of information production—regardless of whether the information is accurate. Anyone can post almost anything, anytime. Viewed from that angle, the *60 Minutes* format is different. It's a closed format (not just anyone can become a CBS reporter) with comparatively high production costs. It's highly formalized, and it's governed by professional standards and procedures. On Wikipedia there are norms, too. But these norms are much less formalized and are integrated into a procedure involving many contributors.

These stories also illustrate how much accuracy of information matters. Accuracy matters because we base decisions on information all the time, as individuals and as polities. And the importance of the accuracy of information in digital format grows over time, given the role that the Web increasingly plays in education and as a general information source. We know, too, that many young people are less able than most adults to evaluate the quality of information on their own. Add up these factors, and it becomes clear that information quality is enormously relevant to the lives of those born digital.

There is no reason to believe that most information found online is of lesser quality than most information that is printed on paper. But what is often quite different are the mechanics by which information is created, reviewed, edited, received, shared, and reused.

Compare Wikipedia to what came before. Wikipedia is a nonprofit enterprise with essentially no staff and tens of thousands of contributors worldwide, most of them amateurs, who make varying levels of contributions to articles. Most of the time, those edits are very small. The *Encyclopaedia Britannica,* perhaps the best-known traditional encyclopedia in the English language, operates very differently. Britannica is a centuries-old, for-profit firm with a relatively small number of professional subject matter experts, science journalists, lecturers, editors, staff members, and the like. These two enterprises are worlds apart.

The extent to which the Wikipedia process of information creation leads to greater or lesser accuracy of information than the Britannica process is hotly debated.[4] Partisans of the Web-based approach point to the fact that the crowds can be immensely wise. The fact of having so many contributors, even if they are all rank amateurs, leads to great richness of some entries and greater accuracy overall.[5] The partisans of the classical approach note that the entries are written by the world's experts on any given topic and are eminently stable. Albert Einstein, after all, wrote the space-time entry for the thirteenth edition of *Encyclopaedia Britannica;* and it's hard to beat that.[6]

The deeply respected scientific journal *Nature* ran an experiment in 2005 designed to answer the question of which approach leads to greater accuracy. The researchers assembled a team of people they considered to be experts, and had them examine entries on science-related topics in both Wikipedia and the online version of the *Encyclopaedia Britannica.*

Nature's team found many inaccuracies in both encyclopedias. Although the *Encyclopaedia Britannica*'s entries tended to have fewer errors than those of Wikipedia, the difference was not as significant as many had expected. Of 42 entries checked, the investigators deemed that the average entry in Wikipedia contained about 4 errors, whereas the average *Encyclopaedia Britannica* article had about 3.[7] The team also found that there were only 8 "serious errors" among the 42 articles, 4 within each encyclopedia. As for factual misrepresentations, "omissions," or "misleading statements," the examiners determined that the Wikipedia entries contained 162 such errors, whereas the *Encyclopaedia Britannica* articles contained 123.[8]

Many people were surprised that Wikipedia did so well in a head-to-head comparison with the *Encyclopaedia Britannica*. After all, the *Encyclopaedia Britannica* has a long tradition and a reputation for high quality. Its contributors are considered highly qualified experts in their respective fields. The encyclopedia also has professional editors to "police" the articles before (and after) they are published. Wikipedia, of course, has no equivalent mechanism for formal fact-checking or peer review—just lots and lots of volunteers, most of whom are never even known to the general public by name.

Information quality matters, but this study seemed to show that quality can derive from fundamentally different processes. Whether *Encyclopaedia Britannica* or Wikipedia is more accurate on any given topic is not the key point. The information environment is growing far more diverse and complex as we proceed in the digital age. For Digital Natives, much turns on the individual's ability to navigate through all this information of varying qualities. Those who come to understand the dynamics of information production in the digital era will be better prepared than anyone else to thrive in the integrated digital world. And the best way to learn these dynamics is to participate in information production directly.

With its tens of millions of users, Wikipedia is the most visible symbol of a much broader shift away from information mediated by powerful firms like Britannica and Brockhaus, the classical equivalent in the German-speaking world. This same phenomenon in the information-creation and information-retrieval business plays out in many other ways. Consider, for instance, any blog. Check out www.technorati.com and type in any search term that appeals—and compare the results to the print edition of a daily newspaper. Or click on homemade clips found on YouTube and contrast them with a show on TV. And what about the latest podcast from podcast.net or iTunes, versus the traditional radio network? In today's world, more and more people—often amateurs—produce more and more information. Sometimes that information is of high quality; sometimes it is not. The production of digital information is highly decentralized, and traditional gatekeepers (like editorial boards, for example) are assuming a reduced role as power-brokers.

The democratizing effect of the Internet is a great thing on many levels. The creation of a diverse information environment seems finally within reach. More people can participate directly in informing the world about events that matter. But this same dynamic—the broad access to the ability to publish, edit, or promote material online—also gives rise to hard questions. Why do so many people think this new environment is better than what came before? It's particularly important to answer this question in light of the risks posed by democratized production for society and culture.

For decades, the policy paradigm in the United States—and to a somewhat lesser extent in Europe—has been: "More information is better information." The underlying premise of this approach traces back to the writings of John Milton and John Stuart Mill, in whose work one finds the seeds of an argument about a "marketplace of ideas." In the twentieth and twenty-first centuries, others have extended this line of argument, contending that the Internet can create a marketplace of ideas that will serve society well. In this view of the world, ideas and information are like goods in a bazaar, from among which consumers can choose. Through this process, the market will set the correct value for various properties, and good information will be more highly valued than bad information. In the strong form of this argument, the more diversity and choice, the better.[9]

Many believe the pendulum has swung in the opposite direction. Today's challenge is no longer to make sure that we have *enough* information available. The problem is that those born digital may have access to *too much* information—a challenge addressed in the next chapter. We're experiencing an extraordinary thing: a real-time test of the proposition that more information, from more voices, is "better" for a society.

It's not clear that the marketplace of ideas works particularly well in a digital world. In cyberspace, the good does not always win over the bad and the ugly. It's not the case that all players in this market—especially our children—are equally well equipped, skilled, or trained to deal with the tussles over quality that play out in real time on the Web every moment of every day around the world. The costs of the process of getting to the truth matter, too.

The debate over information-quality issues online is ongoing. There's no dominant theory of what to do about it, and there are plenty of open questions. It is one of the thorniest issues raised by Internet culture—and we argue with our students and colleagues about it all the time. That said, there are two simple propositions that are easy to subscribe to: First, the question of information quality goes right to the heart of what it means to have a free society; and second, it's impossible to discuss the information-quality problem in the abstract.

Information quality goes directly to the heart of what it means to have a free society. Unfortunately, not all Digital Natives see it this way.

In conversations with Digital Natives about information quality, questions like "So what?" and "Who cares?" are common refrains. The majority of the population born digital doesn't perceive quality of information as an important issue, it seems. This statement by a Digital Native we interviewed is symptomatic: "Google's like, a lot of people use it so I think just use it. You just randomly click one—if it doesn't make sense then I'll just go back and click another one." When we asked this high-school student how she knows that one can trust what a website says, she answered: "I didn't think about that, I just . . ."[10]

In some instances, Digital Natives may care about information quality. They may care when they get back bad grades from papers they prepared using Wikipedia. And they are concerned about the reliability of information on people they meet online. But in most cases, it appears that they do not care about the question of accuracy. This disinterest in the quality question is difficult for an older generation to accept.[11]

Of course, the fact that Digital Natives aren't concerned about information quality doesn't mean that it doesn't matter. Many young people don't worry about the carcinogenic properties of tobacco, either—but that doesn't mean they're not hurting themselves by smoking cigarettes.

Kids are using the Web to access enormously important things—like information about their health. According to one survey, 31 percent of teens aged twelve to seventeen are using the Internet to get health information online, and the number is growing.[12] In the category of Internet users aged eighteen to twenty-nine, 79 percent have looked up health-related issues on the Web.[13] More than 20 percent of teens indicated that they look for online information in topic areas they think are hard to talk about, including sensitive issues such as drug use, depression, sexuality, and the like.[14] As one of our high-school girls put it: "I know like for myself and a lot of girls not—we don't have a lot of sex ed at our school so, you know, sometimes we'll Google 'Birth Controls' and understand how it works or things like that."[15]

There's little doubt that in these cases the quality of information matters, and that teens seeking it should indeed care about it. But there are thousands of websites and forums with health information that is not based on any science whatsoever—a fact that worries not only parents, but also MDs. Internet users in general (we don't know the exact numbers for teens) are not very vigilant when it comes to quality checks of sensitive health information. The vast majority of health seekers, for instance, don't check the source and date of the health information they find online. Food labels, as one study found, get more attention than information quality indicators on the Internet.[16]

Of course, health information is not the only thing Digital Natives are looking up on the Internet. There are other types of information they're searching for online. Consider these findings: Over three-quarters of the teens between the ages of twelve and seventeen are using the Internet to get news and information about current events. Over half of this age group goes online to seek information about colleges, universities, and other schools they're thinking about attending, and about a third is looking for information about jobs online.

All of these kinds of information may be important to the lives of our children. And we think that it's important for young citizens to get reliable news, accurate information about the colleges they're applying to, and a real picture of the institutions that they interact with. If kids are reading about depression, it's important that the source of information is credible. And so on. They increasingly make important decisions based on information they find on the Web—decisions that can change the course of their lives, in some cases. (So do adults, by the way. Fully 45 percent of Internet users—about 60 million Americans—say that online information has played an important or crucial role in at least one important decision they've made in the recent past.[17]) When it comes to addressing their problems, more people turn to the Internet than to any other single source of information and support, including experts, family members, government agencies, or libraries.[18]

It's essential that all of us be able to differentiate good information from bad. By virtue of their age and education level, Digital Natives are more susceptible than adults to the threats posed by inaccurate information. If our children are not themselves concerned about the issue of information quality, then we need to intervene on their behalf. As parents and teachers, we should be concerned about it even if they don't perceive it as an issue. Because we all know: There's wonderful stuff out there, but also a great deal of misinformation that can do significant harm to those unable to see it for what it is.

It's impossible to discuss the information-quality problem in the abstract. The context in which someone is seeking information is crucial to understanding what elements of quality matter.

It's almost impossible to define what "quality" means when it comes to information. Many scholars from various disciplines have tried to figure it out. Librarians, pedagogues, physicians, psychologists, people doing research in knowledge management, journalists, and even lawyers have tried to define it. The result of all these efforts: We have a much better understanding of what quality *may* mean. We have a list of more than seventy quality criteria available for assessing information—ranging from whether it is "functional" (that is, concise, consistent, timely, and objective, for example) to whether it has "aesthetic" value (attractiveness, beauty). An array of sophisticated frameworks have been devised to show the interplay between the different elements that constitute high-quality information. "Information visualization," for example, is a relatively new field that explores the aesthetics of information in terms of how it is presented and experienced as a visual display. But there are also simple definitions and rules of thumb.

A common definition for information quality is "fitness for use." But what makes the discussion about information quality so challenging—and quality regulation so difficult and dangerous, as we will see later in the chapter—is the fact that "information" becomes highly complicated when we talk about it in the human context.

First, every piece of information has a unique relationship to the person who is using it. If a Digital Native is looking for, say, online information about her stomach pain on WebMD, she brings with her a particular demographic, educational, and cultural backdrop. All this is relevant when it comes to information processing. It shapes how our Digital Native is searching for information, what type of information she is looking for, and what level of quality she seeks in that information. In German, there's a great word to describe exactly this phenomenon: Any aspect of human information processing—from searching for information to making quality assessments (for example, about its relevance)—depends on the individual's *Vorwissen*, which roughly translates into "prior knowledge." But that also means that it's very hard to make general statements about information processes. *Vorwissen* is something very subjective, and so is information quality. A piece of information about Japanese history, for example, will be perceived one way by a Digital Native who is coming to the topic for the first time, and another way by her father who happens to be a professor in the field.

The second characteristic of information is its contextuality. The same piece of information can have a completely different quality in different contexts for the same recipient. Imagine a situation where someone has to undergo surgery. Let's assume one scenario where it's a scheduled surgery and another one where it's an emergency treatment. The patient's information needs will be significantly different in these two scenarios. The surgeon's detailed description of how the operation is done, for instance, might be perceived as extremely relevant in one case, but much less relevant in the other. The context can change the value of the information, making it essential or nonessential, potentially harmful or inconsequential.

There is no generalizable, abstract answer to the question of what information quality is. When speaking about information quality, we always need to ask: "Quality" viewed from what perspective and in what context? True, in several cases of the seventy or so quality criteria, it might be easier to find consensus among many people and across different contexts as to what quality means. The fact that Seigenthaler wasn't involved in Kennedy's assassination is a case in point. But even with regard to the same aspect of information quality ("accuracy"), it immediately becomes difficult to make generally accepted statements that are clearly "right" or "wrong" when we turn to more complex informational situations like the 60 Minutes segment mentioned above. That's even more the case where a Digital Native faces the challenge of assessing the quality of highly complicated and dynamic subject areas like health information. Ask a physician about young patients who bring information from the Internet with them to an appointment, and the information-quality concerns come spilling out. According to one survey, 41 percent of primary-care physicians reported that patients arrived in their office with inaccurate information they found online.[19]

Assessing the quality of information is a difficult task for anyone. It requires that various factors be taken into account, ranging from previous bits of knowledge to contextual information. And the task of making quality judgments gets cognitively more demanding as the complexity of the information increases. Where there is interplay among a lot of factual elements, for instance, or in situations where normative judgments are required, deliberate quality assessments become so complicated that people often avoid them altogether. One survey showed that young people were particularly likely to avoid making quality judgments in these cases.[20]

For children, these evaluation processes are especially difficult to navigate. Distinguishing between high- and low-quality information is harder for kids than for adults for several reasons. The simplest reason is that their brains are not as fully developed. Another is that many young people have shorter attention spans than many adults. Attention is essential to the careful assessment of information quality. And research also shows that young people face the added challenge of having fewer experiences of their own against which to compare the information they are assessing. The net result: Though sorting information is hard for everyone, it's particularly tricky for most young people.[21]

Neuroscientists have shown that teenagers don't have a fully functioning prefrontal cortex, an area of the brain heavily involved in the selection, interpretation, evaluation, modification, and ordering of semantic information. This suggests, among other things, that teenagers are less well-equipped to foresee the consequences of their actions and to plan ahead. In particular, the fact that the prefrontal cortex is still under construction, so to speak, has an impact on teens' ability to evaluate risks and their willingness to take them. In simple terms, since teenagers are not yet fully hardwired, their ability to select, evaluate, and sort out information is limited compared to the ability they will have once they are fully grown. And as scholars have concluded, the intelligence of children is fundamentally different from that of adults. The stage of biological and moral development that a child is in matters for his or her ability to assess information accuracy with precision.[22]

There are different stages of being a Digital Native. Just as there are differences between adults and young people, there are differences among age groups of young people when it comes to quality assessments on the Internet. To add a further layer of complexity, children who spend more time online—Digital Natives—are more likely to be better equipped to make judgments about information quality. Studies show that children who have the most extensive access to the Internet are more likely than their less experienced peers to take a skeptical view of the kinds of information that they draw from Web-based sources like Wikipedia. A possible way to explain this phenomenon is that children with unrestricted access have the time to experience knowledge production as a collaborative process, while young people who access the Web, for instance, through computers in the library need to get the information very quickly and thus don't have the time to evaluate their sources carefully. Quality of education also seems to be a factor in how capable a Digital Native is in assessing information.[23]

This is good news for older and more sophisticated Digital Natives, because they spend lots of time connected to the network and are most likely figuring out how to interpret social cues online. Our worry is that it's bad news for the children who spend less time online, or who haven't learned the skills they need to navigate information sources in cyberspace. One study confirms that there is a relationship between time spent online and the ability to evaluate online information. Although younger children—depending on their stage of development—don't always recognize that some information on the Web is incorrect, older kids with lots of Web experience actually evaluate online information quite critically. According to the study, experienced surfers are more critical of online information, less confident in the information, and less enthusiastic about the information than their peers with less Web experience.[24]

However, adolescents with a lot of Web experience often base their evaluations of online information on personal preferences, which are only sometimes a good guide. Visual aspects, such as personal color and design preferences, rank among the top evaluation criteria for judging the depth of online information, often more than, for instance, the sources cited. Further, information quality tends to be equated with information quantity. Young people tend to think that sites with names they recognize have more accurate information than sites that they haven't heard of before.[25] One of the kids we asked about judging online information responded this way: "I normally go by what—well, one of the things I go by is—if it looks like it took a long time to make—I mean generally someone doesn't spend more than twenty-four hours doing something that's a complete lie, although I backed up with different sites."[26]

The ability to make quality judgments about information on the Internet is not an innate skill. Spending more time online makes Digital Natives more critical about the quality of online content, but time online alone is not a complete answer. There are digital-media literacy skills that can be taught. One experienced college student, for instance, described his approach when judging the quality of online news as follows: "There are many biased websites. . . . So I try to check all of them. And as much as possible, I try also if possible to—to see whatever video footage there is on YouTube. Like if—if there's an interview with whoever, if—if, because that's firsthand information. So and then if it's not someone so I can make my own opinion about it. I—I look for the sources." This technique—looking for firsthand information—is something that younger kids could learn to do. Another routine and tech-savvy user, when referring to Wikipedia, told us about his quality cues: "I go to Wikipedia. If you look at a Wikipedia article, you can usually tell if it's reputable or not because reputable articles will have lots of citations. They will have—they will usually have a large body of text that's coherent and that's obviously written by a good writer. You can also go to the history page, look at who's edited it. And if you know that person then, okay, you know that they're probably reputable. If it's edited by lots of anonymous people, then it might not be that reputable."[27]

So Digital Natives learn how to evaluate information quality as they grow up, partly as a result of the process of maturation, and partly as a result of gaining experience online. But these twin processes do not solve the problem completely. The problem remains for younger Digital Natives and for those who are on the other side of the participation gap—those who are young, but not Digital Natives.

The information-quality problem leads to inquiries about cognition and the accuracy of the information itself. It also gives rise to a conversation about ethics. Ethically questionable information, whether online or in other sources, can do harm to impressionable children. Hate speech—white supremacists raging about ethnic minorities online, for example—is the most obvious example. The sale of Nazi propaganda is another. Some (but by no means all) adults believe that Internet pornography falls into this category. The many efforts to solve these problems through traditional law have failed, putting the onus to sort these ethical problems back on families and communities.

Ethical quality judgments are likely to vary across communities, cities, regions, and countries. What is acceptable speech in one state is often unacceptable in another. For instance, it is considered acceptable to criticize anyone in the United States, so long as your critique is accurate, but in Turkey, one is breaking the law if one speaks ill of the state's founder, Ataturk. The same goes for those who would criticize the king in Thailand. What is perceived to be harmful to young people varies greatly by region, too. Many states allow pornographic images on ordinary television programs, for example, while others do not. Ordinarily, it comes down to social norms, which vary by community, to define acceptable forms of behavior and types of information that are permissible to be communicated to others.

Digital Natives are growing up in a world where information is much harder to contain in any given jurisdiction. On the Internet, a person in one country might publish something online that someone in another country could instantly access, but that would violate the community norms in his region. Neither law nor technology has worked very well to protect the receiver in the second state from seeing the information conveyed by the first. This global phenomenon—that most information, regardless of its ethical quality, can be published from anywhere on the planet and is accessible more or less everywhere else—places further pressure on Digital Natives to make good decisions about what information to believe and what to discard.

Information quality varies not only in terms of accuracy, timeliness, and objectivity. Depending on the type of information, there's also a values-based dimension associated with it. Pornography or hate speech on the Internet obviously does not raise issues of accuracy or reliability so much as they raise issues of normative criteria like morality, mutual respect, fairness, and freedom from malfeasance. And although it might be tricky to reach a broad consensus about the "facts-related" quality of a given piece of information, given the many different contexts in which it might be received, it's even harder to determine whether a given bit of information is ethically acceptable in a given community. The Internet only makes these age-old challenges trickier to meet.[28]

There's a raging debate about what to do about information quality on the Web. Some argue that the answer is greater professionalism online, just as in the case of the *Encyclopaedia Britannica* and other traditional forms of media. Others contend that the Internet is self-healing, as

Wikipedia is, and that a combination of technological innovations and social techniques will lead to better information over time. In the strong form of this argument, the Web enables anyone to sort ideas and information better than ever before by finding the connections and relationships that separate the information wheat from the chaff.[29]

This debate animates the various approaches to dealing with information quality and how to support Digital Natives as they make their way through an increasingly complex, digitally mediated world. There's a spectrum of approaches, with laissez-faire on one end and an information order approach on the other.

Proponents of the laissez-faire approach believe that information quality should not be regulated in any way. They argue that tussles over the quality of digital content—like the Seigenthaler controversy—are merely transitional. These problems will be resolved through the marketplace of ideas over time. The right "level" of quality will be determined through competition between good and bad content. Law has little role to play here. Also, commercial players like Google or YouTube would not intervene directly. Rather, they would improve the capacity of their services—for example, by increasing the number of indexed websites, news feeds, and the like—and leave it to the end user to make any form of quality assessment.

At the other end of the spectrum, some argue for substantial interventions by the state or other institutional players to improve the quality of information online. The advocates of this approach don't trust the marketplace of ideas. In fact, they argue that there is an acute and harmful *market failure* when it comes to information quality (the fact that kids have a very hard time making fully informed decisions is a good example), which in turn calls for a set of rules, standards, and principles we can use to make sure there is high-quality information available on the Web. They therefore argue that governments should play an active role in regulating information quality on the Internet. If this approach were taken, laws and regulation would be put into place in order to promote a high level of quality, on the one hand, and to fight undesirable content—such as hate speech or pornography—on the other. Under such a regime, the state might impose an obligation on ISPs to block and filter certain kinds of low-quality content, but also provide—for instance, through a state-owned media enterprise—a digital "service public" to its citizens.[30]

Neither of the extreme approaches makes sense for dealing with the complex information-quality challenges we face in the digital age. This is one of the issues societies have always grappled with. But there is a fair amount that can be done to improve information quality in the digital age. The best approach to shaping our information ecosystem is somewhere in the middle of the spectrum between laissez-faire and fully interventionist.

But what is the effective middle ground when it comes to dealing with information quality online? The answer is to empower communities to improve the quality of information found online. In structural terms, this means establishing a model of distributed governance. Under this approach, no single force would be in charge of creating a robust information-quality environment. Neither would the development of such an environment be left to the free market alone. Instead, what's needed is a blended regulatory approach under which all categories of key stakeholders and actors, private and public, would play a role in creating a viable information ecosystem. The goal is to establish adequate mechanisms and institutions to deal with information quality issues in the digital age.[31]

As with the other hard problems in this book, many actors—parents, teachers, coaches, companies, lawmakers—need to work together to make progress on this highly distributed problem. This blended approach would involve a private component—Digital Natives, their peers, and their parents—and a public component. The public components would include various actors turning to the four modes of online regulation: markets, social norms, code, and law.

Markets

Markets need to play a role, but not nearly so great a role as purists believe, in taking care of the quality problem. That's the theory of the "marketplace of ideas." Information goods are valued and traded like other goods in a marketplace, the theory goes, and the market works more or less efficiently. Everyone—including but not limited to Digital Natives—examines, compares, evaluates, and finally chooses among different pieces of information, whether news, health information, or information about any other topic, in any medium. In this process, they try to achieve the best value for the costs that they incur, whether those costs are financial, time-related, or measured some other way. Only the best information will survive as we pick out information with the best value/cost ratio.

Although this idea sounds compelling as a theory, it doesn't work in practice for most people. It may work for the most astute Digital Natives, but it's pretty clear from our conversations with young people that it will not suffice as a complete solution for most of them. Research shows that adults, too, have a hard time determining the quality of a given piece of information—and whether this level of quality actually meets their needs.

People can only evaluate the quality of a given piece of information after consuming it, not before. It's called an "experience good." To give an example: We can only evaluate the quality of an article about cancer by reading through it. The author—the creator of the work—knows much more about the quality of the article than any reader could, even after the reader has read it. It is very hard to assess the quality of a piece of health information before experiencing it, and sometimes, even after experiencing it. How can one determine how much the author knew while writing it? There's an information asymmetry—a phenomenon that may lead to the failure of the marketplace of ideas.

Reputation and rating systems can help to mitigate these problems with the pure market solution to information-quality problems. And these systems are key elements of many Web 2.0 applications. Reputation and rating systems are used in commercial and noncommercial settings alike.[32]

Rating systems allow users to build an opinion about the quality of the digital content they're interested in—content like books, video clips, music, expert advice, online magazines, health information, and so on—without the need to experience the quality by consuming it. When a user logs in to YouTube and watches a video, that user can post comments and responses and rate it with up to five stars. YouTube's system aggregates user feedback with all the other feedback received from the viewers of the clip and disclosed to all the other YouTube users. Another example: AllExperts.com, a free Q&A service on the Web, offers expert knowledge in return for expert rating. Each profile shows an expert's general prestige

and average ratings from other users of the service based on quality criteria such as clarity of advice, timeliness, expertise, and other factors. There
are dozens of other examples of rating systems that function in similar
ways, ranging from the online magazine Slashdot to Apple's iTunes Store
or Amazon and eBay. The market, in short, is coming up with some very
intriguing mechanisms to solve some of its own problems.

Quality labels and trustmarks also help to mitigate the problems of the
marketplace of ideas. As in the offline world, labels—and brands—in cyberspace convey information about the characteristics, components, or effects of a product or service. In the online world, however, labels are used
for different purposes. For example, they may be designed to signal the
accuracy of information. Other labels are used to ensure compliance with
e-commerce rules and regulations. Yet another category of labels is used
to rate the content of websites to protect minors from harmful content.
And so forth. Often, certification or accreditation programs provide such
labels and make sure that the products or services deserve the certificate
they get. Among these accreditation and certification programs, to name
just one example, is the American Accreditation HealthCare Commission
(URAC), an independent nonprofit organization that advocates for higher
quality health-care information on the Web. So, for instance, if a teenage
girl went to www.kidshealth.com, which is accredited by URAC, to learn
more about the antihistamines that her physician prescribed, she'd have a
better chance of getting more accurate information than if she went to a site
that was not accredited, because URAC sets forth rigorous quality and accountability standards for health-care providers.

Deploying rating systems and certification programs makes all manner
of sense. These two promising sorts of mechanisms can take us much of
the way toward a solution to information-quality issues on the Web, especially if they work in step with one another. Even within these two categories, however, one can see a tension. On one side there is a reliance on
what the professionals approve of and recommend; on the other, there is
an amateur-oriented approach that allows ordinary people to decide what
is good or not-so-good. Certification relies on a few experts making quality decisions. Reputation or rating systems tend to rely on a broad set of
amateurs making decisions and use advanced technologies to aggregate

the crowd's wisdom. Certification programs are expensive, hard to scale, and often have a more difficult time gaining consumer acceptance than do reputation systems. Reputation systems are especially popular among both younger users and experienced users. They are a key part of the feedback loop that Digital Natives are so fond of.[33] Those less familiar with the Web, and less likely to participate themselves, may prefer the stamp of approval that a trusted organization can convey. Together, these two approaches offer great promise.

Social Norms

Social norms, here as elsewhere, have a crucial role to play in solving the problems of digital information quality. Norms are important forces that shape the behavior of online communications—ranging from e-mail to weblogs and virtual world behavior. In some instances, social norms are so effective that they even overwrite legal norms, as they do in the peer-to-peer file-sharing context. The same types of norms can also promote the creation of high-quality information.

Take a Digital Native, for instance, who decides to edit an article on Wikipedia about a controversial candidate for the local mayor's office. She recently met the candidate and didn't like him at all. The first thing the Digital Native would learn is that Wikipedia—although it doesn't have an editor-in-chief in the traditional sense—has policies and procedures in place that are designed to achieve the project's goal of creating a reliable and free encyclopedia. The most important norm is the broad adherence to the so-called neutral point of view (NPOV) policy, held by Wikipedians to be an official, "absolute and non-negotiable" Wikipedia policy. It requires "that articles should be written without bias, representing all views fairly."[34] This policy, like the other community norms, are developed and enforced by the members of the Wikipedia community.

The NPOV policy often, but not always, effectively governs information quality on Wikipedia. In the case of the article about the mayor, if she failed to describe the candidate and his achievements without biases, her edits to the article would be undone by other members of the Wikipedia community as soon as someone noticed the problem. If she violated this rule repeatedly, she could be excluded from the Wikipedia community and prohibited from making further contributions.[35]

Norms within the Wikipedia community also help to resolve quality disputes among users. The Wikipedia community adheres to formal procedures to resolve such disputes. In cases where disputes cannot be resolved in discussion forums, a mediation committee can be called in to facilitate, and an arbitration committee deals with the most serious cases and violations. The arbitration committee has the power to impose binding solutions, including banning certain individuals from editing Wikipedia articles. Wikipedia founder Jimmy Wales has the ultimate veto right and can reverse the committee's decision. Don't like his decision? That's just how it goes.

Some online community norms work better than others to govern information quality. Not all norms are much of a constraint. But in strong communities, where norms are clear and participants adhere to them, they can be very powerful. Digital Natives often participate in such communities, whether in World of Warcraft or on Slashdot (for computer geeks). Community norms online are associated with different levels of specificity, formality, and enforcement schemes. They range from codes of conduct for bloggers to "Netiquette" and usually work best in online communities where the members have close ties (close-knit or "intermediate-knit" groups, as researchers call it). Whatever you call them, it is these types of groups that develop the community norms that are most helpful in terms of information quality. As these norms take hold, for example, some sources earn a reputation for higher credibility than others.

Code

Well-designed computer code can help Digital Natives and others make better judgments about information quality. Code generally governs activity in cyberspace more than any other force. Many of the mechanisms that Digital Natives might use to deal with the quality challenge are technologies invented or marketed by companies. Filtering software, kid-friendly browsers and services from ISPs, search engines for kids, and syndication and aggregation services are only a few cases in point. The design and development of new interfaces that take into account the heuristics used by Digital Natives when they make quality judgments is another crucial area of future work.

The current market environment sets strong incentives for companies to develop kid-friendly technology and, ultimately, to help them find high-quality content. But not all producers of content are yet doing enough to clarify when their own content is appropriate for children, much less to indicate the quality or credibility of the information they publish. Beyond market incentives, it also seems within the bounds of corporate social responsibility to help address the legitimate quality concerns that many parents of Digital Natives have. Quality-enhancing initiatives by leading Web 2.0 services, including, for instance, MySpace and Facebook, are pointing in the right direction.

More than half of the Internet-connected families with teenagers use a single type of technology—filters—to protect their children from harmful and objectionable online content.[36] That number is growing. One survey found that filters tend to be used by parents who themselves use the Internet frequently, especially parents of middle-schoolers. Filters can be located directly on the individual computer and may take the form of a kid-friendly Web browser, or software such as NetNanny and CyberPatrol, which work with standard Web browsers like Firefox or Internet Explorer. Server-side filters, by contrast, reside not on the individual computer, but on the server of the network itself. They provide roughly the same level of filtering for all the users of a network.

Filtering means delegating to others the task of figuring out what a young person should see or not see online. The core task, for the company providing the service, is to compile a black list of websites (usually, URLs) that will be blocked. In other cases, the company comes up with keyword lists. In this model, the filtering program scans the Web and identifies objectionable words—some of them context sensitive—then creates and updates a list of inappropriate sites based on this information. Internet content rating is a third method. Here, the filters work hand in hand with content-rating systems that qualify Web content, often based on questionnaires. With the results, the system can provide machine-readable labels to the website provider that can be read and interpreted by the filtering programs. Microsoft's Internet Explorer, for instance, provides a filtering function called "Content Advisor" that, among other things, recognizes the respective labels of the Internet Content Rating Association (ICRA), one of the most prominent self-rating systems for online content. The primary problem with filtering outside the home is that someone else makes the decision as to what a user should and shouldn't see. An ancillary problem is that Internet filtering is always either underinclusive or overinclusive. No technological approach yet developed is perfect.[37]

Filtering technology is one example—albeit a highly imperfect one—of how code can help us to deal with the information-quality challenge outlined in this chapter. Though filtering is designed to ensure a certain level of quality and usually addresses the ethical dimension of the quality problem, other technological innovations have a broader impact. Other technologies are much more promising and bring less baggage with them.

Search engines, the wildly powerful gatekeepers of the digital world, play the greatest role today in sorting what most Digital Natives and others see online from what they don't see. Search engines increasingly influence what information we will "consume." The advancement in search technology has already vastly improved the quality of the Internet experience for most users. In particular, the latest generation of search engines helps us to deal with one of the core characteristics of information quality: its contextual nature. These cutting-edge search engines learn from our search behavior and that of like-minded peers. They are increasingly personalized services that "know" about our informational needs and quality requirements and make adjustments to results over time based on these behaviors. Even if a single Web searcher does not make good information choices, over time, the theory goes, preferences will reveal much about the reliability of online information sources that can inform future search results.

Search engines specially designed for kids have emerged, too. The search engine "Ask for Kids," for example, is a natural-language search tool for children that allows them to ask questions and perform Web searches, and that in turn provides answers that have been vetted for appropriateness. Yahooligans, another search engine of this type, is designed for children aged seven to twelve. It prevents objectionable sites from being displayed and bans adult-oriented banner advertising.

The market for digital searching is highly robust. The runaway success of Google (and Lycos, Yahoo!, Ask, and others before them) has ensured that better and better technologies are forthcoming all the time. Future search technologies are certain to make further important contributions to our experiences on the Internet.

Like search engines, content syndication and aggregation tools allow Digital Natives to sort through information online based on quality judgments made over time. Digital Natives want to be up to speed when it comes to the topics they're interested in. They may read literally hundreds of blogs from authors around the world. How can they keep up with all the new blog posts, you might wonder? They essentially "subscribe" to the blogs they're interested in and have short descriptions of new posts ("blurbs") automatically delivered to them via RSS technology. MyYahoo! and Bloglines offer simple versions of this service. This type of application, which collects RSS feeds from various sources in certain intervals, is called an "aggregator." Aggregators not only eliminate the need to check whether new content has been posted on a website but also provide additional features (such as keyword filtering) that help to design a personalized information environment.

Although no single innovation could fix all the quality problems on the Internet, there's much we can do using technology to address the information-quality challenge. Search technology, syndication, and aggregation, especially when combined with ratings and recommendation technologies, are promising. These tools work best when they can blend the aggregated human judgment—the wisdom of the crowds—with the best technical approaches.

We should never underestimate Digital Natives' willingness to learn about the challenges they face online and their ability to adjust to them. The most sophisticated kids we've talked to are using rating systems, content aggregators, and applications that can help to create an information niche with an appropriate level of information quality. But many young people are completely unfamiliar with the tools most helpful for sorting wheat from chaff online. Many tools are limited because they are poorly designed for use by anyone who is not a serious nerd; they too often require a high degree of technical skill.

Code can be used for harmful ends as well as helpful ones, and this complicates its role in the information-quality debate. Many young people, as we learned in our focus groups—particularly the youngest or least sophisticated about technologies—use search engines as a crutch: Whatever comes up first in Google must be accurate. Syndication and aggregation technologies may just encourage people to surround themselves with information they agree with—the problem of the "Daily Me." As wonderful as digital technologies are, we shouldn't let ourselves be fooled into thinking that any technology can single-handedly solve any problem as multifaceted as the information-quality problem.

Law

Law should be the last resort for dealing with online information-quality problems, and many approaches to solving these problems through law should be avoided entirely. In particular, new laws that seek to make *ex ante* regulations—regulations that prohibit certain kinds of things from being published—are not promising in this context. In the United States, these laws have a hard time passing constitutional muster, and with good reason: It's extremely hard to write a law that will block someone from saying something before they say it without prohibiting lots of speech that is protected by the First Amendment.[38]

That said, lawmakers still have a role to play. Depending on the legal tradition and cultural context, lawmakers may want to legislate by setting some minimum standards when it comes to online information. The Council of Europe's Cybercrime Convention is a good illustration of this type of legislation. Many similar laws across Europe achieve a standard-setting function by banning, for instance, extreme forms of violence or prohibiting kids' exposure to hard-core pornography.

The law can help address harms after the fact and can create incentives for people not to publish inaccurate information. Consider the Seigenthaler story. If Seigenthaler had decided to sue the station manager of the delivery service company in Nashville who manipulated the Wikipedia biography, the legal system would have had to deal with it. Liability for information that damages someone's reputation is a good example of *ex post* ("after the event") regulation. This type of law generally doesn't cause too much of a headache: For instance, one would be hard-pressed to come up with a good reason why defamation laws should not also apply to false statements of fact published on the Internet, assuming the traditional test for defamation is met. The same holds true for other forms of liability for false information. In these cases, law might in fact make a small contribution to the cause of trying to ensure higher levels of information quality than we now have online.

As a general rule, though, *ex ante* regulation to improve information quality through law should be avoided. These are instances where the law sets information-quality standards "in advance." By necessity, these standards are abstract. There are several reasons to disfavor this form of regulation.

First, laws are usually tied to local values, but the Internet is a global medium. It's very unlikely that an international consensus about "good" and "bad" information can ever be achieved. The application of varying national laws to information-quality problems with global reach would almost certainly lead to inadequate results. The enforcement of quality norms in the online world would be very difficult to carry out in any sort of consistent way, and in some cases, it would be impossible. The limits of national law-enforcement in a global network, as well as the user's ability to move to a jurisdiction with more relaxed information-quality regulations, are two impediments to using this approach. Finally, law is ill suited to dealing with information quality because information is so varied and comes from so many sources and perspectives; it has a strong subjective component and is highly contextual. Trying to regulate information quality by law would be like trying to nail Jell-O to the wall.[39] Law tends to be more abstract, devising general rules and remedies but with only limited means of taking specific contexts and subjective judgments into account.

Though we must not overestimate what law can achieve when it comes to information quality, there are extreme cases where the law may be very helpful, even in the form of *ex ante* regulation. The law may play its role best in extreme cases where there is broad societal consensus, over a wide territory, that we want to protect young people (along with the rest of society) from very disturbing pictures, texts, posts, and the like. The Council of Europe's Cybercrime Convention, for example, allows the law to assure a certain absolute minimum standard for information quality by banning some of the ugliest forms of hate speech or pornography.

We can and should use each of the four primary modes of regulation—markets, norms, code, and law—to address the information-quality problem that Digital Natives, and all of us, face. The market, norms, and code should have large roles, while the law should function as a backstop to cover extreme cases and to enable people harmed by low-quality information to achieve just outcomes. If information quality is to improve in our digital era, many people will have to use these modes in concert.

For the time being, education is the best way to help Digital Natives manage the information-quality problem. Digital literacy is increasingly a critical skill for Digital Natives to learn. We are not yet doing what we can, or even what we need to do, to teach Digital Natives to be media literate in this new, more complex information environment.

A true laissez-faire approach, where we rely solely on the marketplace of ideas, isn't going to cut it, especially when it comes to young people. The way forward is to solve this issue from the bottom up, with education at the heart of the effort.

Through education, we need to pass along a healthy skepticism when it comes to any information, whether online, on the television, or accessed through any other medium. Digital Natives, like the rest of us, must develop the skills they need to analyze and cross-reference information before they rely upon it in any way that matters. The ability to separate credible information from less credible information, especially in the digital environment where a new and different set of cues is at work, is too rarely addressed in the curricula our children encounter, and it needs to be. Our Digital Natives will succeed wildly if they can synthesize the information they find in the digital world; too many of them will founder if they cannot.

Parents and other family members can make the crucial difference in terms of helping young people to assess information quality on their own. Tools like kid-friendly browsers that parents can install on their home computers to protect their children from inappropriate content help a good deal, for starters. It's clear, though, that the use of technology alone is not enough. We as parents need to *care* about the Internet usage habits of our children. We need to learn about the kinds of pages they visit, to hear about both their positive and negative online experiences, and to establish rules or make informal agreements where necessary. In other words, we as parents need to learn, listen, and get involved in an active way in order to help our kids navigate the Internet successfully.

Teachers also bear an enormous responsibility when it comes to the information-quality challenge faced by those born digital. Despite good intentions and promising initiatives, media and information literacy curricula have yet to be widely deployed. This step is necessary if we're to be successful in preparing young people to handle the challenges of information quality online. Many current training programs for teachers focus on the use of checklists that are meant to guide Digital Natives through the quality-evaluation process. These quality checklists are limited in their usefulness. They are too often ignored by students when learning on their own. While the checklist approach certainly has its place in the curriculum, it seems crucial to work with multiple methods—taking into account children's level of cognitive development, their interests, habits, and heuristics—as part of more comprehensive educational strategies aimed at strengthening Digital Natives' skills to critically evaluate the quality of online information. Such a strategy would not only address the problem of credibility but also provide guidelines and help with regard to other aspects of information quality, including ethical issues. We as parents should make a strong case that such programs should be developed at our kids' schools, beyond experiments and pilot studies. We don't have a second-best option on this score.[40]

Parents, teachers, and Digital Natives shouldn't have to go it alone. The state can't solve the problem, but it certainly can help. Given the great importance of education and media literacy programs, governments should make an extra effort to push this agenda and allocate the resources necessary to build and run such programs. Very few schools have even considered adding digital literacy to their curricula, much less started to do so.

The government can also become part of the solution itself through the digital information it produces. Nearly every local government has a website, but these vary enormously in terms of what they provide. By establishing procedures that ensure the quality of public-sector information, governments actively contribute to a high-quality information environment. The government should also support high-quality public broadcasting services that use the Internet—digital "service publics"—to play a role much like the one the BBC plays with its online offerings in Great Britain. These approaches would ensure that there was quality information available on a broad range of topics for Digital Natives, while also serving the information needs of the rest of society.[41]

Fundamentally, parents and educators are best positioned to help kids deal with information-quality issues. Children need to be taught critical thinking in general. Evidence suggests that as they learn these skills, they are better able to make assessments of information online as well as offline. We don't need to teach them anything fundamentally new. But the need for critical thinking is even greater now than it was twenty years ago, when kids had library cards instead of Web access. The material at the library was already hand-picked for its suitability and accuracy. We need to be teaching kids these skills earlier, and in ways that work for them in the digital environment as well as in traditional environments.

8

OVERLOAD

I think the reason why print magazines are still very popular is because you kind of have the feeling, okay, this is like one issue, and this is what happened this week. And on the Internet . . . there's no beginning and no end.

—HARVARD STUDENT, EIGHTEEN YEARS OLD

I N 2007 ALONE, 1,288 X 10^{18} BITS, OR 161 BILLION GIGABYTES, OF DIG-
ital content were created, stored, and replicated around the world. In lay terms, that's 3 million times the amount of information in all the books ever written, or twelve stacks of books reaching from the Earth to the Sun, or six tons of books for every living person. It would require 2 billion of the highest-capacity iPods to store all of that information. In 2003, researchers estimated the world's information production to be around 5 billion gigabytes. Current reports predict that the world will generate 988 billion gigabytes of digital information in 2010. Most astonishing of all is not the absolute size of the information environment, but the rate of

growth. Every year, the amount of digital information grows even more rapidly than in the year before.[1]

These gigabytes are a product of the billions of Web pages and sites run by millions of companies, nongovernmental organizations (NGOs), governments, universities, and ordinary people. Google, for instance, had indexed more than 6 billion items on the Web by 2004, including over 8 billion Web pages, 1.19 billion images, and 845 million Usenet messages. Blog search engine Technorati is currently tracking 105.6 million blogs— roughly 120,000 new ones are created worldwide each day—and more than 250 million pieces of tagged social media on platforms such as Photobucket and YouTube.[2]

The amount of information available on the Web is staggering—and potentially debilitating. There are limits, in cognitive terms, to how much information people can process. A person's short-term memory, for instance, can hold roughly seven items at once. Our minds have an estimated maximum processing capacity of 126 bits per second. Clearly, there is an enormous gap between the growing sea of information, on the one hand, and limited human attention and information-processing capacity, on the other. Digital Natives are learning to cope with this gap, but it is a long and slow process for even the most sophisticated Internet users.

There are certain risks to be considered if the strategies and technologies designed to help us cope with these enormous amounts of digital content fail. Internet addiction, information fatigue syndrome, and information overload are among the terms being thrown around to describe the new psychological diseases of the digital age. To some, these new threats mark the dark side of the brave new world with an ever-growing amount and diversity of information.

Information overload is a very real and uncomfortable phenomenon, and there's still a great deal that researchers don't know about its effects on young people. It's true that the sheer amount of information available in digital format can be overwhelming. The constant use of digital technologies can place a strain on families, friendships, and classrooms. And it sure makes for some shocking headlines. Some news accounts stretch the truth to suggest that its extreme form—Internet addiction—is a major health hazard for most Digital Natives. Even if information overload does prove to be a societal concern over time, there may be ways to mitigate its effects. Some of these, particularly the community-oriented approaches, could work if we decided to invest in fighting the problems that accompany the wealth of information that we have at our disposal in the digital era.

S ome recent headlines from around the world:

- "A South Korean games addict died after playing nonstop for 86 hours."[3]
- "An overweight 26-year-old man from north-eastern China has died after a ceaseless gaming session over the Lunar New Year holiday."[4]
- "A 30-year-old man has died in the south China province of Guangzhou after apparently playing an online game continuously for three days."[5]

Internet addiction is the extreme form of information overload. As with extreme cases of any other type, it gets more than its fair share of attention. Especially in East Asia, there is a growing worry about the effects of the digital information environment on the health and mental well-being of children. Particularly at risk, it appears, are "gamers"—those young people who play a lot of video games and their close cousin, online games. A 2007 poll found that 8.5 percent of youth gamers in the United States could be classified as pathologically addicted to playing video games.[6] In an online British study that same year, 12 percent of gamers demonstrated addictive behavior.[7] In summer 2006, the first inpatient clinic for computer game addicts in Europe opened its doors;[8] Korea, meanwhile, already has more than forty game-addiction counseling agencies registering thousands of cases per year.[9] According to government estimates reported in the press in 2006, 2.4 percent of South Koreans aged nine to thirty-nine are addicts, and another 10.2 percent are borderline cases.[10] In June 2007, the American Medical Association (AMA) debated whether video-game overuse should be considered an addiction. The organization ultimately decided not to formally designate it as such; the measure it adopted instead did say, however, that playing too many computer games has become a problem for many people, both children and adults. In a study released in 2006, Stanford University researchers reported that 13.7 percent of the adults they interviewed said they found it difficult to stay away from the Internet for several days at a time. According to the same study, 8.2 percent said they used the Internet as a way to escape problems or relieve negative moods.[11]

Clinicians have begun to develop diagnostic criteria to determine whether a child is at risk for Internet addiction. The types of questions make intuitive sense. Does the child feel preoccupied with the Internet, anticipating the next session online? Does the amount of time required to feel satisfied seem to grow? Does he or she lie about time spent online to deceive friends or family members? Has Internet usage jeopardized relationships? These types of questions can help clinicians and parents determine whether limits need to be set for Internet usage, or, more radically, whether treatment may be in order.[12]

Psychologists distinguish between "specific" pathological use of the Internet and "generalized" pathological use. Specific pathological use refers to a fixation on a particular aspect of Internet use, such as online gambling or pornography. Generalized pathological use, in contrast, involves a more general dependency or obsession with use of the Internet, which may, however, manifest itself with respect to a particular function of the medium, such as chat rooms, e-mail, or Web-surfing in general.[13]

The increasing power and attractiveness of the Internet for purposes like escape and self-expression is part of the problem for some young people. The Internet's interactive quality leads some Digital Natives to prefer their "second life" to their first. For some, the Internet allows for escape from the frustrations of real life. Internet use can turn into a coping strategy, especially in the case of online gaming addictions. Young people who have a preexisting disposition or psychopathology, such as depression, social anxiety, or substance dependence, are at particular risk.[14] Some young people become overly focused on their online selves. Research suggests that some may also overgeneralize specific positive events associated with

Internet use, which can cause them to develop the belief that *only* the Internet holds positive experiences for their lives.[15]

There is no single, reliable, global study that proves that a certain percentage of children and teenagers are, in fact, "addicted" to the Internet. Online addiction significantly affects some Digital Natives, and it will no doubt remain an item on the policy agenda in the years to come.[16] In the German-speaking part of Europe, experts recognize Internet addiction as a particular problem of young users. Specialized treatment centers have begun to treat addicts to online games, chatting, or Web-surfing. According to a recent study that involved a systematic look at the treatment outcomes with Internet addicts, cognitive behavioral therapy is the most promising approach.[17] Much work remains to be done to understand how Internet addiction works and how to treat specific cases.

Though there's not enough hard evidence to put Internet addiction at the top of the list of things that we worry about, there are less dramatic aspects of information overload that are worth paying close attention to in the years to come. These problems don't make headlines, but they do merit serious thought. How to prepare our kids to combat them is the most serious question, since the information environment isn't getting any smaller.

Information overload may seem particularly acute in the digital era, but concerns about it are not new. In the 1950s, cognitive psychologists researched the limited capacity of the human mind when it comes to short-term memory. These studies yielded some valuable insights. Among the most famous ideas to come from them is the notion that we can only keep roughly seven items at once in our working memories.[18] Around the same period, sociologists started to describe the information overload phenomenon as such based on observations of people living in large cities.[19] One sociologist found that residents of cities had less capacity to react to new situations with the same energy as they once had; evidently, they had developed a filter for information and stimuli.[20] Because they were bombarded with so much information, they became desensitized as they sought to shield themselves from excessive stimuli in the form of media, ideas, communication, and so forth. In the pre-Internet days, researchers characterized this as the "disease of cities."[21] It was a disease where the ability to make decisions was jammed by the clamor for attention of so many forms of information.[22]

Research conducted since the mid-1970s has examined the phenomenon of information overload more closely. Broadly defined, information overload occurs when the amount of information that is available exceeds a person's ability to process it (he or she is "receiving too much information"). It's no surprise to anyone who spends time online that the explosion of the Internet dramatically increased the possibility of overload, and in recent years the problem has become both widespread and more recognized. And it's not only that the amount of information has exploded. The availability of just-in-time, highly relevant information, often accessed on devices like cell phones and Sidekicks (or, for professionals, BlackBerries), which are located on our bodies at all times, has also become crucial for economic survival in a modern society. Digital Natives both experience overload and contribute to it inasmuch as they have a penchant for creating information online.

The formal research about kids and information overload is thin. Most research has focused on information overload in the lives of adults. There is promise, though, in a strand of research initially published in 1998, through which scholars have started to investigate whether children have experienced information overload situations as well. One survey of Texas elementary school students, for instance, showed that at least 80 percent of fourth-graders and eighth-graders had experienced information overload—girls and fourth-graders being more likely to suffer from it than boys and eighth-graders.[23]

The effects of information overload, in the worst cases, can be severe. They range from increased heart rates, increased blood cholesterol, migraines, and retarded reading skills to reduced attention span or restlessness, among other symptoms. The negative effects of having too much information amount to what's called "technostress." In addition to psychological impacts, technostress can have secondary physical effects. Technostress can diminish one's well-being, decrease one's appetite, cause insomnia, suppress immune functions, and so forth.

It's no surprise that parents worry about children suffering from such symptoms. Information overload can seem threatening. In the survey of students at the Texas elementary school, some students described experiencing feelings such as confusion and frustration when overloaded; others reported being mad, angry, or furious. Indeed, psychological effects like stress, anxiety, depression, low motivation, and sometimes even panic rank high among the consequences described in the overload literature.[24] Information overload can adversely affect learning as well. Several studies have suggested that information overload reduces children's attention spans, leads to frustration in children, and ultimately lowers their level of motivation.

The unprecedented amount of digital information and the means of coping with it may have a negative impact on Digital Natives' relationships. As a general matter, survey data suggest that those who have more interactions online tend to have more intense face-to-face interactions than those who do not engage in so much online interaction.[25] However, kids who spend a large amount of time on their Sidekicks, or instant messaging with friends, can strain social relations, particularly in families.[26] The lure of digital communications can undercut family time. Multitasking may prove to be one of the most dramatic areas of change in family interaction within the past few decades.[27]

Although children and teenagers are, on average, spending more and more time on the Internet every year, there is no evidence that they have simultaneously cut back on the hours they spend with traditional media like TV, music, or print. By multitasking, Digital Natives have simply come to consume more media content in the same period of time.[28] One study released in 2005 showed that nearly one-third of young people either talk on the phone, use instant messaging, watch TV, listen to music, or surf the Web for fun "most of the time" that they're doing homework—and the trend is growing.[29] Multitasking tends to be bad for learning (though there are a few exceptions). According to psychologists, kids learn better if they pay full attention to the things they want to remember. Recently, the adverse effect of multitasking on children's ability to learn new facts and concepts has been supported by brain-imaging studies.[30]

The jury is still out on whether the higher levels of distraction associated with multitasking are outweighed by the overall gains in productivity from the use of digital technologies. In one study, for instance, researchers examined the effects of multitasking in the classroom. Students in one group were allowed to use their laptops during the lectures, while those in another group were not. While the group of students with laptops was obviously distracted by having access to the Web, e-mail, IM, and other digital tools, traditional tests of memory revealed that their performance in the class overall was not adversely affected by the disruption. Other factors—including class structure, dynamics, and "expertise" in multitasking—apparently also played a role in determining the impact of multitasking on learning.[31]

One of the primary reasons to be concerned about too much information being accessible to young people is the possibility of negative effects on decision-making. An individual's ability to make adequate decisions heavily depends on the amount of information that person is exposed to. Life experience suggests that more information increases the overall quality of decisions. If a decision-maker gets too little information, he or she can't see the full picture and runs the risk of making a decision without having taken important information into account. But the positive correlation between the amount of information and the quality of decision-making has limitations. At some point, additional information cannot be processed and integrated. In fact, the extra information may result in information overload, with consequences that include confusion, frustration, panic, or even paralysis. Like the rest of us, young people face the paradox of choice. As behavioral economics teaches, the more the options, the greater the chance that a person will make no decision at all, as studies have shown in many different contexts.[32]

Information overload limits the ability of young people to make good decisions in some contexts. One study confirmed this limiting effect on cognition among Web-surfing students between the ages of fourteen and sixteen years old.[33] In particular, websites with a lot of text can cause young people to feel overloaded, according to the study. Text-only sites are often left unexplored (again, no surprise).[34] To make the relationship between "amount of information" and "decision quality" even more complicated, recall that websites with large amounts of information are often considered to be more accurate than sites with less information. The one common finding of these studies is that too much information leads to suboptimal decision-making by Digital Natives and others.

There are five general causes of information overload, several of which suggest that young people may be more at risk than older people of suffering its effects.[35] First, the development and use of information technologies— everything from the high storage capacity of computer systems to the proliferation of television and cable channels and the explosion of the Web itself—is what has made information overload possible. Digital Natives, as we've seen, often spend large amounts of time online. E-mail, in particular, is often cited as a source of information glut. Second, in the management context, the organizational design and workflow of a company are drivers of information overload. As traditional corporate hierarchies break down, and as the popularity of e-mail continues to increase, more people share ever more information with more and more colleagues. The rise of interdisciplinary teams only exacerbates this problem, as more people need to be kept in the loop than ever before. The decentralization of management structures can increase the amount of information that needs to be processed. Third, the nature of the tasks that someone undertakes may lead to information overload. The newer and more complex the task, and the greater the amount of information that needs to be taken into account in order to perform it, the more likely it becomes that a person will suffer from overload symptoms. Fourth, the varying quality of information matters, too. Uncertain, ambiguous, or complex information might contribute to information-overload symptoms. Last, factors such as personal skills, qualifications, experience, and motivation are important elements that determine whether—or, more precisely, when—information overload occurs. This last cause is the most important.

Many of these factors apply to young people as aptly as they do to adults, or even more so, in some cases. Younger kids with lower skill levels and less experience, for instance, are more likely to suffer from information overload than their Digital Native peers are—despite the fact that Digital Natives likely spend more time online.[36] The technological environment, the quality of information, and the complexity of the task to be completed can be determining factors. Even organizational factors may play a role, when we think of schools and curriculum design.[37]

Information overload is a fast-growing problem in the digital age. There is no end in sight to the growth of the amount of information and the frequency with which we tend to access it. For young people who are just learning about the world, this trend is reason for concern. Even if there's no data to suggest that there is a major health or other societal issue at the moment, the hallmarks of a big problem in the making are plain. It makes sense to step in front of this problem before it grows too large to handle—or, better yet, to put Digital Natives in a position to solve it for themselves over time.

Young people growing up in a digital era, whether or not they are Digital Natives, will face information overload throughout their lives. We must, of course, provide them with the skills and tools they need to *avoid* information overload in the first place. But we also need to develop strategies that will be effective against information overload when it inevitably occurs.

The research on how people cope with life in big cities, conducted by sociologists and psychologists, offers helpful starting points. American psychologist Stanley Milgram was among the pioneers of the field. He addressed the psychological effects of what he called, in an article title, "The Experience of Living in the Cities" in great detail, identifying several reaction patterns people tend to have in response to heavy information load. Milgram's contribution, among other things, was to focus our attention on the allocation of less time to each piece of information, the use of filtering devices, and the creation of specially designed institutions to absorb inputs.[38]

Since Milgram's time, researchers have identified other coping strategies that work for some people, but which come at certain costs. One study of early Internet communities, called Usenet groups, has shown that users are more likely to respond to simpler messages in overload situations; they are more likely to end active participation if they receive too much information; and they are more likely to generate simpler messages as overload increases.[39] Studies involving online learning have also often found that certain users end up printing out online materials in an attempt to reduce overload. The process of using technology to interface with educational content inevitably produces distractions from the most relevant information required for the desired learning process. As a simple coping mechanism, students who experience overload sometimes benefit from printing materials in order to eliminate the distractions of the technology. The cost to the environment of the extra printer paper will likely be offset by the gains in terms of the Digital Native's sanity.[40]

By necessity, everyone practices simple filtering mechanisms. We ignore certain information because of its source, its form, or its apparent contents. A 2003 study involving young people in Flanders found that many young Internet users tend to limit the number of websites they visit in order to avoid information overload. We have seen this same dynamic in our own conversations with young people.

The problem with our tendency to favor some sources of information online over others is that it gives certain websites much more influence than others. Studies show that very few Internet sites get attention from very many people, and the vast majority of sites get very little attention from anyone. In economic terms, attention online takes the form of a power-law, or Pareto, distribution. This power-law distribution is popularly referred to as the "80/20 rule." That is, in the Internet context, we might expect that roughly only 20 percent of the available websites will receive 80 percent of all Web traffic. One famous study of weblogs found that, out of 433 weblogs, the top 2 sites (that's 0.46 percent of the weblogs studied) received 5 percent of all inbound links. The 12 most popular blogs (less than 3 percent of the total) received 20 percent of all inbound links. And the 50 most popular sites (still less than 12 percent of the total) accounted for 50 percent of inbound links.[41]

Most blogs, which are usually written by amateur creators rather than professional journalists, receive little or no attention from the vast majority of Internet users. Given this fact, one might question whether there really is an information-overload problem at all; people seem to find their way to useful information and to ignore the extraneous. However, the fact that perhaps only 20 percent of the weblogs in existence will receive the most attention does not change the fact that there are many weblogs available to readers with a great deal of information of a diverse nature. And any one of the weblogs within the "long tail" represented by the other 80 percent may hold the information that a particular Web surfer is seeking at a given point in time. On the flip side, many weblogs would indeed prove to be red herrings that distracted the surfer from the information he was seeking. The power-law distribution among weblogs is an expression of one of the natural coping strategies for the information glut—namely, the tendency to ignore a great deal of the information available.

In addition to ignoring and filtering out certain information, children use strategies that researchers have given unusual names, like "chunking" and "twigging," to avoid information overload. The Texas elementary school study revealed that a typical fourth-grader will first choose material fitting criteria they've set for themselves. The student then is likely to "chunk" large amounts of information into a common shape. From there, the student often tries to compress the large chunk of information into something understandable, or to enlarge it in order to find commonalities. Students in the eighth grade preferred first to omit material, then to filter, and finally to chunk the information. The eighth-graders proved much more able than the fourth-graders to separate information they wanted from information they would ignore, making a decision on each piece as it reached their consciousness.[42]

Most, if not all, of the strategies used when information overload occurs share the shortcoming that some information will be lost. Even the most astute Digital Natives often can't tell whether information deserves to be ignored, rejected, or forgotten. This dynamic is the same whether they are doing research online or offline. The phenomenon has to do with a basic feature of information that we've mentioned before: It's an *experience good*. In order to tell whether or not information is relevant, important, and interesting, we need to process it. The most common responses to overload situations, however, are strategies designed just to avoid information processing; they therefore carry an inherent risk to the researcher of missing something that matters. This risk is usually not mitigated by deliberate selection of information.[43]

Kids as well as adults have bounded rationality when making information choices, as a mountain of research has shown.[44] Information-seeking has a strong affective component and is by no means only a cognitive activity. As we saw in the context of the information-quality debate, personal preferences shape information-seeking: Young people choose one website over another based on strong personal preferences such as color, design, sound, and likes or dislikes.[45] In one 1997 study, researchers discovered that fifth-graders basically ignored websites with more than one or two pages of text, focusing instead on sites with pictures and colorful graphics.[46]

The solutions we employ may also give rise, in turn, to new problems. The most prevalent concern—though much disputed—is whether young people will use these new filtering and searching technologies to surround themselves only with information that they are likely to agree with. Critics of the way the online environment is evolving worry that in the face of so much information, we may be encouraging our children to narrow their frame of vision rather than to expand it. The shorthand term for this problem, as we mentioned previously, is the "Daily Me." When traditional newspaper readers read the local paper cover to cover, they were confronted with the information that the editors felt they should see. Through careful selection by experts, or pure serendipity, readers were exposed to alternate viewpoints and topics that edified them. In the nightmare scenario, our young people, in coping with information overload, will use new technologies to tailor their information environment to their own preferences. They would rarely be confronted, in this conception, with information that challenged their viewpoint or forced them to think critically. While the evidence is inconclusive on this score, it is plainly something that we ought to keep in mind as we meet the challenge of information overload.

Digital Natives, like the rest of us, have found their own techniques for dealing with information overload. We have little choice in the matter: Every person must devise coping strategies. Though it's an imperfect solution for an imperfect world, one thing is clear: We are all learning to live with the onslaught of digital information. Most of the time, humans manage to adapt.

Technology plays an enormous role in the information-overload problem, but it can also be a major part of the solution to the problem. Digital Natives rely on technology, both consciously and unconsciously, to make choices among the billions of pieces of information available on the Internet. In this way, it helps them to cope with the information overload threat.

Search engines top the list of tools that Digital Natives, like the rest of us, use to deal with the massive amount of information now at our disposal online. Search tools were the first response to the digital information explosion. They've come a long way since "Archie"—the first pre-Web search tool—was developed in 1990 by a group of McGill University students. The first big breakthrough happened around 1994, when the first full-text search engine, called WebCrawler, was introduced. WebCrawler let users search for any word in any Web page and became popular within months. The powerful search engines we use today, including Google, Yahoo! Search, MSN Search, and A9, to name just a few, soon appeared.

The underlying technologies of search engines—web crawling, indexing, and searching—have become more sophisticated over time, allowing users to find the information they are looking for more precisely and efficiently every year. These engines are the invisible hands that help most Web users cope with the staggering amount of digital information available to them. First, they allow users to locate content conveniently based on self-defined search terms. In previous eras, the user had to know the exact title of the document he or she was looking for on the Internet, and extensive, exhaustive, and time-consuming browsing was required. But now, using Internet-era technologies, a word or two will turn up highly relevant information from around the world. Second, search engines help us to determine the relevance of a given piece of information without requiring that we experience it fully. The most prominent example of such a system is Google PageRank, which ranks Web pages essentially according to their popularity and determines the order in which the results are listed in response to a query. Viewed from that angle, search engines are important selection tools that allow Digital Natives and adults alike to quickly locate the information that seems most "relevant."[47] Search engines help Digital Natives pinpoint just a few websites among the billions that are available online in just moments—the latest news on a young person's favorite baseball team, for example, is just a few keystrokes away.

Syndication technologies work alongside search engines to help sophisticated users cope with information overload. A software protocol called Really Simple Syndication, or RSS, is designed to bring information to the user's attention even if the user is not really searching for it at the moment. If a website—for example, a news site, a blog, or a particular social network site—works with this protocol and offers an RSS feed, a user can "subscribe" to the feed in order to receive periodic updates from that source once new content has been added. All incoming feeds are then aggregated and displayed on a single page in the users' RSS reader. This type of push-technology eliminates the pressure on a Digital Native to check out his or her favorite websites continuously. Digital Natives may have dozens, if not hundreds, of favorite Web destinations. RSS makes it easy to locate all these sources into a single view, offering a free, best-of-the-Web home-delivery service. But even among the most sophisticated groups of Digital Natives, surprisingly few use RSS and related syndication and aggregation technologies yet.

A third, and increasingly important, mode of finding the "needle in the haystack" online is to use various types of recommendation systems. Sophisticated recommendation systems can help to mitigate information overload. Imagine, for example, that a teenager buys most of his books on Amazon.com. When he logs in to Amazon, he is greeted with a series of books and other items that a computer program thinks may appeal to him. He may also receive regular e-mails to suggest that he come to Amazon to see his recommendations. The recommendations that Amazon provides are based on various factors, including the types of books he has bought in the past and the purchases that other people with similar reading interests have made. Amazon's sophisticated recommendation engine, applying a system known as "collaborative filtering," saves the customer time and helps him fight information overload, because—if it's working well—he doesn't have to browse through millions of titles on Amazon to find his next book.

Another example of this sort of service is Digg.com, a website that draws news and information from around the Web to the attention of its users based on what other users enjoyed reading. Digg users submit digital content—everything ranging from news to images to podcasts and videos. Their peers (other Digg users) vote on how much they like what has been submitted. If a submission receives enough votes ("Diggs"), it is promoted to the front page of the popular portal and becomes visible for millions of visitors who come to the Digg.com homepage.[48]

These systems form part of what Silicon Valley people often call the "social web," a major force in fighting information overload. These recommendation engines come in various flavors, but the idea is the same: Find a group of people with similar interests (for example, music tastes) online and help them locate the content they're interested in. Thousands of eyes see more than two can. Recommendation and peer-review systems enable people to group items that are more likely to appeal to others. Through this process, the most salient pieces of information find their way to Internet portals and, over time, garner more attention as more people recommend them to others.[49] StyleFeeder users do the same for clothing and other fashion items, iTunes users do it for music, and so forth. Search engines, RSS technology, and recommendation systems help Digital Natives find and receive those pieces of information they find interesting.

Human and technical filtering of information is a final technique for fighting information overload, and it's one that everyone uses to some extent. We mentioned filtering in the previous chapter as a means to ensure certain levels of information quality. But filtering also can reduce the threat of information overload. Consider, for instance, spam filters in e-mail programs, which save us a lot of time and leave our attention intact to deal with relevant information. Other types of filters have been developed and implemented as well, helping to further reduce the amount of information we need to process. RSS readers, for instance, often let users define what messages they don't want to be displayed even if they have subscribed to a feed. And some search engines provide filtering functions to eliminate irrelevant or unwanted information (for instance, the "safe search" function on Google, which eliminates some results), or to limit the search to certain sectors or areas (for instance, only websites whose domain names end in ".edu").

These tools and techniques help Internet users to limit the amount of information they must deal with, and, to one extent or another, to identify the information that best suits their interests. These tools, unthinkable even a few decades ago, seem unspectacular to the small number of Digital Natives who use them so extensively. However commonplace they may seem to the most advanced technology users, though, the fact remains that search engines and RSS technology are both ingenious new mechanisms. Their evolution over the past few years has made the Internet much easier to use than it was at first. It's hard to imagine how we would navigate the sea of information without these innovations.

Many of the new information-navigation tools are based primarily on how information is organized (or disorganized, for that matter) in the online space. Traditional classification systems for information have broken down during the transition to the digital era. Gone are the card catalogs of yesteryear. Traditional "experts" are still classifying things, now online, but they have been joined by groups of passionate amateurs who are inventing their own information order.

One method of user-based categorization that is frequently used is tagging.[50] Tags are essentially keywords that are associated with a piece of information—for example, a photo, blog post, or video—in a keyword-based classification scheme.[51] Tagging, in other words, is like creating a label for online content. Here's an example: After creating an account on a site like Del.icio.us, each user can put customized virtual labels onto websites of his choice—for instance, someone could label a website with travel information about Boston as "Red Sox Country." Once the label is added, anyone who looks for "Red Sox Country" in the Del.icio.us search bar can find the Boston travel information website—as well as all other websites that are similarly tagged. This technique helps Digital Natives find information based on descriptions of their choice.

Tags have a social dimension as well as a personal dimension, which makes them useful to other people after the person doing the tagging has left his mark. Once aggregated, tags become part of a bottom-up, highly evolutionary categorization system created around shared semantics among users rather than experts.[52] By creating a new, user-driven orientation and navigation system for digital information, tagging is expected to help prevent and/or manage information-overload situations in the future. This idea is known as a "folksonomy," as opposed to a formal "taxonomy" created only by experts, as in John Dewey and his famous decimal system.

Technology-enabled responses that make use of peer knowledge and the "wisdom of the crowd" are a key to addressing the challenges faced by

Digital Natives and triggered by the digital information explosion. In fact, technological innovation is a solution to a problem created by technology.[53] Though we believe there's great power in social technologies to help solve the information-quality and information-overload problems, not all observers share our optimism. Critics note that computational responses may in fact make matters worse. These technologies, they argue, have the potential to add to the overload problem by creating even more information to distract users' attention. For instance, when many people create many different tags representing Boston—like Red Sox Country, the Hub of the Universe, Beantown, and so forth—the result may be more clutter rather than more clarity.[54]

As in the case of each of the tough problems we've considered in other chapters, many different parties have roles to play in solving the information-overload issue.

Technology companies—small and large—that develop and market the tools that help us to organize and manage the endless ocean of information on the Web are essential players in this narrative. Their technologies are critical tools for Digital Natives because they enable them to navigate digital environments while shielding themselves against information overload. Their primary contribution in developing new hardware and software products is to provide innovative platforms that allow Digital Natives, and the rest of us, to control the digital inbox. We want to receive only as much information as we can process, at a time that is convenient for us and of the quality we desire.

The next generation of technology tools in the works offers substantial promise in this regard. These technologies prompt talk of "Web 3.0." Leading technologists have a vision of a "Semantic Web" that functions like an extension of the World Wide Web. In this Semantic Web, digital information can be understood, interpreted, and used by "intelligent" software agents that help users to manage the vast amount of information online. Others describe this future in simpler terms: Computers are going to make it easier to tap into the wisdom of the many human beings who are together shaping the information environment.

However one describes this future, the research and development teams of many hip tech companies are working very hard to improve upon the tools that help Digital Natives avoid getting swamped by the ever-growing amount of information in cyberspace. Technology companies are also working with academics to address the manifold issues associated with the current information explosion and to explore new ways to address information-overload problems.

Here, as elsewhere, the answer is not to "pass a law." At a glance, it's difficult to see what states and governments might do to protect Digital Natives from the information-overload problem. The law, in a traditional sense, does not have an obvious role to play in the overload problem. But even though classic regulation is unlikely to help, states can do a few things to contribute to a sustainable digital information ecosystem.

Governments should focus on doing what they can to be part of the solution, rather than part of the problem. The public sector is itself an important producer and distributor of information. Governmental agencies and bodies create many types of information, ranging from health reports, meteorological information, travel advisories, and every sort of statistics to new laws and regulations (which itself is information). In addition, laws of various sorts—"transparency laws"—require private actors like companies to disclose certain kinds of information.[55] In many instances, the state can provide information in a way that allows for efficient processing. Researchers have started to look into what they call "collaborative transparency," where the government provides data in a useful format (for instance, as part of an e-Government strategy) and in such a manner that it may be easily accessed and efficiently analyzed by interested citizens.[56]

Moreover, governments can actively fight the pollution of the information environment. As in classical environmental protection, governments around the world—from Australia to the United States—have enacted laws to ban certain types of pollution that have adverse consequences—in economic terms, that produce "negative externalities." For instance, there are anti-spam laws on the books in several dozen countries around the world. Unfortunately, anti-spam laws share the fate of many laws in cyberspace: They don't work particularly well, in no small part because they are hard to enforce. The most active spammers are often difficult to trace and usually operate in jurisdictions without efficient law enforcement. Similar types of laws against information pollution might be more effective. Consider, for instance, legislation that enables individuals to place themselves on do-not-call lists, which tend to be more effective in terms of helping consumers than anti-spam laws.

Finally, governments can also work with technologists to encourage development of better navigation and filtering systems. Though the government should not be in the position of mandating technologies of this (or almost any) sort, the overall legal framework should be designed so as not to discourage this sort of innovation. For instance, copyright law is currently in tension with innovative attempts to develop navigation tools. The most restrictive copyright laws work at cross-purposes to innovation in the information technology space. In setting copyright policy, lawmakers should take the costs of information overload into account, particularly when it defines when it should be permissible to provide small samples of copyrighted materials in order to index, tag, or otherwise organize or review that information.[57]

Though there's no law that any one country could pass that would address the problem of information overload on the World Wide Web, that doesn't mean that governments should sit back and do nothing. States can try to be part of the solution rather than part of the problem, whether through their role as information producers or through their laws, policies, or regulations and procedures.

Education offers the most promise in terms of helping young people cope with information overload. Parents and teachers must work with kids to teach them the skills they will need to manage all the information that can enrich their lives in a digital era.

The first step toward solving the information-overload problem is awareness. Often, as our conversations with kids taught us, young people are not aware of the overload problem—or they may be aware of it, but frame it in completely different terminology, or attribute its symptoms to another cause. As in other areas of their digital lives, through education Digital Natives can gain a deeper understanding of both the promises and the challenges that lie ahead. (The quiz on our website, or the Wikipedia entry on information overload, might be good starting points here.) Once young people are aware of the problem, it's much easier for them to start learning to use the tools, applications, and strategies that can help them avoid overload. And they can learn more ways to cope with overload on their own as they develop their skills in handling and processing information.

Second, children should understand that there is very little they can do while multitasking that they could not perform more effectively without multitasking. This fact may seem counterintuitive to many Digital Natives, since multitasking often makes them feel more productive and less stressed.[58] And many parents and teachers may be poor role models in this regard. But to make strides against information overload, we should find ways to help young people distinguish between situations where it's good for them to concentrate on one task, and situations when multitasking might not be harmful to learning.

This learning needs to take place in the home as well as in schools. Parents' strategies for dealing with the massive amount of information and the threat of overload may look different from family to family, depending on both demographics and social norms within the family. Some families might decide to turn off all electronic devices, including cell phones, iPods, IM-devices, and so on, while having dinner together. Others may limit the time their children can stay online in the evening, or move the computers their children use to the living room, out in the open, rather than allowing them to be tucked away in the children's bedrooms. The effectiveness of these strategies will no doubt vary by the age and temperament of the young person in the equation.

Of the many things parents can do, two are particularly important. Parents need to be focused on the online behavior of their kids, watch for information-overload symptoms, and be ready to intervene. They should also have open conversations with their children to find out about their online behavior and how they use their favorite digital technologies. That does not mean banning their use of cell phones or confiscating their iPods. It means learning about the ways in which kids live their digital lives, knowing how they find the information they are looking for, observing how they take breaks, and facilitating a dialogue about what it means to live in a world in which digital information—in the amount of six tons of books for every person—is created per year.

Second, parents need to lead by example. We, as parents, teach our kids how to "become our own filter," as one author put it.[59] We can show them when it's time to switch off our cell phones and laptop computers, when it's best to refrain from checking e-mails on our BlackBerries (realistically, our "Crackberries," as some of us have come to call them), and how to focus on one thing at a time instead of doing several things at once. Indeed, multitasking is not a new phenomenon (although the order of magnitude that it reaches has changed dramatically from the generation born "analog" to those born "digital"). Most of us drive cars while listening to the radio or make dinner while watching TV. And sometimes, that might be fine. But parents should consider what happens when their child turns sixteen: Do they really want their son or daughter talking on the cell phone—or text-messaging—behind the driver's wheel? Leading by example might be difficult in this particular area, as we know firsthand, but it's definitely worth an effort.

Kids should be learning these skills in school, too. Educators can and should play an important role in raising awareness at a very basic level, both among children and among their parents. Teachers can make parents more sensitive to the overload issue, for instance, and provide suggestions for how to address the issue at home.[60]

Most important, teachers can include information overload as another important item on their teaching agenda—ideally, of course, as part of tailored media and information literacy programs for children. The American Library Association's Information Literacy Standards are a great starting place for developing a program that also addresses information-overload issues.[61] Either in ordinary classroom settings or in specific bibliographic sessions, teachers can inform Digital Natives and their peers about the problem. Teachers can also introduce the range of possible responses as well as the use of the tools and techniques—including heuristics (rules of thumb) that help in preventing or at least limiting the overload. This type of training is particularly important when it comes to younger children and those less experienced in navigating the digital world.

Many of the strategies to cope with overload that children can learn are closely interconnected with time-management strategies. Here, too, teachers in general, and school librarians in particular, can teach young students how large amounts of information can be skimmed in a relatively short amount of time and, for instance, how prioritization works. Finally, schools themselves might adjust their information-relevant policies in ways that take into account the limited processing capabilities of Digital Natives. These policies may range from curriculum development and assignments to the question of to what extent the use of laptops, WiFi, and cell phones (text messages!) should be allowed in classrooms.[62]

We are confident that this is a problem that we can solve as a society, if we work together. No one actor can solve it alone, and no one solution, without the others, will do the trick. We need to reflect carefully on the potential consequences of our rush to build more and more computing capacity while increasing bandwidth and pushing toward ever more ubiquitous computing. The credo of the past—"the more information the better"—needs to be supplemented by a set of carefully designed strategies, tools, and techniques that support our children in their attempts to adjust to an information ecosystem we've created for them.

Good things often come with the bad. The danger of information overload is simply the flip side of many of the most wonderful aspects of the digital era. It's terrific, for instance, that more and more young people are expressing themselves online, but this prolific expression can add to the amount of information that others must process. The huge diversity of sources available in the online world, and the fact that no one gatekeeper controls too large a share of the online attention, are also to be cheered. This democratizing effect of the Internet is plainly in tension, however, with our desire to manage the crush of information—of varying qualities—with which our children will interact every day of their lives.

Information overload is an issue that we need to grapple with, but it's by no means the biggest issue for Digital Natives. Though information overload is not causing terrible harm to the vast majority of young people in wired societies, it will be a persistent challenge. Over time, human beings have shown a remarkable ability to adapt to new communication technologies, especially as the sheer volume of information began to grow after the introduction of the printing press in the fifteenth century. Television and radio, though more recent, also turned up the volume, as did the Internet. Effective tools, credible brands, and a wide range of skills have arisen to help people navigate the surging rivers and growing ocean of information. We take information overload seriously. Though there are plenty of other concerns that are much more alarming, such as the prevalence of violence in society, there is certainly room for technological innovators and others to devise ways to help our children come to grips with the sheer magnitude of information that awaits them every day on their computers and other digital media.

9

AGGRESSORS

O N APRIL 16, 2007, SEUNG-HUI CHO OPENED FIRE ON THE VIRGINIA TECH campus. He killed or wounded thirty-two of his fellow students and faculty members. Cho's rampage, the worst shooting incident of its kind, led to worldwide mourning. The victims came from cultures and continents around the globe.[1]

Hours after the tragedy, the finger-pointing began. In talk show after talk show, pundits speculated about the role of violent video games in prompting Cho to commit such a grotesque crime. One analyst repeatedly blamed the game Counter-Strike, a so-called first-person shooter game in which the player simulates a counterterrorist agent hunting down terrorists. In an interview on *Larry King Live,* Dr. Phil McGraw blamed video games. But students who had lived in the Virginia Tech dorm with Cho said, in fact, that they'd never seen him play video games, much less Counter-Strike. Psychologists who analyzed Cho and other school shooters pointed instead to a very different set of factors as the root causes of these crimes, such as feelings of acute rejection and preoccupation with death. Soon, much attention surrounding the shooting turned to the missed warning signs. Students and adults alike had felt uncomfortable with a series of morbid plays that Cho had written, for example, but no one had realized the seriousness of his condition or state of mind. The talk about violent gaming as the cause of the tragedy eventually quieted down.[2]

We are quick to blame video games whenever a young person commits a violent act. Many of these games are, without a doubt, shocking. One young person in Australia even made a perverse game called "V-Tech Rampage" about the Virginia Tech shooting, in which the gamer is prompted to recreate Cho's steps and shoot his victims, identified by name, in order. There is little to like in these games, and much to worry about. But we need, all the same, to be sober in our analysis of what is cause, what is effect, and what we ought to do to protect our children from the underlying problem: violence and violent images *throughout* our society.[3]

T he jump to a quick conclusion about the connection between video games and violent acts by young people is commonplace. As early as 1999, the FBI reported that one of the characteristics of school shooters is "the inordinate amounts of time playing video games with violent themes," and the fact that they seem to be more interested in the violent images than in the game itself.[4] Since then, over a dozen shootings worldwide have been linked to violent games and Internet content. In the tragic Dawson College shooting of 2006, where a young adult killed one person and injured more than twenty others, the murderer's online posting about his moods, and his digital profile, with links to websites with violent content, came under public scrutiny.[5] In the case of a Finnish school shooting in 2007, where a teenager killed eight people, the massacre had been *pre-*announced only hours earlier in a YouTube video.[6] In an incident in Switzerland in 2007, in which a young man in his early twenties randomly shot a sixteen-year-old stranger to death at a bus stop, the police reportedly confiscated boxes with ego-shooter games in the offender's bedroom.[7]

There is no doubt that there can be a connection between aggressive thoughts, violent behavior, and the use of digital technologies. In some instances, Internet applications, such as blogs or personal websites, have been used as outlets by the young person to express his (and it almost always is a "he") aggressive thoughts and beliefs that ultimately led up to a violent act. In other cases, online discussion groups, chat rooms, websites, and the like have been (mis)used by young people to glorify the acts of violence that were carried out by peers. In other instances, online games allow players to carry out their own violent acts using avatars—on-screen characters that are part and parcel of their emerging sense of identity.

Research does in fact show that there is a relationship between violent content (ranging from violent music to aggressive online games) made accessible through digital technologies and the formation of aggressive thoughts and beliefs that might ultimately result in violent behavior of children and teens. We as parents and teachers indeed should be concerned about the connection between violence displayed on Digital Natives' screens and the real-world consequences of this type of media use. The key questions, it turns out, are what exactly we should worry about, how much we should worry about it—and what we can do to prevent harm.

But this topic is by no means just about the Internet. The debate about violent media content and its potential impact on children has a lot of history that's worth revisiting. The introduction and widespread adoption of TV has led to a heated controversy over the past fifty years about the impact of violent pictures and movies on young viewers. And for good reason: A 1992 study showed that the average child in the United States at that time witnessed more than 8,000 killings and 100,000 violent acts on TV by the time he or she finished elementary school.[8] And a 1997 study found that a teenager living in a household with cable TV or a video recorder saw, on average, 32,000 murders and 40,000 attempted murders by age eighteen. The problem is by no means an exclusively American one: Nearly 80 percent of German TV programs feature scenes of violence.[9] It is unclear just how much these viewing times have changed with the rise of the Internet. It is likely that the new sources of violent images, such as video games, have only increased the types of media on which the images are available—and made the violence more interactive (more on that later)—not reduced the number of violent images overall. These numbers alone illustrate the order of magnitude of the media violence challenge we're dealing with.

Hundreds of studies have been carried out over the past few decades to study the impact of violent TV and film content on children. Though screen violence doesn't translate *directly and invariably* into violent behavior, these studies do confirm that there is a positive correlation between exposure to violent media content and raised levels of aggression.[10] There is, for instance, compelling evidence that brief exposure to violent sequences on TV leads to short-term increases in children's aggressive thoughts, emotions, and behavior, including physically aggressive behavior serious enough to harm others.[11] Other studies have confirmed that the physical aggression, verbal aggression, and aggressive thoughts of young people correlate with the amount of TV and film violence they regularly watch.[12] And longitudinal studies have established that high levels of exposure to violent TV programs in childhood can promote aggression in later childhood, adolescence, and even young adulthood.

Experts in the fields of psychology, sociology, and media analysis have performed extensive studies of *why* violence observed through media increases aggression and violence in the real lives of young people. One of the most comprehensive theoretical models helpful to understanding this phenomenon is called the extended General Aggression Model (GAM). This model helps us to break down the types of effects that violence in media can have on aggression. The model also helps to distinguish acute, short-term effects from long-term effects.

The first factor is the collective effect of a series of situational variables. These variables influence aggressive behavior through different psychological processes. Violent media show kids how to act aggressively. As cognitive psychologists and neuroscientists have demonstrated, children begin to imitate other humans at a very early age in order to develop skills, including social (or antisocial) behavior.[13] Children can learn from whomever they observe, including parents, brothers and sisters, peers, and characters in the mass media. This type of observational learning often happens without much awareness that any learning is going on. A child who observes others acting aggressively is more likely to perform the same aggressive behavior immediately afterward. The likelihood that he will mimic aggressive behavior increases if the perpetrator he observes is similar to him or attractive to him, if he identifies with the perpetrator, or if the context of the aggressive behavior he observes seems realistic and has some sort of a rewarding consequence.[14]

The second factor that determines why observed violence can lead to aggression is that children can become primed to respond to a stimulus that causes them to act in a certain manner. The things that we think and feel and the ways in which we behave are often the result of a network effect that unconsciously takes place in our brains. Through an associative network, a trigger in the environment—or a "stimulus," as psychologists call it—can activate, or "prime," an already existing set of aggressive thoughts, angry emotions, or behavioral patterns (so-called scripts). Exposure to violent media content, in other words, makes existing aggressive schemas more available and "colors" other pieces of incoming information.[15] Often, such priming effects are short term. But what makes this of particular concern in the case of children is that repeated priming makes these responses more likely to occur on an ongoing basis. In this way, aggressive thoughts, emotions, and behavioral scripts may become a long-lasting part of the normal internal state of a child. This installation of an aggressive bias, in turn, increases the likelihood that a child will interpret any social encounter in "aggressive terms" and respond in kind.

The third factor is that watching violence on a screen is arousing for many kids. Both their heart rate and blood pressure rise with exposure to violent imagery. High arousal, generated by violent movies or, say, first-person shooter games increases the likelihood of aggression because it can amplify a child's tendency to respond in an aggressive manner. In other words, if a child has aggressive tendencies, he is more likely to behave even more aggressively when screen violence leads to arousal. Further, when a child is highly aroused after viewing violence, he is likely to emotionally overreact later in time. For example, a little provocation from a classmate that would normally trigger mild anger might now be experienced as intense anger, since the emotional response stimulated by the violent movie watched at home is being misattributed to the provocation at school.[16]

The findings of studies that focus on violent television and movies are likely to apply to Internet violence as well. Much empirical work remains to be done in this important area before we can draw firm conclusions.

But a growing body of research shows that several of the new digital media formats—including, for instance, violent music texts, hate websites, and violent movies on cell phones—are likely to have effects similar to the ones researchers have shown in the context of television and movies. This holds especially true for computer games and console-based video games, which have gained much attention recently. Many of the most popular video games sold today—including Soldier of Fortune, Doom, Mortal Kombat, Resident Evil, Gunman Chronicles, Wolfenstein 3D, Duke Nukem 3D, and BioShock—invoke superrealistic scenes of violence and feature massively aggressive actions.[17]

When playing these games, kids are no longer observers. They become active participants in violent fantasy worlds. They are prompted to become virtual killers. This interactivity marks a difference between the digital environment and what came before. This difference may render the effects of violence on young people stronger than they were with passive media such as TV. The implications are frightening, inasmuch as somewhere between 70 and 90 percent of young people in the United States play video games.[18]

In the course of our research, we interviewed a number of Digital Natives who are also avid gamers. They struck us as smart, thoughtful, articulate young people. But one of the most striking features of these conversations was the way in which they would switch seamlessly from a commonplace discussion of Internet use (such as sending instant messages) to a discussion of their online gaming (in environments such as Counter-Strike). In the same voice as they would describe sending a message to a friend, they told us about how they enjoyed playing "first-person shooter" games where the object was to kill other players. What was remarkable about these conversations was the extent to which IMing a friend seemed directly parallel to playing a game about killing another human being. The same tone, the same voice, the same sense that nothing about these interactions was out of the ordinary.

Digital Natives, like those who grew up before them, experience violence in the culture all around them. Research suggests that there are negative effects of this exposure. Online, just as in video games, those effects may play out in different ways, as Digital Natives put themselves in the position of the violent actor, rather than watching someone else control the actor. There is no doubt that it will be increasingly important to understand the phenomenon of online gaming as these characters become more and more intertwined with the identities of our children.

Parents have reason to worry about video games; nonetheless, it's important that parents know how to differentiate between the kinds of video games. First, there are tens of thousands of games across dozens of platforms.[19] These games are neither all the same nor all bad.[20] Many of them in fact hold great promise for use in educational settings. Go to freerice.com for an example: Here, for each word puzzle a kid (or anyone else) solves, a donor gives free rice to the hungry, paid for by advertisers and donors. PBSKids.org has many more games that kids love and that also teach them useful things. (The commercial influence over some of these games and the privacy implications are another story.)

Second, the social context of game playing also needs to be taken into account. Laboratory-based experiments with gamers have been critiqued for not adequately representing the social context of game play: According to surveys, 60 percent of gamers are playing with friends and 25 percent with a spouse or parent.[21] Because of this social aspect, there are tremendous opportunities for peers and parents to help put the games into context for the young people playing them. Of course, there is the possible downside of a culture of violence emerging among peers playing these games socially, as well.

The characteristics of the individual child matter a great deal when it comes to assessing the likelihood that exposure to media violence will lead to aggressive behavior. Age, for instance, is an important factor. Although the relationship between age and effects is complicated, studies suggest that the impact of media violence is greatest in the group of very young children (up to five years of age). Although gender doesn't seem to make a big difference, according to recent studies, it can influence the types of aggression associated with early exposure to media violence.

Some children may be more likely to be aggressive by nature than others, and this tendency may in turn be aggravated by media. As one might predict, highly aggressive children show even greater effects when exposed to violent content than relatively nonaggressive kids. More aggressive children are also more likely to consume violent media, including violent computer games[22]—an effect that psychologists describe as "reciprocal determinism." A child's intelligence, too, may be a factor.

Second, the environment in which a child is raised can have an impact on whether exposure to media violence translates to aggressive behavior. Children from cultures with strong sanctions against violence are less likely to learn and imitate aggressive behavior from the media than those from cultures where such sanctions are not in place. One interesting study demonstrated, for instance, that Israeli children raised on a kibbutz with strong antiviolence norms were less likely to be affected by TV violence than Israeli kids raised in less pacifist suburbs.[23] This will come as no surprise to anyone: Communities and contexts matter to how kids grow up.

The socioeconomic status of children and their families may matter, too. It's a matter of scale, primarily: Kids raised in poor families in America watch more TV on average than children raised in wealthier families. Young people in lower socioeconomic brackets may be exposed to violence on television more often than those in higher brackets. By the same token, children from wealthier families are likely to spend more time online than those from poorer families.

Media violence is not going to affect every young person in the same way. It is not a 1:1 correlation, by any means. But the overall point is valid: There's reason for concern about violence in our society, and the online world can be a new, additional source of media violence.

The Internet does not prompt a sharp break with the recent past in terms of the effects of media violence. In many cases, what we're seeing is a migration to the Internet from video games once played on TVs or gaming consoles. Many forms of violence that have previously been consumed on TV screens are now simply displayed on the computer screen as a result of media convergence.

There are a few things that are new in the Internet era that we should pay attention to as we move forward. One change is the shift from video games played against computers to games played against—and with—other humans. Another is the enhanced level of interactivity of the games.

There is greater realism than in the past, and the avatar has become part of the player's identity, to some extent. We do not yet know the impact of either of these changes on Digital Natives and their level of aggression, but they are factors worth watching.

We expect the debate about media violence to expand in scope, too, because some parts of the population that we call Digital Natives are not only recipients of media violence, but also involved in the distribution and the production of violent materials. Digital Natives might produce a violent video that they post on YouTube, which in turn their friends share with others. They might code a video game, as the creator of the disturbing V-Tech Massacre did. There are plainly dark sides, too, to the creativity that young people undertake as part of online culture.

Even though the scope of the media violence problem has expanded in the digital era, for the most part the solutions to the problem haven't changed much just because the problem has migrated to a new technology. Return to the model of the concentric circles used throughout this book. There's a role to play for Digital Natives, their peers, parents and teachers, technology companies, and the state in limiting and addressing the effects of media violence.

We should start by being realistic about what we expect on this score from Digital Natives themselves. In a perfect world, all young people would moderate their own exposure to violent media for their own sake. This, of course, is unrealistic, especially when it comes to younger children. As anyone who watches television knows, it's almost impossible to avoid exposure to episodes of intense violence—one needn't watch extreme wrestling to see horrific images. They're on the evening news, in advertisements, and laced throughout popular television shows of almost every variety. It's too much to expect that kids will keep themselves away from all aggressive content in a world where their peers swap digital files in school and compare their scores in their favorite violent games.

As with television violence in the past, much of the responsibility lies in the hands of parents to keep young kids, at least, away from violent media and to provide context to the older kids who are inevitably going to encounter it. It's essential that parents set limits on the use of media likely to involve violent imagery, from television to movies to video games, online or on the console. It's also important that parents give common-sense advice to kids about how to think about what they are seeing.

Parents should start by playing the video or online game up for discussion themselves and evaluating it before letting their kids get involved with it. This is guaranteed to be a learning experience for the parent as well as the child. Parents should also avail themselves of video-game ratings, as flawed as they are, to prevent their kids from being exposed to harmful games. These things are much easier said than done, but they are important steps on many levels. They help kids steer clear of the most violent games and help parents and their children build a connection based on shared experiences in new media.[24]

The role of educators is similar to that of parents, but educators can be helpful in more formal settings as well. Well-designed media literacy programs, as discussed in other contexts, can help manage the negative effects of media violence on kids. An early study at the elementary-school level suggests that a strategy that combines education about the effects of violence with interventions aimed at changing media usage and parental monitoring might be promising.[25]

The private sector needs to do more than it is doing today. Companies also need to be doing their part to create a safe digital information environment for Digital Natives. But not everything they have done is having a salutary effect. In an ideal world, companies would not create and market media products and games that can lead to aggressive behavior in children. But forbearance of this sort seems unlikely.

Technologies can be part of the solution. Some digital technologies in place today have a generally positive effect on keeping kids from media violence. Kid-safe browsers, parental control tools, safe Internet access services for children, and the like are helpful tools. YouTube, MySpace, and other conscientious companies are using a reasonably effective combination of new technologies and human beings to detect and remove violent content where a certain threshold is met—and investing a great deal of money, time, and effort in the process.[26] Other content-oriented services, such as online gaming sites, might work on common symbols or warning messages that would help parents, teachers, and young users better assess the content of the service. Naturally, however, the companies' willingness to contribute to solutions depends much on their underlying business model.

Voluntary rating systems can help, too, up to a point. Rating systems for television, film, music, and video games in the United States have raised awareness about violence in media. But at a systemic level, this rating process suffers from major flaws. A system that bases ratings on age has the perverse effect of encouraging some degree of underage consumption. Further, the rating criteria have allegedly become more lenient over time and have been frequently applied in an incorrect way. Finally, parents too often lack the knowledge to understand the different rating systems or implement them in the home.[27]

In general, these efforts by some, but by no means all, companies don't work, and there are structural problems that make them unlikely to work. Kids always want to look at stuff they shouldn't be looking at and playing games that may not be terrific for them. Many companies also aren't really giving it their best effort. The companies that make video games and online games are plainly making a great deal of money from these violent products, and they aren't about to become major parts of the solution voluntarily.

With the private sector leading only in modest ways, governments need to jump in on behalf of kids. For starters, governments should mandate ratings and expand them to include a broader set of online games than have been included in such systems in the past. If ratings by the private sector are failing for one reason or another, a government-sponsored entity could rate products prior to distribution and sale. The United Kingdom has adopted such a system.[28]

Governments can play a role through educational efforts, whether via schools or at the level of general public awareness. Governments can also help to foster collaborative efforts by public and private parties to work to reduce unwanted exposure by young kids to extreme violence. The Safer Internet Plus program, sponsored by the European Commission, is one such initiative that combines a series of helpful educational and leadership functions by governments.[29]

If all else fails, governments should restrict the production and dissemination of certain types of violent content in combination with instituting mandatory, government-based ratings of these materials. The production and distribution of extreme types of violent content—including, for instance, so-called snuff movies, in which people are filmed being killed—can and should be banned by law. Similar restrictions on access to such materials, based on age ratings, are in place in Germany, the United Kingdom, Canada, and Australia, among other places. These types of controls must be very narrowly tailored to pass constitutional muster in the United States, appropriately enough, given the force and breadth of First Amendment protections. We already have most of the legal tools needed to mitigate the effects of this problem, but rarely are these tools used effectively across the relevant platforms that mediate kids' exposure.

Too often, the Internet is the metaphor for all that is hard to understand about youth culture. The challenge of parsing out what's different about the Internet and its usage by young people is nowhere more important, or more difficult, than in the context of aggressive behavior.

Digital Natives have much to gain from the way they interact with information online, but we cannot afford to be blind to the very real hazards they face as well. The digital world involves fewer barriers to violent content, allows young people to communicate directly with others about their violent thoughts, and offers a platform for highly realistic role-playing that can involve extreme violence. Although much more research still needs to be done, there is plenty of reason to advocate limits on the amount of exposure our kids have to violence in online media and games.

But even as we worry about our children's exposure to violent video games, we need to be careful not to panic—and not to overreach with the restrictions we put in place. Violence in the media is not new to the digital environment. Since time immemorial, children have played games in which they pretend to kill each other—cops and robbers, cowboys and Indians, pirates on the high seas, toy soldiers waging war against other toy soldiers. Kids are attracted to guns and violence. Some of the violence that we see in the media in modern society—whether online or on the TV or in movies—is far more gruesome than cops and robbers. It's crucial to help them put both their own instincts and what they are watching others do into perspective.

The best regulators of violence in our society, whether online or not, are parents and teachers, because they are the people closest to Digital Natives themselves. Parents and teachers have the most time with kids—and, ideally, their trust. As in other contexts, parents and teachers need to start by understanding what their Digital Natives are up to. From there, it's important to set limits, especially for young children, on gaming and exposure to violent activities. Parents and educators can and should work overtime to channel the interest of Digital Natives in interactive media into positive directions. But companies need to step up, too, and to exercise restraint in terms of what they offer kids. And despite the hard free-speech questions implicated by these kinds of interventions, the government also needs to be involved. As we've emphasized throughout the book, the answer isn't to shut down the technologies or reactively to blame video games for every tragedy, but rather to teach our kids how to navigate the complex, fluid environments in which they are growing up. That's easier said than done, but we don't have much choice but to take this problem head on. The stakes could not be higher.

10

INNOVATORS

I N A FEW SHORT YEARS, FACEBOOK HAS ROCKETED FROM A DORM-ROOM IDEA
to a household name, and its creators—Mark Zuckerberg and his
friends from Harvard—have become legends in the history of technology
entrepreneurship. Without much capital, and (mostly) independent of big
partners, they've created a platform in three years that now figures near the
center of the Web 2.0 movement. Facebook has become a "social utility,"
to use the company's own terminology, that fuels and documents tens of
millions of human relationships. The company's meteoric ascent is already
the subject of entire books of its own.

In the fall of 2007, Harvard dropout Bill Gates' Microsoft invested $240
million in Harvard dropout Zuckerberg's Facebook. Microsoft didn't even
get a full 2 percent of Facebook's stock for its investment of a quarter-billion
dollars. Microsoft's investment valued Facebook's total worth at $15 billion.
Although Facebook's earnings were not what they would ordinarily need
to be to justify such a valuation, Gates wanted a stake in Facebook because it made strategic sense for Microsoft to align itself with the world's
most promising social network—and to keep Facebook's shares out of
archrival Google's hands. Along with equity in Facebook, Microsoft bought

itself a sweet advertising deal that enabled it to connect with customers via one of the most important environments in the social lives of Digital Natives.[1]

Zuckerberg has achieved an iconic status among young Americans. He has appeared on the cover of *Newsweek* and in fawning articles across the Web. Even in the formal business press, Zuckerberg is photographed wearing the casual clothes favored by college students headed to the dining hall for an early-afternoon Sunday brunch; his fame stems in part from the fact that he is one of the very few billionaires who wear flip-flops to work.

D igital Natives are transforming businesses. To date, their biggest impact has been through their entrepreneurship, as Mark Zuckerberg's Facebook demonstrates. But Digital Natives are making huge waves as employees and consumers, too—and the magnitude of these changes will grow over time as they continue to enter the workforce, become managers themselves, and earn more money to spend in the marketplace.

In each of these roles, Digital Natives are causing disruption in the short term. This disruption stems in part from their use of technology and their shifting relationship to information. Over time, though, their creative destruction will begin to look more constructive than it does today. Even though these kids seem, at best, unusual—and sometimes plain old unpromising—they're remaking the culture of business in meaningful, and ultimately socially beneficial, ways.

The most visible effect that Digital Natives are having on business is as entrepreneurs who threaten to take down giant, long-established industries. The music industry, Hollywood, the television and cable industries, even newspapers—each is suffering through some very challenging years at the hands of businesses started by Digital Natives and their Digital Native customers.

There is no real evidence that Digital Natives are more entrepreneurial than those who toiled in bygone days. But while a kid thirty years ago might have been able to invent a new whirligig, the Internet era has given rise to something new: a cadre of really young kids whose innovations have had a global impact. So, even if there aren't more young entrepreneurs than there used to be, they are capable, more than any young generation in the past, of reshaping the global economy. The age of gerontocracy is over.

These Digital Native entrepreneurs have been successful in no small part because they know this hybrid analog-and-digital world extremely well. They know how to thrive in it. They know how their peers are living their lives in digitally mediated ways. And they are figuring out ways to exploit the trends of a digital age. The businesses that they are creating are becoming some of the most important services for the highly connected Digital Natives of our times.

Digital Natives are becoming entrepreneurs at a time when the conditions make it cheaper and easier than ever to start a business. The economic conditions of starting a business that offers a service in cyberspace—low upfront costs, minimal capital requirements, and scalability—are important prerequisites of the larger trend toward the democratization of innovation. A cool idea, coding skills, a few friends, and enough start-up capital to pay your Web-hosting bills are the basic ingredients needed to create a new business in the new economy.

Shawn Fanning started Napster while he was still in college. It began as a straightforward application of technology and turned—extremely rapidly—into a big, disruptive business. His idea was simple and innovative: offer a free, online space where anyone could swap music files. Most likely, the money didn't figure into his calculus much at the start. Fanning brought to his work an outsider, devil-may-care attitude, revealed in e-mails to his colleagues at the time—e-mails that became public when his company was sued. What he developed turned out to be illegal to operate the way he was doing it, but it was a powerful innovation. Napster, version 1.0, unleashed a great deal of energy in the digital media space, much of it previously bottled up in Digital Natives. In Napster's wake, Bram Cohen, by all accounts a prodigy of a software developer and still in his mid-twenties, created the revolutionary BitTorrent system. Cohen's innovation took Fanning's work a few steps further, allowing for far faster sharing of rich media files across digital networks. The music-recording and movie industries claim that they have suffered billions of dollars in losses because of illegal file-sharing on systems like Napster and BitTorrent.[2]

A nanosecond later in historical terms, Chad Hurley and his friends created YouTube, the simple yet innovative idea that let anyone post a movie to the Internet (and for which Google paid $1.65 billion only a few years after its founding). YouTube has already had a happy ending for its founders: They've had their big payday from Google and no judge has—yet—said they have to shut their service down. Viacom, the giant media company and a big copyright holder, has filed suit against YouTube for alleged violations not all that different from what brought Napster down. YouTube, like Napster, has been followed by many similar services—with names like Metacafe, Daily Motion, and VideoEgg, among many others—each innovating fast and hard to offer a better service in the video-uploading and -sharing space. At their core, each of these services does exactly the same thing: They let you upload a video file to the Internet and share it with other people. The television and cable industries, along with the recording industry and Hollywood, fear their heyday may be a thing of the past if Hurley's YouTube continues to take viewers and listeners away from traditional modes of content distribution.

These young entrepreneurs are not businessmen in the traditional sense. They are, more often than not, visionary kids who happen to be skilled in computer development themselves. They have big, ambitious ideas that they can implement on their own, without having to ask anyone's permission. They don't need to build a big new production facility to go to market. Their visions are often infused with a strong techno-libertarian streak—that the Internet is a place where creativity and innovation flourish in ways that resist traditional, hierarchical modes of control—which appeals to their Digital Native customer base. The best entrepreneurs of the digital world, whether or not they are Digital Natives, have learned to tap into and exploit a counterculture that values and celebrates this creativity and innovation. These are not the company men of the 1950s; they are often rebels with a deep-seated instinct to stick it to "The Man."

From the viewpoint of the recording industry, Hollywood, or the newspaper business, the digital revolution certainly doesn't seem like a good thing. These Digital Natives may be innovators, but they are threatening a way of life. People are losing their jobs. This process is not new; this kind of creative destruction has repeated itself throughout history in the wake of disruptive technologies. What's different here is that Digital Natives can cause this creative destruction on their own, without pausing to worry about the implications. And the revolution in information technologies is enabling them to carry out this destruction to occur at a shockingly rapid pace, in markets that span the globe.

Despite its destructive effects, this digital entrepreneurship, which often involves development of new platforms for further innovation, will drive forward the societies and economies in which it is taking place. Mark Zuckerberg and his peers unleash transformative change and innovation through the platforms that they build. The types of innovation to which these new services give rise are productive for economies. Their success undercuts certain markets and costs some people their jobs, but it creates new industry sectors and new jobs for others. Their innovations lead to productivity gains, greater enjoyment of creative works, possibilities for greater self-expression and participation in political and cultural life, and the rekindling of old friendships (via new social networks). Many of these innovations let others build yet more innovative things on top of them, from which each party (the platform maker and also the one building upon the platform) can profit. This notion of "generativity," or "open innovation," is part of what makes the Internet unique. And it is part of what is enabling the innovation to take place so quickly.[3]

Digital Native entrepreneurs who build the most disruptive businesses often unleash the greatest amount of change. The drivers of innovation are countercultural to begin with and tap into the broader counterculture of their Digital Native peers. The resulting change takes place in Internet time—at a blistering pace, often too fast for traditional industries to react strategically, other than through lawsuits.

As entrepreneurs, Digital Natives go about the business of business in ways quite different from their parents and grandparents. Digital Natives work well collaboratively as entrepreneurs just as they do when writing wiki entries or creating YouTube videos. Information technologies make it easy for them to collaborate—even at great distances and when they are working asynchronously (as it does for older people).

Facebook was not the work of Zuckerberg alone. Though he is the most famous of the founders, he relied on the skills of several college friends to get Facebook off the ground. Dustin Moskowitz, one of Zuckerberg's co-founders, remains a senior technologist at the company. Chris Hughes served as the spokesman for the company right from the start, and he only left to put his social-networking skills to work as the online organizer for Barack Obama's presidential campaign. These cofounders are not the only ones to claim Facebook as their idea. Another group of Harvard students, from the same era, claim that the idea was theirs in the first place and that they had been working together with Zuckerberg before Facebook took off. They sued Zuckerberg and his friends for all manner of intellectual-property violation and other infractions. (After a messy lawsuit got underway, Facebook eventually settled these claims out of court.)[4]

The collaboration that fuels businesses in the digital age also pulls customers into the act of creating and refining products and services online. Digital Natives have this figured out. Even if one person is the visionary and the coder and the business-development person rolled up in one, Web-based businesses often rely upon the contributions of the users of the service over time. That's the story that we've heard, time and again, with the digital businesses started by Digital Natives. Innovation can mean building on the shoulders of giants who came before, but it can also mean trusting the company's users to point the way to sustained innovation over time. Often, this refinement takes place asynchronously, in physical spaces all around the world, and in a manner that is only loosely coordinated. These services—like Facebook, Napster, and YouTube—are highly independent from the powers-that-be, yet connected in deeply social ways that are obvious to their Digital Native participants and founders.

The biggest breakthrough in Facebook's short history was its decision to trust not just its users, but also other computer-application developers. In 2007, Facebook opened up its platform to allow others to develop applications upon it. In technical terms, Facebook offered computer engineers the ability to interoperate with the site through an Open Application Programming Interface, or Open API.[5] Within a few months, more than 5,000 applications had been developed and integrated into Facebook. For instance, someone who wanted to allow users to play a game that looked like Scrabble could develop the game and offer it within Facebook to Facebook users. It's similar to Microsoft's idea to let anyone develop a computer program that can run on Windows, such as Intuit's TurboTax or H&R Block's TaxCut. Just as at one time, all software developers wanted their programs to work on Microsoft Windows, anyone developing a Web service today has to consider rolling out a "Facebook app" alongside the ordinary service on their own site. Facebook's decision has quickly changed the face of computing in the Web 2.0 era.

This story of interoperability—a boring-sounding, technical term, admittedly—means that people who do not work for Facebook can drive competition and innovation within and across popular social networks. Interoperability enables a new process of communicating and sharing new discoveries in computing to take place. By making these systems work together online, developers have new incentive to innovate and to collaborate. Digital Natives are a big part of this movement. Facebook, to be sure, is only one of many to open up its service to third-party developers. Google, Yahoo!, and other Web giants have made their platforms open in this way. (Microsoft was a leader in this regard, having decided to let anyone develop a computer program that could run on Windows.) There are now entire businesses that consist of mash-ups of other services, such as Zillow (which tells you how much your home and your neighbor's home is worth) and Scrabulous (which lets you play online Scrabble with other Facebook users). There are now businesses that exist solely to create applications for others that can work in Facebook: Two major venture capitalists have announced a special fund to invest in Facebook applications. These efforts tap into the innovative side of the counterculture of the Web.[6]

Digital Native entrepreneurs benefit, too, from the low costs of creativity online. Digital Native entrepreneurs have thrived by making online creativity and sharing easier and more fun. From the perspective of an economist, it's much more cost-effective to become a creator of digital content than it was to create similarly complex works in previous eras. The availability of technology and content has soared. At the same time, the cost of creation, dissemination, storage, and usage of digital content like text, music, video, photography, and the like has plummeted. Costs associated with the relevant technologies continue to fall. And Digital Natives are flocking to many of these services. These are trends into which the founders of Facebook, YouTube, and other Web 2.0 services have been able to tap.

The decline in the cost of computing equipment affects nearly every phase of the creative process. In the 1980s, for instance, a start-up rock band would have spent roughly $50,000 to purchase or rent the necessary recording equipment to make an album. Today, a rock band simply needs a laptop computer and some additional pieces of hardware and software, which might cost less than $1,000, in order to produce—as "amateurs"— a professional album.[7] More important, the same equipment opens the door to a large-and-ready marketplace for music. The costs of storage devices have also declined dramatically. Innovation in storage technologies and the lower costs of data-storage space have in turn enabled new types of hosting services for user-created content to emerge—platforms that are particularly popular among Digital Natives.[8] In August 2006, the *Wall Street Journal* reported that the video-sharing platform YouTube hosted about 6.1 million videos, consuming an estimated 45 terabytes of storage, "about 5,000 home computers' worth—and requir[ing] several million dollars' worth of bandwidth a month to transmit."[9] Roughly half of YouTube's registered users are under twenty years of age, and it is a site that simply couldn't have existed a few years ago. The technology wasn't there and the costs of operating the service would have been prohibitive.

This phenomenon is self-perpetuating. Digital Natives are into online creation; their peers (and others) who are entrepreneurs discover ways to capitalize on this penchant, creating newer and better ways for Digital Natives to create on line; and these services then facilitate even more avenues for creativity and economic opportunities for entrepreneurs, especially those who are attuned to the feedback from their customers. These online services, like YouTube, are democratizing creativity.[10] At the same time, for-profit companies are increasingly looking to user-created content as a way to make money—always a potent driver of innovation and creativity.[11]

Digital Natives are particularly good at creating services and products that will appeal to other Digital Natives. Together, they are creating important markets. Not all Digital Native entrepreneurs are quite as famous as Fanning, Zuckerberg, Cohen, and Hurley, but many—in places around the world—have figured out the same tricks.

Two high-school kids, Catherine and David Cook, and their older brother Geoff Cook, were frustrated with the costs and the design of their own yearbooks. So, in 2005, they founded myYearbook. In three years, myYearbook became one of the most popular and fastest-growing online enterprises. The service connects more than 1.7 million young users around the world. As many online successes did, they started small. They launched as a yearbook for a single local high school. Not even a year later, thousands of new members were signing up for the service each day. Venture capitalists have provided more than $4 million in funding, and myYearbook.com soon became one of the top-ranked websites for teenagers.

Very often, the businesses that Digital Natives start look very similar to businesses that do well in other sectors of the economy, too, but are geared toward catering to Digital Natives. Ben Kaufman, a high-school student, noticed that many of his friends carried around iPods. In 2005, at age eighteen, he started a company called Mophie that makes accessories for iPods, such as cases, belt clips, armbands, splitters, and silicon skins. Its products can be found in Apple stores and elsewhere and are distributed in about thirty countries worldwide. After receiving venture capital and multiplying revenues, in 2007 Ben turned to his customers to get them to help him design a next generation of new iPod accessories.

The phenomenon of young digital entrepreneurs is by no means unique to the United States. The next Facebook may not start up in Silicon Valley or on an Ivy League campus. The low barriers to entry in this emerging culture of entrepreneurship and innovation mean that the next Google or Facebook may well come from India, China, Russia, Brazil—or a smaller developing country. The culture of entrepreneurship among Digital Natives is just as promising in Shanghai, in Dublin, and in parts of the Gulf as it is in most of the digital hubs of the United States. We've been there and met with young entrepreneurs just as impressive as those we've met in Boston or San Francisco. A half-dozen places in India may well emerge as the next hotbeds of innovation by Digital Natives.

Take for instance, Bellamy Benedetto Budiman from Jakarta, Indonesia. After playing around at creating websites, he decided to open his own design studio at the age of sixteen. That was back in 1998. Today, that company, Neuro-Designs, provides design and production services as well as web-hosting for clients in Indonesia. The company is also a supporter of godote.com, which provides a common forum for Indonesian designers where they can interact, share designs, and exchange ideas. Budiman himself acts as a moderator for the site's forum.

The shift is on: In a few short years, businesses have gone from ignoring informal groups of Digital Natives getting together online to obsessing about ways to monetize their enthusiasm. Established media conglomerates and big Internet companies, like NewsCorp, Google, Sony, and Yahoo!, have become interested in deriving revenues from user-generated content services. Big media companies sniffing around this space see this movement as big business. Several have invested significant amounts of money to acquire online services that make it possible to upload creative content to the Web and to connect with one another based on common interests. The nature of the disruptive effect of digital creativity—and what they're doing about it—varies among market players, depending upon their respective business models and strategies.[12]

The firms most likely to thrive are those that are balancing experimentation and enthusiasm for the new environment, on the one hand, with continued revenue generation from traditional modes of operation, on the other. Some Digital Natives are figuring this out; some innovative older people, like the marketing geniuses at Apple, are figuring it out, too. In so doing, they build credibility in the online space without sacrificing the ability to generate a sustainable stream of revenues.

Even when they are not starting big, disruptive new enterprises, Digital Natives are changing the way business is conducted. Digital Natives offer feedback, often quite harsh, but in a way that can help brands to refine at the margins, or to innovate in wholly new ways—if in fact businesses can find a way to listen to the feedback. Companies that provide no feedback loop to their Digital Native customers are missing an opportunity to learn. But they may also be jeopardizing the appeal of their brands altogether. As Digital Natives become a force as consumers and enter the workforce in large numbers, their use of technology can lead to improved products and higher workforce productivity. They also pose fundamental challenges to

existing business models when they are ignored, as the recording industry has learned the hard way.

Digital Natives are good at collaboration, online and offline, and sometimes will do so for free on behalf of companies willing to listen to them.[13]
Digital Natives are putting into practice the idea of bottom-up innovation
better than any population of consumers before them. Many of them are
critical consumers, who provide feedback on their experiences. Marketers can find the feedback streams from Digital Natives all over the
Web, sometimes full of unwelcome invective.[14] Their complaints about
a given product—"Taco Bell used to be great, but now they stink"—are no
longer confined to the schoolyard or the dinner table. They're out in the
open, for anyone to read. They're also out there for anyone to aggregate.
Or, as is the case with the most compelling critiques, to link to and build
off of. (Think we're kidding? Check out, for instance, BurritoBlog.com, a
site dedicated to a running critique of Taco Bell and others in the burrito
industry, or just do a Google search on "burrito complaints.")

The feedback loop is an essential feature of services that Digital Natives
come to love. Marketers who learn to listen to their feedback will be able
to cash in by becoming completely in step with their customers. Companies are learning that it's much better to offer customers a place to give direct feedback at their virtual doorstep than to ignore complaints and let
them crop up everywhere. Microsoft learned this lesson when it released
an important new browser, Internet Explorer 7, in 2006. In the Internet
era, a sense had developed among young people that Microsoft was a be-
hemoth that often acted like the monopolist that it was; Microsoft no
longer looked like the nimble, responsive start-up darling that it once did.
But when Microsoft released IE 7, it explicitly set up a process for feedback
from users about bugs and enhancements. The comments flowed in, Microsoft responded, and the product improved and thrived.

Facebook executives have shown that they are masters at this process of
gathering feedback from Digital Natives and, most of the time, acting on it.
In 2006, two years into its growth phase, Facebook introduced a new feature called the News Feed. Instead of going to a friend's page to see what was
new on their profile, the news would be broadcast to each friend's page. So
when logging on to Facebook, the user would be greeted with the aggregated news flowing from everyone in his or her immediate social network.

A good friend broke up with his girlfriend (finally). Another friend is at her favorite café this morning. The lecture in microeconomics class is particularly boring today.

The feature seemed like a clever idea. But Facebook's users were immediately up in arms. It didn't sound like a feature, it sounded like a bug. Worse, it sounded like a violation of their privacy. Within hours of the News Feed feature rolling out, a Facebook group formed within Facebook itself to criticize the move. It turned out to be a huge group: Hundreds of thousands of users signed up. The ringleader was a student from Northwestern University named Ben Parr, aged twenty-one at the time.[15]

The first reaction of Facebook's executives was to acknowledge the uprising within the community. Mark Zuckerberg wrote to the group: "Calm Down. Breathe. We Hear You." Their second reaction, after a bit of thought, was just the right one. Zuckerberg wrote another blog post to the community with a first line that read: "We really messed this one up." Facebook did exactly what a sensible company should do, but so few will do: Its executives listened to their customers, and they made sensible adjustments to its service accordingly. News Feed has turned out to be an enormous success, well post-launch, and the privacy settings of most people on Facebook have not been used to block the feeds from issuing. Facebook's team listened to the community and got it right in the end. The same story has repeated itself with the rollout of an advertising feature at Facebook called Beacon. One can imagine this process repeating over time, and Facebook continuing to succeed if they continue to listen well to their enormous customer base.[16]

Digital Natives can be pushy customers. They can also be very generous, in a way, with their criticism. When this feedback is encouraged and rendered constructive, it can help to strengthen products and build long-term customer relationships. Those who don't set up processes for feedback, customer reviews, and the like are ignoring both their customers and an opportunity for improvement at their peril.

There is a third way in which Digital Natives are transforming business as usual: as employees. Many would argue that they're not transforming it for the good. Employers often complain that they don't understand the ways in which Digital Natives work, communicate, and manage information. Or even when they do understand it, they don't like it.

The behavior of Digital Natives in the workplace does not always have to be simply accepted. Many traits that are truly mystifying to bosses who grew up analog can be resisted. The casualness of e-mail and texting language spills over, for instance, often inappropriately, to business environments where formal language and structured correspondence serve a purpose. Digital Natives who furtively spend much of the day social-networking on the Internet or reading gossip on TMZ.com may be downright infuriating—and a total waste of time on the company's dime. These aspects of Digital Native culture just need to be changed when Digital Natives become employees, through rule or incentive systems.

But to dismiss the habits of Digital Natives entirely out of hand would be a big mistake for employers. Many of the attributes that make Digital Natives annoying as employees may also make them more likely to be effective as employees, too, for those with an aptitude—and the patience—to manage and mentor them effectively. Raised in a digital world that thrives on collaboration, Digital Natives can be stymied by—and disrespectful of—the hierarchical structure of most workplaces. In some cases, there are teams that can be highly efficient with less hierarchy, such as computer-programming teams. Digital Natives who multitask constantly can seem unfocused to employers. Yet some Digital Natives can put their ability to juggle tasks to work to make them more productive in high-stress jobs. Think of what it takes to succeed as an event planner or as the manager of a fast-food restaurant, where computers process orders and where attention needs to be split across multiple tasks in short time frames.

Digital Natives already make up an important, productive part of the workforce. As in the home or in school, they may have much to learn from those who are older and wiser. But they also bring to their work facilities digital tools that will help businesses succeed in unexpected ways. Just like parents and teachers, employers need to listen carefully to what Digital Natives are saying and watch what they are doing differently, to push back and give guidance where they are plainly messing up, and to lean into what they are uniquely capable of doing.

D igital Natives have already transformed the economy in fascinating ways, and we're only at the beginning. As more Digital Natives come of age, we will see innovations in productivity, consumer-driven innovation, and new platforms for creativity that we can't foresee today. Cultures that promote the kind of innovation that Digital Natives are pioneering will reap the benefits in untold ways and for a long time to come. In the short term, Digital Natives' entrepreneurship, work habits, and consumer patterns will be disruptive—indeed, already have been. Digital Natives will in time revitalize the industries that they are challenging, create new jobs to replace those they are threatening, and offer new services to customers around the world.

Established businesses need not, ultimately, be threatened by Digital Natives and their puzzling ways. Firms that build strong, trusting bonds with their employees and customers will thrive. Those successful firms will learn to operate in the largely open, globally connected online marketplace in a digitally networked world. They will tap into the creativity of Digital Natives while, at the same time, refusing to give in to the excesses— occasionally, lawlessness—of the digital counterculture.

11

LEARNERS

I N THE LATE 1990S, HARVARD LAW SCHOOL INVESTED A LOT OF MONEY TO renovate and modernize some beautiful old classrooms. Among other things, the school's administrators decided to install new chairs. The old ones were incredibly uncomfortable—hard, plastic, and form-fitting. The chairs harkened back to an earlier era of education, when students were expected to sit still and ramrod straight, responding to hard questions and taking notes as the hoary old professor at the front of the room drilled the laws of evidence into their brains.

Having decided to update the chairs, Harvard Law School decided it would make sense to install an Ethernet jack at each student's seat, along with an electric outlet for laptops. This renovation happened to coincide with the dot-com era, in which students were jumping ship to start their own Internet companies. Even law firm associates and partners were bailing out to join dot-coms. Not to be outdone by other schools preparing their lawyers for practice in a digital age, the Harvard Law School administration decided that a modern classroom ought to have Internet access at every seat. But the faculty hadn't focused on what the effect of access to the Internet during class would be.

Immediately after they were installed, the law school faculty ordered that the Ethernet jacks—the on-ramps to the Internet—be turned off. Students could plug their laptops into the electrical sockets and take notes, if they must, but the notion of a classroom full of students surfing the Web during a Socratic teaching session on the hearsay rule made professors uneasy.

A decade later, no one uses the Ethernet jacks in the renovated classrooms. But the students are most definitely on the Internet during Evidence class—pretty much all of them, actually. Students access the Net through the wireless networks that blanket the Harvard campus (and much of the city of Cambridge, for that matter). During class, the students are online, reading the news on CNN, sending instant messages, accessing Wikipedia to learn (maybe) what happened in that case they didn't read for class. There's no meaningful way to stop them from doing so, short of banning laptops in the classroom or situating teaching fellows at the back of the room to keep an eye on every screen. Some faculty members do just that; others seek to harness the Web for pedagogical purposes; and others are still scratching their heads about it all, wondering what happened, so quickly and with so little deliberation, to legal education.

Harvard Law School is far from alone. The educational establishment is utterly confused about what to do about the impact of technology on learning. Schools at every level of education have done the same thing that Harvard Law School did. Some schools have distributed a laptop to every student, and then wondered what to have them do with the computers (or regretted what the students *did* do with them). Others have spent tens of thousands of dollars to equip every classroom with SmartBoards, a terrific newfangled computerized chalk-board that sits at the front of the room, only to wonder, after the checks were cashed, whether the SmartBoards belong there. Now that wireless Internet access blankets many campuses and urban areas, schools are wondering whether to boost the signals or to find ways to try block them from bleeding into the classrooms (almost certainly a futile task).

Forward-looking schools know that technology infrastructures are likely to be worthy investments over time. But very few have any idea how to use them—and, just as important, when *not* to use them—at the present moment. And very few schools have figured out the connection between how young people are learning in general in a digital age, in both formal and informal settings, and their own missions.

In order for schools to adapt to the habits of Digital Natives and how they are processing information, educators need to accept that the mode of learning is changing rapidly in a digital age. Before answering the questions about how precisely to use technology in schools, we must understand these changes. To do so, it's necessary to expand the frame to all learning, not just the kind that happens in the classroom.

Learning itself has undergone a transformation over the past thirty years. The Internet is changing the way that children—and college students—gather and process information in all aspects of their lives. For Digital Natives, "research" is more likely to mean a Google search than a trip to the library. They are more likely to check in with the Wikipedia community, or to turn to another online friend, than they are to ask a reference librarian for help. They rarely, if ever, buy the newspaper in hard copy; instead, they graze through copious amounts of news and other information online.

We're not quite sure yet what the implications of these changes will be over the long term. There are a lot of excellent questions to be answered about how kids are learning in a digital environment and how that compares to the way they learned in a predominantly analog world. Does reading websites, instead of books and broadsheet-style newspapers, actually change the way people process information, in the short and long terms? Do kids end up remembering the information that they gather online more or less effectively than they remember material they read on a printed page? Is the way that kids read these days a cause or an effect of diminishing attention spans (or both)? What is the role of teachers and librarians in a world with so many experts opining freely on the Web, to whom Digital Natives are turning for information? Are kids learning anything of value while playing all those video games that consume so much of their free time? There is a vast phalanx of psychologists, neuroscientists, and educational theorists—among others—working on these and many other questions about how new technologies are affecting the ways that Digital Natives absorb and retain information.

Adults are worried about how kids are learning. In the absence of clear data, a lot of parents and educators are fearful of the effects that digital technologies are having on our children and their ability to learn. Parents and grandparents worry about kids not reading books cover to cover the way they used to. Librarians worry that kids are only looking at a narrow range of sources, to which they've been referred by a single monolithic corporation (Google, or the search-engine-of-the-year). Senior faculty members at universities worry that their graduate students are failing to find highly relevant Lionel Trilling articles because some online databases don't go far enough back to include his work. Slogans, in headline format, they fear, dominate the information seeping into young people's brains, with kids developing too few analytical skills along the way. Kids, the worry goes, are channel-surfing through their education, and their brains are being rewired in the process.

Just because Digital Natives learn differently from the way their parents did when they were growing up doesn't mean that Digital Natives are not learning. Take, for example, the way that Digital Natives learn about events in the news. Many older people assume that because Digital Natives are not reading newspapers and magazines, but instead absorbing news all day long on various websites (and from comedy programs and other unconventional sources), their understanding of current events is superficial and limited to headlines. And worse, these headlines, parents and teachers worry, come from biased websites, rather than authoritative organizations like the *New York Times* or the big television networks, NBC, ABC, and CBS. If it's not outright wrong, the version of the story Digital Natives encounter online must be superficial, many people fear.

These assumptions are wrong, because they underestimate the depth of knowledge that Digital Natives are obtaining on the Web. They also miss a key feature of how Digital Natives experience news: interacting with information in constructive ways. Digital Natives often access much more information about a topic they are interested in than kids of previous generations ever could have. A recent study of young people and their news-gathering habits confirms these changes. The study found, for example, that young Americans don't read the daily newspaper. Digital Natives pick up bits and pieces of news and information as they go about their day, not in a single sitting at the breakfast table in the morning or in front of the television in the evening. And often, they in fact engage more with the material than those who are used to more traditional news formats, by virtue of writing a post about the idea on a blog or sharing it with a friend on Facebook or over instant messaging.

Just because Digital Natives don't learn things in the same way that their grandparents did does not mean that the way that they are learning is not as effective. There is no evidence to suggest that they are learning less than their grandparents did, or that they are more superficial in their learning. In fact, Digital Natives are quite sophisticated in the ways that they gather information. The people to be worried about are those who are growing up in a digital age but who are not learning these sophisticated information-gathering and information-processing skills, or creating things of their own based on what they learn and sharing it with others.

Digital Natives gather information through a multistep process that involves grazing, a "deep dive," and a feedback loop. They are perfecting the art of grazing through the huge amount of information that comes their way on a daily basis. Imagine an eighteen-year-old college freshman interested in the Middle East. (Yes, many Digital Natives are interested in public affairs in regions other than their own.) Her boyfriend comes from an Arabic-speaking family, and she is hoping to travel to Egypt next summer. When she opens her browser, Google is her home page. It features headlines from sources that she has preselected, on topics of her choosing. She might even have plugged keywords into Google or Technorati (a similar service that primarily tracks blogs) so that those services could send her alerts when relevant stories appear. She grazes all day through the news feeds that she sees on her Facebook profile, posted by friends or others. She might see headlines about the region by grazing through news from major news outlets online (CNN, MSNBC, the *New York Times*, *Al-Jazeera*, and so forth). She'll also probably have a few favorite specialized websites or discussion boards—for instance, Mideastyouth.com—which she'll glance at in the course of the day. Chat rooms and e-mail listservs might serve a similar function.

And, of course, her computer isn't the only medium through which she will learn about the news in the Middle East in a given day. Her cell phone might serve up headlines that come through like text messages to her handset, bleeping at her as they arrive (if she's a sports fan, this is how she gets changes in a game score, too). She will hear news on the radio or watch it on the television in a gym or a student center at her university. She also watches television news programs that star comedians, such as Jon Stewart or Stephen Colbert.

While grazing, the Digital Native will absorb a headline or a bit more—perhaps a paragraph—about any given story. The most important features of information in this context are speed, accessibility, and how well it has been sorted. The information is valuable insofar as it is timely, relevant, and easy to process. The fact that it can be accessed from anywhere—that Facebook news feed is channeled through a cell phone that is constantly attached to a Digital Native's body—is equally important. And the interface through which the Digital Native gets this information is more useful and attractive the more it can enable her to sort through the vast rivers of information flowing around her all the time.

With some of the stories she sees, she decides she wants to go beyond the headline, to learn more about a topic or event—to take a deep dive. In this way, she is searching for what's behind the headline, what the facts are, what it might mean for her, what the people involved looked like, and so forth. It might mean clicking on a hypertext link, loading up a video, or downloading a podcast to listen to on the train. The deep dive helps her to make sense of the news, to put it into a frame or better context, to offer an analysis of it, to introduce relevant other voices.

The deep-dive stage in the news-gathering process for a Digital Native is where news organizations, especially powerful and wealthy institutions—those able to afford bureaus and the like—can add the most value. Some blogs fill this role, too. CNN, the BBC, the *New York Times, The Economist,* Talking Points Memo—these are increasingly powerful brands in a world of more and more information sources. Global Voices online is an example of a trustworthy brand that is less well known, but equally important in terms of providing context to stories that our hypothetical Digital Native encounters as she seeks news and information about the Middle East.

Global Voices is a global nonprofit citizens' media organization that seeks to aggregate, curate, and amplify the global conversation online and to shine light on places and people other media often ignore. The key factor is not speed in this context, though timeliness is important; the key factors are accuracy, trustworthiness, insight, analysis, new angles, and relationships.[1]

Some will go further, meaning that they will actively engage with the information, sometimes in new ways. The eighteen-year-old college student may be enraged by what she reads and want to "talk back" to the news. The logical next step is to jump into the debate somehow. This last stage—the feedback loop—is not for every Digital Native, and certainly not for every young person. It is also the hardest for traditionalists to grapple with. Some Digital Natives take this next step to engage more meaningfully with the facts and the context of what they read.

The form of a Digital Native's feedback loops varies. She might write a post to her blog to critique a story she saw on CNN. She might comment on someone else's blog, or on a wiki or bulletin board. Or perhaps she'll send an e-mail to a listserv or to a network news program. If she's especially creative or passionate about a subject, she might create her own podcast or video-log (or vlog). The idea is that she may react publicly to the story or remake and retell it in some fashion. Digital tools enable her to have an impact on the way the story is told. This feedback loop should be taken seriously.

The feedback loop might also involve passing the information around to friends and family. Digital information has a social life in the hands of Digital Natives. They share it with one another, post stories to their profiles in social network sites, and talk about it on instant messaging or on blogs. It's not every young person who engages with information in this interactive way, but it's more than most parents and teachers think. The same instinct that leads a new Web user to circulate so many e-mail jokes (and scams) animates the news- and information-sharing behavior of Digital Natives. The difference between a Digital Native and one's aunt with the new e-mail account in this regard is that the Digital Native is likely more sophisticated about what she shares and how.

Generally speaking, this increased level of engagement with information and the world around her is good for her own learning process. If we can encourage it, there's no doubt that this feedback loop will redound to the benefit of society at large over time. If Digital Natives are rewarded for leading lives more engaged in the civic sphere, we'll all be better off. It's a long shot, but it's one worth taking—and one that won't happen unless we pay attention to fostering the positive behavior that it involves.

While the effects of this mode of learning—both in gathering and recreating information—pose real problems for print and other content-owning industries, those with strong brands should be able to thrive. There's no evidence that Digital Natives have less interest in news and information than their parents and grandparents. It's just that Digital Natives are not engaging with news and information in the same way as it has historically been offered by these industries. Studies of the user-generated content environment show that the news items that spur the most conversation on blogs and similar sites are often first published by mainstream news providers such as the *New York Times*. The *Times* is an example of a company that has invested heavily in an accessible, effective online format for its world-class news. Its senior leadership has a strong vision for how the news will be provided and how people will engage with it in the future. Good things in new formats will enable strong brands to lead in a digital era.[2]

There are no hard data to suggest that Digital Natives are smarter than anyone who came before them. Neither is there any sign that kids are dumber, or in any way less promising, than previous generations of kids. Digital Natives are doing the same things their parents did with information, just in different ways. While they may not be learning the same things through the same processes, it's not the case that Digital Natives are interacting less with information. They are simply coping with more information, and that information comes to their attention in new ways—offering new possibilities for engagement.

Some of the concerns that parents and teachers have about how kids are learning in a digital age have merit. These are real problems that need to be addressed.

First, we know that Digital Natives multitask. At Harvard, most students have a laptop in front of them, connected to the Internet, at all times. As teachers at the front of the room, we can tell that students are using the

Internet during a seminar to IM one another, read news online, and otherwise amuse themselves. There's an obvious concern about students not paying enough attention to the task at hand—namely, in this case, learning about the law. With a world of information and connections to friends at their fingertips at all times, the temptation to stray from the course is great. As we saw in the previous chapter, multitasking is almost always bad when a student is trying to learn new things or doing something that requires a lot of attention. One of the reasons that Harvard professors didn't want access to the Internet in the classroom was that they didn't want students to be distracted by playing solitaire (or, thanks to Internet connectivity, hearts) on their computers during class. Faculty members often wish the students were still sitting up ramrod straight in those uncomfortable chairs and hanging on every word.

Some parents and teachers worry, too, about Digital Natives having shorter attention spans than children in previous decades. There are real issues brewing here. Many kids do read shorter works. They are migrating from things like extended format magazines and books to the Web. On the Web, short formats ordinarily work better than long formats, whether in text, audio, or video. By and large, it is a sound-bite culture. Ditto for text messaging, instant messaging, and even e-mailing.

Many of the young people we interviewed stressed their preference for instant messaging and texting, for instance, as a mode of communication with others. Much has been said of the increasingly short attention spans, not just of our youth but of anyone in society. All news seekers are rewarded for flitting about from sound bite to sound bite, and these bites are coming from more and more sources. For Digital Natives, the phenomenon is the same, only amplified.[3]

A third and unrelated concern we've heard from teachers is that the innovative use of technology leads to a "copy-and-paste" culture—a practice that is in tension with traditional educational ethics. According to insiders, technology-enabled cheating is on the rise on college campuses, especially in technical disciplines, where students increasingly work together on assignments when they are required to submit their "own" answers.[4]

These phenomena are obvious to anyone who teaches or manages Digital Natives in a classroom or a workplace. These fears are realistic. Many adults who have migrated to the Web do just the same things. Things are moving and changing quickly in the digital age. It's hard to know what the future will hold, and more than a bit scary.

Given what we know about how kids are learning in the digital age, there are many things that schools can do to harness what is great about how Digital Natives relate to information. There's also a lot we can do to address the problems that are cropping up.

We don't need to overhaul education to teach kids who are born digital. There is a temptation among those who love technology to promote radical changes in the way we teach our students. It's easy to fetishize technology. That instinct is wrong. Learning will always have certain enduring qualities that have little or nothing to do with technology.

The use of technology in teaching makes no sense if it's just because we think that technology is cool. It's easy to understand how we get to this place. The thinking goes like this: It's fun and cool to blog; lots of people are doing it; we know that kids get some information from blogs; therefore, blogging must have a place in our schools. This orientation is a mistake. We should figure out, instead, how the use of technologies can support our pedagogical goals. Blogging might, or might not, be part of the approach we end up taking. The right way to look at it is to ask whether blogging can meet a need that we have in our teaching. We need to determine what our goals are, as teachers and parents, and then figure out how technology can help us, and our kids, to reach those goals.[5]

The things that schools and teachers do best should not be scrapped in the rush to use technologies in the classroom. In every field, there are aspects of the curriculum that should be taught without screens or Net connections. In our field of law, for instance, the computer has no place in a classroom where a wonderful teacher is firing questions at a first-year student, quizzing him about contracts. Surveys among Digital Natives indicate that students have a preference for a moderate use of technology in the classroom.[6] The way that students learn to think critically, much of the time, is through old-fashioned dialogue, with people exchanging views and looking in depth at a topic, questioning and exploring issues in a face-to-face, real-life setting: Our teaching, in such cases, should not necessarily be mediated by new technologies. This is the hardest job that teachers and principals may face: how to avoid the trap of shunning the technology, on the one hand, and embracing it in places where it does not belong, on the other.

There are ways that we can get Digital Natives interested and take advantage of the particular ways that they learn. Let's take advantage of the fact that they have computers in front of them and the skills to use them. Schools should make it a priority to figure out the right way to integrate technology into the curriculum for the given skill level of students. These approaches should seek to optimize, in the classroom environment, what we know Digital Natives to be doing in learning both inside and outside the formal school setting.

The most important thing that schools can do is not to use technology in the curriculum more, but to use it more effectively. We ought to experiment with ways in which technology ought to be part of the everyday curricula in schools—but only where it belongs. The technology should only be applied in support of our pedagogy, not for its own sake. This basic orientation suggests that holding "computer classes," while possibly a sensible add-on to some curricula, is not as good of an idea as the notion of building technology into the ordinary curriculum where it can help. Programs where students are doing applied work, research and writing, arts and music, and problem solving are obvious places to seek integration.[7]

As part of these curricular changes, schools need to focus on bringing the kids on the other side of the participation gap up to speed.[8] The New Media Literacies curricula are designed for this purpose. Instead of worrying about the "digital divide" in terms of just access to technologies, schools need to adopt affirmative strategies to teach kids who otherwise are being left behind by the digitally mediated world to function effectively within it.

To bridge this gap, schools should encourage kids to learn by doing in digital environments. Young people, whether they are Digital Natives or not, can learn by creating digital works ranging from the utterly simple to the highly elaborate. The idea is to build on their penchant for developing online profiles and other materials in MySpace, Facebook, blogs, and

YouTube. Music classes can be transformed by letting kids listen to Beethoven and then having them create their own master work (or maybe not) using inexpensive software on a computer, like FL Studio or, for the more daring, Audacity.[9] Writing, poetry, art—in each instance a teacher can orient Digital Natives in a digital space and encourage them to build something new or improve on something old. In social studies or a class on politics, students could be prompted to take digital speeches of candidates for office and remix them into contexts that make them meaningful to the student. In so doing, students could learn about copyrights—their own as well as others'. This mode of teaching students by encouraging their talents for online creativity will no doubt present challenges for many teachers who are not comfortable in the digital world. But the payoff could be substantial, for student and teacher alike.[10]

Schools should also use digital technologies to encourage team-based learning. The school of the future will put students in digitally supported environments where they can work, and learn, in teams. Digital Natives are proving, all the time, that they can build communities around ideas, good and bad. Interaction and a sense of community are the key requests of those born digital when it comes to online learning, as surveys indicate.[11] The work world will require them to collaborate in order to succeed, whether they are starting a new business or nonprofit or taking a staff position in an existing one. Collaborative technologies like wikis are cheap and easy to use. As students research, write, and create collaboratively through online environments, they will be learning skills that will serve them well over time, even as digital economies evolve.

Schools also ought to incentivize and reward experimentation by its faculty. Principals and deans should strive to make it easy for faculty to experiment with new technologies in support of their teaching. Teachers know best what problems they need to solve and what opportunities they want to seize. Most schools develop a mode of supporting modest use of modest tools by a handful of faculty. School leaders need to have enough vision and enough support for experimentation for creativity to take hold and flourish, in step with curricular reform.[12]

Experimentation by faculty might include creative use of gaming in the classroom, for instance. Many parents and teachers complain about the short attention spans of their kids; but those same kids seem to have more than adequate attention spans when it comes to gaming. The technologies themselves can be used to address the problems to which their use contributes—such as short attention spans.[13] Schools can find ways to tap into the Digital Native love of gaming. There is a movement building around "pro-social gaming," for example, which has enormous promise as a concept. In reality, most of the games invented so far with a socially oriented purpose have been less than compelling. The notion of finding ways to use games, in certain instances, to teach math or science has a place in future curricula.

There's an enormous amount we can learn from what is engaging Digital Natives, and we should apply that learning to our efforts to rethink curricula. One simple idea, for any class that involves writing of some sort, is to put digital technologies to work as a feedback loop for students to comment on the material they are studying or on the ideas of their peers. The technologies to do so are free or cheap, and students already know how to use them.

Finally, the school of the future should be better connected to the world at large. It's a big world. We learn too little about people and places far from us. One of the ways that the Internet can be used for free is to help people to explore the world without having to buy a plane ticket. Digital Natives know how to connect to people who are geographically far from them. In the simplest form, the Internet provides access to deeper, richer information about other cultures.

A great way for a classroom teacher to enable students to listen in on what people in another culture are saying, and to communicate with them, is to use Global Voices. A simple class project would be to follow the news in a place that students are studying in class and to require students to post comments on stories about what happened that week in Kenya or Mongolia—or any other place they are studying. Project Lingua at Global Voices ensures that many articles are translated by users into multiple languages, and sometimes a fascinating discussion on a given word-choice in one language or another accompanies the piece.[14] Kids can effectively travel abroad by using the Internet.

Those schools with more in the way of resources can experiment more extensively than those with fewer resources, and more elaborate systems will pay off for students who perform at a high level. The computer science program at the elite Chapin School in New York City, which encourages the integration of digital tools across the curriculum, is one exceptional example. They have set up creative online spaces that look like MySpace pages, only more structured and learning-oriented.[15] Most schools can't afford Chapin's level of experimentation, but for those that can, the opportunities are endless—and well worth pursuing.

Schools of the future will need faculty of the future. We both teach at fancy universities. Our schools have invested a lot of money installing new technologies. But no one has ever offered to teach either of us how to apply those technologies in our teaching. There are great people we can go to if we have a question about how to get on the network, connect a computer to a projector, or perform any other task related to getting the technology to work. But very few schools of any sort take the simple first step of giving teachers adequate training, or any training at all, to help them teach using technologies in a way that supports their specific pedagogical mode. The trainers don't need to be expensive outside consultants. They could well be the most tech-savvy teachers in each department, just sharing examples of how they've successfully deployed the technology in their own teaching. One could even imagine ways to work Digital Natives into helping teachers learn to teach more effectively using some of these technologies. We know this is much easier said than done, especially for schools strapped for cash and teachers hard-pressed for time. But it is a worthy and obvious place to start.[16]

Television didn't transform education. Neither will the Internet. But it will be another tool for teachers to use in their effort to reach students in the classroom. It will also be a means by which students learn outside of the classroom.

The changes for libraries over the past couple of decades have been even more radical than the changes in the classroom. Libraries are the facet of education that will change the most in the digital age.

Librarians have no choice but to ask hard questions about acquisitions, given the increasing importance of digital resources to the library's core users. The problem is that both digital works and traditional print materials cost money. The ideal scenario—in which a collection includes a hard-copy version and digital version of every book, for searching, cataloging, borrowing, and citation—is implausible. This is, at a certain point, a zero-sum game of resources. The cost of acquiring an increasing number of works in two formats and maintaining dual systems (analog and digital) is prohibitive.

Many libraries are already being transformed. Some are devoting less and less room to books, and more and more to computers and printers. In the process, many libraries are becoming more like bookstores with every passing year. Digital technologies allow them to know more about what their patrons are reading, just as bookstores use them to track their customers' preferences. The need to spend on digital works and services—in part to meet the demand from Digital Natives—is concurrently reducing the amount of money available to spend on books. Libraries are teaming up with one another to acquire books for just-in-time delivery to patrons, rather than maintaining the old system of each library having its own copy of each book on the shelf. We are witnessing the Amazonification of libraries.

Digitization has meant that books—in their classic, bound format—aren't the only way to convey information. Patrons have more options than they used to. Just as iTunes offered customers an à la carte approach to obtaining music, publishers are signing on to allow people to buy one chapter at a time. Google lets customers sample many books before buying them. More profound, kids who can't afford books can read John Locke in digital format for free online, and many other public domain works besides.

Books are not dead; culture is not collapsing. There is no need to worry about the future of the book just yet. Books for many people remain a very good technology. Hard copies of books are important on many levels. Many people prefer to read hard copies of books to digital forms of books, despite massive investments in technologies like e-Ink at the MIT Media Lab. Books don't run out of batteries on airplanes, as an Amazon Kindle can in the middle of a gripping novel. Some people, including Digital Natives, still like to curl up with books in bed, collect them on bookshelves as signs of their knowledge (or for easy access), take them to the beach, and so forth. Books represent a stable format, unlike the constantly changing digital formats that imperil digital record-keeping processes over the long term. Books are the cornerstone, for now at least, of the large and important publishing industry, whose leaders play a significant role in democracies and cultures around the world. Books have the advantage, under U.S. and European law at least, of being covered by the first-sale doctrine and the principle of exhaustion, respectively (you can give them away, or lend them, or sell them in a secondary market). But books have downsides, too—the slow fire phenomenon (whereby books of a certain vintage are deteriorating quickly), the high cost of production (compared to their digital counterparts), and the high cost of storage and distribution.

The libraries of the future will also need the librarians of the future. Libraries will be staffed increasingly by those who can serve as guides to Digital Natives. At a fundamental level, the services provided by the library ought to adjust to the way that Digital Natives are accessing information. There's never been a greater need for reference librarians than there is today, when Digital Natives are relying so heavily on Google, Wikipedia, and the places to which those sites point them.

The job of the librarian of the future should in part be to help to create a self-service information environment that allows students to navigate the increasingly complex array of choices for getting the information they need. In addition to maintaining access to traditional pools of knowledge (such as books, journals, and case studies), librarians should help Digital Natives figure out how to manage the rivers of digital information that they encounter every day (RSS feeds of current information that is useful for a short window, but less so with the passage of time, for example). Right now, libraries are focused on the pools. Librarians could profitably help patrons have greater access to the rivers, and to use them more effectively.

Libraries should serve as a digital heritage center. The works of Digital Natives, and of everyone else living in the digital age, may well be less likely to be preserved than the writings of ninth-century monks on sturdy parchment. Librarians should think in terms of collections that will preserve this digital heritage for future generations. The collection of digital resources by every library, historical society, museum, and other collecting institution can help on this front. This is what it means to gather resources for the public in a digital era. In a world where our children are born digital, these collections can be freely online and available to anyone, any-where in the world—not just those within walking or driving distance of each library. And these collections should take the form of a digital com-mons, without the constraints of physical distribution, from the start. As Digital Natives are creating many of the artifacts that successive genera-tions will wish to study, this will be their legacy.[17]

The role of libraries is increasing, not decreasing. The job may take on different contours, but its importance is only rising as Digital Natives grow up saturated in the information environment of the digital age.

Schools and libraries should start by putting the learners first. Teachers and administrators need to get serious about figuring out how kids are learning, and they must build digital literacy skills into their core curric-ula. Librarians should embrace the crucial role that they can play in guid-ing Digital Natives through the increasingly complicated world of digital information.

Our children find information in digital formats and are processing it in ways that those who came before them could only have imagined. This information is sometimes surrounded with far less context than in the past, while at other times, it is surrounded with far more. Our challenge is to help them make sense of these new contexts and new meanings, and to think synthetically and critically, rather than letting them lose their way. Digital Natives may be able to lead us into these new environments and show us how they work, but parents, teachers, and librarians still need to teach children and students how to interpret the signals they pick up with such perception.

We find ourselves in a period of transition. Digital tools will find their place in schools and libraries. We have managed transitions of this sort before. The hard part, during the transition, will be to discern what to pre-serve about traditional education and what to replace with new, digitally mediated processes and tools. Sometimes, this will mean teaching kids to use computers; sometimes, computers will have no place in the room. We need to get much better at telling the two apart. Only then can we exploit what we know about how kids are learning in the digital age.

12

ACTIVISTS

I MAGINE A DEVELOPING COUNTRY THAT IS STARTING TO GET SOME ECO-
nomic traction, with a growth rate of 6 or 7 percent per year. The president, up for reelection, faces a stiff challenge from a popular opposition
leader. The challenger, a charismatic tribesman with a wide following, campaigns hard. The election is extremely close. After the vote, the president
arranges for a quick swearing-in and abruptly declares himself the winner. Supporters of his opponent cry foul. Violence erupts across the country. The major city is thrown into turmoil. The country's main port shuts
down.

During the election, a group of citizens used the Internet and their cell
phones to tell the story of what was going on through firsthand accounts.
These activists, some of them Digital Natives, took photographs of events
as they broke and posted them to the Web. They critiqued the formal accounts coming from the government and from the mainstream press. They
organized their opposition over cell phones and in e-mail, in the process
connecting people who never before would have found one another and
orchestrating meetings and rallies in far more efficient ways than they
could have without the technology.

In the aftermath of the election, activists on both sides of the dispute continue to chronicle the violence and to tell the story of what is taking place for a global audience. The world's press relies, in no small part, on the most reliable of these firsthand accounts for the articles that people outside of the country read in their local papers in London, Tokyo, and Washington, D.C.

This story is no mere hypothetical. In Kenya in early 2008, a period of violent political unrest followed a contested election.[1] Skilled political activists, taking advantage of Kenya's partially networked environment, provided firsthand accounts of the election and its aftermath that helped to shape what people in Kenya and others around the world came to know about what happened in those heady days.

In Kenya, Internet and cell-phone penetration is relatively low by global standards, but the country's elites are online. Just as important, there is a large diaspora community of Kenyans who use the Internet as a primary means of communication. Within the wired subpopulace of Kenyans, there is a growing, vibrant community of people who are writing and posting digital media to the Web in highly sophisticated ways, geared toward having a political impact. Young people played a leading role in the election narrative. But Kenya is not the only developing country where the Web, and young people, are beginning to influence the course of important events.[2]

The new mode of activism, made possible by the use of networked digital tools, leads to benefits for citizens of established democracies, countries in transition, and authoritarian regimes alike. First, as the Kenyan example demonstrates, it is possible to harness the Internet's power to render more transparent the actions of a specific government. This transparency matters both in times of crisis—in an unruly election, for example—and in times of orderly governance. Second, the Internet can provide a means for ordinary citizens to participate in the way that public events are told to others, set into context, understood by people far and near, and remembered for posterity. The traditional hierarchies of control of news and information are crumbling, with new dynamics replacing the old. These new dynamics will lead to a more responsive politics.

The ability of networked activists to transform politics in some countries could prove to be the single most important trend in the global Internet culture. The early signs of a culture of civic activism among young people, joined by networked technologies, are cropping up around the world. If these early signs turn into a bigger movement, politics as we know it is in for big changes.

Presidential campaigns have drawn a lot of attention to the role of Digital Natives in politics, but these campaigns are only the very beginning of the story. Howard Dean's presidential primary run in 2004 is the paradigmatic example. Led by campaign manager Joe Trippi and visionary organizers like Zephyr Teachout and Jim Moore, the Dean campaign used the Internet to harness grassroots energy, to pull new people into the campaign, and to raise a great deal of money online. Barack Obama's 2008 campaign has done all that the Dean campaign did, and more, online. Participation in electoral affairs is a starting point and has led to a lot of hype, but it is also not the most important aspect of how Digital Natives are participating in civic life.

The Internet has not fundamentally changed the nature of political action, nor has it brought millions of new people into civic life. The Internet provides tools that empower people, young and old, to have a greater level of direct, personal participation in the formal political process—if they want to. No new technology is going to make someone have a conversion experience. What the Net provides is an increasingly useful, attractive platform for those who are predisposed to be active in civic life. The Internet makes possible new and occasionally astonishing things for a set of highly empowered individuals. Young people can gain access to far more information than ever before. They can reach out to other people far more efficiently. With huge ambition, one or two people can establish a news operation that can put huge pressure on mainstream news providers, offer alternative viewpoints, and reach a global audience on a modest budget.

That said, we must acknowledge up front that our argument about the political potentialities of the Internet is not data driven. The data do not support the argument that Digital Natives, or anyone else, are, in large percentages, using new technologies for purposes of civic activism. The story of the effect of Internet use on politics is just now breaking; these issues are playing themselves out, right now, in different contexts around the world. The terrain is unsettled. The scholarly field studying these issues is nascent. Empirical evidence is more or less nonexistent. Our interviews and focus groups suggest that the percentage of Digital Natives doing new things online in the activist realm is modest, at best. Most studies that others have conducted regarding the levels of participation have confirmed what we found. The fault lines in the relevant debates are becoming clear, but there's no consensus as to the likely outcome or impact. Though our instinct is to be hopeful, our frame of reference needs to be skeptical.

It is also important to recognize that the story of civic engagement online is not solely about Digital Natives. It can be, and should be, a story about people of all ages. The single best thing that could be accomplished online would be a connection across generations, especially one that is geared toward taking advantage of the networked public sphere in the public interest.

New technologies are transforming certain aspects of politics. The fundamental rules still apply, but the way the game is played is changing. Digital Natives are, in many cases, leading the way. The big impact will occur if the rest of their generation around the world follows suit.

D igital Natives have been at the forefront of the movement to change politics through use of digital tools. Though the Internet doesn't change everything when it comes to politics, in a few instances use of new technologies has made a notable difference in terms of *how* campaigns are conducted. Examples where the netroots have made a difference include South Korea in 2002, Ukraine's Orange Revolution in 2004 and 2005, and the presidential primary elections in 2004 and 2008 in the United States.

The use of the Internet to deepen the participation of individuals in formal political campaigns comes at a welcome moment in history. Over the past twenty years, there's been a lot of hand-wringing about the purported decline in voting among young people in the United States. At the same time, there has been a recent increase in other kinds of civic involvement that point to opportunities that Internet-based activism could exploit. This divergence suggests that it isn't that kids are apathetic. It's just that they are interested in changing the world through ways other than voting.

During the last thirty years of the twentieth century, the youth vote fell precipitously. In 1972, fully half (50.3 percent) of all eligible Americans aged eighteen to twenty-four voted in the election that gave Richard Nixon his landslide victory over George McGovern (the percentage for all age groups combined was 55.2).[3] In 2000, only about one-third (37.3 percent) of eligible young Americans voted in the excruciatingly close general election between George W. Bush and Al Gore (this time, the percentage for all age groups was 51.3).[4] The decline among young voters occurred even though the voter-registration process had become dramatically easier—through motor-voter, same-day registration, aggressive registration drives, and ubiquitous registration forms. This is not just an American phenomenon. Youth in the United Kingdom were also less likely to vote in elections than older citizens.[5]

But by other accounts, many young people demonstrated that they are more engaged than ever—just in ways other than voting. During this same period, young people got involved in public service outside the political sphere more extensively than ever before. Young volunteers stepped up the time they spent helping out in AIDS hospices and homeless shelters, teaching in Head Start centers, providing disaster relief in developing countries, and doing other good works. So while the number of young Americans voting in the presidential elections declined between 1972 and 2000, increasing numbers of young people were participating in public service before they graduated from college.[6]

Although these trends were emerging even prior to 9/11, that event—and the consequent outbreak of war—meant that a lot of people, particularly young people, were galvanized in ways that the Internet was poised to take advantage of. Some were nudged into political activism by a sense that America was increasingly becoming isolated in a post-9/11 world at precisely the moment when we should be drawing closer to other cultures.[7] Others—particularly youth outside the United States—were stirred to action by the reaction of the world's lone superpower to the terrorist crisis. The polarizing effect of a world divided between sharply differing ideologies at the start of the new millennium created an environment that drew people into the debate, including youth.

The decline in the youth vote and the concurrent rise in youth participation in other civic activities set up a dynamic that those promoting use of the Internet could exploit. The Internet offers a way for young people to be engaged in civic affairs that combines the political with the cultural, social, and technological. It also provides a medium through which the creativity of Digital Natives can affect politics. For some young people, interest in politics on the Net offered a path that would lead them back to the polls, too.

Politicians didn't see this potential to engage young people in campaigns right away. Most got off to a slow start in using the Internet as part of their campaigns, but the most savvy among them have caught on quickly of late. American political campaigning on the Internet began in earnest in the 1996 presidential election in the United States and has been surging ever since. Candidates, particularly Republicans in the early days, established their own websites during the campaign cycle. Little more than virtual billboards, these websites offered campaign material that would ordinarily be printed on leaflets, but in an electronic form. In the 2000 presidential election, candidates' Internet presences began to develop beyond just a Web page, a photo, and a list of issues. Internet users in the 2000 election cycle could further connect with politicians through making online donations, seeing a candidate's speaking calendar, and viewing photos of political events.[8]

The 2004 presidential election cycle in the United States marked a watershed in participation in online politics, which continues to this day.[9] New participants, many of them young people, entered the political process, and campaigns deployed new information technology tools with vast potential. A fresh crop of young, wired leaders joined the political fray. For many of the young new politicos, faith in the grassroots organizing potential of the Internet—also called the "Net roots"—is an essential motivating force. They didn't get involved in politics because of the technology, but the technology became the medium that drew them together. The Internet became the common network, both literally and figuratively, of a new generation of activists who came of age in the 2004, 2006, and 2008 election cycles. In 2004, the percentage of young voters surged (to

47.7 percent). This percentage still lagged behind the percentage for all age groups combined (55.3 percent), but it signaled the possibility of a new trend.[10] By 2008, candidates didn't just have their own websites, they had entire Web strategies, Web teams, and multiple points of presence online, including Facebook and MySpace accounts and YouTube videos of speeches.

The Internet enables traditional political campaigns to be more efficient and to increase online participation, but it does not change campaigning altogether. Big-time political campaigns are still largely about fundraising (both online and off), which in turn pays the bill for copious amounts of television advertising. The political process hasn't changed fundamentally just because more money is being raised online. But the Internet has become an essential component of the all-important fundraising process, largely through small donations. In 2000, Senator John McCain's campaign made headlines when it raised nearly $7 million online.[11] Senator John Kerry's campaign raised $45 million online in the first five months of 2004 alone, with an average contribution of just over $100.[12] Kerry's total online fundraising during the primary topped $80 million.[13] Barack Obama has eclipsed records yet again in 2008, raising a total of more than $235 million by May 2008, the vast majority of it online—in the primary alone.[14] Internet fundraising works primarily because it makes donating easy—no checks, stamps, or envelopes. Many campaigns take donations via Paypal, which means it takes only a single click of the mouse to donate to a favorite candidate. In turn, the new technologies enable candidates and their organizers to reach out to donors and likely donors more easily and less expensively than in the past. The Internet helps motivated organizers to develop relationships with those who are inclined to help, but who are too busy, too shy, or otherwise disinclined to reach out to others themselves. It's much easier to send someone an e-mail to ask for money than it is to call someone up or knock on doors, and it's easier for the average voter to click on a link to donate instead of having to go write out and mail a check.

Fundraising is only one of the ways that technology has changed the campaign process; online organizing is in fact the area where the greatest, most lasting transformation can occur. A volunteer for the Ron Paul campaign, for instance, can manage an outreach effort, coordinating thousands of volunteers, from a home computer and an ordinary network connection. These new tools haven't changed the fundamental machinery of a campaign, by any means, but they have increased flexibility and autonomy. A Web-savvy volunteer ran the entire Texas operation for the Obama campaign until the campaign leadership determined that they might have a shot at winning the prized state. At that point, the campaign swooped in to establish a formal presence a few weeks ahead of the primary—while retaining many of the structures that the all-volunteer team had set in place. Similarly, all the classic aspects of campaigning—going door-to-door using detailed walk-lists, arranging for speeches by surrogates, managing get-out-the-vote (GOTV) efforts—allow for forms of participation mediated by new information technologies. The use of these technologies may draw young people into the campaigns, but the participatory acts are not fundamentally altered in the process. It's much the same activity, perhaps done more efficiently or more attractively, but it can draw some young people, particularly Digital Natives, into the political process in a fresh way.

Just as in social networks and in gaming environments, the Internet makes it possible for young people with common interests to find one another and to connect, in politics it enables young people to connect who are on the same page politically and who want to work for the same cause or candidate. In a previous era, these young people might never have found one another; the Internet makes heretofore impossible connections possible, and these connections can lead to collective action around shared ideas at much faster speeds than ever before. They are facilitated by the powerful search tools and social networking features of the Internet. All of this has had a multiplying effect when it comes to enabling young people to engage in political activity in democratic societies.

The formal political sphere is only the most obvious context in which young people are getting involved in civic life. Digital Natives are using new technologies to participate in civic life outside of campaigns in ways that are potentially more constructive to societies on an enduring basis. One of the bigger stories is how young people are using these new technologies to jumpstart their own work in social causes. The networked environment is conducive to getting the word out to friends about a topic of public interest. Participation is not different, just more connected. As one student told us, she uses a MySpace page and a Facebook group to coordinate a growing network of young people interested in peer-education work on teen-dating violence. When students are working on issues of political engagement, such as raising awareness about the humanitarian crisis in Darfur or the interests of Latino/as in a given American city, they told us that their first outreach is through e-mail, instant messaging, and social networks from Facebook and MySpace.

Critics argue that the highly visible activism in social networks doesn't add up to much. It doesn't really mean much, these critics say, when a Digital Native joins a "cause" on Facebook. Often, that's true: It is nothing more than a convenient way to make a statement, the digital equivalent of a "Save the Whales" bumper sticker. Viewed from this angle, it can be a relatively cheap way to speak out by a simple mouse-click, but it doesn't accomplish much. As one college student put it: "Today it's more like people writing their names on a big list . . . [T]he effect is lower when it's not face to face, when it's not physical. . . . You can let millions of people know with just one click what's happening. But, it's hard to get all the million people involved just because of that click."

It's true that it doesn't always mean much when a Digital Native "friends" a politician in MySpace or Facebook. The "friendships" between young people and politicians online are more like style choices—accessories on a social network profile—than like knocking on doors or phone-banking for a favorite cause. But neither are these acts the most important parts of the story; they're just some of the most visible. The act of joining a Facebook group may lead to participation that is bigger and better than merely clicking on "accept" in an online invitation. Some Digital Natives venture outside of Facebook to use specially designed applications such as TakingITGlobal, YouthNoise, Zaadz, or UNICEF Voices of Youth, all of which promote civic engagement and community involvement. These sites are the starting place for something bigger than a personal statement about a public issue, and once young people do get started, they are more likely to begin to engage in some sort of *action*.

The medium is not the message when it comes to the political lives of Digital Natives. Internet engagement sites are usually only facilitators, rather than places of action; the civic engagement activities that result from online interactions often happen in the *offline* space. That said, the relevant online tools make activism less daunting and anonymous for those Digital Natives who already have an interest in civic engagement. These online tools simply make it easier for them to connect with like-minded people, or to share information and get organized.[15]

Digital Natives are shifting many of their core social activities from the offline space to the hybrid online-offline world. These social activities include, for some, political activism. Sometimes this activism expresses itself through traditional political campaigns. More often, and more important over the long term, this activism is expressed through a wide range of civic activities. This is not an apathetic bunch; it's just a group of young people getting engaged in civic life on their own terms, in their own ways.

The second big shift in participation online is the move away from a broadcast media model and toward a more diverse, participatory media model. In the new media environment, Digital Natives (and many other users, too) are no longer mere readers, listeners, or passive viewers. Instead, affordable Internet technology and highly interactive, easy-to-use applications have enabled individuals to become active users and participants in public conversations. As a consequence, it's no longer a few professional journalists or powerful media conglomerates with strong commercial interests who define what we as a society talk and care about. Rather, the public agenda in the digital age is increasingly influenced by the observations, experiences, and concerns of all of us in our roles as citizens. Many Digital Natives are at the forefront of this trend; they take participation for granted as part of their media environment.

Without owning a press or having the capital to rent one, an individual activist can bring a topic into the public discourse by breaking an important story through a credible, firsthand account. The activist can shed light on issues that would otherwise have remained covered up, or that had emerged but been purposely buried again. These activists can get word out to others who need it fast, on devices that are cheap and ubiquitous.

With the right command of these services, people who have traditionally been outside the mainstream of civic life can today command greater authority, and have far greater impact, than they could in an environment where the news media were tightly controlled.

Digital activists are chipping away at the corporate control of the media infrastructure.[16] In the television era, people heard from the candidates but rarely met them. The conversation was mediated primarily by the TV stations. It is still true that few people meet the candidates, compared to those who experience their words through electronic media. TV remains the primary battleground on which campaigns are waged, both through advertising and news coverage. During the 2004 election, presidential candidates spent $2.66 million on Internet ads versus $330 million on traditional television ads.[17] But nonetheless, the Internet has allowed citizens to sneak past the editorial cordon that has separated them from candidates in the past. In this sense, the Internet represents a continuation of a trend begun with the introduction of television into politics in the 1960s. Prior to that time, party bosses controlled access to and the message of the candidates. Both television and the Internet are part of a broader trend toward a more direct relationship between candidates and individual voters. The major political parties, along with labor unions, are part of the hierarchical framework of American politics that is under great pressure in the digital era.

Even as traditional hierarchies are breaking apart, powerful, consolidated interests still play a disproportionate role in politics, especially in America. Strong brands still have it in their power to make or break candidates. As in the commercial space, the Internet often causes first *disin*termediation, then *re*intermediation. The forums are slightly different in the digital age and modestly more diverse. Cable networks like Fox and CNN have expanded the group of networks with the power to influence elections; people like Glenn Reynolds of Instapundit, Markos Moulitsas Zúniga of the Daily Kos, Matt Drudge of the Drudge Report, Charles Johnson of Little Green Footballs, and Arianna Huffington and her colleagues at the Huffington Post are giving the mainstream newspapers a run for their money in the online text media world; and even small bloggers and video creators can become stars with the power to move discussions in elections.

It's not just the relationship with the candidates that is changing in a digital age, but also the relationship of citizens to mainstream media—and to one another. Digital technologies make possible a more interactive relationship between people and media.[18] Thanks to Internet technologies, Digital Natives and others are presented with near-constant opportunities to take on a more active relationship with information—not just passively accepting what is fed through the broadcast medium, but rather engaging with it and recreating it in intriguing, creative ways. The result might be a more energized citizenry with closer ties to the public discussion about politics.

This phenomenon of citizens telling the stories of politics themselves, through digital media, could have a profound and lasting impact on democracies. Instead of thinking in terms of classical participatory politics, we should expand our frame to include the kinds of political involvement in which Digital Natives specialize. One aspect of this broader conception of participation is the making and remaking of narratives of a campaign or of other important public events. This broader frame encompasses notions of semiotic democracy. In a semiotic democracy, a greater number of people are able to tell the stories of their times. This broader group of people participate in the "recoding" and "reworking" of cultural meaning.[19] For example, instead of just receiving a newscast of the day's events in politics from one of three mainstream news channels, citizens can themselves take the video clip of a candidate's speech, interpret it themselves, and remix it into a video that they share with friends—or with the rest of the world on YouTube. In a semiotic democracy, the story can be reinterpreted and reshaped by any citizen with the skills, time, and access to digital technologies to do so. The idea of semiotic democracy sounds academic, but it might just be the most profound difference made possible by the Internet for our time.

The fact that Digital Natives and others have this opportunity to participate actively in the news, information, and entertainment creation and dissemination process doesn't mean that they will avail themselves of it. The Internet isn't going to solve the problem of civic disengagement. Not everyone will be taking advantage of these opportunities—indeed, the data suggest that most of them are not at present. But as events around the world in recent years have shown, when a lot of people care passionately about something, the Internet can become an extraordinarily powerful tool of organization, recruitment, and participation in the telling of the narratives of our society.

As wonderful as the Web, social networks, and blogs may turn out to be for civic participation and a more diverse news and information environment, there are reasons to worry about the overall impact of Internet use on democracies. As we encourage young people to participate in civic life online, we need to recognize also that there are some potential hazards involved with online activism.

The first concern is the "Daily Me," a problem that we've discussed in previous chapters. In his influential book, *Republic.com,* Cass Sunstein argued that in the digital age, citizens simply tailor their environment in such a way that they hear their views reinforced over and over again, rather than exposing themselves to new ones.[20] Weblogs, and the related technologies that allow individuals to aggregate a personal series of news feeds, though terrifically empowering to those who write them, have the potential to intensify angry partisanship disputes rather than engendering serious thought and discussion. The blog culture has been blamed for the exacerbation of the divide between "red" and "blue" America in the period leading up to and immediately following the 2004 election. It is not clear, however, that online politicking is in fact to blame: A recent Pew study found that those who got their political information from the Internet had a wider view, not a narrower one, of political issues and events than those who primarily relied upon offline sources.[21]

There is also reason to worry that the quality of the information in the online political discourse is not as uniformly high as it was in the broadcast era. There is a lot of ostensibly political content on the Web that contributes nothing to civic discourse—for instance, the ubiquitous "Obama Girl" video that became an online sensation during the run-up to the 2008 primary season. There is also a lot of content that profoundly detracts from political conversation by misleading the public. During the 2004 election cycle, for instance, a rumor spread from Drudge across the Web and throughout the chattering classes that John Kerry had an "intern problem";

eventually, the rumor was proven not to have the slightest merit. The networked public sphere is full of gems as well as less valuable content. The pressure on young people to sort the good from the bad is only going to continue to grow.

Finally, the prevalence of commercial forces in the networked public sphere is a cause for concern.[22] The intrusion of marketing, with its powerful underlying data-mining technologies, is only the beginning of a growing trend toward the commercialization of spaces where Digital Natives network online. To the extent that political life is migrating increasingly to the Internet, commercial forces can control the environments where important public discourse is taking place. Presume that YouTube, Metacafe, Daily Motion, and Facebook take enormous market share from television and cable providers, and that these platforms become the way in which young citizens get their news about public life. These platforms can set the rules for how this news and information is provided, what advertising can be run alongside it, and how much people pay to access or provide the information to others. This fear of commercialization is not new to the Internet; it just may take on greater importance than it has to date as attention continues to shift online.

Each of these concerns is worth paying attention to, but none of them should diminish our enthusiasm for the potentialities of online politicking and what Digital Natives are doing in civic life online. In many ways, these are the same problems that we deal with in regard to television. People can choose from Fox or CNN depending on their politics. There's plenty of gossip on television, just as there is on the Web (consider the extensive coverage of Obama's education in a madrassa). Certainly, advertisers and other commercial forces exert enormous clout when it comes to what we see on television. But most of us haven't thrown out our televisions. Nor should we fear the move of political discourse to the networked public sphere. The challenge is to repeat as few of the mistakes of the past as we can during this period of transition—and to take advantage of as many opportunities as we can in this new environment.

The use of the Internet doesn't just promise to strengthen existing democracies; in fact, its most important effects are being felt in the making of new ones. The use of the Internet in politics is much more likely to be transformative in the near term in places with extremely hierarchical political systems. The growth of civic participation and the opening of the media market to new voices leads to increased transparency. It means that individual citizens have greater autonomy as political actors. In autocratic regimes, where the public information space has traditionally been tightly controlled, the impact of the changes wrought by Internet use are likely to have a greater marginal impact than in established democracies.

The potential of the Internet to destabilize authoritarian regimes is so obvious that many such regimes restrict access to it or use it is as a mode of surveillance—or both. Some regimes use Internet technologies such as Internet Service Providers to block access to the Web and to disallow people from sending messages on certain topics.[23] Others use the Web to spy on citizens and to punish them for their political views or activities. There are currently more than two dozen countries in the world—including China, Iran, and Uzbekistan—that are actively refining these practices of censorship and surveillance online.

Since 2001, countries that do not want their citizens to use the Internet for political purposes have blocked access to certain websites and banned the publication of sensitive material online. In China, for instance, citizens seeking information about freeing Tibet, the controversy surrounding Taiwan's independence, or the 1989 massacre in Tiananmen Square will not see as much online as someone searching for the same information from New York. Those who do publish on sensitive topics may well find their content taken down quickly; they are lucky if they don't find themselves in jail. In Thailand, citizens are not free to criticize the king, online or offline; the same goes for criticism of Ataturk, the founder of Turkey. In much of the Middle East and North Africa, citizens are unable to access information about certain religious practices. Opposition groups in the former Soviet states have found their websites inaccessible during the run-up to key elections.

States are also increasingly using surveillance, coupled with censorship, to clamp down on the use of the Internet for civic engagement. In many countries—such as Iran, Vietnam, and China—surveillance of the Internet is a way of life. Dozens of bloggers and other online activists around the world have been put in jail based on their online activities. While these technologies empower young activists, they can also get them into a lot of trouble.[24]

Despite repression in dozens of countries that censor the Internet, the digital environment is, in most cases, serving as a locus of reform efforts. Smart technologists and digital activists have devised ways around every censorship and surveillance program in place in the world today. The Internet has become a major battleground between those who seek to consolidate power and those who wish to see it more broadly distributed. The global crew of Digital Natives is a far better bet than the dictators in the long run.

N ot all Digital Natives are rushing to the Internet to debate politics or to create new online ways to raise awareness about atrocities in the Sudan—but enough are doing creative things online that we should be excited by the prospects. There are seeds of change that ought to be nurtured.

The most promising examples of this change are efforts initiated by young people for their peers. These initiatives demonstrate the use of new technologies to inject energy and excitement into civic affairs. TakingIT-Global has established an active online network of 200,000 young people taking action in their local communities around the world. They've connected with each other in at least 200 different countries to support each other's work on HIV/AIDS, peace issues, technology policy, and a host of other causes. GuerillaFunk Recordings supports hip-hop artists who use the Web and new technologies to challenge orthodoxies, discuss hard issues about race (in very controversial ways, sometimes), and raise awareness about corporate control of the media environment. Scoop08 has aggregated the work of 400 young people to cover the 2008 political campaign in the United States. Alexander Heffner and Andrew Mangino, the two teenage cofounders of Scoop08, have, in the process, launched a new kind of newspaper that puts young people in the posture of reporters and pundits. These young writers interview leaders, write columns, and publish online cartoons. Generation Engage provides young people with access to politicians and to civic organizations that match their interests—giving students a direct voice, over iChat and other technologies, with global leaders. Each of these organizations, and many others like them, are tapping into the global youth civic culture to inspire political involvement— not always of the traditional variety.[25]

Long after the 2008 elections, the 400 students engaged in Scoop08 are likely to continue speaking out online. Along with mainstream media outlets and data-miners and citizen journalists, these young activists will continue to shine light on what's going on in politics. Most important, their work will have an impact on the world in which they live. Encouraged by the response to their own participation, these students—and the many millions of other young people currently engaged in online activism around the world—will learn to love civic involvement in a networked public sphere. In the best possible scenario, both these young activists themselves and the world in which they act will be improved in the process.

13

SYNTHESIS

E-mail from John to Urs, on BA Flight 285 from London to San Francisco, November 27, 2007

It's down to the final chapter. We first drafted this chapter the old-fashioned way, for starters, but I think we ought to scrap that version. It was your idea to write this last section by e-mail instead. I think it's an inspired idea. I'll start, right now, and send a first message to you, and you'll reply, and so forth. We'll sew it together into a chapter at the end. Let's see if it works.

I'm high above the middle of the Atlantic right now, as I type, traveling from Europe back home to the United States. This seems an auspicious place to start. I'm precisely between our respective homes, in geographic terms.

My friend and coauthor: After a few years of writing and research about those who are born digital, we've got most of a book. This "book" is, right now, a collection of ideas, wrestled into the form of a digital file in a shared corner of cyberspace, accessible only to a few people. This collection of ideas and words we've assembled will soon be transformed: printed on paper and bound and shipped to Borders bookstores and straight to customers who order it online at Amazon. Perhaps our readers will be scrolling through its pages in digital format, on a Sony Reader or an Amazon Kindle. Or maybe, especially if they're Digital Natives, they'll discover these ideas on our wiki—on the Web at http://digitalnative.org—where we've done much of our research in public, and maybe add something to our collective knowledge by recording something new there.

This last chapter is in no way a Conclusion. To me, this chapter is instead a synthesis of what we've said in this first version of *Born Digital*. As we "finish" this iteration of our book, I've got the acute sense that this is version 1.0. Part of me wants to put the words "version 1.0" right on the cover of the book. Whether or not we do that, the point seems to me critically important: This book is part of an ongoing conversation, not a conclusion to anything.

I think of this book as an invitation to conversation. It's an invitation sent out especially to parents and teachers of Digital Natives and would-be Digital Natives. I think they—we—are essential to the happy resolution of the many conflicts that we describe in this book. Parents and teachers have lots to worry about, I know, much of it unrelated to the privacy or Web-surfing habits of their kids. But this is important, and more so with every passing day.

As of today, and surely subject to change, I'm absolutely convinced of three things about the population born digital.

First, the ways in which some—by no means all—young people are interacting with information, with one another, and with institutions is changing rapidly. The consequences of these changes are enormous for the future of our societies. It's not a foregone conclusion that it will turn out well. There's a lot we've got to get right if we want to give our children, and our societies, bright futures.

Second, I'm certain that there is a global culture in the making, which joins people from many corners of the globe together with one another based upon common ways of interacting over information networks. The emergence of this common culture is part and parcel of the trend toward globalization. The consequences of this second notion, of an emerging global culture, ought to be overwhelmingly positive. It is a dramatic amplification of the diplomatic and cross-cultural benefits gained by the invention of the telegraph, millions of international student exchanges, and the rise of the globally networked economy. As we celebrate the emergence of this global culture, we need to recognize that a sharp divide has formed between those with both the access and skills to participate in this digital culture and those without either.

Third, while there's no one-size-fits-all solution to the issues that we worry about—privacy, safety, piracy, overload, and so forth—the best and most enduring solutions are community-based efforts. These are big, gnarly, complicated, subtle issues, every one of them. We have to be flexible in how we approach them, to think creatively, to work together. We have to draw on the wisdom of Digital Natives themselves in the process. They are our greatest hope, hands down.

Over to you: If someone is skimming this book—we suspect some of the Digital Natives we talked to in our research will be among the skimmers—what would you hope they would take away from it? If someone reads just this one chapter, what should they learn?

E-mail from Urs to John, on a Train from St. Gallen to Zurich, Switzerland, November 28, 2007

Many thanks, John, for your thoughts on our book from above the Atlantic. You're asking a tricky question, because you and I were born in 1972. We weren't born digital, and we've written this book with parents and teachers in mind who would like to learn in greater detail how kids are using digital media and what the possible consequences of these usage trends are. So, what then can Digital Natives take from this book if they decide to download and browse it?

First, I hope that Digital Natives skimming this book would see the digital world they're living in from a new—or at least different—perspective. It's as if they were to board an airplane and look down from 30,000 feet on their own neighborhoods, cities, countries, and even continents. We've probably all had this experience once: While it's hard on the ground to imagine how our living spaces are connected with—and sometimes disconnected from—one another, it's quite clear from a bird's eye perspective how highways, railways, rivers, or sometimes even a mountain range, can connect and separate our social spaces.

In other words, I would hope that our Digital Native readers would start drawing new connecting lines when browsing through chapters such as Identity, Privacy, and Safety, or Creators, Learners, and Activists. As they begin to see the big picture painted in this book and start recognizing the interactions among the topics covered in the chapters, Digital Natives may rethink their own (and often very implicit) mental maps of the digital world that they have when navigating cyberspace.

Second, at least some Digital Natives on this journey might discover new terrain. Most of the Digital Natives we've spoken with over the past years, for instance, don't have a deep understanding of the phenomena we explore in the chapters on information quality and overload. However, I think we've shown in this book why it really matters that Digital Natives start to think about quality issues and problems such as the information glut and exposure to violent games and images.

Ultimately, it would be great if we could help our young readers avoid some of the less-visible pitfalls of the digital world, or at least raise awareness for some of the possible long-term consequences of the present digital lifestyle, if one thinks for example about online privacy and safety issues. On the other side, a glance into chapters such as Creators, Innovators, or Activists might encourage Digital Natives to make better use of the new opportunities before us to shape our culture, or participate in economic or political activities.

Third, I would hope that Digital Natives would seriously take into account one of the fundamental arguments that we've built upon throughout this book: that it is to a large degree in our own hands—most of all, their own hands—to shape the future of the Internet. True, the digital world in which we live is a complex mixture of deliberate actions by governments, companies, and users, sometimes not-so-deliberate choices by users, and historic contingencies. But the digital future and how our kids live in it is not necessarily determined by the past. Indeed, in some of the areas discussed in this book we're right now at a tipping point; we are moving toward an Internet that in ten years will look significantly different from what we see today.

Now, the basic point here is that not only politicians or companies are responsible for thinking about this future. Digital Natives themselves have in many instances the power to shape the future of their digital lives in important ways. It's a shared responsibility, and often Digital Natives are best positioned to address and even solve some of the thorny problems outlined in this book.

Now, John, knowing that we're on the same page with regard to the last point, in what areas in particular do you think Digital Natives can make a real difference? On the other hand, what are the limits of this notion of self-responsibility when it comes to kids? Where is it unrealistic that this approach will work?

E-mail from John to Urs, This Time on BA Flight 213 from London to Boston, December 4, 2007

I've spent the past few days with an extraordinary group of people, many of them Digital Natives, most of them from Arabic-speaking parts of the Middle East and North Africa. What struck me about what they told me was their strong belief that they are global citizens. Every one of the people I met shared a commitment to making the world a better place. I've had the same experience in Istanbul, Turkey, in Shanghai, China, and in many other places around the world. The spirit of innovation, entrepreneurship, and caring for society at large that we've seen in certain young people in our own backyards—in Western Europe and the United States—is alive and well in cultures that span the globe.

What I most hope to see in the next several decades is Digital Natives applying this innovative, collaborative spirit to solving some of the problems that we've introduced in this book. Through creative and responsible use of digital technologies, Digital Natives are themselves best positioned to address the issues we've raised. And they are best positioned to make the case that the Net ought to remain broadly open and free from excessive proprietary control. They can make this case by showing the world what they can do together, using these technologies in creative ways to make new things possible and to solve problems through collective action. If they do, we will all be richly rewarded by the future innovations that they will build on this openness.

To get more specific, Digital Natives could make a big difference in each of the clusters of problems and opportunities discussed in this book.

When it comes to identity formation, privacy, and safety, Digital Natives need to develop the skills to know what kinds of information about themselves to share with whom, and in what contexts. These are hard skills, and the situations they will face are likely to be complex and dynamic. While Digital Natives themselves can't solve these issues, a good dose of common sense will go a long way much of the time. Peers can help peers who don't get the message, too.

Digital Natives have an enormous role to play in the online creativity and piracy debates, to be sure. Digital Natives will be best served by putting themselves in the role of the creator of digital media. In the process, they will be showing off what they can do with these tools, shaping their own cultures, and learning a perspective that they might not now have. I believe strongly that, if they are regularly in the role of creators, they will come to respect the intellectual property rights of others over time—as they will have developed rights of their own—and to understand the power of sharing certain rights with others for the greater good. And they'll lead the way to sustainable business models that reward creators for their efforts while preserving the interests of the public at large.

I'm hopeful that Digital Natives will develop the critical thinking skills that will help them to overcome the overload and quality issues they'll encounter throughout their lives. These problems are the ones hardest of all to solve through law or other centralized action, in my view. The best hope is for skills development among Digital Natives, coupled with community-based innovations. Digital Natives ought to figure out how to apply new digital technologies, like tagging systems, and work together as communities to assess sources and methods of information production that will improve the ecosystem over time, as well. It's a long shot, I know, to pin any hope on something as ill-defined as critical thinking skills and development of healthy skepticism about information sources, but I'm pretty sure there's not a better way on balance.

In terms of the opportunities that we pointed to—for innovation, learning, and activism—Digital Natives just need to do the things we've seen a few of them doing, to spread the word virally among their peers as to what's possible. We've pointed to examples of a few extraordinary young people doing very cool things. The real promise lies in whether these few will become many.

What I worry most about is that the promise of what's possible will be overshadowed by a few truly horrible acts that happen to be mediated through digital technologies. Digital Natives, like all human beings, sometimes treat one another badly. Digital technologies can make it easy to hurt someone in ways that are very painful and hard to undo. Aggressive behavior online isn't necessarily bad; it can lead to positive social change. But it can also lead to harm. (And it's true, also, that some criminals use the Internet as a way to harm young people, but we should not blame the network for this but rather the underlying problem.) Digital Natives can do their part by acting accountably and caring about one another when they use digital technologies, not to mention in the rest of their lives.

I worry, too, about the gap in access, literacy, and participation. The digital "haves"—those who are both born digital and who have the opportunities and skills to make use of the technologies—need to realize that there are digital "have-nots" in every culture, and that it matters. Whether for self-interested reasons or altruistic motives, Digital Natives ought to work to bridge the access, literacy, and participation divides that bedevil societies. If left alone, these digital gaps will cause other unhealthy gaps in society to widen.

So Urs, though you're not a Digital Native, you're a parent and a teacher. You know well the possibilities and limitations of these roles. What specifically would you suggest parents and teachers do about the issues we've raised in this book?

E-mail from Urs to John, on BA Flight 498 from Seattle-Tacoma to Boston, December 5, 2007

In the course of researching this book and while traveling the world over the past few years, we've spoken to hundreds of parents and teachers in the United States, in Western and Eastern Europe, and in the Middle East, Africa, and Asia about both the hard problems you've just mentioned as well as the opportunities outlined in the previous chapters. While they often expressed different opinions on each of the issues and were more or less optimistic about the digital future of our kids, I've left all the conversations with a very strong sense that the parents of Digital Natives and teachers who educate kids born digital care a great deal about all the issues we've discussed here. And I think that's the first important step that we, as parents and educators, can do: to care about the digital lives and lifestyles of our kids, even if we belong to a generation that knows very well how to live without Google, YouTube, or Wikipedia.

Especially from parents with teenage kids I've often heard sentences like, "Well, you know, I'm still wrestling with my computer, and I often ask my son how to do things like, say, set up a WiFi at home or how to set up a free e-mail account." I think sentences like that touch upon a second point that seems very important. In order to help address the problems outlined in this book and encourage their children to make use of digital opportunities, parents and teachers need to improve their knowledge of digital technologies in the first place. In my opinion, it's not enough to care about the things we've described here. We have to do it, too. One also has to gain a firsthand understanding of how the technology that our kids are using works, and how Digital Natives live their digital lives. Of course, we hope that this book contributes in one way or another to closing this knowledge gap between the generations, but certainly learning about digital technology and our kids' use of it in their daily lives has to continue.

The third point I want to make is that parents and teachers alike ought to engage, to take this issue head-on with their kids and their students. It seems crucial to me that kids are asked to talk about their online experiences both at home and at school. The format of these conversations, of course, might vary. At the breakfast or dinner table, parents should engage in a very open and informal discussion with their kids about the services they are using, about their favorite websites, about the ways in which they communicate with their friends, whether they often use Wikipedia, whether they've witnessed something that worries them. Very much in the same spirit as we ask our kids about the things they've done at school, we should also show honest interest in their digital experiences, wherever and whenever they might have had them.

The parents who are having the most success don't only talk about these things, they let the kids also show them online how things work, what their favorite sites look like, etc. In return, of course, we should also share our experiences and talk about the issues we encounter. In the classroom, the discussion may take a different form and can be more topical. Depending on the age of the kids and the particular setting, one can imagine special sessions dedicated to the discussion of issues such as online privacy or online aggression. Ideally, of course, such conversations would be linked to media and information literacy programs—something I will return to in a moment.

Fourth, parents and teachers alike should not hesitate to intervene if they learn about issues that their kids experience online and with which they are not comfortable. If you learn, for instance, that your ten-year-old is playing violent video games online every evening, you definitely should step in and have a very serious conversation about it. Like we teach our kids to wear a helmet when riding a bike, or not to get into a car with a stranger, or to call us anytime they face a problem while away from home, we can also ask them to follow rules and respect certain norms while surfing the Web or making connections online. Digital technology—for instance, kid-safe browsers or parental control technology—may assist parents in enforcing rules where they think it's particularly important. It's important to remember that for the generation born digital the boundaries between offline and online, between what many of us still call the "real world" versus the "online world," are blurring. In response, we as parents and teachers should not treat the two as separate worlds just because we are more familiar with one of them. In my view, there is no good reason why parents should have less (or more!) responsibility for their children with regard to the things they're doing online versus the things they do on the street, in our backyards, at school, etc. It goes without saying, of course, that the degree of responsibility changes with the age of our children.

Finally, let me turn to another important aspect. I think it's important that parents and teachers work in concert to support Digital Natives when they consider making use of the new opportunities before them as well as to help them—very much along the lines of what you've said before—to avoid the dangerous zones of cyberspace and the pitfalls. I think of it as a shared responsibility. Like in other areas of education, we as parents and teachers need to team up and work together in a strategic way to create an optimum learning environment for our children when it comes to media education and information literacy. An important prerequisite, as we've documented in this book, is of course that schools recognize their part of the responsibility and intensify their efforts to introduce curricula that specifically address digital media issues. Here, much more work needs to be done. This collaboration between schools and homes, of course, needs to be dynamic and, as in other areas of learning (say, for instance, biology or math or sports), needs to carefully take into account the particular stage of our children's development. Let me close by saying that for me personally it's one of the most interesting and exciting things for the months and years to come to assist parents and teachers in dealing with this educational challenge before us, and I very much hope that our joint research teams will be on board, too.

But now, John, let me turn over to you. I recently returned from a trip to Seattle, where software giant Microsoft has its headquarters, and I will, in a few minutes, touch down in Boston, the home of many cool and innovative software companies. Over the past few years, you've had many conversations with executives of such companies and given advice to some of them. What, from what you've learned, is their responsibility and respective contribution when it comes to challenges like privacy and safety, or online piracy?

E-Mail from John to Urs, from Terra Firma in Cambridge, Massachusetts, December 15, 2007

One of the most interesting things about studying the Internet, for me, is the realization that the dividing line between the public and the private, in digital space, is blurred, if not disappearing altogether. Our assumptions about the rights and responsibilities of actors on either side of this line require reexamination. So, if we want to understand how the personal information of Digital Natives is controlled, we have to figure out the relationship between these users and the companies to whom they entrust massive amounts of information about themselves.

The critical message to technology companies is that they need to see it as in their self-interest (and certainly in society's interest) to be part of the solution to some of the problems we've raised. As we have written this book, debates have raged about the role of companies in holding and sharing personal information about their customers. MySpace has been the primary target of parents who fear that their children will expose information about themselves on MySpace's pages to people viewing those pages who might do them harm. Facebook has experimented with sharing information about its users with other users, and with other companies, which has raised the hackles of its critics and some of its users. The battle over the sharing of copyrighted music and movies online, now mostly between copyright holders and uploaders of content to various digital services, continues to rage. The role of a wide range of private players, like Yahoo!'s news operation or the Wikimedia Foundation's global distributed community, in conveying the news and information to young people online has only continued to grow.

In each of these instances, companies share some of the responsibility for the fact that these issues are arising. Social networks (and search engines, for that matter) make their money by running advertisements against pages on which their users, many of them young, place information about themselves, their friends, and their worlds. These services in turn are implicitly asking for a huge amount of trust from those young people, a trust that neither the companies, nor society at large, can afford for them to betray. As a consequence, these companies have a major role to play in solving the hard problems we grapple with in this book, and with which Digital Natives may end up grappling all their lives. In most cases, the law, for various reasons, is unlikely to force all companies to play such roles.

What does this mean in practice? It means that companies need to factor into their decision-making the impact of their business affairs on their Digital Native customers. We know that a certain group of young people, from cultures around the world, are more likely to share information about themselves online than in the past. MySpace, Facebook, CyWorld, studiVZ, Google, and their ilk need to make it much easier than it is today for these customers to control the information about themselves. They need to take the time to reach out to their customers, to bring them into the conversation about privacy, and to earn the trust that they are asking their Digital Native customers to place in them. The recording industry needs to find the reset button on its relationship with Digital Natives; that one cannot be fixed through marginal change. And content providers need to find ways to partner with libraries, schools, and others to shape the information environment to ensure that our kids are learning the new media literacy skills that they need to thrive.

There's a related message in this book for anyone hiring or managing a Digital Native. Many of the conversations we've had with companies have centered on the challenges of recruiting, hiring, and managing Digital Natives. There's no doubt that the challenges that employers face are here to stay, for the foreseeable future, anyway. But I'm convinced that the astute human resources managers will succeed brilliantly: There is enormous talent in this generation entering the workforce, and the Digital Natives among them will be innovative, productive employees if managed well.

Corporate leaders who seek to harness this innovative spirit stand to gain mightily from what Digital Natives have to offer. Digital Natives may seem to be a threat to your business, whether as competitors, employees, or customers, because of their occasionally disruptive ways. They may post information that you perceive to be "yours" someplace online where you do not want it. They may launch services that undercut your pricing. They may stir up discontent in the ranks of their fellow staff members. They may complain loudly and publicly about your lousy service.

The hardest message is this last one: Listen to these Digital Natives. Invite them into your company, either virtually or in the flesh. Hire some of them. They are the future, like it or not, and they have some great ideas. Sometimes, we know, they have a hard time conveying those ideas in productive ways. That's something we can all work on together. But an attitude of "those damn kids . . ." is definitely a loser. With low barriers to entry for new market players, with essentially no barrier to entry for speech that can be spread to the four winds, these Digital Natives are a force to be reckoned with—or, better yet, to be brought into the fold in constructive ways.

So, counselor, help us to understand: Where does the law belong in this picture?

E-mail from Urs to John, on LH Flight 454 from Frankfurt to San Francisco, December 18, 2007

In 1996, John Perry Barlow, an American essayist and former lyricist for the Grateful Dead, wrote a provocative essay titled "A Declaration of the Independence of Cyberspace," which was presented at the World Economic Forum in Davos, Switzerland. It became an instant classic. Barlow essentially argued that governments ought to stay out of cyberspace and that the law as we know it from our offline world doesn't apply to the new social space created by a network of computer networks. Obviously, his vision hasn't come true. Law also governs cyberspace. Throughout this book, we've drawn attention to many instances where the law plays an active role in the mix when it comes to the regulation of our Digital Natives' New World. Recall, for instance, the ways in which traditional doctrines from copyright or trademark law have been applied to the new lifestyles of Digital Natives. Or consider, taking another example, data protection laws. In other areas, we've even witnessed how governments have stepped in to enact Internet-specific laws. The Council of Europe's Cybercrime Convention is an example that belongs to this category, the legal protection of digital rights management systems is another one.

We've also discussed in what contexts and under what conditions law can be used as an instrument to solve some of the thorny problems addressed in this book. In particular, we've argued that tougher laws may help protect our kids from online predators, or that the law can be used to set the right incentives for Internet companies so that they undertake best efforts to protect the personal information of Digital Natives. We have also discussed instances where law plays an enabling function, for instance, when it comes to the reform of copyright law that could support new forms of creative expression on the part of Digital Natives and contribute to semiotic democracy, or the application of competition law to keep entry barriers low and enable digital entrepreneurs to bring their innovative ideas and business models to the market. Thus, it's important to understand that law in the Internet context, too, not only has a constraining function by outlawing certain forms of behavior (e.g., stalking Digital Natives), but also a leveling power and enabling effect that can help us to better realize the opportunities we've outlined in this book.

However, we've also made the argument that law often doesn't hold the greatest promise for dealing with the challenges that Digital Natives face in cyberspace. In problem zones such as information quality and information overload, for instance, the role of law is very limited. Indeed, education- and technology-based approaches are often much better suited to make a contribution to problem solving. Why, then, does law often not work that well when it comes to the digital lives of our children? One general answer is that the Internet is a global medium and that laws are still very much limited by national boundaries. We've seen, for instance, that privacy legislation varies significantly from continent to continent. This tension between a "global Internet" and "local laws" makes it difficult to address many of the challenges we've touched upon in a coherent and comprehensive manner. Further, it is often more difficult and costly to enforce the law when it comes to the Internet as opposed to the offline world. Law enforcement, too, is (still) very much tied to a particular geographic area where the government has "jurisdiction." And sometimes it's simply difficult in cyberspace to trace the individuals who behave badly in the first place. All this may result in a gap between the law on the books and law in action when we seek to use law as a means to help protect Digital Natives.

Whether law is a good approach to deal with a certain problem or can at least work in concert with other strategies—as part of a "blended approach," something we've advocated in this book—needs to be decided on a case-by-case basis. In any event, lawmaking is a resource-intense and costly process, and therefore we should carefully prioritize the instances in which we call for new laws—or law reform, for that matter—in response to the challenges experienced by the generation born digital. We've proposed specific aspects within the clusters of online privacy, safety, and creativity as possible candidates. The challenge then is at least threefold. First, we must appropriately design each legal intervention so that it is as effective and efficient as possible (lawmakers, too, have a variety of tools at hand, ranging from self-regulatory to command-and-control types of legislation). Second, we must synchronize the legislative process with the rapid pace of development of Internet technology and the dynamic use of it by Digital Natives. And third, we must avoid unintended consequences of well-intended laws, and keep these laws open to improvement.

Let me make a final point. While several of the points I've just made may seem to be rather "technical," or the stuff that only lawyers should care about, it's important to recognize that the basic question you've asked— What is the role of law when shaping the future of the Internet?—is again one that we as parents, teachers, or coaches of Digital Natives need to elaborate and answer together. We can't simply delegate it to our senators or the executive branch. Lawmaking in the digital age, too, is a shared responsibility, especially when it comes to the future of our children.

We've come a long way and covered a lot of ground by now, John. If you take two steps back and focus on the big picture, what are the two or three most important take-away points from this book that you would like to propose to our readers who have joined us on this journey?

E-mail from John to Urs, in a Snowstorm in Cambridge, Massachusetts, December 20, 2007

The way that many young people are using information technologies is changing the way the world works. We don't yet know the full impact of these changes, but we know that they are profound and will alter all manner of dynamics over the coming decades, if not centuries and beyond.

The reason I wanted to write this book is to put a stake in the ground. My view is that these changes are by and large a very good thing for global society. But whether or not you agree with me, now is the time to take stock of what we, as societies, want to encourage about these changing behaviors, what we want to discourage, and what safeguards we need to put in place to mitigate the harms that our children face during this period of transition from an analog world to a heavily digital world. We need to talk about the interventions we are making and consider their long-term implications for our children's lives.

What's so good about being born digital? The central concept, to me, is the extent to which young people have a much greater ability to shape the culture in which they are growing up. Power dynamics are shifting in many, though not all, contexts to favor the individual and the nimble, small, ad hoc group as against the large, slow-moving institution. This shift in power relates to the long movement in history against certain forms of hierarchies. At the same time, new hierarchies are emerging.

In the remaking of these hierarchies, I hope to see the seeds of creativity, innovation, and entrepreneurship that we see in our children grow into lasting change that serves the broad, global public interest. A big hope, I realize, and bordering on the Pollyanna-ish. But I don't think it's impossible for us to shape the institutions of law, learning, and technology development in ways that will nurture hope of this sort, rather than work at cross purposes to it.

The core concept is an expanded sense of what we mean by "democracy." In using the tools with which they are so proficient, our children are in a position to shape the way we understand their cultures, which is the idea of semiotic democracy. They can make those in power more accountable, both through their work in the marketplace and by shining a bright, digitally enabled spotlight on corruption. They can leverage new networks to create groups of like-minded activists to prompt change on the great, international issues of their day: global warming, poverty, epidemics, and so forth.

Yes: They—we, who use these tools, too—can abuse these powers, too. That's why this moment, as things are still a bit in flux, is so crucial. Let's look around the corner, anticipate these changes, and help to shape institutions and behaviors that will be in all of our interests. Most of all, let's not mortgage their future for our present.

The last word is all yours.

E-mail from Urs to John, back in St. Gallen, Switzerland, December 21, 2007

I decided to write these lines from one of the places where I spent a lot of time some years back, when studying at the University of St. Gallen. It's a small art nouveau restaurant called "Wienerberg," just across the campus.

Sitting in the middle of the crowded restaurant, I can't avoid overhearing a conversation among a group of friends—most of them in their early sixties—at a table next to me. Coincidentally, they have an argument about . . . the Internet. One person, who seems to be a local businessman, tells how he recently spent a vacation on the Maldives, where he nonetheless was able to conveniently carry out all his financial transactions using a Swiss bank's e-banking system. One of his friends, roughly the same age, apparently dislikes the idea and explains over the third glass of wine that he has no trust in the Internet whatsoever. He still uses a yellow account-

ing booklet, like my grandpa did, when paying bills at the local post office. His progressive friend argues that he's completely outdated. At this
point, others jump in, and I can't follow the discussion any longer.

When I started to study law here at St. Gallen in the early nineties, I
didn't have an e-mail account. I remember very well sending my first e-mail
only a few months later over the brand new university e-mail system. Today,
the Internet has become an important tool that I use every day (yes, even
on vacation). I'm using it to get the daily news, to book my flights and ho-
tels, to do research, to share my thoughts on my blog, to communicate
with you, John, and so forth. After only a handful of years, it's already hard
to imagine a life without the Internet. Even more so for our graduate students. They almost exclusively use the Internet to communicate with us,
to brainstorm about possible topics for their term papers, to submit their
exams, to receive their grades—and more recently even to add professors
as friends on studiVZ and Facebook.

Now imagine what happens when our own kids will turn fifteen in
2016 or so. By that time, they are likely to spend somewhere between
1,200 and 1,500 hours per year (if they're not addicts like their dads!) on
digital technologies. Five years later, at age twenty, they will have accu-
mulated at least 10,000 hours as active users of the Internet, if the current
user statistics still apply. This amount of time, in turn, is roughly equivalent to what a musician is expected to practice in order to become, say, a
professional piano player or cellist. Today, we can only speculate what our
children will do online, but it seems likely that they will experience the Internet as an inherently social space, as a computer-based network of
human networks, with its distinct opportunities and challenges.

This book marks the beginning of a long conversation about the future
opportunities and challenges associated with the Internet as a social space,
a space that is increasingly inhabited by users who are part of a population born digital with different habits, attitudes, and beliefs. Looking at
the three stories above, it seems plain to me that something fundamental
happens when we move from one generation to the next while the Internet becomes ubiquitous and continues to evolve rapidly. This book is an
attempt to better understand what this "something" could mean to all of
us—and what its implications for our children might be. We've used the

term Digital Natives as a metaphor, as a hermeneutic tool, to invite readers to join us on this journey and engage in a debate about the promises and limitations, opportunities and challenges, potential benefits and possible downsides of the evolving global network that we call cyberspace. And we very much hope that this conversation among parents, teachers, coaches, and citizens—among people who care about the future—continues, across generations and boundaries.

ACKNOWLEDGMENTS

We both have been blessed with extraordinary research teams and colleagues. For the past few years, our respective teams have been working together on this project on a daily basis across the Atlantic. We racked up a lot of frequent flier miles to work together in person, but our collaboration took place mostly in cyberspace, using our online project wiki (at http://www.digitalnative.org/) as well as a platform called Basecamp, e-mail, instant messaging, Facebook, and Skype. Several of our team members—some of them Digital Natives—have participated in a visiting program that our two institutions put together, spending months on the opposite continent. These interactions across cultures have heavily influenced our thinking and writing on this topic and challenged our methodological approaches, cultural biases, and local orientations.

At the Berkman Center for Internet & Society at Harvard Law School in Cambridge, Massachusetts, our team has been led by Miriam Simun, with terrific effectiveness. Research fellows danah boyd, Corinna di Gennaro, and Shenja van der Graaf taught us a great deal through their own work, helping us to refine the methodology, carry out much of the research, understand our own results, and situate our findings in the work of others (though all errors and omissions are our fault, not theirs).

Erin Mishkin played a crucial role in getting the project off the ground— and by finding Miriam to replace her. Colin Maclay and Catherine Bracy both gave excellent feedback on drafts and helped to pull together and manage our teams. Seth Young, Lexie Koss, Eszter Hargittai, Dena Sacco, Gene Koo, Carey Andersen, Sebastian Diaz, Danny Silverman, Issac Meister, and nearly every Berkman Center staff member and fellow supported this effort in one way or another. Teachers and administrators at schools throughout the Boston area deserve our thanks for allowing us to talk in-depth with their students in our focus groups and interviews. The John D. and Catherine T. MacArthur Foundation provided institutional support and funding for our study of the copyright implications of what Digital Natives are up to; our beloved program officer, John Bracken, as always, offered provocation and key connections along the way.

At the Research Center for Information Law at the University of St. Gallen in Switzerland, we received support and help from a fantastic team. Nadine Blättler contributed to the earliest draft chapters and helped to shape the idea behind this book. James Thurman, our resident U.S. researcher on the European team, has patiently (as always) built bridges across cultures—and writing styles. Sandra Cortesi provided invaluable advice and helped us to better understand the psychology and sociology of Digital Natives. Silke Ernst, Daniel Häusermann, Richard Stäuber, and more recently Jan Gerlach have been great companions on this and many of our other journeys. Our collaboration and joint efforts across the Atlantic have benefited from the support of the Swiss National Science Foundation.

An extremely fun and helpful group of research assistants helped produce this book: Katya Apekina, Jesse Baer, Olivia Balagna, Rosalie Fay Barnes, Greg Dyer, Chen Fang, Charlie Frentz, María Frick, Ben Ganzfried, Ilan Goldbard, Francesco Iberg, Diana Kimball, Kevin Korzeniewski, Jessica Ma, Megan Moore, Diana Oviedo, Anthony Pino, Robert Sinnott, Aurelia Tamò, and Sarah Zhang. Thanks, too, to our friends at Howard Gardner's Good Play project at Project Zero of the Harvard Graduate School of Education and at Henry Jenkins' New Media Literacies project at MIT.

We are particularly grateful to our colleagues for the inspiration we have found in their work and for their guidance and criticism on this project. In particular, Terry Fisher and Jonathan Zittrain gave helpful feedback on an early draft; we owe much to each of them on very many levels. The influences of Yochai Benkler, Lawrence Lessig, and Charles Nesson as well as the inspiration of Herbert Burkert and Jean Nicolas Druey will be evident in these pages to the careful reader who knows their work. Elena Kagan, the dean of Harvard Law School, made summer research for two years possible and has been a die-hard supporter of the work of the Berkman Center. Bernhard Ehrenzeller, vice president of the University of St.

Gallen, has supported the collaboration between our two institutions from the first day we presented the idea to him.

Lara Heimert and her team at Basic Books have been nothing short of a wonder. We can imagine neither a stronger supporter for this project nor a more exquisite editor than Lara. She already had our everlasting respect and gratitude, but she cemented both during this process. (Lara even got into Facebook in the process of editing this book; perhaps a little *too* into Facebook.) Her editorial, marketing, and publicity teams are first-rate. Thanks, too, go to our agent, Cynthia Cannell, for seeing so clearly a book project where there was nothing but a series of puzzles and our desire to work them out.

Most certainly, not least, we thank our families for their extraordinary patience through the long haul of this book project. Their commitment and ongoing support has made it possible for us to work (probably too) hard on this book; we are deeply grateful for that and much else besides. We dedicate our book to Ananda and Dave, Jack and Emeline: May the digital era prove to be a wonderful age in which to have been born.

NOTES

Introduction

1. Throughout this book, we adopt the definition of "social network sites" as established by danah boyd and Nicole Ellison in "Social Network Sites: Definition, History and Scholarship," *Journal of Computer-Mediated Communication* 13, no. 1, article 11 (2007), http://jcmc.indiana.edu/vol13/issue1/boyd.ellison.html. In this article, boyd and Ellison establish a stable working definition for social network sites (SNSs), offer a history of some of the major shifts in the development of SNSs, and include a literature review of work done in this scholarly field.

2. We rely very heavily on the work of Henry Jenkins in drawing attention to this participation gap, and on the social science research of Eszter Hargittai in describing its contours.

Chapter 1

1. For a scholarly overview of many of the key issues that we address in this chapter, see David Buckingham, ed., *Youth, Identity, and Digital Media* (Cambridge: MIT Press, 2008), a series of fine essays on the changing nature of identity for young people in a digital age. See also Nicola Döring, *Sozialpsychologie des Internet,* 2d ed. (Göttingen: Hofgrede, 2003), pp. 325–402. Döring explains how a given media environment impacts the types of identities we develop, how we communicate about these identities, and how we perceive the identities of others. The medium has an influence on both the personal identity and the social identity.

2. See, for example, D.A. Huffaker and S.L. Calvert, "Gender, Identity, and Language Use in Teenage Blogs," *Journal of Computer-Mediated Communication* 10, no. 2 (2005), http://jcmc.indiana.edu/vol10/issue2/huffaker.html.

3. S.L. Calvert, "Identity Construction on the Internet," in S.L. Calvert, A.B. Jordan, and R.R. Cocking, eds., *Children in the Digital Age: Influences of Electronic*

Media on Development (Westport, Conn.: Praeger, 2002), pp. 57–70. See also Buckingham, *Youth, Identity, and Digital Media,* pp. 1–22.

4. Calvert et al., *Children in the Digital Age,* pp. 57–70.

5. The social connections that Digital Natives develop in the outside world can also be strengthened through the virtual world. Patti Valkenberg, "Preadolescents' and Adolescents' Online Communication and Their Closeness to Friends," *Developmental Psychology* 43, no. 2 (March 2007): 267–277.

6. Digital Immigrants—as opposed to Digital Natives—are people who were not born digital, and who do not live a digital life in any substantial way, but are finding their way in a digital world.

7. The findings of a study that analyzed the Facebook behavior of more than 4,000 Carnegie Mellon University students are illustrative, if not definitive. According to the authors, 90.8 percent of the profiles contain an image, 87.8 percent of the users reveal their birthdate, 39.9 percent list a phone number, and 50.8 percent list their current residence. In addition, 62.9 percent of the students reveal a relationship status other than single, naming their partner and sometimes even providing a link to the partner's Facebook profile. See Ralph Gross and Alessandro Acquisti, "Information Revelation and Privacy in Online Social Networks (The Facebook Case), ACM Workshop on Privacy in the Electronic Society (WPES)," November 7, 2005, www.heinz.cmu.edu/~acquisti/papers/privacy-facebook-gross-acquisti.pdf.

8. Kai-Lung Hui, Bernhard C.Y. Tan, and Chyan-Yee Goh, "Online Information Disclosure: Motivators and Measurement," June 2005, http://www.comp.nus.edu.sg/~lung/motivators.pdf.

9. The risk depends on the type of personal information disclosure, which in turn is linked to different types of "self." See Bruce Jay Forman and Brian Withworth, "Information Disclosure and the Online Customer Relationship," http://brianwhitworth.com/foreman2005.doc.

10. For statistics on identity theft, as well as practical advice on how to prevent and recover from identity theft, see Terri Cullen, *Complete Identity Theft Guidebook: How to Protect Yourself from the Most Pervasive Crime in America* (New York: Dow Jones, 2007).

11. Adam N. Joinson, "Knowing Me, Knowing You: Reciprocal Self-Disclosure in Internet-Based Surveys," *Cyber Psychology and Behavior* 4, no. 5 (2001).

12. Platform design matters a lot when it comes to the disclosure of personal information. Some of the social network sites, such as Xing, remind users as to what percentage the user profile has been completed. We'll discuss a similar instance of "charismatic code" in Chapter 8 in the context of P2P file-sharing platforms.

13. Judith Donath and danah boyd, "Public Displays of Connection," *BT Technology Journal* 22, no. 4 (October 2004): 71–82.

14. See danah boyd and Nicole B. Ellison, "Social Networking Sites: Definitions, History, and Scholarship," *Journal of Computer-Mediated Communication* 13, no. 1 (2007).

15. The relationship between revelation of personal information and cooperative behavior is also emphasized—albeit from a completely different perspective—in the work of our colleagues Judith Donath and danah boyd, who have studied why people display their social connections on social network sites like Facebook or MySpace.

16. Classic concepts such as Havighurst's developmental tasks (Robert J. Havighurst, *Development Tasks and Education,* 3d ed. [New York: D. McKay, 1972]); Lerner's observations regarding the mechanisms used by adolescents to shape their identity context (Richard M. Lerner, *Concepts and Theories of Human Development,* 3d ed. [Mahwah, N.J.: Lawrence Erlbaum, 2001]); Erikson's stages of identity development and notion of crises (Erik H. Erikson, *Identity: Youth and Crisis* [New York: Norton, 1968]); or Rosenberg's theory on conceiving the self (Morris Rosenberg, *Conceiving the Self* [New York: Basic Books, 1979]), among others, are important points of reference when it comes to the proposed perspective of developmental psychology on the information disclosure phenomenon. Much work has to be done by psychologists to "apply" these basic theories to the emerging phenomena we're observing in the digital space.

17. See, for example, H. Tajfel, *Social Identity and Intergroup Relations* (Cambridge: Cambridge University Press, 1982); H. Tajfel and J.C. Turner, "The Social Identity Theory of Inter-Group Behavior," in: S. Worchel and L.W. Austin, eds., *Psychology of Intergroup Relations* (Chicago: Nelson-Hall, 1986).

18. Sherry Turkle, a professor at MIT, has written extensively on these topics. See Sherry Turkle, "Can You Hear Me Now?" *Forbes,* http://www.forbes.com/free_forbes/2007/0507/176.html. (This article is not just on youth, but it includes a section devoted to adolescence and an important consideration of the drawbacks

of mobile technology.) See also her chapter "Always-on/Always-on-you: The Tethered Self," in James Katz, ed., *Mainstreaming Mobiles: Mobile Communication and Social Change* (Cambridge: MIT Press, forthcoming), and the PDF file at http://web.mit.edu/sturkle/www/Always-on%20Always-on-you_The%20Tethered%20Self_ST.pdf.

19. danah boyd, "Why Youth (Heart) Social Network Sites: The Role of Networked Publics in Teenage Social Life," in David Buckingham, ed., *Youth Identity, and Digital Media,* John D. and Catherine T. MacArthur Foundation Series on Digital Media and Learning (Cambridge: MIT Press, 2007), pp. 119–142. Also available at http://www.danah.org/papers/WhyYouthHeart.pdf, p. 2. See also Shelly Turkle, *Life on Screen: Identity in the Age of the Internet* (New York: Simon and Schuster, 1997).

20. Multiple identities online are not an entirely new phenomenon in the construction and maintenance of social identity. Erving Goffman, a sociologist who wrote extensively about identity in the 1970s, describes an individual as comprising many different identities—a "back stage" and "front stage" identity, for example, as well as the different roles one holds in various environments and situations. To identify the particularities of such identity performance online, we must consider that these multiple identities are being constructed *consciously* and *explicitly,* that the different "roles" or "identities" are recorded and visible simultaneously, that we must learn to negotiate multiple roles simultaneously as we negotiate various audiences to one identity space, and that the "back stage" identity has very much entered the "front stage." The collapsing of the online and offline worlds might suggest that this distinction is less useful than it once was.

21. Focus group data, female high-school students, age sixteen (F1), sixteen (F2), and seventeen (F3).

22. Focus group data, male high-school student, age seventeen.

23. danah boyd, "Viewing American Class Divisions through Facebook and MySpace," Apophenia Blog, June 24, 2007, http://www.danah.org/papers/essays/ClassDivisions.html; E. Hargittai, "Whose Space? Differences among Users and Non-Users of Social Network Sites," *Journal of Computer-Mediated Communication* 13, no. 1 (2007), article 14, http://jcmc.indiana.edu/vol13/issue1/hargittai.html.

24. The word "avatar" originally comes from Hindu mythology and denotes the earthly incarnation of a deity in human or animal form. See, for example, "avatar" in Merriam-Webster online, http://www.merriam-webster.com.

25. See "Create an Avatar," http://secondlife.com/whatis/avatar.php.

26. See http://www.gamespot.com/news/6181920.html.

27. David Barboza, "Ogre to Slay? Outsource It to the Chinese," *New York Times,* December 9, 2005, http://www.nytimes.com/2005/12/09/technology/09gaming .html?_r=1&oref=slogin.

28. Social network sites already provide tools to make more radical identity transformations as they might be needed—for instance, when a Digital Native graduates from college and enters into worklife. However, by no means do all users change their self-presentation when transitioning from college into the workforce. Researchers on this topic therefore suggest that the designer of social network applications should develop and improve the tools that support bridging across multiple and heterogeneous social communities. See Joan Morris DiMicco and David R. Millen, "Identity Management: Multiple Presentations of Self in Facebook," GROUP '07, November 4/7, 2007, www.joandimicco.com/pubs/ dimicco-millen-group07.pdf.

29. See Google's low rating on privacy: Privacy International, "Privacy Ranking Report of Internet Service Companies," 2007 (http://www.bespacific.com/ mt/archives/015065.html#015065). See also Victor Mayer-Schoenberger's article about data not being forgotten: "Useful Void: The Art of Forgetting in the Age of Ubiquitous Computing," Working Paper Number RWP07–022, http://ksgnotes1 .harvard.edu/Research/wpaper.nsf/rwp/RWP07-022.

30. Focus group data, female high-school student, age seventeen.

31. The identities of Digital Natives represent the images of themselves as projected into cyberspace. These images, in turn, shape the ways in which they are perceived. Digital identities are complex composites. As pieces of personally identifiable data compiled to some sort of public "user profile," they include explicit information about (real or faked) personal identities (for example, user name, age, hobbies, musical tastes, and the like). At the same time, and more implicitly, they are linked to a Digital Native's social identity or identities, either as signals of group membership (for example, groups on social network sites) or as constitutive elements when a new social identity emerges through online

behavior (postings, conversations, ratings, and so on). This also makes clear that digital identities are only one aspect of a person's identity, and that digital identities interact in several ways with other elements of identity. See Thierry Nabeth, "Understanding the Identity Concept in the Context of Digital Social Environments," CALT-FIDIS working paper, January 2005, http://www.calt.insead.edu/project/Fidis/documents/2005-fidis-Understanding_the_Identity_Concept_in_the_Context_of_Digital_Social_Environments.pdf.

32. Focus group data, male high-school student.

33. Judith S. Donath, "Identity and Deception in the Virtual Community," http://smg.media.mit.edu/people/Judith/Identity/IdentityDeception.html. Donath writes: "In the electronic domain, the design of the environment is everything. Whether or not you know that other people are present or privy to a conversation, whether or not you can connect an on-line identity to a real-world identity, whether you have only a faint notion of the personalities around you or a vibrant and detailed impression—this is all determined by the design of the environment."

34. Henry Jenkins, an MIT professor and leading scholar in this field, refers to the new digital divide as the "participation gap," because lack of access prevents individuals from engaging with their peers. Henry Jenkins, Katherine Clinton, Rani Purushotma, Alice Robison, and Margaret Weigel, "Confronting the Challenges of Participatory Culture: Media Education for the 21st Century," 2006, http://www.projectnml.org/files/working/NMLWhitePaper.pdf.

35. In *Life on the Screen: Identity in the Age of the Internet* (New York: Simon and Schuster, 1995), Sherry Turkle describes the Internet as a laboratory for exploring and experimenting with different versions of "self." Later research has demonstrated that the Internet serves as a space in which to express the "true self" in situations where the user meets strangers—that is, interacts with individuals whom he or she hasn't already met face to face. See John A. Bargh, Katelyn Y.A. McKenna, and Grainne M. Fitzsimons, "Can You See the Real Me? Activation and Expression of the 'True Self' on the Internet," *Journal of Social Issues* 58, no. 1 (2002): 33–48.

36. PBS's *Frontline* covered one such story in depth, where "Jessica Hunter was a shy and awkward girl who struggled to make friends at school. Then, at age 14, she reinvented herself online as 'Autumn Edows,' an alternative goth artist and model who posted provocative photos of herself on the Web, and fast developed a cult following. 'I just became this whole different person,' Jessica tells FRONTLINE.

'I didn't feel like myself, but I liked the fact that I didn't feel like myself. I felt like someone completely different. I felt like I was famous" (http://www.pbs.org/wgbh/pages/frontline/kidsonline/).

37. The work of Yochai Benkler, especially *The Wealth of Networks* (New Haven, Conn.: Yale University Press, 2006), includes extensive consideration of the concept of the "networked public sphere," and danah boyd has made similar arguments about "networked publics" in "Why Youth (Heart) Social Network Sites," pp. 124–126, and elsewhere.

38. See boyd, "Why Youth (Heart) Social Network Sites," for a discussion of "imagined audiences."

Chapter 2

1. The term "digital dossier" was popularized by Daniel Solove, *The Digital Person* (New York: New York University Press, 2004).

2. See, for example, Eli Saslow, "Teen Tests Internet's Lewd Track Record," *Washington Post,* May 29, 2007, page A01, www.washingtonpost.com/wp-dyn/content/article/2007/05/28/AR2007052801370.html.

3. Don Slater, "Social Relationships and Identity On-line and Off-line," in Leah A. Lievrouw and Sonia Livingstone, *Handbook of New Media: Social Shaping and Consequences of ICTs* (Thousand Oaks, Calif.: Sage Publications, 2002), pp. 533–543.

4. One couple reportedly posted ultrasound images of their unborn baby on Facebook. See "Australian Fetus a Facebook Internet Star," http://www.reuters.com/article/lifestyleMolt/idUSL1516879520070815.

5. Solove, *The Digital Person.*

6. See http://blog.facebook.com/blog.php?post=2406207130.

7. Schoolchildren in the United Kingdom are being tracked through RFID tags in their clothing. Thomas Claburn, "U.K. Kids Get RFID Chips in School Uniforms," *InformationWeek,* October 25, 2007, http://www.informationweek.com/news/showArticle.jhtml?articleID=202601660.

8. Kim Zetter, "School RFID Plan Gets an F," *Wired,* http://www.wired.com/politics/security/news/2005/02/66554; Laurie Sullivan, "Apparel Maker Tags RFID for Kids' Sleepwear," *InformationWeek,* July 13, 2005, http://www.informationweek.com/story/showArticle.jhtml?articleID=165701942; Electronic Privacy

Information Center, "Children and RFID Systems," http://www.epic.org/privacy/rfid/children.html; Barry Levine, "Meet the Cell-Phone Tracking Parents," *Mobile Tech Today,* June 5, 2006, http://www.mobile-tech-today.com/news/Meet-the-Cell-Phone-Tracking-Parents/story.xhtml?story_id=130004F6VD1U; and Ilene and Michael Berson, "An International Perspective on the Techno-Tracking of Children: The Promise and Perils for Safety and Privacy in the Digital Age," http://www.netsafe.org.nz/print/print.aspx?f=news_default.aspx.

9. Xeni Jardin, "Your Identity, Open to All," *Wired,* May 6, 2005, http://www.wired.com/politics/security/news/2005/05/67407 (on the aggregation of digital and offline IDs into a single service).

10. Focus group data, male college student, age twenty.

11. "The potential risks include harm to the physical, psychological, and social well-being of children and young people resulting from engagement with pornography, misinformation, violent and/or racist material, and solicitation by adults to engage in abusive cybersex or to meet offline face to face. The concept also recognizes the ability of children and young people to be active initiators of, and participants in, deviant or criminal online activities such as cyberbullying, cyberstalking, and the creation and dissemination of pornography." Rachel O'Connell and Jo Bryce, "Young People, Well Being, and Risk Online," Council of Europe, 2006.

Chapter 3

1. George R. Milne, Andrew J. Rohm, and Shalini Bahl, "Consumers' Protection of Online Privacy and Identity," *Journal of Consumer Affairs* 38, no. 2 (Winter 2004): 217–232. The data from this survey shows the extent to which college students are protecting themselves online; the study concludes that adequate measures are not being taken.

2. See R. Gross and A. Acquisti, "Information Revelation and Privacy in Online Social Networks," Preproceedings version, ACM Workshop on Privacy in the Electronic Society (WPES), 2005, http://www.heinz.cmu.edu/~acquisti/papers/privacy-facebook-gross-acquisti.pdf. Gross and Acquisti discuss various reasons why Open Social Network (OSN) users are willing to post personal information online, and why they generally do not change the default privacy settings. They provide supporting empirical evidence based on a study of Carnegie Mellon undergrads. See also Seounmi Youn, "Teenagers' Perceptions of Online Privacy and Coping Behaviors: A Risk-Benefit Appraisal Approach," *Journal of Broadcasting*

and Electronic Media 49, no. 1 (March 2005): 86–110. This empirical study of how high-school students respond to privacy concerns online suggests that teens engage in a risk-benefit analysis when deciding what information to divulge.

3. See danah boyd, "Facebook's 'Privacy Trainwreck': Exposure, Invasion, and Drama," Apophenia Blog, September 8, 2006, http://www.danah.org/papers/ FacebookAndPrivacy.html. See also Alison George, "Living Online: The End of Privacy?" *New Scientist,* September 18, 2006, http://www.newscientisttech.com/ article/mg19125691.700;jsessionid=CMGJNHBLPFLJ.

4. Mary Madden, Susannah Fox, Aaron Smith, and Jessica Vitak, "Digital Footprints: Online Identity Management and Search in the Age of Transparency," December 16, 2007, Pew Internet and American Life reports, http://www .pewinternet.org/PPF/r/229/report_display.asp. This report shows that 60 percent of American adults have profiles on social network sites and describes a pattern of sharing information in ways that are strikingly similar to the ways that many Digital Natives share information online.

5. See Emily Nussbaum, "Say Everything," *New York,* http://nymag.com/news/ features/27341/.

6. Ellen Nakashima, "Enjoying Technology's Conveniences But Not Escaping Its Watchful Eyes," *Washington Post,* January 16, 2007, http://www.washingtonpost .com/wp-dyn/content/article/2007/01/15/AR2007011501304.html.

7. There remains the problem of the cache. This Digital Native might enter in a blog post that she later removes, but it could be archived in the cache of a search engine or in an archiving service, like archive.org. The problem of the persistence of digital information is closely related to the ubiquitousness of the information.

8. "Deep Web," http://en.wikipedia.org/wiki/Deep_web. See also http://chimp rawk.blogspot.com/2007/05/facebook-public-profiles.html, which is about technology design flaws that can result in supposedly private profiles showing up in the public Web.

9. http://harvard.facebook.com/privacy.php.

10. See http://news.bbc.co.uk/1/hi/technology/6980454.stm.

11. Tim O'Reilly, "What Is Web 2.0?" September 30, 2005, http://www.oreilly net.com/pub/a/oreilly/tim/news/2005/09/30/what-is-web-20.html.

12. Amanda Lenhart and Mary Madden, "Teens, Privacy and Online Social Networks: How Teens Manage Their Online Identities and Personal Information

in the Age of MySpace," April 18, 2007, http://www.pewinternet.org/PPF/r/211/ report_display.asp.

13. Robert O'Harrow, Jr., "ID Data Conned from Firm," *Washington Post,* February 17, 2005, http://www.washingtonpost.com/wp-dyn/articles/A30897 -2005Feb16.html.

14. Bob Sullivan, "ChoicePoint to Pay $15 Million over Data Breach," January 26, 2006, MSNBC, http://www.msnbc.msn.com/id/11030692/.

15. See http://epic.org/privacy/choicepoint/.

16. For a strong form of this argument, see Simson Garfinkel, *Database Nation* (Sebastopol, Calif.: O'Reilly, 2000).

17. Associated Press, "Lexis Nexis Owner Acquires ChoicePoint," February 21, 2008, http://www.foxbusiness.com/markets/industries/retail/article/lexis-nexis -owner-purchases-choicepoint_488603_7.html.

18. Privacy Rights Clearinghouse, "A Chronology of Data Breaches," December 4, 2007, http://www.privacyrights.org/ar/ChronDataBreaches.htm.

19. The definitive book on this topic is Jonathan Zittrain, *The Future of the Internet—and How to Stop It* (New Haven, Conn.: Yale University Press, 2008).

20. Michael Arrington, "AOL Proudly Releases Massive Amounts of Private Data," August 6, 2006, http://www.techcrunch.com/2006/08/06/aol-proudly -releases-massive-amounts-of-user-search-data/.

21. Michael Arrington, "AOL: This Was a Screw-up," August 7, 2006, http://www.techcrunch.com/2006/08/07/aol-this-was-a-screw-up/.

22. See http://www.chicagotribune.com/business/chi-fri-breaches-mar28,0,442 0914.story.

23. Cassell Bryan-Low, "U.K. Data Breach Has Banks Alert for Fraud," *Wall Street Journal,* November 23–25, 2007.

24. Organisation for Economic Co-operation and Development (OECD), "Participative Web and User-Created Content: Web 2.0, Wikis and Social Networking," 2007, p. 104.

25. News Roundup, "In Study, Facebook Users Share with Stranger," *Wall Street Journal,* August 14, 2007, http://online.wsj.com/article/SB11870598778049 6951.html. According to this article, "Sophos PLC, a computer-security firm, found 41% of Facebook users were willing to divulge personal information—such as phone numbers, home addresses and email addresses—to a complete stranger."

26. "About," http://www.riya.com/about. The site says that "Riya is a new kind of visual search engine. We look inside the image, not only at the text

around it. Use Riya to . . . Find similar faces and objects on many images across the web."

27. Eli Saslow, "Teen Tests Internet's Lewd Track Record," *Washington Post,* May 29, 2007, A01, http://www.washingtonpost.com/wp-dyn/content/article/2007/05/28/AR2007052801370.html.

28. Wallys W. Conhaim and Loraine Page, "Getting to Know You Online," *Information Today* 22, no. 7 (July/August 2005).

29. See http://www.washingtonpost.com/wp-dyn/content/article/2007/01/15/AR2007011501304_2.html.

30. See http://cq.cx/verichip.pl. See also Annalee Newitz, "The RFID Hacking Underground," May 2006, http://www.wired.com/wired/archive/14.05/rfid.html.

31. http://www.consumerreports.org/cro/health-fitness/health-care/electronic-medical-records-306/overview/index.htm.

32. John J. Doll, "The Patenting of DNA," *Science* 280, no. 5364 (May 1, 1998): 689–690, http://www.sciencemag.org/cgi/content/full/280/5364/689; Francis S. Collins, "Personalized Medicine: A New Approach to Staying Well," *Boston Globe,* July 17, 2005, http://www.boston.com/news/globe/editorial_opinion/oped/articles/2005/07/17/personalized_medicine/.

33. See Joseph Turow and Michael Hennessy, "Internet Privacy and Institutional Trust: Insights from a National Survey, *New Media and Society* 9, no. 2 (April 2007): 300–318.

34. European laws generally protect individuals more completely against corporations than U.S. laws do. See Bob Sullivan, "'La Difference' Is Stark in EU, U.S. Privacy Laws," MSNBC, October 19, 2006, http://www.msnbc.msn.com/id/15221111/. See also J. Fernback and Z. Papacharissi, "Online Privacy as Legal Safeguard: The Relationship among Consumer, Online Portal, and Privacy Policy," *New Media and Society* 9, no. 5 (2007): 715–734.

35. See Steve Lohr, "Google and Microsoft Look to Change Health Care," *New York Times,* August 14, 2007, http://www.nytimes.com/2007/08/14/technology/14healthnet.html?ex=1187841600&en=4d2de0ebb10e453c&ei=5070. See also Declan McCullagh and Elinor Mills, "How Search Engines Rate on Privacy," *CNET News,* August 13, 2007, http://news.com.com/How+search+engines+rate+on+privacy/2100-1029_3-6202068.html and http://openmic.org/node/62.

36. Sabena Suri, "Looking for Love on All the Wrong Facebook Pages," *CNET News,* August 2, 2007, http://www.news.com/Looking-for-love-on-all-the-wrong-Facebook-pages/2010-1025_3-6200052.html.

37. Presentation by Chris Kelly, General Counsel of Facebook, NYC Bar Association, February 5, 2007, and subsequent conversations. Notes on file with authors.

38. See danah boyd, "growing up in a culture of fear: from Columbine to banning MySpace," November 2, 2005, http://www.zephoria.org/thoughts/archives/2005/11/02/growing_up_in_a.html.

39. See, for instance, Sonia Livingstone, "Strategies of Parental Regulation in the Media-Rich Home," *Computers in Human Behavior* 23, no. 2 (March 2007): 920–941. See also Sonia Livingstone and Magdalena Bober, "UK Children Go Online—Listening to Young People's Experiences," 2003, http://www.children -go-online.net; Veerle Rompaey and Keith Roe, "The Home as a Multimedia Environment: Families' Conception of Space and the Introduction of Information and Communication Technologies in the Home," *Communications* 26, no. 4 [2001]: 351–369).

40. See David Johnson, Susan Crawford, and John Palfrey, "The Accountable Net: Peer Production of Internet Governance," *Virginia Journal of Law and Technology* 9 (2004), http://cyber.law.harvard.edu/home/uploads/336/Accountable Internet.pdf. The work of Judith Donath and her team at the MIT Media Lab on the importance of design to privacy and identity protection is extremely instructive.

41. For a discussion of efforts by Facebook to monitor potential predators, see "In Study, Facebook Users with Strangers," *Wall Street Journal,* Eastern edition, August 14, 2007, B3. For a discussion of MySpace's reaction to safety and privacy concerns on the site, see Beth Snyder Bulik, "Q&A with MySpace's Gold . . . or Marketing on Online Steroids," *Advertising Age* 77, no. 23 (June 5, 2006).

42. Focus group data, female high-school student, age seventeen.

43. For a discussion of China's increasing problem with online privacy infringements, see Ding Wenlei, "Dark Side of the Net," *Beijing Review* 50, no. 37 (September 13, 2007): 22–23, http://www.bjreview.com.cn/special/txt/2007 -09/07/content_65690.htm.

44. For a discussion of free-speech concerns raised by the Children's Online Privacy Protection Act, see Charlene Simmons, "Protecting Children while Silencing Them: The Children's Online Privacy Protection Act and Children's Free Speech Rights," *Communication Law and Policy* 12, no. 2 (Spring 2007): 119–142. Companies across the European Union, and in Portugal and the United Kingdom, in particular, have advocated for a better balance between the right to data protection and the freedom of expression and information. See Flash

Eurobarometer 147, "Data Protection in the European Union, Executive Summary," p. 10, http://ec.europa.eu/public_opinion/flash/fl147_exec_summ.pdf.

45. The *Lindqvist* decision by the European Court of Justice is illustrative in this regard. Mrs. Lindqvist, a part-time catechist in the parish of Alseda in Sweden, set up an Internet home page to allow parishioners preparing for their Confirmation to obtain the information they might need. On the website, Mrs. Lindqvist posted information about herself and eighteen colleagues in the parish, sometimes including their full names, sometimes only their first names. She described in a funny way the jobs held by these colleagues as well as their hobbies, and posted in several cases family circumstances and telephone numbers. She also mentioned that one colleague had injured her foot and was on half-time on medial grounds. The Court ruled that the act of posting this information fell within the scope of the data-protection directive and was not covered by any of its exceptions. Consequently, Lindqvist was correctly penalized for violating privacy laws under Swedish law. Ruling available at http://curia.europa.eu/jurisp/cgi-bin/form.pl ?lang=en&Submit=Submit&docrequire=judgements&numaff=C-101%2F01&datefs =&datefe=&nomusuel=Lindqvist&domaine=&mots=&resmax=100. For a critical reading, see Flora J. Garcia, "Bodil Lindqvist: A Swedish Churchgoer's Violation of the European Union's Data Protection Directive Should Be a Warning to U.S. Legislators," *Fordham Intellectual Property, Media and Entertainment Law Journal* 15 (2005): 1204.

46. See "Useful Void: The Art of Forgetting in the Age of Ubiquitous Computing," John F. Kennedy School of Government–Harvard University, Faculty Research Working Papers Series, No. RWP07–022 (April 2007), http://ksgnotes1 .harvard.edu/Research/wpaper.nsf/rwp/RWP07-022/$File/rwp_07_022_mayer -schoenberger.pdf. In an official 2003 survey among European companies, 37 percent of the respondents indicated that they believed the requirements of the data-protection law were too strict in certain respects, and 34 percent estimated that the data-protection laws were not necessary except for certain sectors of activity. See Flash Eurobarometer 147, "Data Protection in the European Union, Executive Summary," p. 2, http://ec.europa.eu/public_opinion/flash/fl147_exec _summ.pdf.

47. Consider the work of the Identity Gang, found online at http://wiki .idcommons.net/index.php/Identity_Gang.

48. Others have commented on the benefits of a liability-based scheme; see, for instance, Alessandro Acquisti, "Privacy and Security of Personal Information:

Economic Incentives and Technological Solutions," http://www.heinz.cmu.edu/
~acquisti/papers/acquisti_eis_refs.pdf.

49. The literature relating to online privacy is vast. For selected additional
readings on privacy that we found helpful, see Sonia Livingstone, "Mediating the
Public/Private Boundary at Home: Children's Use of the Internet for Privacy and
Participation," *Journal of Media Practice* 6, no. 1 (2005): 41–51,
http://eprints.lse.ac.uk/506/; "Teen Blogs Exposed: The Private Lives of Teens
Made Public," http://www.google.com/url?sa=t&ct=res&cd=1&url=http%3A%2
F%2Fwww.soc.northwestern.edu%2Fgradstudents%2Fhuffaker%2Fpapers%2FH
uffaker-2006-AAAS-Teen_Blogs.pdf&ei=QCaFRu-oC6LSeuz9yOQB&usg=AFQ
CNFy4-txN2Y49QHkgZDHbYB8nx3j6Q&sig2=UXHVPZsnMw8EZmJrxCkSqA;
Kenichi Ishii, "Links between Real and Virtual Networks: A Comparative Study of
Online Communities in Japan and Korea," *CyberPsychology and Behavior* 10, no.
2 (April 2007): 252–257 (which focuses on real-world versus virtual world
relationships, which seems related to online versus offline identity, and concludes
that there is a cultural component to how users perceive the interactions between
the two); Becky Hogge, "Beware of Online Friendship," *New Statesman* 136, no.
4850 (July 9, 2007) (on the efforts of Digital Natives to carefully manage their
online identities, suggesting they think of online identity as separate, or at least
different, from offline identity); Brock Read, "Information Technology," *Chronicle
of Higher Education* 52, no. 20 (January 20, 2006), A38–A41 (on efforts by some
universities to combat and educate students about privacy abuses on OSNs); Parry
Aftab, "Online Safety at School," *PC Magazine* 23, no. 13 (August 3, 2004) (on
efforts of schools to protect kids while using campus computers); Josephine Rossi,
"Good or Bad, Profiles Attract Attention," *T+D* 60, no. 12 (December 2006): 12–
13 (on the impact that personal profile online postings can have on the professional
prospects of candidates); and Carina Paine, Ulf-Dietrich Reips, Stefan Stieger, Adam
Joinson, and Tom Buchanan, "Internet Users' Perceptions of 'Privacy Concerns' and
'Privacy Actions'," *International Journal of Human-Computer Studies* 65, no. 6 (June
2007): 526–536 (which includes the results of a survey showing the wide range of
privacy concerns that users have as well as the reasoning behind these concerns).

Chapter 4

1. Marilyn A. Campbell, "Cyber Bullying: An Old Problem in a New Guise?"
Australian Journal of Guidance and Counselling 15, no. 1 (2005): 68–76, http://
eprints.qut.edu.au/archive/00001925/.

2. An article on theage.com reported: "Up to 30 per cent of South Koreans under 18, or about 2.4 million people, are at risk of internet addiction, says Ahn Dong-hyun, a child psychiatrist at Hanyang University in Seoul, who has just completed a three-year government-funded survey of the problem. They spend at least two hours a day online, usually playing games or chatting" (http://www.theage.com.au/articles/2007/11/25/1195962828227.html).

3. I. Berson and M. Berson, "Challenging Online Behaviors of Youth: Findings from a Comparative Analysis of Young People and New Zealand." *Social Science Computer Review* 23 (2005): 29, http://ssc.sagepub.com/cgi/content/abstract/23/1/29.

4. Patrick Wintour, "Move to Ban Happy-Slapping on the Web," *The Guardian,* October 21, 2006, http://technology.guardian.co.uk/news/story/0,,1928106,00.html.

5. Gustavo S. Mesch, "Youth Pornographic Consumption: How Similar and Different Are from Other Internet Users," Paper presented at Oxford Internet Institute conference on cyber safety (2005), http://www.oii.ox.ac.uk/microsites/cybersafety/extensions/pdfs/papers/gustavo_mesch.pdf.

6. Simon Johnson, *Keep Your Kids Safe on the Internet* (Columbus, Ohio: McGraw-Hill/Osborne, 2004), and corresponding website at http://www.keepyourkidssafe.com/. See also the website of the United States Internet Crime Task Force at http://www.usict.org/safety.asp.

7. Janis Wolak, Kimberly Mitchell, and David Finkelhor, "Unwanted and Wanted Exposure to Online Pornography in a National Sample of Youth Internet Users," *Pediatrics* 119, no. 2 (February 2007): 247–257.

8. According to some studies, there is reason to be concerned: Researchers have established links between young people who access porn online and unhealthy attitudes toward sex. See, for example, Tori DeAngelis, "Web Pornography's Effect on Children, *Monitor of Psychology* 38, no. 10 (November 2007), http://apa.org/monitor/nov07/webporn.html.

9. Janis Wolak, quoted in Daniel DeNoon, "Internet Porn Reaches Most Teens," *WebMD Medical News,* February 5, 2007, http://www.webmd.com/content/Article/131/118149.htm?pagenumber=1.

10. Elinor Mills, "Google, Sun, Others Band to Fight Spyware, Adware," http://www.news.com/Google,-Sun,-others-band-to-fight-spyware,-adware/2100-1029_3-6030750.html.

11. StopBadWare, "Trends in Badware 2007—What Internet Users Need to Know," http://www.stopbadware.org/home/consumerreport.

12. For links to information about how to protect your computer from badware, see our site http://www.stopbadware.org.

13. H. Bengtsson and L. Johnson, "Perspective Taking, Empathy, and Prosocial Behavior in Late Childhood," *Child Study Journal* 22 (1992): 11–22.

14. Nancy Willard, "I Can't See You—You Can't See Me: How the Use of Information and Communication Technologies Can Impact Responsible Behavior," 2004, http://www.cyberbully.org/docs/disinhibition.pdf.

15. Focus group data, female middle-school student, age thirteen.

16. J.R. Suler, "The Online Disinhibition Effect," *CyberPsychology and Behavior* 7 (2004): 321–326, http://www.rider.edu/~suler/psycyber/disinhibit.html.

17. R. Kowalski, S. Limber, A. Scheck, M. Redfearn, J. Allen, A. Calloway, J. Farris, K. Finnegan, M. Keith, S. Kerr, L. Singer, J. Spearman, L. Tripp, and L. Vernon, "Electronic Bullying among School-Aged Children and Youth," paper presented at the annual meeting of the American Psychological Association (APA), 2005.

18. National Crime Prevention Council Cyberbullying Research Report, 2006, http://www.ncpc.org/cms/cms-upload/ncpc/file/V2_Bullying%20Whats%20New%20and%20What%20To%20Do.ppt.

19. Amanda Lenhart, "Data Memo: Cyberbullying and Online Teens," June 27, 2007, http://www.pewinternet.org/pdfs/PIP%20Cyberbullying%20Memo.pdf.

20. For a treatment of cyberbullying in the college and law school context from the perspective of a dean, see Darby Dickerson, "Cyberbullies on Campus," *University of Toledo Law Review* 37, no. 51 (2005–2006).

21. Lenhart, "Data Memo."

22. danah boyd, "cyberbullying," April 7, 2007, http://www.zephoria.org/thoughts/archives/2007/04/07/cyberbullying.html.

23. Amy Benfer, "Cyber Slammed," 2001, http://archive.salon.com/mwt/feature/2001/07/03/cyber_bullies/index.html.

24. Erin Mishkin, "A Closer Look at Cyberbullying: Is It a Girl Thing?" 2005 (not published, on file with authors).

25. Lauren Collins, "Friend Game," *The New Yorker*, January 21, 2008, http://www.newyorker.com/reporting/2008/01/21/080121fa_fact_collins.

26. http://www.missingkids.com/en_US/publications/NC167.pdf.

27. Amanda Lenhart and Mary Madden, "Social Networking Websites and Teens: An Overview," 2007, http://www.pewinternet.org/PPF/r/198/report_display .asp.

28. Elisheva F. Gross, "Adolescent Internet Use: What We Expect, What Teens Report," *Applied Developmental Psychology* 25 (2004): 633–649, http://www.cdmc .ucla.edu/downloads/Adolescent%20Internet%20usepdf.pdf. See also Elisheva Gross, Jaana Juvonen, and Shelly L. Gable, "Internet Use and Well-Being in Adolescence," *Journal of Social Issues* 58 (2002): 75–90, http://www.blackwell -synergy.com/doi/pdf/10.1111/1540-4560.00249.

29. Polly Klaas Foundation, "Topline Findings from Omnibuzz® Research," http://www.pollyklaas.org/internet-safety/internet-pdfs/PollingSummary.pdf, Kimberly J. Mitchell, David Finkelhor, and Janis Wolak, "Internet Prevention Messages—Targeting the Right Online Behaviors," *Archives of Pediatrics and Adolescent Medicine* 161 (2007): 138–145.

30. "MySpace, News Corp., Sued by Families Whose Daughters Were Assaulted," *Austin American Statesman,* January 18, 2007, http://www.statesman .com/blogs/content/shared-gen/blogs/austin/theticker/entries//2007/01/.

31. See http://www.consumeraffairs.com/news04/2007/01/myspace_zephyr .html.

32. Focus group data, female middle-school student, age twelve.

33. Focus group data, male middle-school student, age thirteen.

34. See http://www-usr.rider.edu/~suler/psycyber/disinhibit.html.

35. Focus group data, two female college students, both age sixteen.

36. Focus group data, female high-school student, age seventeen.

37. Emma Free, New York City Bar Panel, podcast, February 5, 2007.

38. See www.2smrt4u.com.

39. N. Willard, "Choosing Not to Go Down the Not-So-Good Cyber Streets," paper presented at Pornography and Their Applicability to Other Inappropriate Internet Content meeting in Washington, D.C., 2000, http://www.csriu.org/ onlinedocs/pdf/nwnas.pdf.

40. Berson and Berson, "Challenging Online Behaviors of Youth."

41. Bullying. No Way!, "Researchers and Practitioners: Marilyn Campbell," http://www.bullyingnoway.com.au/talkout/researchers/marilynCampbell.shtml.

42. "Backstory: Look, Mom, It's Me. I'm OK!" *Christian Science Monitor,* December 4, 2006, http://www.csmonitor.com/2006/1204/p20s01-legn.html.

43. Focus group data, junior-high student.

44. Jeff Chu, "You Wanna Take This Online?" *Time.com,* August 1, 2005, http://www.time.com/time/magazine/article/0,9171,1088698,00.html.

45. Candace Lombardi, "MySpace.com, News Corp. Sued in Assault Cases," *News.com,* January 19, 2007, http://news.com.com/MySpace.com%2C+News +Corp.+sued+in+assault+cases/2100-1030_3-6151096.html.

46. Pete Cashmore, "MySpace Tracker Tracks Teens," http://mashable .com/2007/01/16/myspace-tracker-tracks-teens/.

47. See Microsoft Press Release, "Government, Technology and Advocacy Leaders Launch National Get Net Safe Tour to Educate Consumers about Online Safety," May 16, 2006, http://www.microsoft.com/presspass/press/2006/may06/05 -16GetNetSafe06PR.mspx; http://phoenix.bizjournals.com/phoenix/stories/2006/ 08/21/daily14.html.

48. Staysafe.org, http://www.staysafe.org/.

49. "A Junior High Student from Utah Makes a Film and a Difference," http://www.staysafe.org/teens/student_spotlight/predator.html.

50. Lisa Lerer, "Parents Sue MySpace," *Forbes.com,* January 18, 2007, http://www.forbes.com/security/2007/01/18/myspace-lawsuit-assault-tech-security -cx_11_0118myspacesuit.html.

51. Jonathan Saltzman, "49 States, MySpace OK Child Safety Pact," January 15, 2008, http://www.boston.com/news/local/articles/2008/01/15/49_states _myspace_ok_child_safety_pact/.

52. "Tom Reilly Takes On 'Social Network' Sites for Teenagers That Are Playgrounds for Sexual Predators, Owned by Fox Television," http://www .massnews.com/2006_editions/8_august/82906_reilly_takes_on_myspace.htm.

53. See Pete Cashmore, "Legislation Could Ban MySpace in Schools," July 28, 2006, http://mashable.com/2006/07/28/legislation-could-ban-myspace-in-schools/.

54. See http://www.danah.org/papers/AAAS2006.html.

Chapter 5

1. Little Loca has a channel on YouTube at http://www.youtube .com/user/littleloca. She also has a MySpace page at http://www.myspace.com/ littleloca4life. StevieRyan.tv is at http://www.stevieryan.tv/. The article "It Should Happen to You" in *The New Yorker* by Ben McGrath is online at http://www.new yorker.com/archive/2006/10/16/061016fa_fact.

2. McGrath, "It Should Happen to You."

3. See Amanda Lenhart, Mary Madden, Alexandra Rankin Macgill, and Aaron Smith, "Teens and Social Media," December 19, 2007, http://www.pew internet.org/pdfs/PIP_Teens_Social_Media_Final.pdf, p. i. For a 2004 survey, see Amanda Lenhart and Mary Madden, "Teen Content Creators and Consumers," http://www.pewinternet.org/pdfs/PIP_Teens_Content_Creation.pdf, p. i. (finding that 57 percent of online teens have participated in one or more content-creating activities).

4. See Lenhart and Madden, " Teen Content Creators and Consumers."

5. Ibid., p. 9.

6. Organisation for Economic Co-operation and Development (OECD), "Participative Web: User-Created Content: Web 2.0, Wikis and Social Networking," 2007, (hereinafter "OECD Report").

7. Ibid., p. 11 (with references); see also " Surveying the Scenesters: China in the Web 2.0 World," Yahoo! News, November 20, 2007, http://news.yahoo.com/ s/adweek/20071120/ad_bpiaw/surveyingthescenesterschinaintheweb20world.

8. The Pew studies have supplied ample evidence of the shifts in creativity and consumption among teens living in the United States. See Lenhart et al., "Teens and Social Media," p. i; Lenhart and Madden, "Teen Content Creators and Consumers," pp. i, 2. The enduring questions that come out of the Pew work and other studies are: (1) How many young people are truly taking an active part in this creation of online content? and (2) What can we do about the divides that are being created between those who have the skills to participate and those who do not? The work of both Henry Jenkins, on the participation gap, and Eszter Hargittai, in her reformulation of the "digital divide" questions, is extremely helpful here.

9. Consider the findings of CapGemini's report from April 2007 on the creative acts of Digital Natives, in which Digital Natives are defined simply as those in the age group from fifteen to twenty-four, in CapGemini, "Digital Natives: How Is the Younger Generation Reshaping the Telecom and Media Landscape?" http://www.de.capgemini.com/m/de/tl/Digital_Natives.pdf.

10. See, for example, Elliot Eisner, "The Loci of Creativity in Arts," *Studies in Art Education* 2, no. 1 (1960): 22–42. Ignacio L. Götz, in contrast, argues that a person who makes something is always being creative. The question whether the piece of work is new, according to Götz, is a separate question about its originality, rather

314 NOTES TO PAGES 116-118

than a question of creativity. While we sympathize with Götz's definition of creativity, we use the term in Eisner's sense, which represents the mainstream understanding of the concept. See Ignacio Götz, "On Defining Creativity," *The Journal of Aesthetics and Art Criticism* 39, no. 3 (1981): 297–301. For a good overview of the different types of creativity, see, for example, Peter Tschmuck, *Creativity and Innovation in the Music Industry* (New York: Springer 2006), Chapter 10. See also Elliot W. Eisner, "A Typology of Creativity in the Visual Arts," *Studies in Art Education* 4, no. 1 (1962): 11–22.

11. This example has been taken from Urs Gasser and Silke Ernst, "From Shakespeare to DJ Danger Mouse: A Quick Look at Copyright and User Creativity in the Digital Age," http://papers.ssrn.com/s013/papers.cfm?abstract_id=909223.

12. Video available at http://waxy.org/random/view.php?type=video&filename =grey_video.mov.

13. See http://politicalhumor.about.com/library/multimedia/bushblair_endless love.mov.

14. See http://www.jibjab.com/originals/originals/jibjab/movieid/65.

15. See http://www.machinima.com/.

16. The letter is available at http://www.chillingeffects.org/fanfic/notice .cgi?NoticeID=534&print=yes. Recently, J.K. Rowling and Warner Brothers sued a small publisher that planned to publish an unofficial Harry Potter encyclopedia based on the online version of a lexicon written by a fan of Rowling's magical stories. See, for example, Julie Hilden, "J.K. Rowling's Law Suit against Those Who Plan to Publish an Unauthorized Harry Potter Encyclopedia: Who Should Win?" *FindLaw Legal News and Commentary,* April 28, 2008, http://writ.news.findlaw .com/hilden/20080428.html.

17. The creative power of collaboration more generally is well described by Keith Sawyer in *Group Genius: The Creative Power of Collaboration* (New York: Basic Books, 2007).

18. The movement toward mass online collaboration does not come out of the blue. In historical terms, the "Open Source software movement," where typically a large number of software developers are teaming up and working together to create software with free source code, has established a trajectory into which the current Web 2.0 trends, and the habits of Digital Natives, fit neatly. The Open Source movement marked the start of a sea change in how production of information goods occurs. The voluntary contributions of

thousands of geeks around the world add up to more than 100,000 person-years of effort in programming software. Most of the geeks involved in the development of the existing base of Open Source software are Digital Immigrants, not Digital Natives. The Open Source movement has led to the development of extremely sophisticated and important software products. Most people use many of these applications every day online, even though they may not know it. The Linux operating system, the Apache server software, and Mozilla's Firefox web browser, to name just a few examples, were created by "amateurs." These creators are amateurs in the sense that Olympic athletes are "amateurs"—they are highly skilled, in many cases, but they happen not to have been paid cash for their time in developing the software. They often get paid for other things, like developing code in other contexts (sort of like playing basketball for an NBA team in addition to playing in the Olympics for free, if that was allowed by Olympic rules). The computer scientists who have given us free software and the Open Source movement are the first-generation heroes of the digital revolution. They set the stage for the population of highly creative Digital Natives. The Open Source movement's participants have demonstrated in unprecedented ways that great things can be achieved in the new digital world—largely based on highly parallel, unstructured processes of collaboration among thousands of volunteers. For an excellent analysis, see Steven Weber, *The Success of Open Source* (Cambridge: Harvard University Press, 2004).

19. The power of wikis is best described in Don Tapscott and Anthony D. Williams, *Wikinomics: How Mass Collaboration Changes Everything* (New York: Portfolio, 2006).

20. Yochai Benkler, *Wealth of Networks: How Social Production Transforms Markets and Freedom* (New Haven, Conn.: Yale University Press, 2006).

21. See http://teen.secondlife.com/.

22. The music created by Digital Natives can be found today all over the Web, on their own website but also on MySpace, AOL Music, and Yahoo! Music. The band Wilco used a similar strategy, including peer-to-peer networks, to revive their popularity and garner a better deal through the traditional label business. Hip-hop and visual artist Tim Fite released an entire album, *Over the Counter Culture,* for free on his website, despite being on his second major record deal. The band Radiohead released an album entirely for free, asking fans to give them in

compensation whatever they felt like paying. See http://www.timfite.com; also http://www.jsonline.com/story/index.aspx?id=570307.

23. See "Digi:nation—Exclusive Research into Our Digital Behaviour," *Guardian Unlimited,* October 16. 2006, http://www.guardian.co.uk/pressoffice/pressrelease/story/0,,1935330,00.html#article_continue. Three-fourths of online teens in the United States reported having broadband Internet connections at home in 2006. See Amanda Lenhart et al., "Teens and Social Media," p. 16.

24. Lee Rainie, "28% of Online Americans Have Used the Internet to Tag Content," January 31, 2007, http://www.pewinternet.org/pdfs/PIP_Tagging.pdf.

25. OECD Report, p. 13.

26. See http://acs.anshechung.com/index.php.

27. See also Kate Bulkley, "Whose Content Is It Anyway?" *The Guardian,* September 21, 2006, http://technology.guardian.co.uk/weekly/story/0,,1876 697,00.html.

28. Jack Balkin, "Digital Speech and Democratic Culture: A Theory of Freedom of Expression for the Information Society," *New York University Law Review* 79 (2004): 1.

29. William W. Fisher III, *Promises to Keep: Technology, Law, and the Future of Entertainment* (Palo Alto, Calif.: Stanford Law and Politics, 2004), p. 28.

Chapter 6

1. See "Online Music-Swapping Rocks," BBC News, September 10, 2001, http://news.bbc.co.uk/2/hi/entertainment/1535789.stm.

2. For detailed analysis, see Organisation for Economic Co-operation and Development (OECD), "Digital Broadband Content: Music," December 13, 2005, http://www.oecd.org/dataoecd/13/2/34995041.pdf.

3. A good source of information on the legal disputes surrounding the Napster case—one of the most important early legal skirmishes of the Internet era—is the website of the Electronic Frontier Foundation at http://w2.eff.org/IP/P2P/Napster/.

4. The MGM complaint can be found online at http://w2.eff.org/IP/P2P/MGM_v_Grokster/20011002_mgm_v_grokster_complaint.pdf.

5. Ipsos Public Affairs, "Internet Piracy on Campus: American Students and Educators Share Their Attitudes Toward Online Downloading, File-Sharing and Copyright Law," September 16, 2003, http://www.bsa.org/country/Research %20and%20Statistics/~/media/80B03498709F4B7E93E6B2D449795763.ashx.

6. Mike McGuire and Urs Gasser, "Global Music Services Face Local Laws and Expectations," GartnerG2 Report, April 2004, p. 6.

7. Focus group data, middle-school female, age thirteen.

8. Robert C. Ellickson, *Order without Law: How Neighbors Settle Disputes* (Cambridge: Harvard University Press, 1991). Ellickson, a professor of property and urban law at Yale Law School, describes in the book how people organize their lives, regulate their behavior, and structure their coexistence in society.

9. Mary Madden and Amanda Lenhart, "Music Downloading, File-Sharing and Copyright," July 2003, http://www.pewinternet.org/pdfs/PIP_Copyright _Memo.pdf.

10. Business Software Alliance, "Internet Piracy on Campus," September 16, 2003, http://www.bsa.org/country/Research%20and%20Statistics/~/media/80B03 498709F4B7E93E6B2D449795763.ashx.

11. See http://torrentfreak.com/50cent-file-sharing-doesnt-hurt-the-artists -071208/.

12. http://archive.salon.com/tech/feature/2000/06/14/love/.

13. Oliver R. Goodenough and Gregory Decker, "Why Do Good People Steal Intellectual Property," The Gruter Institute Working Papers on Law, Economics, and Evolutionary Biology, vol. 4, no. 1 (2006).

14. Lior Strahilevitz, "Charismatic Code, Social Norms, and the Emergence of Cooperation on the File-Swapping Networks," *Virginia Law Review* 89 (2003), http://ssrn.com/abstract=329700.

15. The lawsuits, as one observer put it, "marked one of the most controversial moments in the recording industry's digital history." John Borland, "RIAA Sues 261 File Swappers," *CNET News*, September 8, 2003, http://news.com.com/2100 -1023_3-5072564.html.

16. http://www.news.com/RIAA-settles-with-12-year-old-girl/2100-1027_3- 5073717.html.

17. John Schwartz, "She Says She's No Music Pirate. No Snoop Fan, Either," *New York Times*, September 25, 2003, http://www.nytimes.com/2003/09/25/ business/media/25TUNE.html?ex=1379822400&en=2947c62fa13b3266&ei=50 07&partner=USERLAND.

18. The quote is from Dennis Roddy, "The Song Remains the Same," *Pittsburgh Post-Gazette.com,* September 16, 2003, http://www.post-gazette.com/columnists/ 20030914edroddy0914p1.asp.

19. http://www.bsa.org/country/News%20and%20Events/News%20Archives/ BSA-Harris%20Youth%20Study%20Fact%20Sheet.aspx.

20. Mary Madden and Lee Rainie, "Music and Video Downloading Moves beyond P2P," Pew Internet Project Data Memo, March 2005, www.pewinternet .org/pdfs/pip_filesharing_march05.pdf.

21. http://www.latimes.com/technology/la-fi-itunes4apr04,1,4873885.story.

22. See "iTunes Store Tops Three Billion Songs," Apple Press Release, July 31, 2007, http://www.apple.com/pr/library/2007/07/31itunes.html. See also http://www .theregister.co.uk/2005/09/07/apple_responds_to_rivals/.

23. The Recording Industry Association of America's Consumer Profile for 2006 is accessible online at http://76.74.24.142/E795D602-FA50-3F5A-3730-9C8A40B 98C46.pdf.

24. At the Berkman Center, we have had a keen interest in Apple's Music Store from the time of its release. It was clear, right from the start, that it was a major breakthrough. Although (or maybe because) the research center is at a law school, we've had a very strong interest in what we call "market-driven" solutions to the digital media crisis. In our view, digital entrepreneurs and innovative businesses generally hold greater promise for developing an adequate response to the entertainment industry's crises than judges and lawmakers. Specifically, the Digital Media Project team was interested in the interplay among the economic forces involved, the technological drivers, and the existing copyright and contract law framework. The iTunes Music Store seemed like a perfect testing ground for our hypotheses, and soon after its launch in the United States, the project team at Berkman decided to take a closer look at iTunes. On June 15, 2004, we released a report on iTunes of over 100 pages examining in some detail and from an international perspective "how copyright, contract, and technology shape the business of digital media." Available at http://ssrn.com/abstract=556802.

25. In a follow-up report to the iTunes case study, our Digital Media team at the Berkman Center began to think more radically about new business models for the digital media world and their respective policy implications—to a great extent inspired by William W. Fisher III's seminal book *Promises to Keep: Technology, Law, and the Future of Entertainment* (Palo Alto, Calif.: Stanford Law and Politics, 2004), to date the most comprehensive study of the conflicts surrounding digital music distribution and possible ways out. See "Content and Control: Assessing the

Impact of Policy Choices on Potential Online Business Models in the Music and Film Industries," January 7, 2005, http://ssrn.com/abstract=654602.

26. This story, with its various phases, is symptomatic of innovation in information and communications technologies. In *Ruling the Waves,* Harvard Business School professor Deborah L. Spar actually describes the exact same patterns—"cycles of discovery, chaos, and wealth"—for a variety of disruptive technologies, "from the compass to the Internet." Spar, *Ruling the Waves: From the Compass to the Internet, A History of Business and Politics along the Technological Frontier* (New York: Harcourt, 2001). See also http://www.riaa.com/physicalpiracy.php.

27. The examples are based on Urs Gasser and Silke Ernst, "From Shakespeare to DJ Danger Mouse: A Quick Look at Copyright and User Creativity in the Digital Age," Berkman Center Research Publication No. 2006–05, June 2006, http://ssrn.com/abstract=909223.

28. http://reviews.cnet.com/4520-6450_7-5021115-1.html.

29. We made this argument in an Amicus Brief in the *Grokster* case; see p. 13.

30. Lawmakers around the world have considered—and, in some instances, enacted—new laws aimed at regulating online piracy in general and P2P networks in particular. In essence, we can distinguish two types of legislative initiatives. Legislation of the first sort seeks to make copyright protection stronger by introducing new forms of protection or bolstering existing ones. Legislation of the second sort isn't about strengthening copyright law as a matter of substance. Rather, it is aimed at making the enforcement of copyright law in cyberspace (and beyond) more effective. Recently, the second type of legislation has become popular both in the United States and Europe. The proponents of this approach argue that there's an enforcement problem in cyberspace and that tougher laws are the adequate response to it.

By giving the commercial interests of the entertainment industry more weight than the interests of users and the public at large, the recent laws and bills maintain what for many of us has become an uneasy tradition. Stanford law professor Lawrence Lessig has written a number of thought-provoking books and articles about the expansion of copyright. The most alarming call to action is his book *Free Culture* (New York: Penguin, 2004), in which he demonstrated how copyright law in the United States and abroad has continuously expanded in scope and duration over the past century, while both the free (unregulated) uses and the limitations on copyright have become smaller and smaller. In this sense, many of the recent laws or recently introduced bills, in one way or another, are variations on Lessig's broader theme: *How Big Media Uses Technology and the Law to Lock Down Culture and Control Creativity* (the subheading of *Free Culture*).

31. See Creative Commons Licenses, http://creativecommons.org/about/licenses.

32. Another example where copyright law is used in innovative ways to strike a new balance among the interests of creators, users, and the public at large is Noank. Noank, initiated by Terry Fisher and former members of the Digital Media Team at the Berkman Center, provides "non-compulsory blanket licenses that monetize and legalize online file-sharing." Noank's motto is "limitless legal content flow." The implementation of this system is currently most advanced in China and Canada, but is expected to launch in other countries, too. Learn more at www.noankmedia.com. (Disclosure: John Palfrey is a noncompensated board member of Noank Media, Inc. He represents the interests of Harvard University on the Noank board. Harvard holds equity in the company.)

Chapter 7

1. See http://www.cbsnews.com/stories/2004/09/08/60II/main641984.shtml.

2. See, for example, Roderick Boyd, "How Four Blogs Dealt a Blow to CBS's Credibility: Bush Show in Doubt," *New York Sun,* September 13, 2004. See also Dick Thornburgh and Louis D. Boccardi, "Report of the Independent Review Panel," on the September 8, 2004, *60 Minutes Wednesday* segment "For the Record" concerning President Bush's Texas Air National Guard service, January 5, 2005, p. 20, http://wwwimage.cbsnews.com/htdocs/pdf/complete_report/CBS_Report.pdf.

3. See, for example, "A Brief History of Lying," BBC News, January 6, 2002, http://news.bbc.co.uk/1/hi/uk/1740746.stm.

4. A recent German study commissioned by the news magazine *Stern* randomly picked fifty articles from Wikipedia and compared them with the online version of the leading German encyclopedia *Brockhaus. Stern* declared Wikipedia the winner in forty-three cases out of fifty. See http://www.focus.de/digital/internet/online-enzyklopaedien_aid_228375.html (5.12.07).

5. For a well-written version of this argument, see James Surowiecki, *The Wisdom of Crowds: Why the Many Are Smarter Than the Few and How Collective*

Wisdom Shapes Business, Economies, Societies and Nations (New York: Doubleday, 2004).

6. See http://www.britannica.com/eb/article-256589/Albert-Einstein.

7. See, for example, Jim Giles, "Special Report: Internet Encyclopaedias Go Head to Head," *Nature* 438, no. 7070 (December 15, 2005): 900–901, http://www.nature.com/nature/journal/v438/n7070/full/438900a.html.

8. Britannica also contested *Nature*'s findings. In a paper titled "Fatally Flawed" (http://corporate.britannica.com/britannica_nature_response.pdf), the encyclopedia argued that many of the inaccuracies that *Nature* had counted against the *Encyclopaedia Britannica* were actually not inaccuracies after all and that the journal had evaluated articles that did not appear in the online version—some appeared in different or older Britannica publications, and at least one did not appear in any Britannica publication. Britannica also complained that *Nature* had refused to release all of its data for examination and had based its reviews on article excerpts rather than full articles—in some instances pulling together excerpts from different articles.

9. See Derek Bambauer, "Shopping Badly: Cognitive Biases, Communications, and the Fallacy of the Marketplace for Ideas," *University of Colorado Law Review* 77, no. 649 (2006).

10. Focus group data, high-school female, age fifteen.

11. That credibility is not a primary concern to young people when using digital media is a problem that has also been diagnosed by other researchers. See Andrew F. Flanagin and Miriam J. Metzger, "Digital Media and Youth: Unparalleled Opportunity and Unprecedented Responsibility," in: Miriam J. Metzger and Andrew J. Flanagin, eds., *Digital Media, Youth, and Credibility* (Cambridge: MIT Press, 2008), pp. 5–27, at p. 18.

12. Amanda Lenhart, Mary Madden, and Paul Hitlin, "Teens and Technology," PEW Internet and American Life Project, July 27, 2005, http://www.pewinternet.org/report_display.asp?r=162.

13. Susannah Fox, "Online Health Search 2006," PEW Internet and American Life Project, October 29, 2006, http://www.pewinternet.org/PPF/r/190/report_display.asp.

14. Lenhart et al., "Teens and Technology."

15. Focus group data, high-school female, age seventeen.

16. Lenhart et al., "Teens and Technology."

17. John Horrigan and Lee Rainie, "The Internet's Growing Role in Life's Major Moments," PEW Internet and American Life Project, April 19, 2006, http://www.pewinternet.org/pdfs/PIP_Major%20Moments_2006.pdf.

18. Leigh Estabrook, Evans Witt, and Lee Rainie, "Information Searches That Solve Problems: How People Use the Internet, Libraries, and Government Agencies When They Need Help," Pew Internet and American Life Project and University of Illinois Graduate School of Library and Information Science, December 30, 2007.

19. Consumers Union of United States, "Get Better Care from Your Doctor," *Consumer Reports,* February 2007, p. 33.

20. As to students' difficulties with evaluating information quality, see Jinx Stapleton Watson, "If You Don't Have It, You Can't Find It: A Close Look at Students' Perceptions of Using Technology," *Journal of the American Society for Information Science* 49, no. 11 (September 1998): 1024–1036. See also Miriam J. Metzger, "Understanding How Internet Users Make Sense of Credibility: A Review of the State of Our Knowledge and Recommendations for Theory, Policy, and Practice," in R. Weingarten and M. Eisenberg, *Proceedings of the Internet Credibility and the User Symposium,* 2005, http://projects.ischool.washington.edu/credibility/Metzger%20Skills.pdf.

21. Matthew S. Eastin, Mong-Shan Yang, and Amy I Nathanson, "Children of the Net: An Empirical Exploration into the Evaluation of Internet Content," in *Journal of Broadcasting and Electronic Media,* June 2006, http://goliath .ecnext.com/coms2/gi_0199-5992261/Children-of-the-net-an.html. The authors of this article summarize these points as follows: "The challenge of identifying credible information on the Internet should be greater among young users. Children are less knowledgeable about the real world than are adults; as a result, they cannot evaluate the legitimacy of most Internet content by comparing the information to their own experiences. In addition, children cannot easily evaluate multiple pieces of information at once and may get distracted by extraneous information." In her book *The Primal Teen* (New York: Doubleday, 2003), *New York Times* medical science and health editor Barbara Strauch reports about relevant recent insights from neuroscience about the brains of children, which are not as fully developed as those of many adults.

22. Another relevant strand of research traces back to Jean Piaget's model of cognitive development. Piaget, a Swiss pedagogue, concluded that the intelligence

of children is fundamentally different from that of adults and that their cognitive capacity is built up in a number of qualitatively different stages as they grow up. Later research showed that Piaget's model of age and development stages was too rigid. It was subsequently replaced by more dynamic concepts of cognitive development. However, it has remained undisputed that the ability of kids and adolescents to master complex cognitive tasks is varied, dependent in part on their stage of development, and, for that matter, more limited than that of most adults. Based on Piaget's work, Lawrence Kohlberg distinguished six stages of moral development. Kohlberg's research suggested that only in the last stage of moral development—the postconventional level (adulthood)—could comprehensive moral assessments be made—that is, assessments where "right" and "wrong" judgments also take into account the circumstances (context) that surround a moral problem. While it has remained difficult to make Kohlberg's model operational, his research still gives us a good sense that making sound moral judgments—an important mechanism when it comes to value-based assessments of information quality, as we'll discuss in a moment—has a lot to do with the stage of biological development that a child or adolescent is in at the time. See also Matthew S. Eastin, "Toward a Cognitive Developmental Approach to Youth Perceptions of Credibility," in Miriam J. Metzger and Andrew J. Flanagin, eds., *Digital Media, Youth, and Credibility* (Cambridge: MIT Press, 2008), pp. 29–47.

23. See http://www.henryjenkins.org/2007/06/what_wikipedia_can_teach_us_ab.html.

24. J. Dinet, P. Marquet, and E. Nissen, "An Exploratory Study of Adolescents' Perceptions of the Web," in *Journal of Computer Assisted Learning* 19 (2003): 538–545.

25. Denise E. Agosto, "A Model of Young People's Decision-Making in Using the Web," *Library and Information Science Research* 24 (2002): 311–341.

26. Focus group data, middle-school male, age thirteen.

27. Focus group data, male college student, age eighteen.

28. An example of this type of challenge, and how it tends to play out in the Internet age, is the Yahoo! France case. The lawsuit, brought against Yahoo!, and first decided in 2000, demonstrates how difficult law enforcement has become in the digital age. Yahoo!, a corporation based in California, provides several Internet services, including an online auction service that allows users to post items for sale

and solicit bids from other users. In this process, Yahoo! essentially plays the role of a "matchmaker," but is not a party to the transaction. At some point, Nazi memorabilia and Adolf Hitler's *Mein Kampf* were being offered for sale on the Yahoo! auction website. French Internet users were able to access these materials on Yahoo.com or through a link on Yahoo.fr, Yahoo!'s French regional site. Two French antiracism organizations filed a civil lawsuit against Yahoo, Inc., claming that displaying Nazi propaganda and offering it for sale was illegal under French criminal law. The Tribunal de Grande Instance de Paris agreed and ordered Yahoo!, among other things, to take all measures to ensure that French users would not be able to participate in Yahoo!'s U.S.-based auction service of Nazi objects.

Yahoo! rejected this injunction. It asked the French court to reconsider the terms of the order and argued that compliance with it was technically impossible. However, the French court affirmed the terms of its order. Later, Yahoo! filed a complaint in a U.S. district court asking the court to officially declare that the orders issued by the French court were neither cognizable nor enforceable under U.S. law. Yahoo! claimed that it was not able to comply with the order to block French citizens from accessing the Yahoo.com auction website without banning Nazi-related material from its network altogether. Yahoo! argued that such a ban would violate its rights under the First Amendment. The U.S. district court agreed with Yahoo! and concluded that it was inconsistent with U.S. law for another nation to regulate speech by a U.S. resident within the United States based on the fact that such speech could be accessed by users in nations with other ethical judgments about the quality of information disseminated over the Internet.

29. See, for example, the debate on information quality in the Web 2.0 environment between authors Andrew Keen (*Cult of the Amateurs* [New York: Doubleday Business, 2007] and David Weinberger (*Everything is Miscellaneous* [New York: Times Books, 2007) in the Wall Street Journal Online, July 18, 2007, http://online.wsj.com/article/SB118460229729267677.html.

30. An approach along these lines is reportedly under consideration by Japan's communications ministry, which suggests introducing a minimum level of regulation to guard against illegal and harmful content by 2010. See Michael Fitzpatrick, ". . . While Japanese Face Web Censorship," *The Guardian,* January 3, 2008, http://www.guardian.co.uk/technology/2008/jan/03/censorship.japan.

31. Urs Gasser, "The Good, the Bad, and the Ugly: An Essay on Information Quality Governance on the Internet" (unpublished manuscript, on file with authors).

32. Reputation systems pose an interesting and still under-researched meta-question: Who or what guarantees the quality of statements on such systems about the qualities of a person, service, piece of advice, or the like? This problem of reputational quality and information quality was recently addressed at an international symposium organized by the Information Society Program at Yale Law School. See http://isp.law.yale.edu/repecon/panels and http://blogs.law .harvard.edu/ugasser/2007/12/087/information-quality-and-reputation.

33. Paul Hitlin, "Pew Internet Project Data Memo, Online Rating Systems," October 2004, p. 4, http://www.pewinternet.org/pdfs/PIP_Datamemo_Reputation .pdf. However, it must be noted that rating and recommendation systems, given their level of complexity, may be difficult to grasp, especially for younger children. See Flanagin and Metzger, "Digital Media and Youth: Unparalleled Opportunity and Unprecedented Responsibility," in Miriam J. Metzger and Andrew J. Flanagin, eds., *Digital Media, Youth, and Credibility* (Cambridge: MIT Press, 2008), p. 16.

34. http://en.wikipedia.org/wiki/Wikipedia:Neutral_point_of_view.

35. Of course, a Wikipedia user could game the system by assuming another identity before posting again. Wikipedia has some controls, including use of IP address tracking, to limit such gaming, but it persists. The problem of authentication remains a difficult one on the Web in general.

36. Amanda Lenhart, "Protecting Teens Online," Pew Internet and American Life Project, March 17, 2005, http://www.pewinternet.org/pdfs/PIP_Filters _Report.pdf.

37. See Ronald Deibert, John Palfrey, Rafal Rohozinksi, and Jonathan Zittrain, *Access Denied: The Practice and Policy of Global Internet Filtering* (Cambridge: MIT Press, 2008), Chapters 2 and 3, describing the limits of any Internet filtration system from policy and technical viewpoints.

38. Our colleague Herbert Burkert at the University of St. Gallen made the point some time ago: Generally, information quality "is a subject best to be avoided by law." But, as he recognized, societies often act collectively as though they cannot afford to heed this general rule. Herbert Burkert, "Law and Information Quality— Some Skeptical Observations," in *Studies in Communication Sciences* 4, no. 2 (2004): 17–28, at p. 17.

39. See Stephan Russ-Mohl, referring to information quality in journalism (in German): "Am eigenen Schopfe. Qualitätssicherung im Journalismus— Grundfragen, Ansätze, Näherungsversuche," in *Publizistik* 1 (1992): 85.

40. On challenges and best practices in this context, see Frances Jacobson Harris, "Challenges to Teaching Credibility Assessment in Contemporary Schooling," in Miriam J. Metzger and Andrew J. Flanagin, eds., *Digital Media, Youth, and Credibility* (Cambridge: MIT Press, 2008), pp. 155–179.

41. For an excellent overview of the modes of government intervention in the credibility domain, see Fred W. Weingarten, "Credibility, Politics, and Public Policy," in Miriam J. Metzger and Andrew J. Flanagin, eds., *Digital Media, Youth, and Credibility* (Cambridge: MIT Press, 2008), pp. 181–202. Weingarten discusses ideas such as policies that restrict content on websites, that require content providers to control and/or authenticate access to its content, or that require public access providers to use filters, as well as policies that promote education and literacy, among others.

Chapter 8

1. IDC White Paper, "The Expanding Digital Universe: A Forecast of Worldwide Information Growth Through 2010," March 2008, http://www.emc.com/collateral/analyst-reports/diverse-exploding-digital-universe.pdf. See also http://www.emc.com/about/destination/digital_universe/; University of California–Berkeley, School of Information Management and Systems, "How Much Information?" 2003, http://www2.sims.berkeley.edu/research/projects/how-much-info-2003/execsum.htm.

2. See http://www.google.com/press/pressrel/6billion.html. See also David Sifry, "The State of the Live Web," April 2007, http://www.sifry.com/alerts/archives/000493.html.

3. http://news.bbc.co.uk/2/hi/technology/4137782.stm.

4. http://www.vnunet.com/vnunet/news/2184523/online-addict-games-himself.

5. http://www.vnunet.com/vnunet/news/2198850/chinese-man-dies-three-days.

6. See Harris Interactive, "Video Game Addiction: Is it Real?" Press Release, April 2, 2007, http://www.harrisinteractive.com/NEWS/allnewsbydate.asp?NewsID=1196.

7. S.M. Grüsser, R. Thalemann, and M.D. Griffiths, "Excessive Computer Game Playing: Evidence for Addiction and Aggression?" *Cyberpsychology and Behavior* 10, no. 2 (2007): 290–292.

8. Sean Coughlan, "Just One More," *BBC News* magazine, June 1, 2006, http://news.bbc.co.uk/1/hi/magazine/5034756.stm.

9. Kimberly Young, "Addiction to MMORPGs: Symptoms and Treatment," http://www.netaddiction.com/articles/addiction_to_mmorpgs.pdf.

10. See Anthony Faiola, "When Escape Seems Just a Mouse-Click Away: Stress-Driven Addiction to Online Games Spikes in S. Korea," Washington Post Foreign Service, May 2006, http://www.washingtonpost.com/wp-dyn/content/article/2006/05/26/AR2006052601960.html.

11. "Internet Addiction: Stanford Study Seeks to Define Whether It's a Problem," Press Release, October 17, 2006, http://med.stanford.edu/news_releases/2006/october/internet.html; see also http://www.washingtonpost.com/wp-dyn/content/article/2007/06/27/AR2007062700995.html.

12. One expert on these dynamics posted a checklist to a blog about the possible signs of Internet addiction:

1. Do you feel preoccupied with the Internet (think about previous online activity or anticipate next online session)?
2. Do you feel the need to use the Internet with increasing amounts of time in order to achieve satisfaction?
3. Have you repeatedly made unsuccessful efforts to control, cut back, or stop Internet use?
4. Do you feel restless, moody, depressed, or irritable when attempting to cut down or stop Internet use?
5. Do you stay online longer than originally intended?
6. Have you jeopardized or risked the loss of significant relationship, job, educational or career opportunity because of the Internet?
7. Have you lied to family members, therapist, or others to conceal the extent of involvement with the Internet?
8. Do you use the Internet as a way of escaping from problems or of relieving a dysphoric mood (e.g., feelings of helplessness, guilt, anxiety, depression)?

See http://netaddictionrecovery.blogspot.com/2007/01/what-is-internet-misuse-and-what-is.html.

13. R.A. Davis, "A Cognitive-Behavioral Model of Pathological Internet Use," *Computers in Human Behavior* 17 (2001): 187–195, at p. 188.

14. Ibid., pp. 189–190.

15. Ibid., pp. 191–192.

16. China has already responded to the problem and limited the time for playing games. The new system will impose penalties on players who spend more than three hours playing a game. Gamers who spend more than five hours will have the abilities of their in-game characters severely limited and will be forced to take a five-hour break for the character to be restored. See BBC News, "China Imposes Online Gaming Curbs," August 25, 2005, http://news.bbc.co.uk/1/hi/technology/4183340.stm.

17. See Kimberly S. Young, "Cognitive Behavioral Therapy with Internet Addicts: Treatment Outcomes and Implications," in *CyberPsychology and Behavior* 10, no. 5 (2007): 671–697.

18. G.A Miller, "The Magical Number Seven, Plus or Minus Two: Some Limits on Our Capacity to Process Information," *Psychological Review* 63, no. 2 (1956): 81–97.

19. See Orrin E. Klapp, *Overload and Boredom: Essays on the Quality of Life in the Information Society* (New York: Greenwood Press, 1986).

20. Georg Simmel, *The Sociology of Georg Simmel,* compiled and translated by Kurt Wolff (Glencoe, Ill.: Free Press, 1950).

21. See Karl W. Deutsch, "On Social Communication and the Metropolis," *Daedalus* 90 (1961): 99–110.

22. Klapp, *Overload and Boredom,* p. 7.

23. See Lynn Akin, "Information Overload and Children: A Survey of Texas Elementary School Students," *American Library Association* 1 (1998), SLMQ Online, http://www.ala.org/ala/aasl/aaslpubsandjournals/slmrb/slmrcontents/volume11998 slmqo/akin.cfm.

24. See Kenneth Einar Himma, "A Preliminary Step in Understanding the Nature of a Harmful Information-Related Condition: An Analysis of the Concept of Information Overload," forthcoming in *Ethics and Information Technology.*

25. See Yochai Benkler, *The Wealth of Networks: How Social Production Transforms Markets and Freedom* (New Haven, Conn.: Yale University Press, 2006), p. 363 (citing Keith Hampton and Barry Wellman, "Neighboring in Netville: How the Internet Supports Community and Social Capital in a Wired Suburb," *City and Community* 2, no. 4 (December 2003): 277.

26. While there is currently little empirical evidence on this particular question, the following story from *Time* (Claudia Wallis, "The Multitasking Generation," March

19, 2006, http://www.time.com/time/printout/0,8816,1174696,00.html) might be symptomatic of what many among us experience daily in one form or another:

> It's 9:30 p.m., and Stephen and Georgina Cox know exactly where their children are. Well, their bodies, at least. Piers, 14, is holed up in his bedroom—eyes fixed on his computer screen—where he has been logged onto a MySpace chat room and AOL Instant Messenger (IM) for the past three hours. His twin sister Bronte is planted in the living room, having commandeered her dad's iMac—as usual. She, too, is busily IMing, while chatting on her cell phone and chipping away at homework.
>
> By all standard space-time calculations, the four members of the family occupy the same three-bedroom home in Van Nuys, Calif., but psychologically each exists in his or her own little universe. Georgina, 51, who works for a display-cabinet maker, is tidying up the living room as Bronte works, not that her daughter notices. Stephen, 49, who juggles jobs as a squash coach, fitness trainer, event planner, and head of a cancer charity he founded, has wolfed down his dinner alone in the kitchen, having missed supper with the kids. He, too, typically spends the evening on his cell phone and returning e-mails—when he can nudge Bronte off the computer. "One gets obsessed with one's gadgets," he concedes.

27. Elinor Ochs, director of UCLA's Center on Everyday Lives of Families, quoted in the *Time* article, ibid.

28. Kaiser Family Foundation, News Release, "Media Multi-Tasking: Changing the Amount and Nature of Young People's Media Use," March 9, 2005, http://www.kff.org/entmedia/entmedia030905nr.cfm.

29. Ibid.

30. "Multi-Tasking Adversely Affects Brain's Learning: UCLA Psychologists Report," Press Release, July 26, 2006, http://www.eurekalert.org/pub_releases/2006-07/uoc—maa072506.php.

31. Helene Hembrooke and Geri Gay, "The Laptop and the Lecture: The Effects of Multitasking in Learning Environments," *Journal of Computing in Higher Education* 15 (Fall 2003): 46–64.

32. Consider, for instance, the research from 2007 and 2008 that shows that at a certain point, the more choices individuals have in terms of mutual fund investments through a 401(k) plan, the less likely they are to decide to invest at all. See, for example, http://www.slate.com/id/2130932/.

33. Denise E. Agosto, "Bounded Rationality and Satisficing in Young People's Web-Based Decision Making," *Journal of the American Society for Information Science and Technology,* January 1, 2002, p. 22.

34. Ibid.

35. Martin J. Eppler and Jeanne Mengis, "A Framework for Information Overload Research in Organizations: Insights from Organization Science, Accounting, Marketing, MIS, and Related Disciplines," Paper #1 1/2003, September 2003, Università della Svizzera Italiana, http://www.bul.unisi.ch/cerca/bul/pubblicazioni/com/pdf/wpca0301.pdf.

36. See Akin, "Information Overload and Children."

37. Ibid.

38. Stanley Milgram, "The Experience of Living in the Cities," *Science* 13 (1970): 1461–1468.

39. Quentin Jones, Gilad Ravid, and Sheizaf Rafaeli, "Information Overload and the Message Dynamics of Online Interaction Spaces: A Theoretical Model and Empirical Exploration," *Information System Research* 15, no. 2 (June 2004): 194–210.

40. Shujen L. Chang and Kathryn Ley, *A Learning Strategy to Compensate for Cognitive Overload in Online Learning: Learner Use of Printed Online Materials,* pp. 106, 111–112, http://www.ncolr.org/jiol/issues/PDF/5.1.8.pdf. There was no correlation between better course performance and heavier reliance on printed material. See p. 110.

41. Clay Shirky, "Power Laws, Weblogs, and Inequality," February 8, 2003, http://www.shirky.com/writings/powerlaw_weblog.html.

42. Akin, "Information Overload and Children."

43. See, for example, Francis Heylighen, "Complexity and Information Overload in Society: Why Increasing Efficiency Leads to Decreasing Control," 2002, draft paper, http://pespmc1.vub.ac.be//Papers/Info-Overload.pdf.

44. As to the use of bounded rationality and heuristics in decision-making, see, for example, Gerd Gigerenzer, Peter M. Todd, and the ABC Research Group, *Simple Heuristics That Make Us Smart* (New York: Oxford University Press, 1999).

45. Denise E. Agosto, "Bounded Rationality and Satisficing in Young People's Web-Based Decision Making," *Journal of the American Society for Information Science and Technology* 53, no. 1 (2002): 16–27, http://www3.interscience.wiley.com/cgi -bin/fulltext/88012976/PDFSTART.

46. See Yasmin Kafai and Marcia J. Bates, "Internet Web-Searching Instruction in the Elementary Classroom: Building a Foundation for Information Literacy," *School Library Media Quarterly* 25, no. 2 (Winter 1997): 103–111.

47. This "gatekeeper function" of search engines is not unproblematic because users usually don't know how, exactly, the relevance of a website is measured. The search engine providers usually keep the underlying algorithms a trade secret. On the role of search engines as the new gatekeepers, see, for example, Lucas D. Introna and Helen Nissenbaum, "Shaping the Web: Why the Politics of Search Engines Matters," http://www.nyu.edu/projects/nissenbaum/papers/searchengines .pdf; Nico van Eijk, "Search Engines: Seek and Ye Shall Find? The Position of Search Engines in Law," IRIS PLUS 2006–02 (January 2006), http://www.obs.coe.int/ oea_publ/iris/iris_plus/iplus2_2006.pdf.en; Eszter Hargittai, "Online Gatekeepers: Myth or Reality," http://tprc.org/papers/2002/82/hargittai-tprc2002paper.pdf; Niva Elkin-Koren, "Let the Crawlers Crawl: On Virtual Gatekeepers and the Right to Exclude Indexing," *Dayton Law Review* 26 (2001): 179.

48. See http://digg.com/about.

49. See Benkler, *The Wealth of Networks,* pp. 12–13.

50. According to a Pew survey, 28 percent of Internet users have tagged or categorized online content such as photos, news stories, or blog posts. See "Pew Report: Online Activities and Pursuits: Tagging," January 2007, http://www.pew internet.org/PPF/r/201/report_display.asp.

51. See http://en.wikipedia.org/wiki/Tag_%28metadata%29.

52. David Weinberger, "Tagging and Why It Matters," 2005, http://cyber .law.harvard.edu/home/uploads/507/07-WhyTaggingMatters.pdf.

53. Among the most prominent critics of such an approach is Neil Postman. See his *Technopoly: The Surrender of Culture to Technology* (New York: Vintage, 1993).

54. Or, as Herbert Simon already eloquently put it in the 1970s: "Whether a computer will contribute to the solution of an information-overload problem, or instead compound it, depends on the distribution of its own attention among four classes of activity: listening, storing, thinking, and speaking. A general principle

can be put as follows: An information processing subsystem . . . will reduce the net demand on the rest of the organization's attention only if it absorbs more information previously received by others than it produces—that is, if it listens and thinks more than it speaks." Herbert Simon, "Designing Organizations for an Information-Rich World," in Martin Greenberger, ed., *Computers, Communications and the Public Interest* (Baltimore: Johns Hopkins University Press, 1971), pp. 37–72.

55. Again, the examples are manifold, including things like product safety information, food labeling, and disclosure of balance sheets of publicly traded companies, to name just a few.

56. See Archon Fung, Mary Graham, and David Weil, *Full Disclosure: The Perils and Promise of Transparency* (Cambridge: Cambridge University Press, 2007), for a detailed discussion of transparency laws in general and the emerging approach of "collaborative transparency." On formats and tools, see also Jerry Brito, "Hack, Mash and Peer: Crowdsourcing Government Transparency," October 21, 2007, http://ssrn.com/abstract=1023485.

57. Frank Pasquale, "Copyright in an Era of Information Overload: Toward the Privileging of Categorizers," in *Vanderbilt Law Review* 60 (January 2007): 135.

58. See Lori Aratani, "Teens Can Multitask, But What Are Costs?" *Washington Post,* February 26, 2007, http://www.washingtonpost.com/wp-dyn/content/article/2007/02/25/AR2007022501600.html, quoting Jordan Grafman, chief of cognitive neuroscience at the National Institute of Neurological Disorders and Stroke.

59. David Shenk, *Data Smog: Surviving the Information Glut* (New York: HarperOne, 1997).

60. This may be particularly important if earlier surveys are correct that only 18 percent of all Internet users have ever received more than eight hours of training in searching for, gathering, and evaluating information and sources, and that more than 50 percent have never received any formal training. See Thomas H. Davenport and John C. Beck, *The Attention Economy: Understanding the New Currency of Business* (Boston: Harvard Business School Press, 2001), p. 202.

61. American Library Association, "Information Literacy Competency Standards for Higher Education" 2000, http://www.ala.org/ala/acrl/acrlstandards/informationliteracycompetency.cfm. See also in this context Christopher N. Carlson, "Information Overload: Retrieval Strategies and Internet User Empowerment," paper presented at the conference "The Good, the Bad and the Irrelevant: The User and

the Future of Information and Communication Technologies," University of Art and Design, Helsinki, Finland, September 3–5, 2003, pp. 169–173, http://www .iwf.de/pub/wiss/2003_ca_Information_Overload.pdf.

62. To be sure, we are not arguing that Digital Natives shouldn't work hard in school—which usually includes ambitious curricula and serious assignments (such as homework). However, especially when it comes to younger children, it doesn't make much sense, in our view, to cross boundaries and create an overload situation with its negative consequences, as outlined in this chapter. Later on, overload situations may be created for good reasons (for example, to train airline pilots) or as part of the learning process itself. For a discussion of learning as in some sense an invitation to overload, see, for example, Kathleen M. Sutcliffe and Karl E. Weick, "Information Overload Revisited," http://www.si.umich.edu/ICOS/ overload%20final%20december%202006.pdf.

Chapter 9

1. See http://www.cnn.com/SPECIALS/2007/virginiatech.shootings/.

2. See http://www.msnbc.msn.com/id/18220228/. The transcript of Dr. Phil McGraw's interview on *Larry King Live* is online at http://transcripts .cnn.com/TRANSCRIPTS/0704/16/lk1.01.html. A description of the study of common factors among school shooters is at http://news.bbc.co.uk/2/hi/ americas/6567143.stm. For a description of Cho's upsetting plays, see http://www.cnn.com/2007/US/04/17/vatech.writings/index.html.

3. See http://www.theage.com.au/articles/2007/05/16/1178995212668.html.

4. Mary Ellen O'Toole, "The School Shooter: A Threat Assessment Perspective," Federal Bureau of Investigations, Quantico, VA, 1999, http://www.fbi.gov/ publications/school/school2.pdf.

5. Allison Hanes, Sean Silcoff, and Graeme Hamilton, "A Killer's Dark Mind: Gunman Fantasized about Rampage," *National Post,* September 15, 2006, http://www .nationalpost.com/news/story.html?id=70ca42a5-f979-446f-a9c3-61949f44c737.

6. "9 Slain at Finnish School after Web Threat," *CBS News,* November 7, 2007, http://www.cbsnews.com/stories/2007/11/07/world/main3464828.shtml.

7. "Polizei fand stapelweise Killerspiele!" *Sonntags-Blick,* December 2, 2007, http://www.blick.ch/news/schweiz/polizei-fand-stapelweise-killerspiele-77543.

8. Aletha C. Huston, Diana Zuckerman, Brian L. Wilcox, Ed Donnerstein, Halford Fairchild, Norma D. Feshbach, Phyllis A. Katz, John P. Murray, and Eli A.

Rubenstein, *Big World, Small Screen: The Role of Television in American Society* (Lincoln: University of Nebraska Press, 1992), p. 54.

9. Anne Marie Seward Barry, *Visual Intelligence: Perception, Image, and Manipulation in Visual Communication* (Albany: State University of New York Press, 1997). See also the findings of the extensive study by Helmut Lukesch and Iris Schneider, *Das Weltbild des Fernsehens: eine Untersuchung der Sendungsangebote öffentlich-rechtlicher und privater Sender in Deutschland,* Band 1 und 2 (Regensburg: Roderer, 2004).

10. It's important to understand, however, that not all types of violent media content have the same impact. A well-studied genre, for instance, are fairy tales, which often contain brutal scenes. Researchers argue that violence in fairy tales actually helps children come to terms with fears that they cannot yet verbalize because they do not have the language skills. Harvard professor Maria Tatar puts it this way: "Children think it's hilarious when the millstone comes down and kills the stepmother. . . . Something complicated is happening when those children are laughing, something that has to do with the fact that they are weak and vulnerable and that they have a lot of anxieties which they don't have the words to talk about," she says. The interactive delivery of fairy tales—a trusted adult usually reads them aloud to a child, fostering improvisation and discussion that's absent in passive entertainment like videos—further enhances their therapeutic qualities. Parents or adults provide their own cultural translations and reassuring explanations that can help allay childhood fears. See Beth Potier, "Once Upon a Time . . . ," *Harvard Gazette,* April 10, 2003, http://www.hno.harvard.edu/gazette/2003/04.10/18-tatar.html.

11. That's the finding of some of the leading researchers in the field who reviewed the meta-analyses carried out over fifteen years that computed the overall effect sizes for randomized experiments aimed at investigating the influence of TV and movie violence on aggression. See Craig A. Anderson, Leonhard Berkowitz, Edward Donnerstein, L. Rowell Huesmann, James D. Johnson, Daniel Linz, Neil M. Malamuth, and Ellen Wartella, "The Influence of Media Violence on Youth," *Psychological Science in the Public Interest* 4 (December 2003): 86. In 2001, the American Surgeon General referred to strong evidence suggesting that exposure to violence in the media can increase children's aggressive behavior in the short term. He concluded that "research to date justifies sustained efforts to curb the adverse effects of media violence on youths." See U.S. Department of

Health and Human Services, "Youth Violence, A Report of the Surgeon General," 2001, http://www.surgeongeneral.gov/library/youthviolence/toc.html.

12. Ibid., p. 86, with further references.

13. Hardwired, because the brains of primates and humans have so-called mirroring neurons, which fire both when an individual acts and when the individual observes the same action performed by another individual. In other words, the neuron mirrors the behavior of the other individual as though the observer were acting. See G. Rizzolatti, L. Fadiga, V. Gallese, and L. Fogassi, "Premotor Cortex and the Recognition of Motor Actions," *Brain Research. Cognitive Brain Research* 3 (1996): 131–141.

14. See generally, for example, Albert Bandura, *Social Learning Theory* (New Jersey: Prentice-Hall, 1977). In the context of media violence and youth, see, for example, Brad J. Bushman and L. Rowell Huesmann, "Short-Term and Long-Term Effects of Violent Media on Aggression in Children and Adults," *Archives of Pediatric and Adolescent Medicine* 160 (April 2006): 349.

15. As one team of researchers put it: "In other words, aggressive primes or cues make aggressive schemas more easily available for use in processing other incoming information, creating a temporary interpretational filter that biases subsequent perceptions. If these aggressive schemas are primed while certain events—such as ambiguous provocation—occur, the new events are more likely to be interpreted as involving aggression, thereby increasing the likelihood of an aggressive response." See Anderson et al., "The Influence of Media Violence on Youth," p. 95.

16. The psychologists call this effect "excitation transfer." See, for example, Bushman and Huesmann, "Short-Term and Long-Term Effects of Violent Media," p. 349; Anderson et al., "The Influence of Media Violence on Youth," pp. 93–96.

17. See, for example, Jeanne B. Funk, Heidi Bechtoldt Baldacci, Tracie Pasold, and Jennifer Baumgardner, "Violence Exposure in Real-Life, Video Games, Television, Movies, and the Internet: Is There Desensitization?" *Journal of Adolescence* 27 (2004): 23–39. However, much work needs to be done on Internet gaming, such as Massively Multiple Online Role-Playing Games (MMORPGs). First studies suggest that, indeed, violence plays a crucial role in youth online gaming as well: Seventeen percent of adolescents name violent features as among their favorite aspects of playing the online game Everquest (ranking it third behind social and game-specific features), whereas only 4.8

percent of adults do the same (ranking it last out of five possible favorite aspects). See M.D. Griffiths, Mark N.O. Davies, and Darren Chappell, "Online Computer Gaming: A Comparison of Adolescent and Adult Gamers," *Journal of Adolescence* 27 (2004): 87–96.

18. See, for example, "Safer Children in a Digital World," The Report of the Byron Review, March 2008, N 6.34.

19. See, for example, www.allgame.com, which lists more than 31,000 games, according to its FAQ.

20. According to a 2001 review of the seventy top-selling video games, almost half of the games contained serious violence. See U.S. Department of Health and Human Services, "Youth Violence," p. 92. However, it's also important to note that not all games that include violence need to be harmful. The most prominent example are probably shooting games that are used to support the treatment and healing process of young cancer patients. See, for example, Jens Uehlecke, "Kampf gegen die Killerzellen, Wirksamer als ärtzliche Unterweisung: Mit neuen Videospielen lernen Kinder, sich gegen tödliche Krankheiten zu wehren," *Die Zeit,* Nr. 2, 3 (January 2008). Generally speaking, the benefits of video games include cognitive benefits (for example, training of visual attention, improvement of reaction times, development of skills such as spatial perception or strategic thinking, and the like) and educational benefits by way of interactive learning. For a good overview, see "Safer Children in a Digital World," N 6.54–6.64.

21. See Interactive Digital Software Association, "State of the Industry Report 2000–2001," p. 7.

22. See, for example, Michael D. Slater, Kimberly L. Henry, Randall C. Swaim, and Lori L. Anderson, "Violent Media Content and Aggressiveness in Adolescents: A Downward Spiral Model," *Communication Research* 30, no. 6 (December 2003): 713–736.

23. L.R. Huesmann and L.D. Eron, eds., *Television and the Aggressive Child: A Cross-National Comparison* (New York: Lawrence Erlbaum, 1986).

24. Douglas A. Gentile and Craig A. Anderson, "Violent Video Games: The Newest Media Violence Hazard," in Douglas A. Gentile, ed., *Media Violence and Children: A Complete Guide for Parents and Professionals* (New York: Praeger, 2003), pp. 131–152.

25. See Anderson et al., "The Influence of Media Violence on Youth," p. 103.

26. See, for example, YouTube's Community Guidelines (http://www.youtube .com/t/community_guidelines). Users must agree with these guidelines according to YouTube's terms of use (see http://www.youtube.com/t/terms). These guidelines say, "Graphic or gratuitous violence is not allowed. If your video shows someone getting hurt, attacked, or humiliated, don't post it."

27. See, for example, Douglas A. Gentile and Craig A. Anderson, "Violent Video Games: The Effects on Youth, and Public Policy Implications," in Nancy E. Dowd, Dorothy G. Singer, and Robin Fretwell Wilson, eds., *Handbook of Children, Culture and Violence* (Thousand Oaks, Calif.: Sage, 2006).

28. For an overview of the U.K. approach and its strengths and weaknesses, see Chapter 7 of "Safer Children in a Digital World."

29. Some strategies—including service public approaches—that are also relevant in this context have already been discussed in the chapter on information quality. See European Commission, "Making the Internet a Safer Place," February 2, 2007, http://ec.europa.eu/information_society/doc/factsheets/018-saferinternet plus.pdf.

Chapter 10

1. John Dvorak, CBS Marketwatch, "Microsoft's Facebook Deal Makes No Sense," October 27, 2007, http://www.marketwatch.com/news/story/microsofts -facebook-deal-makes-no/story.aspx?guid=%7B78F7D965-7474-4A82-BE79-063 A36EEFB8A%7D.

2. See http://www.sfgate.com/cgi-bin/article.cgi?f=/c/a/2006/08/06/BUG60 KAUQ71.DTL.

3. The notion of generativity is developed and described in great detail in Jonathan Zittrain, *The Future of the Internet—and How to Stop It* (New Haven, Conn.: Yale University Press, 2008).

4. Many factors determine whether, when, and how innovation occurs beyond the types of character traits and behaviors that we describe in this chapter. The study of innovation is a broad and fascinating field, with far more depth and angles than those we explore here in this chapter. For instance, there is an interesting set of questions that relate to the type of environment most conducive to innovation of the sort that Facebook represents. One strand of thinking pulls at geographic location and a confluence of talent of specific sorts (some of which Digital Natives often have), drive, capital, and other forms of localized support. See, for example,

Scott Kirsner, "Why Facebook Went West," *Boston Globe,* September 9, 2007, http://www.boston.com/business/technology/articles/2007/09/09/why_facebook _went_west/. A related inquiry is the combination of fields of expertise needed to innovate, which many scholars have taken up from various angles. See, for example, Peter Galison, *Einstein's Clocks, Poincare's Maps: Empires of Time* (New York: W.W. Norton, 2003).

5. This passage is based on O'Reilly's description about how to roll out an Open API (http://radar.oreilly.com/archives/2005/05/web_services_es.html), as well as the Wikipedia community's take on the term (http://en.wikipedia.org/ wiki/Open_API).

6. John Palfrey and Urs Gasser, "Case Study: Mashups Interoperability and eInnovation," Berkman Center Publication Series, November 2007, http:// papers.ssrn.com/s013/papers.cfm?abstract_id=1033232.

7. William W. Fisher III, *Promises to Keep: Technology, Law, and the Future of Entertainment* (Palo Alto, Calif.: Stanford Law and Politics, 2004), p. 23.

8. See Organisation for Economic Co-operation and Development (OECD), "Participative Web and User-Created Content: Web 2.0, Wikis and Social Networking" (hereinafter OECD Report), 2007, pp. 13–14. See also Figure 2 in D.A. Thompson and J.S. Best, "The Future of Magnetic Data Storage Technology," *IBM Journal of Research and Development* 44 (2000), http://www.research.ibm .com/journal/rd/443/thompson.html.

9. See Lee Gomes, "Will All of Us Get Our 15 Minutes on a YouTube Video?" *Wall Street Journal,* August 30, 2006, http://online.wsj.com/public/article/ SB115689298168048904-5wWyrSwyn6RfVfz9NwLk774VUWc_20070829.html ?mod=rss_free.

10. OECD Report, p. 13.

11. The OECD Report puts it as follows: "In the last months, an increased desire to monetise UCC has built up. Especially media companies, the communications industry (in particular mobile operators), and other commercial players have identified the revenue potential behind UCC and are investing substantial amounts of money. . . . This financial interest is also reflected in a further driver: the growing amount of financing and venture capital funding, the latter increasing by more than 40% from the third quarter of 2005 to the third quarter of 2006. According to some estimates, in the first half of 2006, venture

capitalists put USD 262 million in commercial agreements related to participative web technologies." Ibid., p. 15.

12. For an overview, see OECD Report, p. 23.

13. Keith Sawyer, *Group Genius: The Creative Power of Collaboration* (New York: Basic Books, 2007). See also James Surowiecki, *The Wisdom of the Crowds: Why the Many Are Smarter Than the Few and How Collective Wisdom Shapes Business, Economies, Societies and Nations* (New York: Doubleday, 2004); and Don Tapscott and Anthony D. Williams, *Wikinomics: How Mass Collaboration Changes Everything* (New York: Portfolio, 2006).

14. Marketers who feel this way ought to read Rick Levine, Christopher Locke, Doc Searls, and David Weinberger, *The Cluetrain Manifesto* (New York: Basic Books, 2001).

15. See http://www.time.com/time/nation/article/0,8599,1532225,00.html; http://blog.facebook.com/blog.php?post=2208197130.

16. See http://mashable.com/2006/09/06/the-facebook-backlash-begins/; http://www.andrewferguson.net/2006/09/09/a-brief-history-of-the-facebook-privacy-debacle/; http://blog.facebook.com/blog.php?post=2208562130.

Chapter 11

1. See http://www.globalvoicesonline.org/.

2. The work of many researchers shows graphically the importance of strong brands and mainstream voices in setting the agenda for user-generated content. John Kelly, for instance, a researcher at Columbia University, has shown this effect in the U.S. blogosphere and elsewhere. The findings of Clay Shirky, in his famous works on the power law distribution, similarly suggest that strong brands set agendas and drive discourse. See http://www.shirky.com/writings/powerlaw_weblog.html.

3. William Zinsser, in his book on writing, described his reader as someone "assailed on every side by forces competing for his time: by newspapers and magazines, by television and radio, by his stereo and videocassettes, by his wife and children and pets, by his house and his yard and all the gadgets that he has bought to keep them spruce, and by that most potent of competitors, sleep." William Zinsser, *On Writing Well* (New York: Harper, 1998), p. 9.

4. See Ben McNeely, "Using Technology as a Learning Tool, Not Just the Cool New Thing," in Diana G. Oblinger and James L. Oblinger, eds., *Educating the Net Generation* (Boulder: Educause, 2005), p. 4.6.

5. Howard Gardner, a widely respected author and professor at the Harvard Graduate School of Education, has given a lot of thought to how technology can play a part in teaching. He and his research team have for decades been paying close attention to how children learn and what role ethics plays in their lives, online and in real space. Through a project called Good Play, he and his team are interviewing educators and young people about how they use technologies in learning and development. See their publications and further context at http://www.goodworkproject.org/research/digital.htm.

6. According to one survey, roughly 30 percent of students preferred taking courses that used extensive levels of technology, while about 25 percent preferred limited or no use of technology in the classroom. Not surprisingly, engineering students were the ones with the highest rate of preference for the use of technology in the classroom. See Robert B. Kvavik, "Convenience, Communications, and Control: How Students Use Technology," in Diana G. Oblinger and James L. Oblinger, eds., *Educating the Net Generation* (Boulder: Educause, 2005), pp. 7.8–7.10.

7. See, for example, in the context of K-12 curriculum development, Alma R. Clayton-Pedersen with Nancy O'Neill, "Curricula Designed to Meet 21st-Century Expectations," in Diana G. Oblinger and James L. Oblinger, eds., *Educating the Net Generation* (Boulder: Educause, 2005), pp. 9.1–9.16.

8. See http://www.technologyreview.com/Biztech/13473/page1/. See also the work of MIT professor Henry Jenkins, such as *Fans, Bloggers, and Gamers: Media Consumers in a Digital Age* (New York: New York University Press, 2006), and his weblog at http://www.henryjenkins.org/.

9. See http://www.flstudio.com/ or http://audacity.sourceforge.net/.

10. Zephyr Teachout wrote about an idea of this sort in an op-ed in the *New York Times*. She said we should use the changing nature of presidential debates in the United States to make much more material available online that showed the candidates speaking to one another. The idea would be to make the results of mini-debates available for anyone to use. Anyone could remake these files themselves, for example, and repost them. A high-school world history class might splice together the most revealing interactions between the candidates on foreign policy, for example, perhaps with added commentary built in by the remaker of the film. Zephyr Teachout, "Time of Their Lives," *New York Times,* August 17, 2007, p. A23.

11. Joel Hartman, Patsy Moskal, and Chuck Dziuban, "Preparing the Academy of Today for the Learner of Tomorrow," in Diana G. Oblinger and James L. Oblinger, eds., *Educating the Net Generation* (Boulder: Educause, 2005), pp. 6.7–6.10.

12. A group of pioneers in the field of education have developed curricular materials that are a great place for schools to start. Experimental curricula for many subject areas, at many levels of teaching, are under development around the world. Many of these tools are available for free reuse. The BBC launched a multiyear effort, BBC Jam, to develop interactive teaching materials for school-aged children. Howard Gardner, at Harvard's Graduate School of Education and Project Zero, is developing curricula along with Henry Jenkins and the New Media Literacies program at MIT. The MIT OpenCourseWare project offers free access to the teaching materials for nearly all MIT courses. More and more free teaching materials are posted to the Web each year. See http://teachdigital.pbwiki.com/curriculum.

13. Marc Prensky, "Engage Me or Enrage Me," Educause, September/October 2005, http://www.educause.edu/ir/library/pdf/erm0553.pdf.

14. See http://www.globalvoicesonline.org/lingua.

15. The Chapin School's website says: "The goal of the computer science program in the Upper School is to integrate technology throughout the liberal arts curriculum, in conjunction with teachers of all disciplines. A required course in Class 8 solidifies a core of technology skills, emphasizing Flash animation and working with audio. A required course in Class 9 provides each girl with an iSpace Web site which she develops around a chosen area of intellectual expertise. The AP Java elective course in the upper grades provides an avenue for advanced computer programming" (http://www.chapin.edu/academic_excellence_us/curriculum.html).

16. Virginia Tech's Faculty Development Institute, which helps faculty members learn to use teaching strategies that leverage instructional technologies to improve learning, is a great example of a faculty development program. See http://www.fdi.vt.edu/. See also Anne H. Moore, John F. Moore, and Shelli B. Fowler, "Faculty Development for the Net Generation," in Diana G. Oblinger and James L. Oblinger, eds., *Educating the Net Generation* (Boulder: Educause, 2005), pp. 11.1–11.16.

17. Consider the Canadian digital heritage initiative (see http://www.alouettecanada.ca/home-e.php).

Chapter 12

1. See Joshua Goldstein, "Blogs, SMS, and the Kenyan Election," Internet and Democracy blog, http://blogs.law.harvard.edu/idblog/2008/01/03/blogs-sms-and -the-kenyan-election/.

2. See http://www.kenyanpundit.com/; http://www.mzalendo.com/2007/08/03/ outrageous-mp-performance-continues/.

3. See http://www.census.gov/population/socdemo/voting/tabA-1.pdf.

4. Ibid. See also http://www.census.gov/population/socdemo/voting/p20 -542/tab01.pdf; http://www.statemaster.com/graph/gov_201_ele_you_vot_tur- 2000-election-youth-voter-turnout; and http://www.infoplease.com/ipa/A078 1453.html.

5. Sonia Livingstone, Nick Couldry, and Tim Markham, "Youthful Steps towards Civic Participation," in Brian Loader, ed., *Young Citizens in the Digital Age,* (New York: Routledge, 2007).

6. See http://www.compact.org/newscc/2003_Statistics.pdf.

7. One of the most interesting of the Net-driven 527 organizations, Win Back Respect, got traction by joining young activists from the United States with those from other countries with a distaste for the foreign policy of the Bush administration.

8. Steven Schneider and Kirsten Foot, "Web Campaigning by U.S. Presidential Candidates in 2000 and 2004," in Andrew P. Williams and John C. Tedesco, eds., *The Internet Election* (Lanham, Md.: Rowman and Littlefield, 2006).

9. Matt Bai's book, *The Argument: Billionaires, Bloggers, and the Battle to Remake Democratic Politics* (New York: Penguin, 2007), includes an excellent discussion of the role of the bloggers in the 2004 election cycle. Bai comes at the topic from the slant of a Democrat; a similar, though distinct, story could be told from the slant of a Republican.

10. See www.statemaster.com/graph/gov_200_ele_you_vot_tur-2004-election -youth-voter-turnout; http://www.infoplease.com/ipa/A0781453.html.

11. Becki Donatelli of Hockaday Donatelli, McCain campaign consultant, interview of March 10, 2000.

12. See http://www.johnkerry.com/pressroom/releases/pr_2004_0616a.html.

13. See http://www.gwu.edu/~action/2004/kerry/kerrfin.html.

14. See http://www.opensecrets.org/pres08/summary.asp?id=N00009638.

15. Kate Raynes-Goldie and Luke Walker, "Our Space: Online Civic Engagement Tools for Youth," in W. Lance Bennett, ed., *Civic Life Online: Learning How Digital Media Can Engage Youth*, The John D. and Catherine T. MacArthur Foundation Series on Digital Media and Learning (Cambridge: MIT Press, 2008), pp. 161–188.

16. See Dan Gillmor, *We the Media: Grassroots Journalism By the People For the People* (Sebastopol, Calif.: O'Reilly Media, 2004), and Yochai Benkler, *The Wealth of Networks: How Social Production Transforms Markets and Freedom* (New Haven, Conn.: Yale University Press, 2006) for two variants of this story.

17. Michael Cornfield, *Presidential Campaign Advertising on the Internet,* Pew Internet and American Life Project, www.pewinternet.org.

18. Terry Fisher, Lawrence Lessig, and Yochai Benkler, among others, have made the case for this trend from consumers to creators of digital media.

19. See Terry Fisher, "Semiotic Democracy," http://www.law.harvard.edu/faculty/tfisher/music/Semiotic.html.

20. See Cass Sunstein, "The Daily Me," http://www.bostonreview.net/BR26.3/sunstein.html.

21. See Pew Internet and American Life Project, "The Internet and Democratic Debate," October 27, 2004, http://www.pewinternet.org/pdfs/pip_political_info_report.pdf.

22. Kathryn C. Montgomery, "Youth and Digital Democracy: Intersections of Practice, Policy, and the Marketplace," in W. Lance Bennett, ed., *Civic Life Online: Learning How Digital Media Can Engage Youth,* The John D. and Catherine T. MacArthur Foundation Series on Digital Media and Learning (Cambridge: MIT Press, 2008), pp. 25–49.

23. See http://www.opennet.net/.

24. See Ronald Deibert and Rafal Rohozinski, "Good for Liberty, Bad for Security? Global Civic Society and the Securitization of the Internet," in Ronald J. Deibert, John G. Palfrey, Rafal Rohozinsky, and Jonathan Zittrain, eds., *Access Denied: The Practice and Policy of Global Internet Filtering* (Cambridge: MIT Press, 2008).

25. For a particularly optimistic view, see Jennifer Corriero, "Role of Youth Survey," 2003, http://research.takingitglobal.org/roleofyouth/Role%20Of%20Youth%20Findings.pdf, p. 4. She writes, "Overall, the sample of youth in this

survey uncovered an optimistic, forward-looking generation encompassing young of age and youth-minded individuals." See also http://people-press.org/ reports/display.php3?ReportID=232; http://www.washingtonpost.com/wp-dyn/ articles/A59750-2004Oct24.html?referrer=emailarticle; http://www.washington post.com/wp-dyn/articles/A23699-2004Nov3.html?referrer=emailarticle; and http://www.pewinternet.org/PPF/r/141/report_display.asp.

GLOSSARY

Add/friend: Used as a verb to represent the action of requesting acknowledgment of friendship via a social-network site (SNS). *See also* Friends.

Aggregator: A Web service that continuously collects data and information from other websites as updates occur.

Bandwidth: The data-handling capacity of high-speed Internet cables. Over one-third of bandwidth is taken up by streaming video, and this share is growing. As the number of people on a network increases, the average connection speed slows down.

BitTorrent: A Web service that enables downloading of files via a network, or "swarm," of computers. Files are broken up into thousands of pieces that can be downloaded from any other user in the swarm as they become available, unlike the beginning-to-end completion process of P2P. *See* Peer-to-peer.

Blogs: Online journals written by individuals, ordinarily the unedited voice of a single person. The term derives from "*web log.*" Blogs are becoming an increasingly popular source of news. More and more people, young and old, are writing and reading blogs.

Copyright: The exclusive rights of a creator, granted by a government, to reproduce, prepare derivative works, distribute, perform, display, sell, lend, or license their expressive works. The rules relating to copyright vary by country. Copyright holders have used technologies to prevent the unlawful distribution, duplication, and reuse of copyrighted material resulting from the capabilities of the Internet and digital technologies, but with limited success.

Cyberbullying: Harassment involving the use of digital media such as e-mail, text messaging, websites, chat rooms, instant messaging, or pagers to intentionally harm others.

Deep dive: Diving deeper into information learned from "grazing" through particular websites that offer features and options that appeal to the individual's particular preferences. *See also* Grazing.

Digital Immigrant: A person who has adopted the Internet and related technologies, but who was born prior to the advent of the digital age.

Digital information overload: The effect of the abundance of data and/or lack of efficient organization of data. Paradoxically, information overload can make information less accessible because there is too much of it to examine.

Digital literacy: The ability to use the Internet and other digital tools effectively. There is a need for more education so that the gap can be closed between those who have digital literacy and those who do not.

Digital Native: A person born into the digital age (after 1980) who has access to networked digital technologies and strong computer skills and knowledge. Digital Natives share a common global culture that is defined not strictly by age but by certain attributes and experiences related to how they interact with information technologies, information itself, one another, and other people and institutions.

Digital products/accessories: Digital items that can be purchased and gifted. For example, e-cards are digital cards that can be sent via e-mail for occasions like birthdays, anniversaries, and holidays. Facebook, for example, has a feature called Facebook Gifts: small digital icons in hundreds of different designs. Each gift costs one dollar and will be displayed in a specific section of the profile of the friend to which the gift was given.

Digital safety: Safety from dangers specific to the online environment, such as online predators and cyberbullying. The Internet offers youth limitless access and information, but it also presents new dangers and issues of serious concern.

Digital tattoos: Content added to a digital identity in cyberspace and changes made to that identity that are difficult to reverse or erase later in life.

Facebook: A popular social network site launched in February 2004. Facebook has expanded from its origins at Harvard to include all colleges, then high-school students, professional networks, regional networks, and, ultimately, the general public. Its network-based structure makes it significantly different from most other SNSs, which are based on a single open network.

Feedback loop: Dialogues about subjects via blog posts, comments, e-mails, and other forms of communication within digital communities.

Friends: People registered with a social network site who enjoy special privileges such as being able to view each other's profiles and pictures. A user's friends appear on his or her profile. Those who are not friends are prevented from accessing one another's profiles by means of certain privacy settings. *See also* Add/friend.

Grazing: Obtaining new information through websites, RSS feeds, and other types of dissemination of digital information. Information obtained in this way is not always accurate or reliable. *See also* Deep dive.

Groups/communities: Groups that users can join and/or create online, often at social network sites. Many have communicative features such as discussion boards, and often they focus on a particular theme. The themes of the various groups and communities online cover a very broad range of interests, from politics to religion to specific educational, technical, or scientific topics. Some are just for fun.

Instant messaging (IM)/chats: Real-time Internet communication via small pop-up windows with a transcription of the conversation. It is widely used among youth. IM is becoming increasingly mobile with technology like text-messaging and mobile IMs. Chats are real-time instant messaging forums that can manage up to hundreds of people.

Intellectual property: A broad legal term that refers to rights regarding creative works and ideas. The primary doctrinal areas of intellectual property are copyright, patent, trademark, and trade secrets.

Mash-up: *See* Video mash-up.

Media industry: Traditional media strongholds (major record labels, major motion-picture studios, media conglomerates, publishers, and the like).

Media/music services: Photo-sharing, video-sharing, and music-sharing websites that allow users to publicize original content and have more control of what content becomes popular.

Mobile technology: Technology such as cell phones, portable laptops, and Internet communication devices that allow people to access unlimited information from virtually anywhere. Devices, and therefore people, can also be tracked more easily via mobile technology.

MySpace: A popular social network site that as of July 2007 boasted more than 200 million users. The interactive user-submitted network allows friends to share personal profiles, blogs, groups, photos, videos, and music internationally.

Online advertising: Paid announcements for products or services, meant to elicit buyers and/or customers, appearing on websites, as separate pop-ups, or contained in e-mail sent to users. Online advertising is an increasingly lucrative business and the primary source of support for otherwise "free" online services and content. The cost of an ad typically corresponds to the number of website users.

Online politicking: Websites maintained by politicians, political organizations, and the like. The Internet now plays a more significant role for politicians and campaigns than ever before. Many major politicians maintain websites with highly interactive and customizable features.

Online predators: Pedophiles, sex offenders, and others with malicious intent who create false and/or misleading digital identities. The Internet poses new risks for youth who are not wary of the potential dangers and consequences of meeting and communicating with strangers online, revealing personal information online, or arranging real-life meetings with someone met online. Harmful encounters between young people and online predators, however, are very rare, research shows.

Ownership: In the digital era, a philosophical dilemma concerning who should own what when it comes to various types of property (for example, profitable vs. free music).

Participatory culture: A culture in which people are encouraged to share their innovations and creativity. Henry Jenkins, codirector of the MIT Comparative Media Studies Program, makes five key points about participatory culture: (1) There are relatively low barriers to artistic expression and civic engagement; (2) there is strong support for creating and sharing what you create with others; (3) there is some kind of informal mentorship whereby what is known by the most experienced gets passed along to newbies and novices; (4) members feel that their contributions matter; and (5) members feel some degree of social connection with each other, at least to the degree to which they care about what other people think about what they have created.

Peer-to-Peer (P2P): A method of downloading files via a computer-to-computer connection.

Personalization/customization: Features on websites, particularly social network sites, that can be altered, added, and removed to fit users' particular tastes. For example, one's MySpace layout can be altered with HTML, Facebook profiles

can be equipped with hundreds of different applications, and Second Life is
played through customized avatars.

Photo-sharing services: Websites that allow users to post (upload) pictures that
can be viewed by the public or a select audience. In addition to Facebook's
photo-sharing feature, popular photo-sharing websites include Photobucket,
Flickr, Ofoto, and Shutterfly.

Platform provider: The term for the organizations that run websites, which may
include coders, programmers, website developers, business developers, and the
like.

Post/upload: The action of contributing content to a website. One can post a
comment to someone's blog entry, post links to interesting topics, and upload
media files to media-sharing websites, for example.

Profile: The digital interface of a user and the central feature of a social network
site. Profiles can be personalized and contain interactive features such as sections for friends and comments.

Profit-driven websites: Websites with content and organization designed with
profitability as one of the major objectives. Media corporations and websites
dealing with e-commerce are prime examples. An important question to ask in
discussions of the impact of the Internet on Digital Natives and others is, "How
are users' experiences impacted by profit-driven websites?"

Real time: The flow of time in offline, real-life situations. The term is used to describe technology that actively updates and can sustain text-based or Internet
communication at a rate very close to in-person interaction.

RFID: Radio Frequency Identification. Small microchips with RFID technology
are now placed in clothing, library books, and credit cards (among many other
objects). They are magnetically charged and can be physically tracked; some
will set off alarm sensors if not demagnetized.

Rip: The (often illegal) duplication of copyrighted material through software designed for the purpose of bypassing embedded security protection.

RSS: A program, either freestanding or used as an add-on to a news aggregator
such as Google Personalized Homepage, that enables the syndication of updates from websites into a real-time feed. The acronym stands for Really Simple Syndication.

Search engine: A service organizing a vast array of information available on the
Internet into an ordered list based on relevance to the keywords entered. Google

is an example, but many other websites include a search engine for the contents of the site, and other search engines are available. Some specialize in specific types of content (for example, some search engines are specifically designed to list kid-appropriate content).

Second Life: An Internet-based, virtual world released by Linden Lab in 2003. It garnered attention from mainstream media in late 2006 and early 2007. Inspired by the cyberpunk literary movement, Second Life is a user-generated world where people can play, interact, do business, and communicate using an avatar interface and a virtual currency, the Linden dollar, which is tied to the U.S. dollar.

Skype: A peer-to-peer Internet telephony network founded by the entrepreneurs who created the file-sharing application Kazaa and the peer-to-peer television application Joost. The Skype communications system offers free voice and video conferencing. It is notable both for its use of decentralized technology to overcome common firewall and NAT (network address translation) problems and for its use of transparent, strong encryption and extreme countermeasures against reverse engineering.

Social network site (SNS): A site, like Facebook or MySpace, that connects communities of people in order to enable the flow of information among users. Using Web 2.0 technology, users create profiles and interact with and "friend" other users. According to a Pew report in early 2007, 55 percent of youth aged twelve to seventeen use these sites, mostly to reinforce existing relationships.

Telecom industry: The telecommunications companies that control all of the physical cables and networks upholding the Internet and that do business based on government regulations.

User base: An estimate of the number of consistent users on a website, most of whom likely have registered accounts. The number of unique visitors per day is also a widely used performance metric. The larger the user base and site membership, the more appealing the site is for users, investors, and advertisers.

User-directed content (UDC): Content on a website that is organized by users via tagging, rating, and other methods. Users of Web 2.0 sites are playing a growing role in how content is organized on the sites they visit. The participation of users in organizing content makes it easier for other people to discover the content by, for example, using search terms or viewing ratings. UDC also refers to the general schema of content organization on a website.

User-generated content (UGC): Content that is created and uploaded to a website by users, such as text, photos, music, and videos. UGC is a driving force behind the rise of Web 2.0. Such content is being created more and more by average Internet users and is becoming increasingly visible.

Video mash-up: A video collage that consists of clips from multiple video sources, such as movies, TV shows, and video logs.

Video-sharing services: Websites, such as YouTube and Metacafe, that allow users to upload video files, including video clips from popular movies and TV shows as well as original footage. Streaming video now represents over a third of Internet traffic. Despite legal battles concerning copyrighted material, major media conglomerates are uploading their own clips and negotiating advertising and product placement deals with these websites.

Vlogs: Video logs, or video diaries. These are often recorded by youth and general Internet users and then uploaded to video-sharing sites.

Web 2.0: The general term for the highly interactive, "read-write," and user-centric web services that sprang up shortly after the Internet bubble burst in 2001.

Wiki: A stand-alone Web page that functions much like an online Microsoft Word page, to which anyone can easily write or edit information. The popular online encyclopedia Wikipedia uses this technology.

Wikipedia: A Web 2.0 encyclopedia that is one of the most widely used websites for information about millions of topics. The articles can be added or edited by anyone at any time. Topics are user created and content is user provided and user edited.

Wireless network: A network that permits Internet-ready devices to connect without any physical connections.

YouTube: The most widely used video-sharing service in the world, accounting for around 10 percent of all Internet traffic. A *Time* magazine article reported that of all users on YouTube, only 00.01 percent are content creators. YouTube is known for having an abundance of amateur video recordings and funny video clips. A central feature to this website is the "video response," in which people can record video clips and post it as a reply to a specific video ("RE:").

SELECTED BIBLIOGRAPHY

Throughout this book, we cite to specific sources that both support our assertions and challenge them in constructive ways. Here, we note those works that had the greatest influence on our understanding of this complex topic. We commend each of these works to readers who wish to go deeper on any subtopic that we take up in this book.

Introduction

Our reflections on Nicholas Negroponte's book *Being Digital*, roughly a decade after he wrote it, inspired us to write this book. Negroponte, the founder of MIT media lab, speculated in his fantastic book about what "being digital" would mean for the way we live. Our book, in some sense, is a journey back to the future predicted by Negroponte. Three other authors have taken up a very similar topic to this one in recent years, including Don Tapscott (*Growing Up Digital*), Mark Prensky (*Don't Bother Me Mom—I'm Learning*), and Neil Howe and William Strauss (*Millennials Rising*). The John D. and Catherine T. MacArthur Foundation Series on Digital Media and Learning, comprising six books, also has been a rich resource. These books address many of the topics our book covers. Volumes in the series include David Buckingham's *Youth, Identity, and Digital Media*; Anna Everett's *Learning Race and Ethnicity*; Katie Salen's *The Ecology of Games*; Miriam J. Metzger and Andrew J. Flanagin's *Digital Media, Youth, and Credibility*; Tara McPherson's *Digital Youth, Innovation, and the Unexpected*; and W. Lance Bennett's *Civic Life Online*.

Our thinking was also influenced by Sonia Livingstone's *Children and the Internet*; *International Handbook of Children, Media and Culture*, edited by Kirsten Drotner and Sonia Livingstone; Kathryn C. Montgomery's book *Generation Digital*; and Johann Günther's *Digital Natives and Digital Immigrants*. *The Network Society*, edited by Manuel Castells, sharpened our cross-cultural perspective. Nicola Dörig's

Sozialpsychologie des Internets helped us to better understand cyberspace as a deeply social space. We've learned about the limits of our own concepts through the work of Henry Jenkins (*Confronting the Challenges of Participatory Culture: Media Education for the 21st Century*) and Eszter Hargittai, who have drawn our attention to the "participation gap" and its contours—the new type of digital divide. It is this divide that prevents parts of the generation we wanted to describe from participating in the new media environment. The extensive work of our colleagues Yochai Benkler, William Fisher, Lawrence Lessig, and Jonathan Zittrain has influenced this book more than anything else. Particularly, we point to Benkler's *The Wealth of Networks;* Fisher's *Promises to Keep;* Lessig's *Code and Other Laws of Cyberspace* and *Free Culture;* and Zittrain's *The Future of the Internet—and How to Stop It.*

Chapter 1: Identities

The identity chapter builds upon an extensive body of research on identity across disciplines, including psychology, sociology, and law. Our understanding of identity-building in the online environment has its roots in the work of Robert J. Havighurst (*Development Tasks and Education*), Richard M. Lerner (*Concepts and Theories of Human Development*), Erik H. Erikson (*Identity: Youth and Crisis*), Erving Goffman (*The Presentation of Everyday Life*), and Morris Rosenberg (*Conceiving the Self*). We've greatly benefited from the work by Sherry Turkle, including her books *Life on the Screen: Identity in the Age of the Internet* and *The Second Self: Computers and the Human Spirit.* In this work, Turkle traces the impact of computers on human psychology and how our ideas about mind, body, and machines change. In her work in general, she explores the emergence of a new type of identity that is multiple and decentralized.

The research by Farzaneh Moinian on children's perspectives of themselves and their lives in their online diaries has shed light on how new perceptions and possibilities in relation to children's social positions and cultural identities emerge (*Negotiating Identities*). We've also learned an enormous amount from our colleagues Judith Donath and danah boyd, both through their work and through our conversations with them. Of their many important contributions, we'd like to point out their coauthored piece "Public Displays of Connection" (*BT Technology Journal* 22, no. 4 [October 2004]); Judith Donath's "Identity and Deception in Virtual Community" (http://smg.media.mit.edu/people/Judith/Identity/IdentityDeception.html); and danah boyd's "Why Youth (Heart) Social Network

Sites: The Role of Networked Publics in Teenage Social Life" (in David Bucking-ham, ed., *Youth Identity, and Digital Media*). The blog that danah writes, called Apophenia and found online at http://www.zephoria.org/thoughts/, is the best "river" of information on this and related topics. The book *A Crowd of One*, by our collaborator John H. Clippinger, has helped us to put the theme of changing no-tions of identity into a larger historical and social context.

Chapter 2: Dossiers

One of the must-reads when it comes to digital dossiers is Daniel J. Solove's *The Digital Person*. In this book, Solove describes the creation and implementation of databases in which the personal information of Internet users is recorded, ana-lyzed, and preserved, and discusses the privacy threats that result from these "dig-ital dossiers," a term that we reuse as the title of this chapter. A very pessimistic view on a similar phenomenon has earlier been presented by Simson Garfinkel in his controversial book *Database Nation*. Several of the technologies mentioned in this chapter, including RFID and sensors, are described in an easily accessible way in a report of the United Nations, prepared by Mary Rundle and Chris Conley, called *Ethical Implications of Emerging Technologies: A Survey*, found online at http://unesdoc.unesco.org/images/0014/001499/149992E.pdf. How the future could look is described by the technologist Adam Greenfield in his book *Every-ware: The Dawning Age of Ubiquitous Computing*. The loss of control over data as one of the core themes in the digital age—here a consequence from the fact that dig-ital technology enables effective and cheap monitoring of behavior problems—is well described in Jonathan Zittrain's article "What the Publisher Can Teach the Patient: Intellectual Property and Privacy in an Era of Trusted Privication" (*Stan-ford Law Review* 52 [2000]).

Chapter 3: Privacy

The literature on privacy has exploded over the past few decades in terms of both academic work and contributions written for a broader audience. Early books on the subject for general readers include Fred H. Cate's *Privacy in the Information Age*; the essays in *Technology and Privacy: The New Landscape*, edited by Philip E. Agre and Marc Rotenberg; and David Brin's *The Transparent Society*. Of the recent books on this topic, we rely on David H. Holtzman's *Privacy Lost*; Daniel J. Solove's *The Digital Person* and his subsequent *The Future of Reputation: Gossip, Rumor, and*

Privacy on the Internet; and *Digital Privacy: Theory, Technologies, and Practices,* edited by Alessandro Acquisti and colleagues.

Our own thinking has been shaped by the scholarly work of several of our colleagues in the legal academy, including Herbert Burkert, Jean Nicolas Druey, Lawrence Lessig, Viktor Mayer-Schönberger, Paul Schwartz, and Jonathan Zittrain. It's not possible to list all the relevant contributions that these authors have made, but we'd like to point to Paul Schwartz's "Privacy and Democracy in Cyberspace" (*Vanderbilt Law Review* 52 [1999]) and Mayer-Schönberger's "Useful Void: The Art of Forgetting in the Age of Ubiquitous Computing" (Working Paper Number RWP07-022, http://ksgnotes1.harvard.edu/Research/wpaper.nsf/rwp/RWP07-022). For starters, we recommend Chapter 11 of Lessig's *Code Version 2.0.* An excellent article on fundamental aspects of privacy is offered by Jerry Kang and Benedikt Buchner, "Privacy in Atlantis" (*Harvard Journal of Law and Technology* 18, no. 1 [Fall 2004]). With regards to privacy and teens, we'd like to highlight the work by Seounmi Youn, who developed a helpful framework to explain teenagers' perceptions of privacy and their coping behaviors ("Teenagers' Perceptions of Online Privacy and Coping Behaviors: A Risk-Benefit Appraisal Approach," *Journal of Broadcasting and Electronic Media* 49, no. 1 [March 2005]). The work of Alessandro Acquisti and his coauthors, Sonia Livingstone, Judith Donath, and danah m. boyd, has greatly influenced the way we think about online privacy when it comes to Digital Natives. Particularly helpful were Acquisti's "Information Revelation and Privacy in Online Social Networks (The Facebook Case)," ACM Workshop on Privacy in the Electronic Society (WPES), November 7, 2005, www.heinz.cmu.edu/~acquisti/papers/privacy-facebook-gross-acquisti.pdf, and boyd's "Facebook's 'Privacy Trainwreck': Exposure, Invasion, and Drama," Apophenia Blog, September 8, 2006, http://www.danah.org/papers/FacebookAndPrivacy.html. For a general-interest audience, the websites on privacy by the Electronic Frontier Foundation (http://www.eff.org/issues/privacy) and the home page of the Electronic Privacy Information Center (http://epic.org/privacy/) are good starting places to learn more about online privacy.

Chapter 4: Safety

Online safety covers a broad range of issues when it comes to Digital Natives, from exposure to pornographic content to cyberbullying. Most of the academic literature, partly for methodological reasons, focuses on one aspect or another; we haven't found a comprehensive discussion of the safety topic as of today. That said, our writing has been influenced by a number of researchers and publications. Gustavo S. Mesch, "Youth Pornographic Consumption" (Paper presented at Oxford Internet Institute conference on cyber safety, 2005); Janis Wolak, Kimberly Mitchell, and David Finkelhor, "Unwanted and Wanted Exposure to Online Pornography in a National Sample of Youth Internet Users" (*Pediatrics* 119 [2007]); and Kimberly J. Mitchell, David Finkelhor, and Janis Wolak, "The Exposure of Youth to Unwanted Sexual Material on the Internet" (*Youth and Society* 34, no. 3 [March 2003]) have been highly informative, although the results from the various studies differ in detail.

An important study on children's use of mobile telephones to access pornographic and violent content is presented by Petra Grimm and Stefanie Rhein in their book *Slapping, Bullying, Snuffing!* With regard to online predators, we would like to point to an article by Janis Wolak, David Finkelhor, Kimberly Mitchell, and Michele L. Ybarra, "Online 'Predators' and Their Victims: Myths, Realities, and Implications for Prevention and Treatment" (*American Psychologist* 63, no. 2 [February-March 2008]), in which the authors suggest a new set of approaches to the safety problem beyond parental control and self-constraint. We recommend David Finkelhor's book *Childhood Victimization: Violence, Crime, and Abuse in the Lives of Young People,* and the work of Finklehor and his colleagues at the University of New Hampshire. Other leading analysts on whose research we rely for insight include danah boyd, Amanda Lenhart, Adam Thierer, and Michele Ybarra. Among the many good online sources on kids' online safety are http://www.isafe.org/, http://kids.getnetwise.org/, and Parry Aflab's WiredSafety.org. The websites of the attorneys general often also provide guides to Internet safety for parents and educators.

Chapter 5: Creators

From the rich body of literature on creativity we found the work by Robert J. Sternberg particularly helpful. His *Handbook of Creativity* is a great starting point for further reading. We gained various insights and data points for this chapter from our collaboration with the Organisation for Economic Co-operation and Development (OECD) in the context of the study "Participative Web and User-Created Content: Web 2.0, Wikis and Social Networking," 2007. Jack Balkin's scholarship, in particular his article "Digital Speech and Democratic Culture: A Theory of Freedom of Expression for the Information Society" (*New York University*

Law Review 79, no. 1 [2004]), has greatly influenced our understanding of why the shift from passive consumers of information to active users matters so much for society—a theme further explored in the first chapter of William W. Fisher's book *Promises to Keep*. Much of the chapter, like much of the book as a whole, builds upon what Yochai Benkler has taught us. His early pieces, including "Coase's Penguin, or Linux and the Nature of the Firm," (*The Yale Law Journal* 112 [2002]) on the new forms of information production in the digital age, have had a great impact on our thinking. His book *Wealth of Networks* is doubtlessly among the most influential books in our field.

In many ways, Henry Jenkins' *Convergence Culture* has shaped our understanding of what happens when corporate and grassroots media collide. With regard to some of the more specific topics addressed in the chapter, we would like to highlight Steven Weber's *The Success of Open Source,* which provides a unique analysis of the Open Source movement. Don Tapscott and Anthony D. Williams's *Wikinomics* is an easy, accessible read on the power of mass collaboration. Our interest in virtual worlds has been particularly stimulated by Beth Noveck's research on virtual worlds, including a great collection of essays and articles she edited from the Institute for Information Law and Policy Symposium titled *State of Play*.

Chapter 6: Pirates

Our thinking about copyright in the digitally networked environment has been greatly influenced by Lawrence Lessig, whose Chapter 10 in *Code Version 2.0* is a must-read for anyone who would like to understand the role of intellectual property in cyberspace. Lessig's *Free Culture* is another important book in this regard. It shows how information is increasingly monopolized by expanding copyright laws, a theme also explored in Siva Vaidhyanathan's *Copyrights and Copywrongs*. This worrisome development led James Boyle, in *Shamans, Software, and Spleens,* to the idea that there is a need for an environmental movement in information policy.

Among the most extensive analyses of the digital music and movie crisis, with a thorough discussion of possible ways out, is William W. Fisher's *Promises to Keep*. Jessica Litman's *Digital Copyright* offers an excellent introduction to copyright issues in the digital age. An overview of the law and economics of information can be found in Steve Shavell's *Foundations of Economic Analysis of Law*. The most important book with regard to social norms is Robert C. Ellickson's *Order without Law*. For an understanding of the social norms in copyright law, we benefited from

Mark F. Schlutz's "Copynorms: Copyright Law and Social Norms" (in Peter K. Yu, *Intellectual Property and Information Wealth* [2007]). With regard to the (controversial) economic effects of file sharing, we recommend the studies by Felix Oberholzer and Koleman Strumpf (*The Effect of File Sharing on Record Sales: An Empirical Analysis*), on the one hand, and Stan J. Liebowitz (*File-Sharing: Creative Destruction or Just Plain Destruction?*), on the other. Excellent research on the neuropsychology of copyright law has been done by Oliver Goodenough at the Gruter Institute for Law and Behavioral Science (www.gruter.org). For starters, we point to our own interdisciplinary research on digital media issues (visit http://cyber.law.harvard.edu/media/).

Chapter 7: Quality

Our interest in information-quality issues, which led, among other things, to a transatlantic research project, is the result of earlier work by Swiss scholar Jean Nicolas Druey. He prominently introduced the theme into information law discourse and advocates for an "informational ecology" in an era that is obsessed with information (*Information als Gegenstand des Rechts*). The surveys and contributions by Martin Eppler, including his book *Managing Information Quality*, have been particularly helpful in giving us a deeper understanding of the subject. The work of another Swiss scholar, Jean Piaget, has had a great influence on the way we think about the cognitive aspect of information quality as it relates to children.

Equally important have been the insights from Lawrence Kohlberg's work on moral development. We further benefited from a terrific volume by Miriam J. Metzger and Andrew J. Flanagin, *Digital Media, Youth, and Credibility,* which was released just after we wrote the first draft of this chapter. Their work shed light on various fundamental questions as well as specific issues, such as the credibility of health information and the implications for youth. Denise E. Agosto's work, including "A Model of Young People's Decision Making in the Web" (*Library and Information Science Research* 24 [2002]), has also helped to shape our thinking about information quality on the Internet.

Chapter 8: Overload

A number of classics laid the foundation for our research, including the work of Stanley Milgram, who investigated the psychological effects of heavy information load in cities and identified reaction patterns ("The Experience of Living in the Cities," *Science* 13 [1970]); Karl W. Deutsch; and Georg Simmel. Another inspiring sociological source is Orrin E. Klapp, *Overload and Boredom,* which includes a series of essays that explore the impact of information on the quality of modern life. Martin Eppler and Jeanne Mengis's work, including "A Framework for Information Overload Research in Organizations: Insights from Organization Science, Accounting, Marketing, MIS, and Related Disciplines" (Paper #1 1/2003, September 2003, Università della Svizzera Italiana, http://www.bul.unisi.ch/cerca/bul/pubblicazioni/com/pdf/wpca0301.pdf), provided helpful guidance.

At the intersection of philosophy, law, and information ethics, we greatly benefited from Kenneth Einar Himma's publications. From the popular science genre, we recommend David Shenk's book *Data Smog.* In this book, Shenk, a media scholar, explores the various psychological and social effects of information overload and describes strategies for coping with information glut. In offering solutions, we were influenced by David Weinberger's *Everything Is Miscellaneous.* A starting point when it comes to Internet addiction is the website of the Center for Internet Addiction Recovery, http://www.netaddiction.com/. Among the experts in the field is the center's director, Kimberly S. Young (*Caught in the Net: How to Recognise the Signs of Internet Addiction and a Winning Strategy for Recovery*). The work of Keith W. Beard and Eve M. Wolf, as well as the more skeptical views of Mark Griffith and Fionnbar Lenihan, have also influenced our thinking about online addiction.

Chapter 9: Aggressors

An invaluable source for gaining a better understanding of the problem of youth violence and aggression is provided by the U.S. Department of Health and Human Services in "Youth Violence, A Report of the Surgeon General," 2001 (http://www.surgeongeneral.gov/library/youthviolence/toc.html). This report explores the magnitude and cause of youth violence and outlines how it might be prevented. The work by James J. Lindsay and Craig A. Anderson has informed our writing at a conceptual level, especially their General Affective Aggression Model. The extensive research by Anderson, Brad J. Bushman, and their collaborators on the effects of violent media on aggression in children and adults has also informed our work in this chapter. With regard to video games, we recommend the meta-analytic review of scientific literature in Craig A. Anderson and Brad J. Bushman, "Effects of Violent Video Games on Aggressive Behavior, Aggressive Cognition, Aggressive Affect, Physiological Arousal, and Prosocial Behavior" (*Psychological Science* 12 [2001]).

Important work on violent media content—including website content—has been done by Michael D. Slater, including his article "Alienation, Aggression, and Sensation Seeking as Predicators of Adolescent Use of Violent Film, Computer, and Website Content" (*Journal of Communication* 53 [2003]). For an excellent article on screen violence, see Barbara J. Wilson, "Media and Children's Aggression, Fear, and Altruism" (*Children and Electronic Media* 18, no. 1 [Spring 2008]). Probably the most extensive study on violent games is one conducted in Germany: Maria von Salisch, Astrid Kirsten, and Caroline Oppl, *Computerspiele mit und ohne Gewalt: Auswahl und Wirkungen bei Kindern*. Our thinking about screen violence has further been shaped by the German neuroscientist Manfred Spitzer's *Vorsicht Bildschirm!* and Petra Grimm and Stefanie Rhein's *Slapping, Bullying, Snuffing!* Finally, we recommend Aletha C. Huston's classic book (with several colleagues) *Big World, Small Screen* on the role of TV in society.

Chapter 10: Innovators

Our understanding of innovation was heavily influenced by *Open Innovation* by Henry Chesbrough. We rely heavily on the extensive work of our colleague Eric von Hippel, especially *Democratizing Innovation,* and the work by Karim Lakhani, which builds on von Hippel's thinking. Von Hippel and Lakhani both demonstrate how ICTs increasingly empower users to develop their own new products and services. At a fundamental level, user-driven innovation can be seen as a consequence of the generative power of the Internet, a theory advanced by our colleague Jonathan Zittrain (*The Generative Internet*).

One important feature of the Internet is that it enables mass collaboration to take place on the Web, which usually leads to incremental or "small-step" innovations. Keith Sawyer's *Group Genius* provides a good overview of the creative power of collaboration—a theme that, with different nuances, is applied to the networked environment by James Surowiecki's *The Wisdom of the Crowds* and Don Tapscott and Anthony D. Williams's *Wikinomics*. The authoritative text in this context, however, remains Yochai Benkler's *The Wealth of Networks*. With regard to questions about the conditions under which innovation thrive on the Internet, we highly recommend Jonathan Zittrain's book *The Future of the Internet—and How to Stop It*. On Digital Native–specific issues, we greatly benefited from the essays in *Digital Youth, Innovation, and the Unexpected,* edited by Tara McPherson.

Chapter 11: Learners

Our thinking about tech-based learning has been influenced by Jean Lave and Etienne Wenger's *Situated Learning* and by the contributions to *Educating the Net Generation,* edited by Diana and James Oblinger. On specific issues, we benefited from Nicola Dörig's article "Lernen and Lehren im Internet" in B. Batinic (Hrsg.), *Internet für Psychologen,* 2., überarbeitete und erweiterte Auflage, S. 443-478 (Göttingen: Hogrefe, 2000), as well as from a number of journals exploring the use and impact of digital technologies on education and learning. Two sources that informed our writing on the topic are the *International Journal on E-Learning (IJEL)* and the *Journal of Educational Multimedia and Hypermedia (JEMH).* From the many books on e-learning we would like to mention the essays in *Innovation in Open and Distance Learning,* edited by Fred Lockwood and Anne Gooley; Marc J. Rosenberg's *Beyond eLearning,* in the context of organizational learning; and, more recently and in German, Rolf Meier's *Praxis E-Learning.*

We've benefited enormously from the writing and research of Howard Gardner and his team on the GoodPlay Project, which studies how young people who regularly participate in online games, social network sites, and other online communities learn and what role ethics plays in their lives. One interesting paper that resulted from the project is Lindsay Pettingill's "Trust without Knowledge," which discusses how young users carry out research on the Internet. On video games and learning we would like to mention Marc Prensky's *Digital Game–Based Learning* and James Paul Gee's *What Video Games Have to Teach Us about Learning and Literacy.* Herbert Burkert's *The Place of the University: Teaching and Research in the Information Society* (in C. Monville, *Variation sur le droit de la société de l'information,* Bruylant: Bruxelles, 2000, pp. 70–78) offers an inspiring and surprising look at the future of the university and its role in the information society. Interesting contributions on various aspects of ICT usage in the university context can be found in *eUniversity: Update Bologna,* edited by Reinhard Keil and colleagues.

Chapter 12: Activists

In this chapter, as elsewhere throughout the book, much of our thinking is grounded in Yochai Benkler's scholarship, particularly his book *The Wealth of Networks.* Cass Sunstein's exploration of the "Daily Me" and other implications of the digital age likewise have been crucial to our understanding of this field. Sunstein's *Republic.com 2.0* and *Infotopia,* for example, in certain ways press against, and in other ways further inform, the conclusions found in Benkler's work. Articles and essays from two edited volumes have proven to be great sources of knowledge and inspiration: *Young Citizens in the Digital Age,* edited by Brian Loader, and *Civic Life Online,* edited by W. Lance Bennett. *Youth as E-Citizen* by Kathryn Montgomery, Barbara Gottlieb-Robles, and Gary O. Larson, accessible online at http://www.centerforsocialmedia.org/ecitizens/youthreport.pdf, is another important work in this field.

At a more general level, we benefited from the book *Media Consumption and Public Engagement* by Nick Couldry, Sonia Livingstone, and Tim Markham, and from *The Internet Election,* edited by Andrew P. Williams and John C. Tedesco. A classic read on social activism through connectivity that is also worth mentioning in the context of this chapter is Howard Rheingold's *Smart Mobs.* We have benefited from the insights of several scholars on the use of the Internet in politics, including Stephen Coleman, the pollster John Della Volpe, Elaine Kamarck, Pippa Norris, Sunshine Hillygus, and Steven Ward. To learn more about the Internet's effect on democracy, see the website of the Berkman Center for Internet and Society at Harvard University (http://cyber.law.harvard.edu/research/internetdemocracy).

INDEX